45ᵀᴴ REGIMENT
of
VIRGINIA MILITIA

STAFFORD COUNTY VIRGINIA

1781–1856

WITH
BIOGRAPHICAL NOTES
ON OVER 1,600
MILITIAMEN

Jerrilynn Eby

HERITAGE BOOKS
2011

HERITAGE BOOKS
AN IMPRINT OF HERITAGE BOOKS, INC.

Books, CDs, and more—Worldwide

For our listing of thousands of titles see our website
at
www.HeritageBooks.com

Published 2011 by
HERITAGE BOOKS, INC.
Publishing Division
100 Railroad Ave. #104
Westminster, Maryland 21157

Copyright © 2011 Jerrilynn Eby

Other books by the author:
Laying the Hoe: A Century of Iron Manufacturing in Stafford County, Virginia
Men of Mark: Officials of Stafford County, Virginia
They Called Stafford Home: The Development of Stafford County, Virginia, from 1600 until 1865

Militia records used with permission of The Library of Virginia

All rights reserved. No part of this book may be reproduced or transmitted in any form or by any means, electronic or mechanical, including photocopying, recording or by any information storage and retrieval system without written permission from the author, except for the inclusion of brief quotations in a review.

International Standard Book Numbers
Paperbound: 978-0-7884-5267-3
Clothbound: 978-0-7884-8585-5

Introduction

A substantial collection of Stafford County's militia records are housed at the Library of Virginia in Richmond. These span the years 1781-1856 and are nearly complete for most of those years. The county militia records should have been on file in the Stafford Courthouse; if they were, they have long since been lost. Fortunately, after the Revolution, each county was required to file annual militia reports with the state's Auditor of Public Accounts. These reports included the names of officers and rosters of the names of men who failed to appear at one or more of the required summer monthly musters. Had these annual reports not been filed, there would be practically no information about Stafford's militia. The principle value of this collection is that it contains many names that cannot be found in any other official Stafford County records.

County militias were established during the Virginia colony's earliest days. These organizations were comprised of local residents who were frequently called upon to put down Indian attacks or slave uprisings. Companies of the 45th Regiment of Virginia Militia were organized in several different regions of Stafford and each company seems to have had its own muster field. The locations of three of these fields are known.

Nearly every man was familiar with using a gun for hunting or self-defense. For many militiamen, their prior experience with firearms was all the training they had or received. At the outset of the Revolution, these largely untrained militia regiments were swept into a larger organizational structure and pitted against some of England's finest soldiers. By nothing less than a miracle, the Americans succeeded in defeating troops who were far better trained and outfitted.

Having just experienced the forced quartering of enemy troops during the Revolution, America's founding fathers were strongly averse to creating a large standing army. George Washington's soldiers, who had fought so valiantly, were born and bred to the colonial militia system. While Washington recognized the need for better training for the soldiers, he also saw the wisdom of citizen-soldiers who could defend national security without jeopardizing the rights of citizens. George Mason wrote in his Virginia Declaration of Rights that the need for "a well-regulated militia, composed of the body of the people, trained to arms, is the proper, natural, and safe defense of a free state." The debate over militias and trained armies continued for many years.

All able-bodied men above the age of about 18 were automatically considered part of the county militia, though it's not unusual to see boys aged 15 or 16 on the rosters. Few of the men had any formal military training and what little training they did receive occurred during monthly musters conducted each summer. Here their weapons were checked and the men marched in formation to a drummer and fifer. Training was often sporadic and ineffective and there was little or no consistency in training or performance standards. Based upon the Stafford muster rolls, few men even bothered to show up for the musters, perhaps believing that tending their farms or shops was of more importance.

The county militias continued to play an active role during the War of 1812 and, later, when slave uprisings became of grave concern. Many of the men who served in Stafford's militia during the years immediately preceding the War Between the States were willing to fight to defend their soil from a new enemy, but by this time, the importance of having well trained soldiers had become obvious. The county militia companies didn't transfer neatly into the local cavalry and infantry units. Instead, men enlisted in whatever cavalry or infantry unit they chose. After the war, the Stafford's 45th Regiment was not re-established and faded into obscurity. Such functions were accommodated elsewhere in post-Civil War Virginia by resurgent, largely ceremonial units, such as the Richmond Light Infantry Blues. Such units also allowed for the creation of African-American units during Reconstruction and briefly afterward. Over time, there was a resurgent interest in militia units and, in the Rappahannock region, these tended to cluster around Fredericksburg. By at least the late 1890s, National Guard units were formed, finally bringing about George Washington's vision of well-trained militia. The National Guard approach, using local companies as a building block, provided both the inherent cohesiveness of the old militia system as well as more regular training. In later years, Virginia reconstituted a militia force which supported and supplemented the National Guard. During World War II, the militia tradition resurfaced in the Virginia Reserve Militia, constituted in 1942 to guard vital installations, bridges, etc. along the U. S. Route 1 corridor.

For years, the county courts were responsible for appointing the militia officers; however, by the mid-1820s, the militia companies were allowed to elect their own officers. Officers were customarily the wealthier, better educated men of the county. Some served for many years and others resigned their ranks after brief periods.

Stafford's militia records are of more interest to genealogists than to military historians as they contain in excess of 1,600 names and many pages of material dating from periods for which there are no surviving county records. The Library of Virginia has organized the militia collection into three broad categories: officers' commissions; payment records for the War of 1812; and muster rolls listing the names of those who missed one or more of the required summer monthly musters. The vast majority of the names contained in this collection are those who failed to appear at muster, yet these lists are an important source of genealogical material. At the end of the muster season, the lists of "no-shows" were turned over to the Stafford sheriff. It was his job to locate each of the absent militiamen and collect a fine of $2.00 for each missed muster. The sheriff often made notations on the lists indicating whether or not he'd been able to collect the fine and, if not, the reason. Many of the men had "no property to fine" or were "not found." Occasionally, a note was made indicating that the missing militiaman was dead or had removed to another county or state. At the ends of most of the militia rolls were the names of several Quakers who consistently and predictably avoided the musters. These families had been employed at James Hunter's Iron Works near Falmouth and had remained in Stafford even after that facility closed. Fines collected from absent militiamen were used to pay the fifer and drummer, repair damaged weapons, and provide for miscellaneous operating expenses.

The author has abstracted the material from this collection, organized it by year, and attempted to include brief biographical footnotes for as many of the militiamen as possible. This may include birth and/or death years, parents' and spouses' names, places of residence, business interests or occupations, land and/or personal property tax information, wills, Homestead Exemptions, court records, newspaper notices, etc.

Indexing is done by the year/s in which the men were listed and, when possible, the biographical footnotes are inserted the first time an individual's name appears in the records. Men for whom these footnotes have been included will have an index entry in italics followed by an italicized "*n*." (Example: Pearson, Asa *1819n*, 21). This means that Asa Pearson's name will be found in the section headed 1819 and his biographical footnote is included there. His name also appears in 1821.

45th Regiment of the Virginia Militia
Stafford County Virginia's

1781
Colonel—James Garrard[1]
Major—John Gregg[2]
Captain—Mason Pilcher[3]
Lieutenants—Thomas G. S. Tyler[4]
              Henry Ward[5]

1785
County Lieutenant—William Garrard[6]

1786
Colonel—William Phillips[7]
Lt. Col.—John F. Mercer[8]

---

[1] James Garrard (1749-1822) was the son of William Garrard (c.1715-c.1786) and Mary Naughty (born c.1721). James married Mary Ann Mountjoy (1753-1823) and lived at Hampstead on the west side of Poplar Road (Route 616). While a resident of Stafford, James was a member of Hartwood Baptist Church. In January 1775 he was appointed clerk of that body and maintained the church register. He served as clerk until 1780 (Hartwood). It was at about that that he removed to Kentucky where he became governor and left a large family.

[2] In 1783 John Gregg paid taxes on 12 slaves, 26 cattle, and 6 horses. Little is known about him other than he served in the Revolution.

[3] Mason Pilcher (1742-1790) was the brother of Moses, Peter, and Stephen Pilcher (died 1775) and possibly brother to some of the other Stafford Pilchers of the period. During the Revolution, Mason served as a captain in the Virginia militia. He married Bathsheba/Beersheba Pickett. From 1778 to at least 1781 Mason was one of the tobacco inspectors at the Falmouth Warehouse. In 1784 he served as deputy sheriff of Stafford. In 1783 he paid taxes on 8 slaves, 20 cattle, and 6 horses in Stafford.

[4] Thomas Gowry Strother Tyler (c.1740-1816) was the son of Henry Tyler (c.1710-1777). Both he and his father worked for many years as clerks of the court in Stafford. Thomas also operated one of the numerous quarries on Austin Run. He married Ann Fisher Adie (1756-1818), the daughter of William Adie (1729-1797). Thomas and Ann were separated after having seven children. In 1781 Thomas was court marshaled for being "a delinquent and deserting the militia when on duty at Falmouth and Hunter's Forge" (Virginia Executive, p. 91).

[5] In 1782 Henry Ward paid taxes on 250 acres in Stafford. By 1810 he was operating a tavern and "house of entertainment" (gambling) on Gaines Run in Culpeper County. His wife, Juliet Broaddus, died at Stevensburg in August 1812 (*Virginia Herald* Jan. 27, 1810 and Aug. 29, 1812). She was the daughter of William Broaddus and Martha Jones of Culpeper.

[6] William Garrard (c.1715-c.1785) lived at Apple Grove on the north side of Garrisonville Road (Route 610) and owned Garrard's Ordinary just northeast of the courthouse. When he died, he was replaced as county lieutenant by Thomas Ludwell Lee, Jr. The County Lieutenant was responsible for overseeing militia groups in each district.

[7] William Phillips (1744-1797) lived at Traveler's Rest on the north side of Garrisonville Road (Route 610) very near Ruby. He married Elizabeth Anne Fowke (died c.1830) of Fauquier.

[8] John Francis Mercer (1759-1821) was the son of John Mercer (1704-1768) and Ann Roy (c.1729-1770) of Marlborough. From 1782-83 and 1785-86 John Francis represented Stafford County in the Virginia House of Delegates. John was tutored at home at Marlborough, then studied law at William and Mary; he graduated from that institution in 1775. He was admitted to the bar and commenced his law practice in Williamsburg in 1781. During the Revolution, John served as aide-de-camp to Gen. Charles Lee. In 1785 he married Sophia Spigg and two years later moved to West River, Anne Arundel County, Maryland. John died in Philadelphia and his body was brought back to his seat, Cedar Park, in Anne Arundel.

Major—Elijah Threlkeld[9]
County Lieutenant—Thomas Ludwell Lee[10]
Captains—William Alexander[11]
    George Brent[12]
    George Burroughs[13]
    William Hewitt[14]
    Valentine Peyton[15]
    Mason Pilcher
    James Primm[16]
    Joseph Smith
    William Taylor
    Thomas G. S. Tyler
Lieutenants—Benjamin Adie[17]
    Thomas Bowen[18]

---

[9] Elijah Threlkeld (1744-1798) was the son of Christopher Threlkeld, Jr. (1698-1757). He married Mary (Bronaugh) Waugh (died 1799) and resided at Coal Trips, now the Girl Scout camp on Aquia Creek.
[10] Thomas Ludwell Lee, Jr. (1751-1807) was the son of Thomas Ludwell Lee (1730-1778) and Mary Aylett (c.1741-1779:82) of Bell View and Berry Hill in Stafford. Thomas, Jr. married Fanny Carter (c.1760-c.1850) and inherited his father's Potomac Creek farms. He lived there for a time before removing to Coton in Loudoun County.
[11] May be William Pearson Alexander (1758-1804), the son of John Alexander (1711-1763) and Susannah Pearson (born 1717). William lived at Snowden, east of Fredericksburg and on the Rappahannock.
[12] George Brent (c.1760-1804) was the son of Robert Brent (1730-1780) and Ann Carroll (1733-1804). He was born at Woodstock, Stafford County. In 1785 George married Molly Fitzhugh, the daughter of William Fitzhugh (1725-1791) of Marmion, King George County. He served as a lieutenant in the Virginia Line during the Revolution and was present at the siege of Yorktown. In 1792, 50 acres of his Woodstock plantation were taken for the town of Woodstock (also called Aquia).
[13] George Burroughs (c.1750-c.1827) was the brother of Samuel Burroughs. Little is known about this man other than he resided at Dipple on Aquia Creek; he leased this from Gustavus Scott (1753-1800) to whom it had passed from Alexander Scott (1686-1738). He also owned a tract, later called Plumfield, in what is now the Marine Corps reservation. George was a vestryman of Overwharton Parish in 1785 and, possibly, in other years as well. In 1812 he paid taxes on 9 slaves, 9 horses, 1 coach, and 352 acres in Stafford.
[14] William Hewitt (1740-1795) was the son of James Hewitt (died 1763) and Susanna Crump (1723-1797) of King George. He married Catherine Edmonds (1756-1823) and resided on the 200-acre Locust Grove plantation in White Oak. William served as sheriff of Stafford from 1789-1790.
[15] Dr. Valentine Peyton (1756-1815) was the son of John Peyton (1691-1760) and Elizabeth Rowzee (c.1715-1782) of Stony Hill. Valentine married Mary Butler Washington (1760-1822) and lived at Tusculum. During the Revolution, Valentine was a surgeon's mate in the 3rd Virginia regiment. After the war, he operated a boarding school for boys at Tusculum.
[16] James Primm (1754-1820) served as a justice of the peace for Stafford in 1797, 1806-1809, and possibly other years as well. In 1790 James paid tax on 256 acres in Stafford. He was the son of John Primm and Margaret Welch. In February 1776 James enlisted in Capt. William Washington's company. In August of that year he was sent to New York and served under Col. Hugh Mercer. He was discharged in Feb. 1778 at Valley Forge. Upon returning to Stafford James was appointed captain in the Stafford militia. In the early 1800s James and friends Mason Harding and Edward Bethel left Stafford for the "Western Country" ("McInteer vs McInteer"). For Primm, this meant moving to Washington County, Maryland. When he applied for his pension in 1818, James was described as being in "indigent circumstances" (National Archives, Revolutionary War Pensions, #S.35034).
[17] Benjamin Adie (1762-c.1825) was the son of William Adie (1729-1797) and Elizabeth Parrender (1729-c.1842) of Bloomington, Stafford County. Benjamin married Margaret Gibson Gillison (born c.1770). Although he inherited Bloomington from his father, Benjamin lived the latter part of his life in Prince William County.

Jeremiah Kirk[19]
James Lyon[20]
Robert B. Morton[21]
Charles Ralls[22]
William Ross
Thomas Peyton[23]
James Waters[24]
Edward West[25]
Benjamin Withers[26]
Ensigns—William Ball[27]
George Fant[28]
William Haner[29]
James Hore[30]

---

[18] Thomas Bowen died after 1819.

[19] Jeremiah Kirk (died c.1817) was the son of Jeremiah Kirk (died c.1792) and Ann Thomas (born c.1723). In 1785 he married Anne Monroe in St Paul's Parish and by whom he had several children. Jeremiah lived near Holloway's Mill on Potomac Run. In 1804 he paid tax on 120 acres in Stafford that his father had purchased from Charles Carter. In 1812 Jeremiah paid taxes on 6 slaves and 6 horses. The Kirk farm later belonged to George K. Blackburn and became known as Elm Spring. It is located on the north side of Kellogg's Mill Road (Route 651).

[20] James Lyon was a tailor. This may be the same James Lyon (1755-1836) who was a tailor and was born in Falmouth. In 1778 he married Mary Longwill (1748-1794), also of Falmouth. In 1792, and possibly other years as well, he served as a county tax assessor. Three years later, he was appointed overseer of the streets in Falmouth. In 1804 James paid tax on lot #22 in Falmouth.

[21] Robert Baylor Morton (1761-1807) served as a justice of the peace in Stafford from at least 1788-1792. He was the son of George Morton (1717-c.1765) of King George and Lucy Baylor. He inherited land in Orange County from his father. In 1786 he married Mary Mountjoy (1769-1804) in Maryland.

[22] Charles Ralls (died 1804) was the son of John Ralls (c.1747-1785). He married Frances "Frankie" Williams (born 1778), the daughter of George Williams and Mary Barker. The Ralls family resided in the upper part of the county on land that is now part of the Marine Corps reservation. Charles died in Kentucky.

[23] Thomas Peyton (died 1795) was the son of Yelverton Peyton (1735-c.1782) and Elizabeth Heath. From 1787-1792 he served as inspector of tobacco at the Aquia Warehouse.

[24] This may be James Waters (born 1754), the son of William Waters and Jane/Jean Cash.

[25] Edward West (c.1757-1827) lived at Richlands. A gunsmith, he may have been employed at Rappahannock Forge. In 1782 Edward paid taxes on 149 acres of Richlands. Around 1785 he moved from Stafford to Lexington, Kentucky where he became the first watchmaker in that town. A gifted inventor, West was fascinated with steam engines and in 1793 launched a steamboat in the Elkhorn River in Lexington. This was some years before Robert Fulton claimed international attention with his steamboat. West's boat was in operation until sometime after 1816 and, at the time of his death in 1827, was housed in a museum in Lexington (Ranck 183-184).

[26] Benjamin Withers (1762-1830) was the son of John Withers (1713-1794) and Hannah Allen (died 1801). Benjamin and his brother inherited the Withers family land on Potomac Run. In 1812 he paid taxes on 9 slaves, 3 horses, 1 coach, and 500 acres. Benjamin married Ann Markham and later moved to Kentucky.

[27] William Ball (1768-1815) was not of the local Ball family. He was the son of William Ball (died 1782) and Martha Brumfield of Pennsylvania. He married Jane Vernon, the widow of Abner Vernon (died 1792) who had been bookkeeper at Hunter's Iron Works in Falmouth. Abner was a Quaker. In 1792 William was surveyor of the road "from Potomack run to Ackokeek run" (Eby, Men 138).

[28] George Fant (1745-1839), also known as Sullie Fant, was the son of William Fant and Catherine Stewart. In 1791 George was granted a license to keep an ordinary in Stafford.

[29] In 1786 William Haner was employed at the Falmouth Tobacco Warehouse as a prizer (Fredericksburg, "Howe vs Buchanan").

Enoch Mason[31]
Henry Mason[32]
Lewis Mason[33]
Jacob Mentharpe
Richard Morton[34]
Samuel H. Peyton[35]
George Williams[36]

1787
Ensign—Edward Waller[37]

1788
Officers of Troop of Cavalry—Capt. Travers Daniel[38]
Lt. Charles Vowles[39]
Cornet Hancock Eustace[40]

---

[30] James Hore (died 1807) was the son of Elias Hore (1719-1782) and Mary Brown. He married Frances Nelson.

[31] Enoch Mason (1769-1828) was the son of John Mason (1722-c.1796) and Mary Nelson (172_-c.1801). Over a period of years, he purchased numerous tracts in the Roseville section of Stafford and amassed some 2,461 acres. He lived at Clover Hill in the Roseville area of Stafford and married Lucy Wiley Roy (1798-1835). Enoch served in various capacities in Stafford County government.

[32] Henry Mason (1760:70-1840:56) was the son of John Mason (1722-c.1796) and Mary Nelson (172_-c.1801). Henry's estate inventory included 6 horses, 11 cattle, 20 hogs, 1 old wagon, 7 slaves, farm implements, "3 stands of bees," 1 walnut desk, 1 walnut table "out of repair," 6 Windsor chairs, 1 "cherry wood chest," 1 tea board, 3 waiters, a large sugar box, 1 painted pine table, 6 silver teaspoons, 1 Gin case and bottles, 1 Bible, 7 feather beds with bedsteads, 10 pairs of cotton sheets, 1 silver watch, 2 huckerback table cloths, and 1 gig and harness all valued at £839.14.0 (Stafford Deed Book AA, p. 142).

[33] Lewis Mason (1757-c.1834) was the son of John Mason (1722-c.1796) and Mary Nelson (172_-c.1801). He married Mary Bethel (died 1831). In 1783 he paid taxes on 3 horses and 15 cattle; he owned no slaves. In 1805 he was excluded from Hartwood Baptist Church for the "sin of Excessive Drinking Spiritous Liquors" (Hartwood). The 1819 land tax records list him as having a "Lease for Life" on 100 acres of the Parke in Hartwood.

[34] Richard Morton (1771-1812) was the son of Thomas Morton (died 1782) and Ursula Brightwell (c.1725-after 1782). He married Margaret Ursula Waller (1771-1821) of Concord in Stafford. In 1812 he paid taxes on 15 slaves, 2 horses, and 468 acres including Peyton's mill seat.

[35] Samuel Heath Peyton (c.1770-1823) was the son of Yelverton Peyton (1735-c.1782). Samuel lived in various places around Stafford. For some years he resided at Loch Lomond on Potomac Run and near what is now The Glens subdivision. From there he moved to Auburn near what is now Apple Grove subdivision on Garrisonville Road.

[36] George Williams attained the rank of captain in the Revolution. This may be the same George Williams (died c.1826) who by 1805 was a resident of Dumfries in Prince William County. He ran an ordinary/tavern there until at least 1822. George married Catherine Hore (died c.1832), the daughter of Elias Hore (1719-1782) and Mary Brown.

[37] Edward Waller (1768-1818) was the son of William Waller (1740-1817) and Elizabeth Allen (1746-1768) of Concord. He married Elizabeth Chadwell and lived at Concord on Aquia Creek. In 1812 he paid taxes on 7 slaves and 4 horses.

[38] Travers Daniel, Jr. (1763-1813) lived at Crow's Nest on Potomac Creek. He married Mildred Stone (1772-1837), the daughter of Thomas Stone of Maryland, one of the signers of the Declaration of Independence. Travers represented Stafford in the Virginia House of Delegates from 1790-1794. He also served as a justice in Stafford from at least 1790-1796. The 1800 land tax records list Travers as owner of 2,166 acres in three parcels.

[39] Charles Vowles (c.1754-1799) was the son of Thomas Vowles (before 1727-1800) and Susannah Chunn (born c.1730) of St. Mary's County, Maryland. During the Revolution, Charles was a lieutenant of artillery in the Virginia line (National Archives, Revolutionary War Pensions, #R.18,701). Charles died unmarried.

1789

Captain—Mason Pilcher

1790

Captains—William Ball
　　　　　William Williams
　　　　　John Wallace in room of Mason Pilcher, deceased
　　　　　George Faunt in room of Mason Pilcher, deceased
Lieutenants—Robert Bruce[41]
　　　　　　Benjamin Tolson[42]
　　　　　　John West
Lieutenant of Horse—George L. Waugh[43]
Ensigns—Charles Bruce[44]
　　　　　Rubin Franklyn[45]
　　　　　Kenaz Ralls[46]
　　　　　Henry Ralls
　　　　　James Leach[47]

---

[40] Hancock Eustace (1768-1829) was the son of Isaac Eustace (died 1795) and Agatha Conway (1740-1826). In 1789 he married Tabitha Henry (died c.1840), the daughter of the Hon. James Henry (1731-1804) of Fleet's Bay. Hancock lived at Woodford on the north side of Garrisonville Road (Route 610).

[41] Robert Cary Bruce (c.1759-1801) was the son of William Bruce (c.1724-1792) and Elizabeth Grant of King George. He married Roberta M. Cary and lived at Springfield in the lower part of Stafford.

[42] Benjamin Tolson (c.1763-1838) was the son of George Tolson (1726-1785) of Stafford. In 1817 he purchased Bellfair Mills on Chappawamsic Run and operated this large commercial flour mill until his death.

[43] George Waugh (born c.1762) was born at Belle Plain. He was the son of Gowry Waugh (c.1734-c.1783) and Letitia Turberville (born 1736).

[44] Charles Cary Bruce (1768-1845) was the son of William Bruce (c.1724-1792) and Elizabeth Grant of King George. He lived at Springfield in White Oak. His first wife was Anne Kenyon. He married secondly Sarah Jane Mason (c.1787-1839), the daughter of Capt. Henry Mason (1760:70-1808).

[45] Rubin Franklin (1755-after 1833) was born in King George and was a small boy when his father moved his family to Stafford. Reuben remained in Stafford during the Revolution, during which time he served in the Virginia line and in the militia. In 1778 he was drafted into Capt. John Mountjoy's company and marched north to Valley Forge. During his militia service, he was under Capt. James. Reuben deposed, "The [militia] company was raised in Stafford county Virginia and marched down the Potomac river to a place called Brents house, which was burnt by the British under Governor Dunmore whilst we were in sight of it and compelled to retreat." In 1780 he served under Capt. George Mountjoy and in 1781 under Capt. George Burroughs, Capt. James Primm, and Col. William Phillips. At one point Reuben's company was sent to Winchester to guard British prisoners.

In 1786 Reuben bought from William Fitzhugh of Maryland 100 acres on Rocky Run adjoining Fristoe (Stafford Deed Book S, p. 336). This is now part of the Marine Corps reservation. In 1805 Reuben moved to Clarke County, Kentucky (National Archives, Revolutionary War Pension, #S.13,082).

[46] Kenaz Ralls (1763-1845) was the son of Edward Ralls (1724-1785) and Mary Rawleigh (c.1730-before 1804). He married Mary Brown (1765-c.1845), the daughter of Joshua Brown and Alice Lunsford. During the Revolution, Kenaz served in the Virginia militia. By 1824 he had removed to Fauquier.

[47] James Leach (died c.1823) was likely the son of Benjamin Leach/Leitch (died c.1812). James owned part of the large Richlands tract along Warrenton Road (U. S. Route 17). For a number of years he was a deputy surveyor under Travers Daniel, Sr. In 1812 James paid taxes on 8 slaves and 4 horses in Stafford.

1791
Captain—Lewis Mason
Lieutenant—Kenaz Ralls
Ensign—Peter Hansbrough[48]

1794[49]
Lt. Colonel Commandant—George Brent
1ˢᵗ Major—James Primm
2ⁿᵈ Major—William Hewitt
1ˢᵗ Captain Infantry—Thomas Peyton
2ⁿᵈ Captain Infantry—Enoch Mason
Lieutenant Infantry—Isaac Newton[50]
                Robert Hening[51]
Ensign Infantry—William Bronaugh[52]
                William Brent[53]
1ˢᵗ Captain Militia—Thomas G. S. Tyler
2ⁿᵈ Captain Militia—James Hore
3ʳᵈ Captain—William Ball
4ᵗʰ Captain—George Fant
5ᵗʰ Captain—William Williams
6ᵗʰ Captain—Lewis Mason
7ᵗʰ Captain—William Ross
8ᵗʰ Captain—Samuel H. Peyton
9ᵗʰ Captain—Benjamin Withers
10ᵗʰ Captain—Newman B. Barnes[54]
11ᵗʰ Captain—Benjamin Ficklen[55]

---

[48] It's not clear which Peter Hansbrough this was.

[49] In 1794 Col. George Brent asked the governor to supply the Stafford militia with arms from the public weapons in the state arsenal (Box 148, Folder 7).

[50] Isaac Newton (c.1745-1838) was the son of Maj. William Newton (c.1706-1789). From his father he inherited that part of Little Falls plantation on the Rappahannock River that included the house, mill, and quarry. Isaac married Margaret Strother. His will mentioned children Gerrard, Sarah, John, Thomas, and Jane. Sarah and Jane were allowed to live in Isaac's house "so long as they live single & not otherwise." Son-in-law Thomas B. Conway and wife Elizabeth (Newton) received "all the negroes, money, household furniture & other things I gave them in their life time" (Stafford Deed Book LL, p. 226). In 1812 Isaac paid taxes on 13 slaves, 9 horses, and 1 coach in Stafford.

[51] Robert Hening (1771-1828) was the son of David Hening (died 1798) and Mary Waller (c.1741-after 1806) who was the daughter of George Waller (1703-c.1768) of Spring Hill. Robert married Elizabeth Travers Brown, daughter of Rawleigh Travers Brown. In 1804 he paid tax on lots 30 and 36 in Falmouth and on 334 acres elsewhere in Stafford. In 1812 he paid taxes on 6 slaves and 5 horses in Stafford.

[52] William Bronaugh (1775-1859) was the son of Dr. John B. Bronaugh (1743-1777) and Mary Ann Carter. In 1792 he married Lucy Bryan in Fauquier. His second wife was Maria Fitzhugh and he married thirdly Mary Catherine Heath Peyton (c.1778-1853), the daughter of Yelverton Peyton (1735-c.1782).

[53] This may be William Brent (1775-1848), the son of Robert Brent (c.1730-1780) and Ann Carroll (1733-1804). William was born at Aquia and married first Catherine Walker Johnson (c.1786-1822). His second wife was Elizabeth Neale (c.1799-1863) of Charles County, Maryland. William was one of three commissioners appointed to receive subscriptions for Washington's first manufactory, the Columbia Manufacturing Company. He also served as clerk of the courts in Washington, DC.

[54] Newman Brockenbrough Barnes (died 1853) was the son of Thomas Barnes (c.1723-1767) and Winifred Brockenbrough of Richmond County. Newman married in Richmond County Lucy Harrison Ball, the daughter of Capt. Williamson Ball (1736-1793) and Priscilla Churchill. In 1811 Newman was hired as police officer in Falmouth following the resignation of George Kiger, the first one to hold that position (Town 39).

12th Captain—Charles Ralls
Lieutenants Militia—Richard Morton
        Thomas Porter[56]
        Charles Bruce
        John West
        Benjamin Tolson
        Kenaz Ralls
        Henry Mason
        William Stark[57]
        Burket Bowen[58]
        John Smith
        Jeremiah Kirk
        Nathaniel P. Williams[59]
Ensigns Militia—Edward Waller
       John Hore[60]
       Anthony Strother[61]
       James Leach
       Reubin Franklyn
       John Sterne[62]

---

[55] Benjamin Ficklen (died 1821) was the son of Anthony Strother Ficklen (died 1844). He married Susannah Foushee.

[56] Thomas Porter (born 1754) was the son of Calvert Porter (c.1718-c.1790) and Elizabeth Cash of Aquia Creek.

[57] William Stark (1754-1838) was the son of John Stark (1717-1781) and Howson Porter (c.1730-1755). William married Mary Kendall and left a family in Stafford. During the Revolution, he served as an orderly sergeant in Capt. William Harding's company of the Virginia militia and marched from Stafford to Yorktown (National Archives, Revolutionary War Pensions, #R.10,069). In 1812 he paid taxes on 6 slaves and 6 horses. The Stark house is now part of the Quantico reservation. Prior to the government condemnation in 1942, Rock Hill Church Road (Route 644) continued across Garrisonville Road and on to Stafford Store. The Stark house stood in the angle made with these two roads, to the immediate west of Rt. 644 and within a hundred yards or so of Rt. 610. It was a rectangular structure with a stone chimney on one end and a brick chimney on the other. The family cemetery is a short distance northwest of house site.

[58] Burket Bowen (died 1812). In 1790 he paid taxes on 5 slaves and 5 horses and lived in the White Oak area of Stafford.

[59] Nathaniel Pope/Pearson Williams was the son of Pearson Williams. This branch of the family came to Stafford from Maryland in the mid-18th century to work at Accokeek Iron Furnace. In 1812 Nathaniel paid taxes on 5 slaves and 4 horses in Stafford.

[60] John Hore (died 1810) was the son of Elias Hore (1719-1782) and Mary Brown. John married Nancy A. Norman (1773-1848), the daughter of George Norman (1743-1807) and left a will in Stafford. He freed slave Mary "in consequence of [her] faithful services." He also directed his administrator to provide her annually $20, 300 pounds of pork, and three barrels of corn for the remainder of her life. She was also to receive two acres of land and all the wood she needed for one fireplace "and timber to keep enclosed the said two acres" and he asked that a log house be built for her. John left his nephew, Walter Hore, all his interest in Lot 80 in the town of Aquia (Stafford Deed Book AA, p. 16). This was the lot on which stood the old tobacco warehouse and wharf. Hore's estate included 8 slaves, 4 horses, 13 cattle, 14 sheep, 34 hogs, half a seine rope, 1 canoe, 1 still tub and worm, 80 barrels of corn, and 2,000 pounds of tobacco (Stafford Deed Book AA, p. 230).

[61] This may be Anthony Strother (died 1818) who married Betsy Newton (born 1771) in 1793. She was the daughter of John Newton (1740-1812) and Mary Thomas (1744-1812). Anthony was the son of Anthony Strother (1710-1765) of Richmond and Stafford counties and Mary James (born 1736).

[62] John Sterne. In 1812 he paid taxes on 12 slaves, 8 horses, 1 gig, and 798 acres in various tracts 6 and 10 miles west of the courthouse.

8   1794

                    Alexander Walker[63]
                    Charles Kendall[64]
                    William Hay[65]
                    James Adam[66]
                    Joel Mason[67]
                    Lawson Robertson[68]
                    Daniel Hord[69]—in Capt. John West's company
                    Edward Norman[70]—In Capt. John West's company

Falmouth Company—Capt. John Wallace[71]
                    Lt. Robert H. Hooe[72]

1795
Captain of Light Infantry—Isaac Newton—in place of Thomas Peyton, deceased
Captain—John Wallace—in place of Newman B. Barnes, resigned
Lieutenant of Light Infantry—Henry Peyton
Lieutenant of 2nd Company Light Infantry—William Bronaugh—in room of Robert Hening, resigned

1796
Major 2nd Battalion—Enoch Mason—in room of William Hewitt, dec.
Captains—Henry Mason
           Lewis Mason
           William Bronaugh
           Hancock Eustace—1st Battalion of Light Infantry—in room of Isaac Newton, resigned
           Burkett Bowen—in room of Benjamin Withers, resigned
           Robert H. Hooe—Falmouth Company—in room of Newman B. Barnes, resigned

---

[63] Alexander Walker (1771-1830) was a member of the well-known cabinet and clock making family of Fredericksburg. For the last ten years of his life, Alexander owned Clearview adjoining the town of Falmouth.

[64] Charles Kendall (died c.1835) lived on Aquia Run near what is now the village of Ruby. In 1812 he paid taxes on 7 slaves, 5 horses, and 307 acres on Aquia Run 10 miles north of the courthouse.

[65] William H. Hay (died c.1818) lived near Accokeek Run, Potomac Church, and Crow's Nest. He married Margaret Bruce, the daughter of William Bruce (c.1724-1792) and Elizabeth Grant of Caroline County.

[66] James Adam (died after 1817).

[67] Joel Mason (1761-1813) was the son of John Mason and Mary Nelson of Stafford and a brother to Enoch Mason (1769-1828) of Clover Hill. He married Sarah Bourne (c.1771-1835), the daughter of George Bourne of Culpeper. Joel served as a justice of the peace in Stafford from at least 1806-1811 and lived very near Tackett's Mill. In 1812 he paid taxes on 6 slaves, 5 horses, and 407 acres 10 miles west of the courthouse.

[68] Lawson Robertson (1777-1848) is thought to have been the father of William Wildie Robertson (1774-1842) who operated one of the large freestone quarries on Rocky and Austin runs. Lawson married Elizabeth Ralls (1775-1853).

[69] Daniel Hord (died after 1839) was the son of Kellis Hord (c.1744-1815) and Mary (Hord) Hord (born 1744). Daniel later resided in Culpeper.

[70] Edward Norman (1752-1814) was the son of Thomas Norman (c.1712-1785) and Elizabeth Duncombe (c.1714-1771) of Edge Hill. Edward married Jane Stewart (c.1756-1814) and resided at Edge Hill. In 1812 he paid taxes on 8 slaves, 8 horses, and 383 acres on Aquia Creek.

[71] John Wallace (1761-1829) was the son of Dr. Michael Wallace (1719-1767) and Elizabeth Brown (born 1723) of Ellerslie. He married Elizabeth Hooe (c.1766-1850) and resided at Liberty Hall

[72] Robert Howson Hooe (1748-1834) was the son of Howson Hooe (1725-1796) and Mary Dade (born 1727). Robert was born at Buck Hall in Prince William County and was buried in what is now Mayfield Cemetery in Manassas. In Stafford he served as sheriff and justice and in 1804 was county coroner. Robert married Mary Waugh, the daughter of Richard and Matilda Waugh. In 1812 he paid taxes on 23 slaves and 14 horses in Stafford.

1796

Lieutenants—Alexander Walker—in room of Henry Mason, promoted
    Joel Mason—in Capt. Benjamin Ficklen's company
    Daniel Payton
    William Ware—in Hancock Eustace's company—in room of Henry Peyton, resigned
    John Sterne—in Hancock Eustace's company—in room of Kenaz Ralls, removed
    William Hay—in Burkett Bowen's company—in room of Burkett Bowen, promoted
    John Moncure[73]—Thomas G. S. Tyler's[74] company—in room of Richard Morton, resigned
Ensigns—Harris Whitecotton[75]—in room of Joel Mason promoted
    Travers Brown[76]
    James Edwards—in Capt. Ralls' company
    Gustavus Scott[77]—in Hancock Eustace's company—in room of William Ware, promoted
    Enoch Harding[78]—in Samuel H. Peyton's company—in room of John Sterne, promoted
    John Harding[79]—in Samuel H. Peyton's company—in room of Charles Kendall, resigned
    Thomas Newton[80]—in Lewis Mason's company—in room of Alexander Walker, promoted
    Alexander Hay[81]—in Burkett Bowen's company—in room of William Hay, promoted
    Lewis Ficklen[82]—Thomas G. S. Tyler's company—in room of Edward Waller, resigned

1797

Lt. Col. Commandant—James Primm—in room of Lt. Col. George Brent, resigned
Major— William Williams[83]

---

[73] John Moncure, III (1772-1822) was the son of John Moncure II (1747-1784) and was born at Dipple on Chappawamsic Creek. He inherited the adjoining Clermont from his father, but was buried at Dipple. He married Anne Conway (born c.1750), the daughter of George Conway (died 1754) of Wicomico. John represented Stafford in the Virginia House of Delegates in 1797-98, 1805-06, 1808-09, and 1818-19. He also held a variety of posts in county government.

[74] By early 1796 Thomas G. S. Tyler had been captain of the militia for 13 years. He believed that as senior captain he was entitled to a promotion to major, but the county court appointed Enoch Mason instead. In April 1796 Thomas wrote to the governor to complain (Box 148, Folder 9).

[75] Harris Whitecotton (c.1768-1803) was the son of George Whitecotton, Jr. and Mary Harris. In 1790 he married Margaret Shumate (1776-1819) in Fauquier County. Harris was granted licenses to keep an ordinary in 1795 and 1801-1803. Family history holds that he died in 1803 enroute to Augusta County.

[76] Raleigh Travers Brown (1753-1803) married his cousin Million Waugh (c.1763-1799), the daughter of Joseph Waugh (c.1736-1763) and Mary Bronaugh (died 1799). Raleigh and Million resided at Windsor, very near Crow's Nest. Raleigh was one of the tobacco inspectors at Cave's Warehouse in 1778 and served as a Stafford justice in 1781.

[77] Gustavus Scott (c.1753-1800) was the son of James Scott (1715-1782) of Dipple (Stafford County) and Dettingen Parish (Prince William County) and Sarah Brown (1715-1784) of Charles County, Maryland. He married Margaret Hall Caile. Gustavus died in Washington, DC and was buried in Fairfax County.

[78] Stafford was home to a number of Enoch Hardings. This one may be the Enoch (c.1770-after 1826) who was the son of William Harding (1738-1826) and Clarissa "Clarky" Million (1745-1826). In 1812 Enoch paid taxes on 5 slaves, 3 horses, 1 gig, and 104 acres adjoining Hansbrough and 12 miles north of the courthouse.

[79] This may be John Harding (born 1765) who was the son of William Harding (1738-1826) and Clarissa "Clarky" Million (1745-1826).

[80] Thomas Newton (died 1823) was the son of Maj. William Newton (c.1706-1789) and brother of Isaac Newton (c.1745-1838).

[81] In 1813 Alexander Hay paid tax on 70 acres near Crow's Nest "for Thomas Hay." In 1812 he paid taxes on 3 slaves and 4 horses.

[82] Lewis Ficklen (died c.1828) lived next to the Parke Quarter in Hartwood. He was the son of Anthony Ficklen (died before 1810) of Poplar Settlement in Stafford and Elizabeth Bruce. By 1826 Lewis was living in Fauquier. He married Simpha Rosa Enfield Phillips (born 1775), the daughter of Col. William Phillips (1744-1797) of Stafford. In 1812 Lewis paid taxes on 10 slaves and 4 horses.

2ⁿᵈ Major—William Alexander
Captains—John Fox[84]—in room of Thomas G. S. Tyler, resigned
    Garnett Peyton[85]—in room of Burkett Bowen, resigned
    Benjamin Tolson
    Nathaniel P. Williams
    Samuel H. Peyton
    Hancock Eustace
    Lewis Mason—1ˢᵗ Battalion
    Benjamin Ficklen—1ˢᵗ Battalion
    Charles Ralls—1ˢᵗ Battalion
    William Williams—1ˢᵗ Battalion
    Samuel H. Peyton—1ˢᵗ Battalion
    Henry Mason—2ⁿᵈ Battalion
    William Bronaugh—2ⁿᵈ Battalion
    William Williams
Lieutenants—Edward Withers[86]
    Gustavus Scott
    Reubin Franklyn—in Benjamin Tolson's company
    Lawson Robertson—in Nathaniel P. Williams' company
    William Hay
    Charles Bruce[87]
Ensigns—Allen Withers[88]—in room of Lewis Ficklen, resigned
    William Waller[89]
    Sidney Wishart[90]

---

[83] William Williams wrote to the governor complaining that he had been a commissioned officer for twelve years and had commanded a militia company for eight years. He objected to not having been promoted (Box 148, Folder 10).

[84] John Fox (c.1770-1834) was the son of Thomas Fox (c.1710-1792) of King William County. He married Nancy "Ann" Threlkeld (1772-1828), the daughter of Col. Elijah Threlkeld (1744-1798) of Coal Trips on Aquia Creek. From 1798-99 John represented Stafford County in the Virginia House of Delegates. From at least 1791-94 he was deputy clerk of the court in Stafford.

[85] Garnett Peyton (c.1775-1827) was the son of John Rowzee Peyton (1754-1798) of Stony Hill. He resided in the town of Aquia and married Agatha Strother Madison (1782-1865), the daughter of William Strother Madison of Botetourt County.

[86] Edward Withers (1766:70-1830) was the son of James Withers (1736-c.1818) who owned what later became known as Kellogg's Mill on present Abel Reservoir. His first wife was Mary DeJarnett (born c.1776) of Caroline County. He married secondly his widowed sister-in-law, Sophia DeJarnett (1790:94-c.1841). In 1804 Edward became tobacco inspector at Dixon's Warehouse in Falmouth. Edward and Mary were buried at Cherry Grove on Sanford Road (Route 670), which is now a Del Webb subdivision. At the time of his death he lived on the Ficklen Tract near Wiley Honey's Tavern (near the Mountain View Fire Department) (Stafford Deed Book LL, p. 11).

[87] Charles Bruce was fined this year for failing to appear at the muster, but was found to have no property to fine.

[88] This may be William Allen Withers (1773-1828), the son of John Withers (1738-1818) and Virginia Hannah Routt (1740-1774). He married Susannah Waller Bower (1780-1855), the daughter of Michael Bower and Elizabeth Withers. Around 1810 Allen moved to Scott County, Kentucky where he later died.

[89] William Waller (1740-1817) was the son of Edward Waller (1703-1753) of Essex (later of Concord, Stafford County) and Ann Tandy (c.1721-1748). His first wife was Elizabeth Allen (1746-1768). He married secondly Margaret Waller (1744-1777) and thirdly Ursula Withers (1752-1815). In 1812 he paid taxes on 11 slaves, 6 horses, 500 acres on Aquia Creek (Concord) and 200 acres on Potomac Run (near Abel Reservoir). This may be the same William Waller who, during the Revolution, served as a drummer, fifer, and wagoner.

Lewis Bridwell[91]—in Nathaniel P. Williams' company
Stanfield Jones[92]
Thomas Fristoe[93]
Daniel Hord
George Taylor—in Hancock Eustace's company
Sergeant—James Bywaters

Fined for failure to appear at muster:

Name	Company	Note
William Adie[94]	William Bronaugh	
Richard Anderson	William Hay	Fined for failure to appear at muster but had no property to fine.
Nathan Atchison[95]	Samuel H. Peyton	
George Bell[96]	William Hay	Fined for failure to appear at muster but had no property to fine.
Edward Ball[97]	William Bronaugh	Fined for failure to appear at muster but had no property to fine.
Edward Bethel[98]	Benjamin Ficklen	
Jesse Bails[99]	Charles Ralls	Fined for failure to appear at muster but had no property to fine.
Charles Barby[100]	Charles Ralls	Fined for failure to appear at muster but had no property to fine.
Jesse Barns	William Bronaugh	Fined for failure to appear at muster but had no property to fine.

[90] Sidney Wishart (1773-1841) married Ann Eilbeck Cooke (1788-1833), the daughter of John Travers Cooke (1755-1819) and Mary Thomson Mason (1762-1806).

[91] Lewis Bridwell (c.1776-c.1824) was the son of Moses Bridwell (c.1728-1803) and Lucy Lee (born c.1741). He married Elizabeth Stark (born c.1780). Lewis and Elizabeth were born in Fauquier County. In 1812 Lewis paid taxes on 9 slaves, 4 horses, and 1,026 acres on Beaverdam Run of Aquia Run.

[92] Stanfield Jones (died after 1827) was a carpenter. He married Narcissa Burdett Phillips (born 1776), daughter of Col. William Phillips of Stafford. Stanfield later worked as an overseer for James B. Skinker.

[93] Thomas Fristoe (1767-1815) was the son of Daniel Fristoe (1739-1774) who was a minister at Chappawamsic Baptist Church. Thomas married Lydia Wells, the daughter of Carty Wells of Stafford, later Shelby County, Kentucky. Thomas served as a justice for Stafford from at least 1806-1813. In 1812 he paid taxes on 8 slaves, 8 horses, and 327 acres on the south Run of Chappawamsic Run.

[94] William Adie (1766-c.1824) was the son of William Adie (1729-1797) and Elizabeth Parrender (1729-c.1842).

[95] Nathaniel Atchison (born 1756) was the son of Adam Atchison and Elizabeth Byram. In 1785 he paid taxes on 3 slaves, 3 horses, and 6 cattle in Stafford.

[96] George Bell (born 1753) was the son of George Bell and Ann or Mary Hinson of Stafford.

[97] In 1812 Edward Ball paid tax on 1 horse in Stafford.

[98] Edward Bethel (1754-c.1820) was the son of Edward Bethel (c.1720-1758).

[99] Jesse Bails (Bayles, Bailis) (1754-after 1819) was the son of John Bailis and Mary Bailis and was a carpenter (Stafford Estate accounts, 1823, p. 337). He married Jane Lunsford (c.1754-after 1821), the widow of Moses Lunsford, Sr. of Stafford and the mother of Moses Lunsford, Jr. (born 1780). By 1810 Jesse and Jane were living next door to Moses, Jr. in Mason County, Kentucky. During the Revolution, Jesse served under Capt. Marquis Calmese in the 2nd Virginia Regiment. According to a deposition included with his pension application is a statement that Jesse "is extremely poor, and incapable of doing any work of any consequence" (National Archives, Revolutionary War Pensions, W.8345).

[100] May be the Charles Barbee who was the son of Andrew Barbee (born 1759) and grandson of Andrew Barbee (died 1795).

John Beagle[101]	William Bronaugh	Fined for failure to appear at muster but had no property to fine.
Joseph Beagle[102]	William Bronaugh	Fined for failure to appear at muster but had no property to fine.
Thomas Brewin	William Bronaugh	
Bailey Bell[103]	William Williams	Fined for failure to appear at muster but had no property to fine.
John Bridwell	William Williams	
John Barker	William Williams	
William Berry	Henry Mason	Fined for failure to appear at muster but had no property to fine.
William Bobo	William Williams	Fined for failure to appear at muster but had no property to fine.
James Botts	William Williams	Fined for failure to appear at muster but had no property to fine.
Joseph B. Botts[104]	William Williams	
James Bouchard	Lewis Mason	Fined for failure to appear at muster but had no property to fine.
Isaac Branson[105]	Lewis Mason	
Jessey Badger[106]	Benjamin Ficklen	Fined for failure to appear at muster but had no property to fine.
James Billingsley[107]	William Bronaugh	
William Butler	Henry Mason	
Raleigh T. Browne	Henry Mason	
Rawleigh Courtney[108]	Benjamin Ficklen	Fined for failure to appear at muster but had no property to fine.
John Carter	William Williams	Light infantry.
William Chadwell[109]	William Bronaugh	
John Carter	William Bronaugh	
Daniel Courtney[110]	William Bronaugh	
Joseph Carpenter	William Hay	
Jedediah Carter	William Hay	
William Cash	William Williams	Fined for failure to appear at muster but had no property to fine.
James Cloe[111]	Charles Ralls	Fined for failure to appear at muster but had no property to

---

[101] John Beagle (died before 1819). In 1819 his heirs paid tax on 73 acres on Aquia Run in what is now the Quantico reservation.

[102] Joseph Beagle married Gracie ___.

[103] Bailey Bell. In 1828 he leased property from Willoughby Tebbs in northern Stafford, now part of Quantico.

[104] May be Joseph Butler Botts (1774-1848), the son of Joseph Botts (1748-1814) and Catherine Butler (1755-1834). He married Nancy Fristoe and moved to Page County, Virginia.

[105] Isaac Branson (born 1765) was the son of William Branson (born c.1714) and Elizabeth Osmond. Isaac was a Quaker and was born in Stafford.

[106] During the Revolution, Jesse Badger served in the navy (Creel 55).

[107] James Billingsley (1756-c.1844) was born in Stafford, the son of James Billingsley (1726-1776) of Maryland. His first wife was Margaret Primm. He married secondly Ruth Holloway(?). In 1812 James paid taxes on 1 slave and 4 horses in Stafford. He moved to Belmont County, Ohio.

[108] Raleigh Courtney (born c.1764) was the son of James Courtney (1723-1775) and Christine Humphrey (1727-1775).

[109] William Chadwell (died 1813).

[110] Daniel Courtney (born c.1766) was the son of James Courtney and Christine Humphrey. In 1799 he married Lucy Jones in Fauquier. By 1803 Daniel was in Harrison County, Kentucky.

		fine.
John Cooke[112]	William Williams	
Samuel Cocks	Henry Mason	Fined for failure to appear at muster but had no property to fine.
Vincent Cocks, Jr.	Henry Mason	
Enoch Cocks	William Bronaugh	Fined for failure to appear at muster but had no property to fine.
William Crop[113]	William Bronaugh	
James Crop, Sr.[114]	Lewis Mason	
John Crop, Jr.	Lewis Mason	
John Crop, Sr.[115]	Lewis Mason	
Robert Crop	Benjamin Ficklen	Fined for failure to appear at muster but had no property to fine.
William Davis	William Williams	Fined for failure to appear at muster but had no property to fine.
Spencer Dawson[116]	William Williams	Fined for failure to appear at muster but had no property to fine.
William Dent	William Williams	Fined for failure to appear at muster but had no property to fine.
Jesse Doing	William Williams	Fined for failure to appear at muster but had no property to fine.
Mourning Douglas[117]	Benjamin Ficklen	
Edward Duffill	Charles Ralls	Fined for failure to appear at muster but had no property to fine.
Jesse Doyall	William Williams	Fined for failure to appear at muster but had no property to fine.
Joseph Ennever[118]	Henry Mason	
George Fling[119]	Lewis Mason	Fined for failure to appear at muster but had no property to

[111] James Cloe, Jr. (1763-c.1806) was the son of James Cloe, Sr., Scots immigrant, and may have been born in St. Mary's County, Maryland. The younger James is thought to have married Elizabeth Bridwell.
[112] John Travers Cooke (1755-1819) lived at West Farm on the Potomac River and in what is now Wide Water. He married Mary Thomson Mason (1762-1806). John was the son of Travers Cooke (1730-1759) and Mary Doniphan and the grandson of John Cooke (died 1733), the Irish immigrant. In 1812 John paid taxes on 53 slaves, 29 horses, 2,738 acres on the Potomac River and Aquia Creek, 921 acres between Accokeek and Potomac Creek (Marlborough), and 1 coach. He operated a quarry and timber business.
[113] William Cropp (1774-1858) was the son of John Cropp (1753-1830) and Rosie Thomas. He married Mildred Cason, the daughter of William Cason and Agatha (Agnes) Pemberton and moved to Missouri.
[114] James Cropp, Sr. may have been the James Cropp who was born c.1778 and was the son of John Cropp (1753-1830) and Rosie Thomas. On Jan. 26, 1793 James was excluded from Hartwood Baptist Church for "Drinking to Excess and swearing and living a life of Irregularity" (Hartwood).
[115] John Cropp, Sr. (1753-1830) was the son of James Cropp (died before 1780) and Joyce Hinson and lived on Deep Run in the Hartwood section of Stafford. He was the likely builder of Cropp's Tavern. His first wife was Rosie Thomas. He married secondly Eliza Fallis (c.1798-c.1850) of Stafford.
[116] Spencer Dawson (born after 1758) was the brother of Revolutionary War pensioner Christopher Dawson (c.1759-1846). They were the likely sons of Christopher Dawson and Jane George of Stafford. By 1810 Spencer was living in Clark County, Kentucky.
[117] Mourning Douglas (1771-1823) is thought to be the son of Archibald Douglas. Mourning died in Stafford and his widow, Ann "Nancy" Douglas, moved to Alabama with son Archibald (1804-1852).
[118] Joseph Ennever (1770-1848) was born in Dunkirk, French Flanders and came to Virginia in 1787. After the Revolution, he became manager of James Hunter's Iron Works. His first wife was Fanny Potts (1776-before 1818). He married secondly Lucy Latham. Joseph and Lucy were buried at their home, Stanstead, but this cemetery is now in the parking lot of the Fredericksburg Auto Auction.

		fine.
Thornton Fitzhugh[120]	William Hay	
Moses Fritter[121]	William Bronaugh	
Daniel Grigsby	William Bronaugh	
John Gardner	Henry Mason	Fined for failure to appear at muster but could not be found.
Thomas Garnett[122]	Henry Mason	
Jesse Green[123]	Henry Mason	
Joseph Graves	Lewis Mason	Fined for failure to appear at muster but had no property to fine.
Martin Griffin	William Williams	Fined for failure to appear at muster but could not be found.
Moses Grigsby[124]	William Bronaugh	
Walter Guy[125]	William Williams	Fined for failure to appear at muster but had no property to fine.
Joseph Guy[126]	William Williams	Fined for failure to appear at muster but had no property to fine.
Benjamin Guy[127]	William Williams	Fined for failure to appear at muster but had no property to fine.
John Hedgman	William Hay	
John Holloday	William Bronaugh	Fined for failure to appear at muster but had no property to fine.
Martin Heffernon	William Bronaugh	Fined for failure to appear at muster but had no property to fine.
Samuel Holladay	William Bronaugh	Fined for failure to appear at muster but had moved.
John Holloday	William Hay	
James Hore	William Hay	
William Horton[128]	William Bronaugh	Fined for failure to appear at muster but had no property to

---

[119] George Fling (c.1765-c.1842). This may be the same George Fling who was born in Loudoun County, married Amelia Lattimore in 1791, and moved to Perry County, Ohio. George owned land on Austin Run in the upper part of Stafford.

[120] Thornton Fitzhugh (1768-1804) was the son of John Fitzhugh (1727-1809) of Bellair (Stafford County) and Alice Catlett Thornton (1729-1790).

[121] Moses Fritter (1756-after 1833) was the son of Moses Flitter/Fritter and Elizabeth Horton. During the Revolution, he served under Capt. Thomas Mountjoy and pursued the British down the Potomac River after Lord Dunmore's troops burned William Brent's house. He deposed that he wasn't present when the house was burned, "but being stationed in the neighbourhood he saw the flames and was marched under Capt. Mountjoy…to the aid of the sufferers, and under the commands of that officer pursued the British down the Potomac River aforesaid to the distance of 70 or 80 miles." In 1781 he entered service in Capt. William Alexander's company and was engaged at the Battle of Yorktown. In 1783 Moses paid taxes on 3 horses, and 6 cattle in Stafford. In 1790 he paid taxes on 50 acres of land in Stafford. Shortly thereafter, he moved from Stafford to Pittsylvania, then to Mason County, Kentucky, then to Ohio, then back to Mason County, where he spent the remainder of his life (National Archives, Revolutionary War Pensions, #S.1201).

[122] Thomas Garnett (died c.1803). In 1804 his estate paid tax on 708 acres in Stafford.

[123] In 1814 Jesse Green was paid for repairing arms for the militia.

[124] Moses Grigsby (1762-1838) was the son of Moses Grigsby and Mary Matheny (born 1736) of Stafford. During the Revolution, he served in North Carolina. Returning to Stafford, in 1784 he married Abigail Fritter (1761-1860) and moved to Marion County, Indiana. He died in Gibson County, Indiana (National Archives, Revolutionary War Pensions, #W.10069).

[125] Walter Guy (born c.1780) was the son of Moses Guy (born c.1761) of Prince William County. Walter later moved back to Prince William.

[126] Joseph Guy (c.1763-1812) was the son of William Guy (c.1718-c.1792) who may have come from Lancaster County, Pennsylvania.

[127] Benjamin Guy (c.1755-c.1830) was the son of William Guy (c.1718-c.1792).

		fine.
William Hunter	Henry Mason	Fined for failure to appear at muster but had moved to Fauquier.
Samuel Johnston[129]	Henry Mason	Fined for failure to appear at muster but could not be found.
George James[130]	Lewis Mason	
Isaac James	Lewis Mason	Fined for failure to appear at muster but had no property to fine and had moved.
Jeredine	William Williams	"William Brents teacher"
Jessey Jett[131]	Benjamin Ficklen	Fined for failure to appear at muster but had no property to fine.
James Jett[132]	Benjamin Ficklen	
George Jackson	Benjamin Ficklen	
George Jones	William Bronaugh	Fined for failure to appear at muster but had no property to fine.
William Keshaw	William Bronaugh	Fined for failure to appear at muster but had no property to fine.
Peter Knight[133]	Samuel H. Peyton	
Charles Kendall	Samuel H. Peyton	
John Latham, Jr.	Lewis Mason	
James Lavender[134]	Benjamin Ficklen	Fined for failure to appear at muster but had no property to fine.
Benjamin Leach[135]	Henry Mason	
John Leach	Henry Mason	Fined for failure to appear at muster but had no property to fine.
Porch Limbrick[136]	Henry Mason	Fined for failure to appear at muster but had no property to fine.
William Limbrick	William Hay	
Thomas Lowry[137]	William Hay	Fined for failure to appear at muster but had no property to

[128] William Horton (c.1776-after 1850). Lived in what is now the Marine Corps reservation. In 1804 he paid tax on 80 acres. He left a large family in Stafford. From 1815 until at least 1817 he rented part of the Bell's Hill tract to the north and west of the courthouse (Lee, VHS).

[129] In 1785 Samuel Johnston married Peggy Birch in Stafford.

[130] May be George James (born c.1755) who was the son of Thomas James (1729-c.1776) and Mary Bruce. The James family were major land holders in Stafford County and George owned a large tract of land on the south side of Potomac Creek.

[131] Jesse Jett (1776-1860) died in Spotsylvania. Little is known about him.

[132] This may be the James Jett who married Ethelswitha Sanford (born c.1789).

[133] May be Peter Knight, Jr. (1760-c.1840), the son of Peter Knight, Sr. (born 1731) and Rachel Abbot (born 1733). Peter, Jr. married Elizabeth Kendall (1758-c.1840). During the Revolution, Peter served under Capt. William Phillips and Capt. William Harding. In May 1786 Peter bought 300 acres from William Fitzhugh of Maryland. This adjoined Bailey Washington's Windsor Forest and Long Branch of Aquia Run (Stafford Deed Book D, p. 352). According to the Stafford land tax records, by 1819 Peter had moved to Harrison County, West Virginia.

[134] Many of the Lavender family were millwrights and iron workers and seem to have been employed as such at James Hunter's Iron Works on the Rappahannock. Exactly how this James Lavender is related to the others of that name is unclear.

[135] Benjamin Leitch (1754-1812) married Elizabeth Peyton (died after 1811). His estate inventory included 2 slaves, 3 horses, 21 cattle, 31 sheep, 24 hogs, 80 barrels corn, 1 still, 1 cart, 1 loom, 23 casks, 4 window curtains, 5 bedsteads, household and kitchen furniture, 2 cotton wheels, 1 flax wheel, farm implements, carpenter's tools, 1 gun and powder horn, 2 chests, and "Body cloaths" all valued at $1,966.33 (Stafford County Deed Book AA, p. 331). Benjamin lived near Muddy Creek in lower Stafford.

[136] Porch Limbrick (before 1765-after 1820) was the son of William Limbrick (died c.1784) and Letitia Porch (c.1740-c.1804).

		fine.
Joshua Marston	Henry Mason	
Henry Mattox	William Bronaugh	Fined for failure to appear at muster but had no property to fine.
William Mason	Lewis Mason	
Francis McIntosh	Charles Ralls	Fined for failure to appear at muster but had no property to fine.
James McRobertson[138]	William Bronaugh	
Henry Musselman[139]	Benjamin Ficklen	Fined for failure to appear at muster but had no property to fine.
Isaac Newton	Henry Mason	
William Norman[140]	Benjamin Ficklen	Fined for failure to appear at muster but had no property to fine.
Francis Payne[141]	William Hay	Fined for failure to appear at muster but had no property to fine.
John W. Payne[142]	William Hay	
Garnett Peyton	William Bronaugh	
Yearly Porch	Benjamin Ficklen	Fined for failure to appear at muster but had no property to fine.
Aldom Puzey[143]	Henry Mason	Fined for failure to appear at muster but had no property to fine.
Richard Randall[144]	William Bronaugh	Fined for failure to appear at muster but had no property to fine.
Fielding Reddish	William Bronaugh	
Christopher Rogers	William Bronaugh	
Orasid Robertson	Henry Mason	Fined for failure to appear at muster but had no property to fine.
George Robertson	Henry Mason	
Aaron Rogers	Lewis Mason	Fined for failure to appear at muster but had no property to fine.
James Rogers	Lewis Mason	
Robert Rose	Lewis Mason	
Theophilus Rowley	William Williams	Fined for failure to appear at muster but had no property to fine.

[137] Thomas Lowry (1760-1846) was born in St. Mary's County, Maryland. His parents moved to Stafford when Thomas was about three years old. During the Revolution, he served in Capt. George Mountjoy's company of Stafford militia and was stationed at Marlborough. He also served briefly in Capt. Elijah Threlkeld's company. In 1805 Thomas married Nancy Dedmon (c.1780-1860) in Orange County. He left Virginia in 1816 and moved to Clark County, Kentucky.

[138] This name appears variously as "James M. Robertson" and "James McRobertson." The former spelling is likely the correct one as he was the brother of William Wildie Robertson (1774-1842) who ran Robertson's Quarry on Rocky and Austin runs. James resided in or near the town of Aquia and was the likely son of Lawson Robertson.

[139] Henry Musselman (c.1765-c.1815) was the son of Christian Musselman (c.1730-after 1801).

[140] This may be the William Norman who in 1801 married Mary Ann Felder in Prince William County.

[141] Francis Payne (died c.1815). His daughter, Jemima (c.1774-c.1869) married George Curtis, Jr. (c.1767-1844).

[142] In 1812 John W. Payne (died c.1817) paid taxes on 7 slaves and 2 horses.

[143] Aldom Puzey (died c.1825) was a stone mason. He may be Algernon Pusey (1766:84-after 1810) who was listed in the 1810 census as a resident of Falmouth. Some of the Puseys were Pennsylvania Quakers and one may wonder of Aldom might have been one of those employed at Hunter's Iron Works near Falmouth.

[144] In 1804 Richard Randall paid tax on 99 ½ acres in Stafford.

William Sanders	William Bronaugh	Fined for failure to appear at muster but had no property to fine.
Benjamin Shacklett[145]	William Bronaugh	Fined for failure to appear at muster but had no property to fine.
Edward Shelton[146]	William Bronaugh	
William Shelton	William Bronaugh	
Mourning Smith[147]	Benjamin Ficklen	Fined for failure to appear at muster but had no property to fine.
William Smith	Charles Ralls	Fined for failure to appear at muster but could not be found.
Jeremiah Stark[148]	William Bronaugh	
James Stewart	William Hay	
John Shelkett[149]	William Hay	
Jesse Stone[150]	Benjamin Ficklen	
Gabriel Sullivan[151]	William Bronaugh	Fined for failure to appear at muster but had no property to fine.
John Sullivan	William Bronaugh	Fined for failure to appear at muster but had no property to fine.
Thomas Sullivan	Henry Mason	Fined for failure to appear at muster but had no property to fine. He "refused to fall in ranks in June."
Henry Taylor	Benjamin Ficklen	Fined for failure to appear at muster but had no property to fine.
John Templemen	Benjamin Ficklen	Fined for failure to appear at muster but had no property to fine.
William Templeman	Lewis Mason	Fined for failure to appear at muster but had no property to fine.
Thomas Tippett	Benjamin Ficklen	
Mark Walters[152]	William Williams	
James Walker	Lewis Mason	
Bailey Washington, Jr.[153]	Samuel H. Peyton	

[145] In 1783 Benjamin Shacklett paid slaves on 3 horses and 12 cattle. He didn't own any slaves. In 1806 he bought Lot #42 from the trustees of Woodstock (town of Aquia) (Stafford Land Tax Records).

[146] Edward Shelton (1761-1850) was the likely son of William Shelton and Margaret Nelson. William was born in Charles County, Maryland. This may be the same Edward Shelton who from 1815 to at least 1817 rented part of the Bell's Hill tract north and west of the courthouse (Lee, VHS).

[147] Mourning Smith (c.1777-1853) was the son of John Smith of Spotsylvania and was involved with the Rappahannock Gold Mine near Richland Baptist Church. He married Sally Ann Stewart and left a large family in Stafford.

[148] Jeremiah Stark (1749-1824) was the son of Thomas Stark (c.1725-1802) of Stafford. He married Mary King of Stafford. In 1804 he paid taxes on 111 acres in Stafford. In 1809 Jeremiah was dismissed from Chappawamsic Baptist Church. He died in Abbeville County, South Carolina.

[149] During the early to mid-19th century, there were two John Shelketts in Stafford, both of whom had wives named Nancy. One John Shelkett (1793-1857) married Nancy Stark (1786-1834) of Fauquier and lived in the upper part of Stafford. Thye John Shelkett included in the militia records seems to have been the other by that name who died in 1825. He married Nancy Lunsford (c.1780-1870), the daughter of John and Nancy Lunsford of King George County. In 1816 this John was a tenant on Crow's Nest; he later lived on William Hewitt's Locust Grove near Belle Plains (Eby, Will).

[150] Jesse Stone (1772-1841) was the son of Spilsby Stone (1742-1818). He was born in Stafford and married Betsy Wells (1773-1833), the daughter of Carty Wells and Margaret Bush. Jesse was a blacksmith (Stafford County Estate, 1823, p. 170). He died in Nelson County, Kentucky.

[151] In 1812 Gabriel Sullivan paid taxes on 4 horses. By 1826 he was levy free, or exempt from paying the levies.

[152] The Walters and Waters surnames may have been used interchangeably. This may be the Mark Waters who lived on Chappawamsic Run and was included in the Stafford land tax records.

David Waugh	William Bronaugh	Fined for failure to appear at muster but had moved.
Charles West	William Bronaugh	Fined for failure to appear at muster but had no property to fine.
John Woodard	William Bronaugh	Fined for failure to appear at muster but had no property to fine.
John Yost	Charles Ralls	Fined for failure to appear at muster but had moved.

1798

Lt. Col. Commandant—James Primm
Captain of Light Infantry—William Bronaugh—2nd Battalion
                        Hancock Eustace—1st Battalion
Captains—Lewis Mason—1st Battalion
        Benjamin Ficklen—1st Battalion
        Benjamin Tolson—1st Battalion
        Samuel H. Peyton—1st Battalion
        Henry Mason—2nd Battalion
        Garnett Peyton—2nd Battalion
        Robert Hening—2nd Battalion
        John Fox—2nd Battalion
        Hancock Eustace
        William Bronaugh
Majors—William Williams
        Enoch Mason
Clerk of the Court Martial—William Mountjoy[154]

Fined for failure to appear at muster:

Name	Company	Note
John Armstrong	John Fox	Fined for failure to appear at muster but could not be found.
John Armstrong	William Bronaugh	Fined for failure to appear at muster but could not be found.
Enoch Bayles	John Fox	Fined for failure to appear at muster but he had moved.
William Bates	Henry Mason	Fined for failure to appear at muster but was dead and insolvent.
Abram Bloxton	Garnett Peyton	Fined for failure to appear at muster but had moved to Maryland.
John Braniston[155]	Lewis Mason	Fined for failure to appear at muster but had no property to fine.
Thomas Bridwell	Hancock Eustace	Fined for failure to appear at muster but had no property to fine.
Thaddeus Brown	John Fox	Fined for failure to appear at muster but had no property to fine.
William Brown, Jr.	Henry Mason	Fined for failure to appear at muster but had moved.
Isaac Burton[156]	John Fox	Fined for failure to appear at muster but had no property to

---

[153] Bailey Washington, Jr. (1752-1814) was the son of Bailey Washington (1731-1807) of Windsor Forest. In 1812 he paid taxes on 19 slaves, 8 horses, 1 coach, and 561 acres (Windsor Forest). This tract is now part of the Marine Corps reservation.
[154] William Mountjoy (1737-1820) was the son of Capt. William Mountjoy (1711-1777) and Phyllis Reilly (1717-1771) of Locust Hill near what is now Brooke. The younger William inherited his father's Locust Hill property and served as a justice in Stafford in 1774 (and possibly other years as well).
[155] This may well be John Branson (born 1777), the son of William Branson (born c.1714) and Elizabeth Osmond. John was a Quaker. He was born in Stafford and married Abigail Holloway, also from a Quaker family.

1798

William Chadwell	Samuel H. Peyton	Fined for failure to appear at muster but had no property to fine.
Charles Cocks	Henry Mason	Fined for failure to appear at muster & was judged insolvent.
Samuel Cocks	Henry Mason	Fined for failure to appear at muster & was judged insolvent.
Fielding Coppage[157]	Garnett Peyton	Fined for failure to appear at muster but had moved to Kentucky.
Morris Cosby[158]	Benjamin Tolson	Fined for failure to appear at muster but he had moved.
Spencer Dawson	Benjamin Tolson	Fined for failure to appear at muster but had moved to Prince William.
James Dowdall[159]	Lewis Mason	Fined for failure to appear at muster but he had moved.
George Fling	Lewis Mason	Fined for failure to appear at muster but had no property to fine.
Thomas Harding[160]	Hancock Eustace	Fined for failure to appear at muster but had no property to fine.
Robert Harrison	Hancock Eustace	Fined for failure to appear at muster but had moved to Prince William.
Abel Holloway[161]	John Fox	Fined for failure to appear at muster but had died.
Reuben Hord[162]	Hancock Eustace	Fined for failure to appear at muster but he had moved.
George Horton	Robert Hening	Fined for failure to appear at muster but had moved.
John Hutchison	Benjamin Tolson	Fined for failure to appear at muster but he had moved to Maryland.
George Jones	William Bronaugh	Fined for failure to appear at muster but he had moved.
Travers Jones[163]	William Bronaugh	Fined for failure to appear at muster but he had moved.
George Kisshuck	Robert Hening	Fined for failure to appear at muster but had moved.
Thomas Knight[164]	Garnett Peyton	Fined for failure to appear at muster but had no property to fine.
James Lavinder	Benjamin Ficklen	Fined for failure to appear at muster but he was found to be insolvent.
Porch Limbrick	Benjamin Ficklen	Fined for failure to appear at muster but had no property to fine.
Moses Lowry[165]	Hancock Eustace	Fined for failure to appear at muster but had no property to fine.
Enos Monteith[166]	Henry Mason	Fined for failure to appear at muster but had no property to

[156] Isaac Burton married Mary, the daughter of Anthony Marquess. In 1804 he paid tax on 114 acres that had formerly belonged to James Hunter of Falmouth.

[157] Fielding Coppage was the son of Travis Coppage and Elizabeth Helm (1772-1851). Fielding moved to Pendleton County, Kentucky.

[158] Morris Cosby (1769-1814) was the son of Wingfield Cosby (1746-c.1810) and Mary Morris of Louisa County. He was descended from John Cosby of York County and died unmarried.

[159] James Dowdall (1758-1802) owned Spotted Tavern in Hartwood. He married Elizabeth Cropp (1765-1799), the daughter of James Cropp (died c.1778) of Stafford and Joyce Hinson.

[160] Little is known about Thomas Harding. In 1810 he served as a constable in Stafford.

[161] Abel Holloway was a Quaker and the son of Isaac Holloway (1735-c.1809) of Stafford. He married Rachel Branson.

[162] Reuben Hord (died after 1839) was the son of Peter Hord (c.1749-after 1790) of Essex, King George, and Stafford counties. Reuben was killed in Georgia.

[163] Travers Jones was the son of Henry Jones, Sr. Travers had a brother named Charles (Stafford Deed Book GG, p. 10).

[164] In 1812 Thomas Knight paid taxes on himself only.

[165] In 1799 Moses Lowry (born c.1770) was the brother of Thomas Lowry (1760-1846). He married Mary Snapp in Frederick County, Virginia.

1798

		fine.
John Martain	William Bronaugh	Fined for failure to appear at muster but he had moved.
Henly Mattocks	William Bronaugh	Fined for failure to appear at muster.
Joshua Morton	Henry Mason	Fined for failure to appear at muster but had moved.
Edward Mullin[167]	Lewis Mason	Fined for failure to appear at muster but had no property to fine.
James Munns	Robert Hening	Fined for failure to appear at muster but had moved.
James Owens[168]	Henry Mason	Fined for failure to appear at muster but had moved.
James Payne	Robert Hening	Fined for failure to appear at muster but could not be found.
John Payne	Garnett Peyton	Fined for failure to appear at muster but had no property to fine.
John Payne	Benjamin Ficklen	Fined for failure to appear at muster but he had moved.
Jacob Pettit	John Fox	Fined for failure to appear at muster but he had moved.
William Robertson	Robert Hening	Fined for failure to appear at muster but could not be found.
Thornley Schooler	Robert Hening	Fined for failure to appear at muster but had no property to fine.
George Shurlock	Robert Hening	Fined for failure to appear at muster but had moved.
Jesse Simpson	John Fox	Fined for failure to appear at muster but he had moved.
Gabriel Sullivant	William Bronaugh	Fined for failure to appear at muster but he had moved to Kentucky.
George Swope	Robert Hening	Fined for failure to appear at muster but had moved.
William True	Benjamin Ficklen	Fined for failure to appear at muster but he was found to be insolvent.
Stewart Wallace[169]	Robert Hening	Fined for failure to appear at muster but had moved.
Charles West	William Bronaugh	Fined for failure to appear at muster but had moved.
Charles West	Robert Hening	Fined for failure to appear at muster & was judged insolvent.
John Williams	John Fox	Fined for failure to appear at muster but he had moved.

At the annual Officers' Parade and General Muster Presley Cox[170] was paid for his services as a drum major and "for repairs done to a Drum." Joseph Chinn[171] was paid for his services there as a fife major (Auditor, Fines).

1799
Colonel—James Primm
Major—Enoch Mason
Captains—Garnett Peyton
    Benjamin Ficklen
    Samuel H. Peyton
    Benjamin Tolson
Adjutant of Court Martial—Benjamin James[172]

---

[166] Enos Monteith (born c.1780) was the son of James Monteith and Leah Owens. He married Eleanor Thorn (c.1778-1870) and lived in White Oak.
[167] Edward Mullin may have been the son of William Mullin (died 1791) who was employed at James Hunter's Iron Works near Falmouth.
[168] James Owens was the son of Reuben Owens and Sarah Kenney. He married his first cousin, Keziah Monteith.
[169] Stewart Wallace kept a store in Falmouth.
[170] Presley Cox married Sarah Jett (died before 1820), the daughter of Francis Jett (c.1735-1791) and Barsheba Porch (c.1741-1817).
[171] Joseph Chinn may be Joseph James Chinn (c.1775-1821) of Stafford.

1799

Provost Marshall—Richard Morton
Clerk of the Court Martial—William Mountjoy
Enlisted—Thomas Newton

1800
Adjutant—Benjamin James
1ˢᵗ Major—Enoch Mason
Captains—Samuel H. Peyton
          Hancock Eustace
          Benjamin Ficklen
          William Bell[173]—captain of Falmouth Company—in room of Robert Hening, resigned
          Henry Mason
          Daniel Mason[174]
          Lewis Mason
          William Waller—in room of Garnett Peyton, resigned
          John Fox
          John James[175]—in room of Hancock Eustace, promoted
2ⁿᵈ Lieutenant—James McRobertson—in Hancock Eustace's company
3ʳᵈ Lieutenant—William Hill—in Hancock Eustace's company
Lieutenants—Gervis C. Davis[176]—in Benjamin Ficklen's company—in room of Joel Mason, resigned
            John Hore—in Falmouth company
            Lewis Hord[177]—William Burroughs'[178] company—in room of Daniel Mason, disqualified
            John G. Hedgman[179]
            Allen Withers—in John Fox's company—in room of Edward Withers, resigned
            Thomas Fristoe—in room of Reubin Franklyn, resigned
            Robert Crutcher[180]—in Hancock Eustace's company

---

[172] This may be Benjamin Strother James (1768-1825), the son of John James (c.1732-1794) and Ann Strother (c.1730-c.1814). Benjamin, a lawyer, married Jean Stobo (born 1764) and moved to Laurens County, South Carolina.

[173] William Bell (1771-1855) is believed to have been the son of John Bell (c.1748-1830) who owned Bellmeade just north of Falmouth. William lived in Falmouth and from c.1807 to c.1827 he operated a tavern there. He was the first known tax collector for Falmouth, a town trustee, and was also the chief tobacco inspector at Dixon's Warehouse in Falmouth.

[174] Daniel Mason was the son of Daniel Mason, Sr. (c.1725-c.1810) and Elizabeth Nelson. In 1755 Daniel, Sr. leased 200 acres in the forks of Aquia and Cannon runs adjoining land belonging to his wife's family (Stafford Deed Book P, p. 41). Daniel Mason, Sr. owned land near Loch Lomond on Potomac Run which was near Harding's Mill and the "muster field" (*Virginia Herald*, May 17, 1809). In 1812 Daniel, Jr. paid taxes on 2 slaves and 5 horses.

[175] John James (born 1763) was the son of John James (c.1732-1794) and Anne Strother (c.1730-c.1814).

[176] Gervis Davis (died after 1834) was a millwright. By 1815 he lived near Richards' Ferry. In 1819 Gervis paid tax on 283 acres there.

[177] Lewis Hord (died after 1827) was the son of Kellis Hord (c.1744-1815) and Mary (Hord) Hord (born 1744). Lewis was a millwright.

[178] Possibly William K. Burroughs (1782-1836), son of John Burroughs (c.1748-c.1836) of Stafford. William died in Mathews County, Virginia.

[179] John Grayson Hedgman (1782-c.1845) was the son of John Hedgman (1758-1796) and Catherine Grayson (1760-1795). He married his cousin, Hannah Ball (Daniel) Brown (born 1780), the daughter of Travers Daniel, Sr. (1741-1824) and the widow of Raleigh Travers Brown, Jr. From 1842-1845 John represented Stafford County in the Virginia House of Delegates. He also held various posts in county government. John lived near Brooke.

[180] Robert Crutcher (c.1779-1829) was the son of Hugh Crutcher (died 1779) and Frances Coleman of Culpeper County. In 1809 Robert married Tarissa Hamble Phillips (1783-c.1853), the daughter of Col. William Phillips (1744-1797) and Elizabeth Anne Fowke (1747-c.1830) of Traveler's Rest. This old farm,

1800

Ensigns—Thomas Starke[181]—in room of John Harding, resigned
    Archibald Rowley—in Henry Mason's company—in room of Thomas Newton, resigned
    William Horton—William Burroughs' company—in room of Stanfield Jones, resigned
    William Ball
    John P. Fant[182]—in John Fox's company—in room of Allen Withers, promoted
    Henry Williams[183]—in room of Thomas Fristoe, promoted
Clerk of the Court Martial—William Mountjoy

1801

Lt. Colonel Commandant—Lewis Mason
Colonel—Enoch Mason—in room of James Primm, resigned
1st Major—Samuel H. Peyton—in room of Enoch Mason, promoted
2nd Major—Benjamin Ficklen—in room of William Williams, resigned
Captain of Falmouth Militia—William Ball
Captains—John James
    William Starke—in room of Samuel H. Peyton, promoted
    Gervis C. Davis—in room of Benjamin Ficklen, promoted
    Henry Mason
    Lawson Robertson—in room of Nathaniel P. Williams
    William Waller
    John Hore—in room of William Bell, resigned
    John Sterne—in room of Lewis Mason, resigned
    Lewis Hord—in room of William Bronaugh, resigned
    Allen Withers—in room of John Fox, resigned
    Robert Crutcher—in room of John James, deceased
1st Lieutenant—James M. Robertson—in room of Robert Crutcher, promoted
2nd Lieutenant—William Hill—in room of James M. Robertson, promoted
3rd Lieutenant—Martin Bronaugh[184]—in room of William Hill, promoted
Lieutenants—John C. Edrington[185]—in Capt. John James' company—in room of William Ware resigned
    James N. Stewart[186]—in room of William Starke, promoted
    William West—in room of Gervis C. Davis, promoted
    Thomas Alexander—in Henry Mason's company—in room of Charles Bruce, resigned
    Lewis Bridwell—in room of Lawson Robertson, promoted
    Charles Bell—in room of John Hore, promoted
    Rawleigh T. Browne—William Waller's company—in room of John Hedgman, resigned
    Enoch Harding—in room of John Stern promoted
    William Horton—in room of Lewis Hord, promoted

---

one of several in Stafford by that name, was north of Ruby Post Office and is now part of the Marine Corps reservation.

[181] Thomas Stark (1759-1820) was the son of John Stark (1717-1781) and Hannah Eaves (born c.1721). Thomas married Sarah Fristoe (born 1759) and died in Bourbon County, Kentucky. In 1812 he paid taxes on 8 slaves, 4 horses, 1 gig, and 310 acres on Cannon Run 12 miles northwest of the courthouse.

[182] John Penn Fant (1776-1850) was the son of Joseph Fant (1738-1812). In 1802 he married Anna Payne and died in Culpeper. Prior to leaving Stafford, he was a member of Hartwood Baptist Church (Hartwood).

[183] In 1812 Henry Williams paid taxes on 9 slaves, 7 horses, and 300 acres 10 miles north of the courthouse.

[184] Martin Bronaugh was the son of Col. John Bronaugh (1743-1777) and Mary Anne Carter. He married Sarah Bronaugh (1784-1869).

[185] John Catesby Edrington (1775-1820) lived at Myrtle Grove on Aquia Creek. He was the son of William Edrington, Jr. (c.1741-1794). William was born in Stafford and died in Fairfield, South Carolina. John Catesby married Sarah Porter (born 1769), the daughter of Joseph Porter and Jemima Smith. John died in Stafford and was buried at Myrtle Grove. His gravesite is now in Aquia Overlook subdivision.

[186] James N. (may be Norman) Stewart (died 1825) was the son of Charles Stewart (died 1819) and Ann Norman (born 1750). For a number of years James owned Coal Landing on Aquia Creek.

1801

    John P. Fant—in room of Allen Withers, promoted
Ensigns—Elijah Harding[187]—in room of James Stewart, promoted
    Claiborne Fox[188]—in room of Archibald Rowley, resigned
    John Ashby[189]—in room of Lewis Bridwell, promoted
    Lewis Alexander[190]—in room of Charles Bell, promoted
    Fielding Fant[191]—in room of Enoch Harding, promoted
    Ransom Reddish[192]—in room of William Horton, promoted
    Benjamin Pettitt[193]—in room of John P. Fant, promoted
    James Stewart—in Samuel H. Peyton's company—in room of Thomas Starke, resigned
Clerk of the Court Martial—William Mountjoy

1802

Adjutant—Thomas Fristoe
Majors—Benjamin Ficklen
    Henry Mason
    William A. Withers
Captains—Thomas C. Alexander[194]
    Thomas Fristoe—in room of Lawson Robertson, resigned
    Daniel Mason, Jr.—in room of Lewis Hord, resigned
    John Hore
    Robert Crutcher
    John Stern
    Hancock Eustace
    Benjamin Tolson
    William Stark
    William Waller
Captain of Cavalry—Garnett Peyton[195]—in room of Hancock Eustace resigned
1st Lieutenant—James M. Robertson—in Hancock Eustace's company
Lieutenants—Claiborne Fox
    Elijah Harding—in room of James N. Stewart, resigned
    Henry Williams
    Coleman R. Browne[196]—Capt. Thomas Fristoe's company—in room of Lewis Bridwell, resigned

---

[187] Elijah Harding (died 1826) lived on part of the Parke Quarter in Hartwood. He was the son of William Harding (1738-1826) and Clarissa "Clarky" Million (1745-1826). He married Philadelphia ___. In 1812 Elijah paid taxes on 4 slaves, 4 horses, and 117 acres 10 miles west of the courthouse.

[188] Claiborne Fox was the son of Capt. Nathaniel Fox (1748-1819) and Sarah Newton.

[189] John Ashby was the brother of Robert Ashby.

[190] The parentage of Lewis Alexander (died 1827) is uncertain. He lived in Falmouth and in 1808 married Elizabeth Patterson (c.1783-1862), the daughter of Leonard Patterson. Lewis also owned property in Fredericksburg. From around 1811 until at least 1812 he was a trustee of the town of Falmouth.

[191] Fielding Fant (c.1771-1824) was the son of George Fant (1745-1839). At the March term of the Stafford Court, 1793 Fielding was charged with the murder of Thomas Graves. He was accused of hitting Graves in the head with an ax and killing him while Elias Fant, Fielding's cousin was charged as an accessory in fact (*Virginia Herald*, May 9, 1793). Apparently, Fielding was found not guilty as he moved to Kentucky. Around 1794 Fielding married Frances Hardin(g).

[192] Ransom Reddish (c-1778 c.1837) was the son of Joel Reddish (1748-c.1826). His first wife was Mary "Polly" Butler (born 1814). He married secondly Mary Ann Hall and removed to Kentucky.

[193] Benjamin Pettit (died 1801:1805). In 1789 Benjamin was the overseer of the road "from Falmouth to Chapman's Ordinary" (Stafford County Scheme Book 1790-1793, p. 78). Benjamin married Mary Banks and moved to Lincoln County, Kentucky.

[194] Thomas Casson Alexander (died 1817) was the son of William Pearson Alexander (1758-1804) and Sarah Bruce Casson. He married Elizabeth Callaway Innis (born 1785) and moved to Henrico County. Thomas died unexpectedly while on a visit to Falmouth (*Virginia Herald*, May 24, 1817).

[195] Garnett Peyton resigned in favor of James M. Robertson, also an Aquia resident.

Innis Browne[197]—in room of William Horton, cashiered
Rawleigh T. Brown
William Stark
Cornet of Cavalry—John H. Peyton[198]—in room of Martin Bronaugh, resigned
Ensigns—Benjamin Ashby[199]—in Capt. Crutcher's company
William Primm—in room of Ransom Reddish, resigned
Thomas Pilcher[200]
George Williams
George H. Tolson[201]—in room of John Ashby, resigned
Samuel Marquess[202]—in Capt. John Hore's company—in room of Lewis Alexander, resigned

Men fined for failure to appear at muster:

Henry Mason's Company:

William Achors	Benjamin Kennedy[203]	John Patterson
James Bates[204]	George Leach[205]	Lewis Read
Henry Boarn	Daniel McCarty	George Robertson
John Brown[206]	James McCarty	William Stone[207]

---

[196] Coleman Reid Browne (died 1829) was the son of Joseph Browne (died 1806) and Ann Innis. He was also the brother of Innis Browne. Coleman worked as overseer on his father's Stafford plantation. He married ___ Harding, widow of Enoch Harding (died c.1814). In 1812 Coleman paid taxes on 2 slaves and 2 horses in Stafford.

[197] Innis Browne (died c.1840) married Sarah Botts (1787-c.1826), the daughter of Aaron Botts (1746-1790). In 1803 he was a deputy sheriff in Stafford (Eby, Men 141). In 1827 he paid taxes on 324 ½ acres on Beaverdam Run ten miles north of Stafford Courthouse.

[198] May be John Howison Peyton (died c.1815), the son of John Rowzee Peyton of Stafford. John H. Peyton later lived in King George.

[199] It's unclear which Benjamin Ashby this was.

[200] This may be the Thomas Pilcher (c.1787-1832) who was the son of the elder Daniel Pilcher and may the same Thomas who married Elizabeth Bray and died in Tappahannock in 1832 (*Virginia Herald*, Feb. 1, 1832).

[201] George H. Tolson (c.1779-1832) was the son of George Tolson (1726-1783). He married Sythia Combs, the daughter of Capt. Joseph Combs and Mary Rousseau. In 1812 George paid taxes on 6 slaves, 3 horses, and 301 acres on Beaverdam Run of Aquia 12 miles northwest of the courthouse. During the early 1800s, George drove a wagon and team that transported goods between Dumfries, Aquia, and Falmouth.

[202] Samuel Marquess (c.1780-c.1848) was the son of Anthony Marquess. In 1849 he paid tax on land on Falls Run about 10 miles southwest of the courthouse.

[203] In 1813 Benjamin E. Kennedy paid tax on 118 acres adjoining Gabriel Jones, James Withers, and William Waller. This was on the north side of Potomac Run near Mountain View Road.

[204] James Bates married Mary Limbrick, the daughter of William Limbrick (died c.1784) and Letitia Porch (c.1740-c.1804).

[205] George Leach (died c.1834) was granted licenses to run an ordinary from roughly 1815 until his death c.1834.

[206] The 1807 personal property tax records indicate that John Brown was a blacksmith.

[207] This may be William Stone (c.1759-1829) who served three years in the Revolution under Col. George Gibson. In 1777 he enlisted in Capt. Walter Vowles' company of the 1st Virginia State Regiment and fought at White Marsh, Valley Forge, Monmouth, Stony Hook, and Paulus Hook. He was wounded in the thigh by buckshot. He also served a few months in Capt. William Washington's cavalry unit. When he applied for his pension, he owned "no property of any kind [and had] a wife & three Children—a farmer on rented land." In 1818 he was still living in Stafford, but by 1821 was a resident of Caroline. In 1781 he

1802

William Brown, Jr.	Philip Mannen	George Sullivan
William Curtis	Benjamin Newton[208]	Meriweather Taliaferro[209]
William Fletcher	Isaac Newton	Richard J. Tutt[210]
Jacob Gardner	Chandler Pates[211]	
George Hartly	Reuben Pates	

William A. Withers' Company:

Joseph Barber[212]	William Horton	Thornley Schooler
Abraham Blackstone	James Jones	George Thornton[213]
Nathaniel Burton[214]	George Kennedy	Joseph Turner
William Burton, Sr.[215]	William Lakenan	William B. Wallace[216]
William Black[217]	William Lunsford[218]	Archibald Watson[219]
Dennis Doyal[220]	Elijah Marquess[221]	William Watson
Joseph Graves	Joseph Marquess	Charles West
Charles Guy[222]	Samuel Marquess	
Thomas Holloway[223]	Eliot McCoy	

---

married Mary McGuire (c.1761-after 1838). After William's death, Mary moved to Harrison County, Kentucky (National Archives, Revolutionary War Pensions, #W.8752).

[208] Benjamin Newton (born 1769) was the son of John Newton and Mary Thomas. He married Nancy Butler, the daughter of William Butler and Rosanna Courtney.

[209] Meriweather Taliaferro (c.1774-1824) was the son of Joseph Taliaferro and Lucy Alexander. During the War of 1812, he served in the U. S. 20th regiment of infantry as a captain. By 1815 he was a resident of King George where he died at Oakland. In 1819 he paid tax on 300 acres near the King George line. Meriweather left an illegitimate child named Nappertandy that he fathered by Ann Truston. By his will he freed and provided for his slaves (King George Will Book 3, p. 259).

[210] Richard Johnson Tutt (1772-1840) was the son of Col. Richard Tutt and Elizabeth Johnson of Culpeper. Richard married Million Kenyon and kept an ordinary in Fredericksburg. Richard died in Callaway County, Missouri.

[211] Chandler Pates (c.1780-after 1860) later lived in Spotsylvania. He married Lucy Sullivan (died before 1850), the daughter of Francis Sullivan (died c.1830) and Frances Newton.

[212] In 1814 Joseph Barber had a lease for life on 50 acres of the old mine tract near Ramoth Church.

[213] In 1804 George Thornton paid tax on 1,000 acres in Stafford.

[214] Nathaniel Burton (died c.1809). In 1790 he paid taxes on 1 slave and 4 horses in Stafford.

[215] William Burton, Sr. had a son named Fielding Burton.

[216] William Brown Wallace (1757-1833) was the son of Dr. Michael Wallace (1719-1767) and Elizabeth Brown (born 1723) of Ellerslie. In 1787 William married Barbara Fox (1766-1833). During the Revolution, William served in the 1st regiment of artillery and in 1775 in Col. William Woodford's 2nd Virginia regiment. As payment for his service William was granted 200 acres of land and by 1828 was a resident of Kentucky (National Archives, Revolutionary War Pensions, #S.42612). He and his wife died within days of each other.

[217] William Black (c.1777-after 1850).

[218] In 1812 William Lunsford paid taxes on 6 slaves and 5 horses in Stafford.

[219] In 1812 Archibald Watson paid taxes on 1 horse in Stafford.

[220] In 1780 Dennis Doyle leased from Alexander Doyle 106 acres on Whitson's Run. This included the house where George West then lived (Stafford Deed Book S, p. 41).

[221] Elijah Marquess (died 1815) was the son of Anthony Marquess and lived near Yellow Chapel, now Hartwood Presbyterian Church. In 1804 he paid tax on 159 acres he had obtained from James Hunter's estate. In 1812 Elijah and Anthony Marquess jointly paid taxes on 8 slaves, 6 horses, and 1 gig in Stafford.

[222] Charles Guy (born c.1768) was the son of William Guy (c.1718-c.1792) who may have come to Stafford for Lancaster County, Pennsylvania.

[223] In 1804 Thomas Holloway paid tax on 156 acres for John Fox.

William Waller's Company:

John T. Brooke[224]	Alexander Hay	Elijah Payne
William Berry	William Hay	Sarsfield Snoxall[225]
Joseph Boatler	Benjamin James	Jesse Stone
Jeremiah Day	John Leach	Jesse Threlkeld[226]
John B. S. Fitzhugh[227]	James Mitchell[228]	Hosea Wine

Daniel Mason's Company:

James Agin	Ephraim Fritter[229]	William Limbrick
John Beagle	Enoch Fritter[230]	John Martin
Joseph Beagle	Robert Finnall[231]	James Oglevy
Richard Brooks	James Guy	William Payne
Henry Bradley[232]	William Holloday	Christopher Rogers
Harberson Bradshaw[233]	Henry Jones[234]	William Turner
Zachariah Bradshaw[235]	Fielding Knight	James Woodward
Enoch Cox[236]	Valentine Knight[237]	William Young

---

[224] John Taliaferro Brooke (1761-1821) was the son of Richard Brooke and Ann Hay Taliaferro (born 1731). He married Ann Mason Mercer Selden.

[225] Nothing is known of Sarsfield Snoxall, but in 1820 a Townshend Snoxall was listed in the Stafford personal property tax records.

[226] This may be the Jesse Threlkeld who was the son of Margaret (Jett) Threlkeld and grandson of Peter Jett (1717-1784) and Rebecca Ann Bowen (Born c.1717) of King George.

[227] John Bolling Stith Fitzhugh (1778-1825) was the son of Henry Fitzhugh (c.1747-1815) and Elizabeth Stith (1754-1786) of Bellair, Stafford. He married Frances Tabb (born 1794) and lived at Bellair. In 1812 he paid taxes on 25 slaves, 11 horses, and 1 carriage in Stafford.

[228] James Mitchell (died 1822) was of Scottish descent. He owned the 332-acre Berry Hill tract as well as Shepherd's Green, both of which were on the south side of Potomac Run. James left children Eliza (Mitchell) Daniel, Jane (Mitchell) Morton, Margaretta G. Mitchell (1829-1879), William, James, Jr. and Mary E. Mitchell (Stafford Deed Book LL, p. 52).

[229] Ephraim Fritter (c.1790-1861) was the son of John Fritter (born 1752) and was a brother of Barnett Fritter. His modest estate included household and kitchen furniture, farm tools, and carpenter's tools valued at $148.12 (Stafford Deed Book TT, p. 67).

[230] Enoch Fritter (c.1765-c.1845) was the son of Moses Fritter (born 1726:32) and Elizabeth Horton.

[231] Robert Monteith Finnall (1775-1847). His first wife was Margaret Newton (born 1776). He married secondly Mary Rollow (born c.1780), the daughter of Archibald Rollow, Sr. (1775-1829). The Finnalls lived in White Oak.

[232] In 1817 Henry Bradley rented part of the Bell's Hill tract north and west of the courthouse (Lee, VHS).

[233] Harberson Bradshaw (1785-1843) was probably born in Amelia County, Virginia. He left an estate in Stafford. This included household and kitchen furniture, 15 cattle, 3 horses, 1 loom, 1 soap pot, 1 wagon tent, 1 curtain bedstead, 1 clock, 1 silver watch, 1 sidesaddle, shoemaker's tools, and 20 barrels of corn valued at $657.95 (Stafford Deed Book NN, p. 201). Harberson lived near Falmouth. He was a member of Chappawamsic Baptist Church from which he was dismissed in January 1812.

[234] Henry Jones was the son of Lewis Jones. In 1825 Henry served as a constable in Stafford (Eby, Men 145).

[235] Zachariah Bradshaw (born c.1785) was the son of Jeremiah Bradshaw (born c.1753) and Nancy Jeter of Dinwiddie County. He was a brother of Harberson Bradshaw. In March 1839 Thomas Seddon's administrators sold Zachariah 197 acres formerly belonging to William Marquess (Stafford Deed Book LL, p. 416).

[236] This may be the same Enoch Cox who, during the Revolution, served in Posey's Virginia battalion.

[237] According to family history, Valentine Knight was the son of Gustavus Knight (born c.1792). He married Maria Holden and moved to Ohio. This is thought to be the same Valentine Knight who served in the War of 1812 in Ross County, Ohio.

1802

Newton Cox[238]
Mourning Douglas

Benjamin Knight[239]
John Lakenan

Benjamin Tolson's Company:
Robert Ashby[240]	John Dunbar[241]	Sollomon Littleton
Benjamin Adie	Knight Dorson	William Melion[242]
George Brent	Richard Fristoe[243]	William Mountjoy
John Bridwell	John Scot Jordin	Edward Mountjoy
Presly Bridwell[244]	George Lane[245]	Vintson Taylor
Jessey Cooper, Jr.	Robert Lyle[246]	Benjamin Wells[247]
John Dent	John Lunsford	Henry Woodroe[248]

Robert Crutcher's Company
Daniel Bell[249]	Barnet Cooper	Thomas Jackson
Joseph Black	Spencer Cooper[250]	John Knight
Thomas Bridwell	William Dent	George McDaniel
Samuel Blackston[251]	Lewis Edwards[252]	Ozborn McDaniel

---

[238] Newton Cox (died before 1823) was the son of Vincent Cox and Sarah Jones. He married Judith Jett (died 1823), the daughter of Francis Jett (c.1735-1791) and Barsheba Porch (born c.1738).

[239] In 1790 Benjamin Knight paid taxes on 266 acres in Stafford.

[240] In 1812 Robert Ashby paid taxes on 2 slaves and 165 acres on Beaverdam Run.

[241] John Dunbar (died c.1814) ran the Mt. Pleasant/Rock Rimmon freestone quarry on Aquia Creek and sold stone for the new city of Washington. He does not seem to have been related to Robert Dunbar (c.1745-1831) of Falmouth with whom he was in business.

[242] William Million (1774-after 1850) was born in Stafford. By 1820 he was in Fayette County, Kentucky and then moved on to Howard County, Missouri.

[243] Richard Fristoe (1775-1856) was the son of Richard Fristoe (1742-c.1791). The younger Richard married Sarah Harding (1778-1857). Richard and Sarah later moved to Mason County, Kentucky where they died.

[244] Presley Bridwell (c.1780-c.1832) was the son of Simon Bridwell of Stafford. Presley was a member of Chappawamsic Baptist Church from which he was dismissed in 1804. He removed to Nelson County, Kentucky and died in Spencer County, Kentucky.

[245] George Lane (1762-c.1822) was born in Loudoun. He was the son of James Hardage Lane (1735-1787) and Mary Jane Smith (1739-1796). George married Mary Digges Ashmore (1781-1842). For some years he owned Rock Hill Farm in upper Stafford. During the early 1800s, he served as a justice in Stafford. In 1812 George paid taxes on 7 slaves, 6 horses, and 276 acres on Cannon Run 12 miles north of the courthouse. Mary Lane was buried in Evergreen Cemetery in Prince William County.

[246] Robert Lyle (died before 1819). In 1819 his heirs paid tax on 384 acres on South Run of Chappawamsic in what is now the Quantico reservation.

[247] In 1804 Benjamin Wells paid tax on 20 acres "for George Wells."

[248] Henry Woodroe was a merchant.

[249] In 1791 Daniel Bell (1765-c.1840) served as a deputy sheriff in Stafford. He later moved to Mason County, Kentucky. During the Revolution, he served under Capt. James Primm and was present at the Battle of Yorktown. Daniel was granted a pension but never took any of it, asking that it be left as a legacy to his daughter (National Archives, Revolutionary War Pensions, #S.30271). In 1817 Daniel rented part of the Bell's Hill tract to the north and west of the courthouse (Lee, VHS).

[250] Spencer Cooper served in the Revolution but his papers were lost (National Archives, Revolutionary War Pensions, #B. L. Wt. 11985,100).

[251] Samuel Blackstone (died before 1821). In 1821 his estate paid taxes on 298 acres on Aquia Run 3 miles north of Stafford Courthouse.

John Brown   Joseph Guye   Matthew Norman[253]
Senate Byram   James Hewe   John Phillips
Fielding Combs[254]   Baily Jordin[255]   Joseph Wormsly

Hancock Eustace's Company:
James Burroughs   Presly Gill[256]   Samuel Jones
Enoch Brown   Mason Harding[257]   Joel Mason
Jessey Carney[258]   Pitman Hill[259]   Fielding Readish
John Carter   Charles Humphry[260]   James Sinclare
Lewis Crop   Henry Jones   John Suttle[261]
Robert Crop   Isaac Jones   John West
Benjamin Ficklen   Thomas Jones

John Stern's Company:
John Branson[262]   Nathan Holloway[263]   William Primm[264]
Isaac Branson   John Holloway[265]   Robert Rose
William Chadwell   Charles Humphrey   Allen Steaphens
John Harding   Thomas Jones   William Walters
Aaron Holloway[266]   William Jones   Joseph Wright[267]

---

[252] In 1804 Lewis Edwards paid tax on 44 acres on Aquia Creek for Bennett Woodard. In 1800 he was granted a retail license and in 1802 held a license to run an ordinary (tavern/inn) (Eby, Men 252, 269). Prior to 1809 he owned Lot #50 in the town of Aquia (Stafford Land Tax Records).

[253] Matthew Norman (c.1779-1814) was the son of Edward Norman (1752-1814) and Jane Stewart (c.1756-1814) of Edge Hill. Matthew, his brother James S., and both parents died in the epidemic of 1814/15 and were buried at Edge Hill.

[254] Fielding Combs (born c.1752) was the son of John Combs (c.1715-1785) and Seth Harrison Bullitt (1728-after 1819).

[255] Baily Jordan "refuse[d] to fall in the ranks at June Muster."

[256] In 1826 Presley Gill paid taxes on 14 slaves, 7 horses, and 1 carryall and harness.

[257] In the early 1800s Mason Harding, Edward Bethel, and James Primm moved west.

[258] Jessey Carney was the son of Joshua Carney (died c.1811) who resided on Chappawamsic Run. In 1813 Jesse paid tax on 124 acres that is now in the Quantico reservation. In December 1810 Joshua Carney gave Jesse the 124 acres he had bought from Susanna Williams in 1799. This was located on the North Run of Chappawamsic and adjoined Seddon, Ashby, Meadow Branch, South Run of Chappawamsic, Million, and George Carney (Stafford Deed Book AA, p. 246).

[259] Pitman C. Hill (c.1768-1834) was the son of Leonard Hill (died c.1814) who was overseer at Landon Carter's Parke quarter in Stafford. Pitman inherited a portion of his father's Oak Grove farm in Hartwood. He married Fanny (Elliot) Wharton (before 1780-1872), the daughter of Caleb Elliot.

[260] Charles Humphrey (died c.1818) was the son of William Humphrey (died c.1799) and lived near Deep Run between Spotted Tavern and Tackett's Mill. In 1804 he paid tax on 250 acres in Stafford.

[261] John H. Suttle, Sr. (died c.1830) married Susan Barret Conway (died c.1838). He operated a freestone quarry to the west of Stafford Courthouse. His widow later ran a store in the town of Aquia.

[262] In 1813 John Branson, of the Quaker Branson family, paid tax on 122 acres adjoining Holloway.

[263] Nathan Holloway (1781-after 1850) was a Quaker and the son of Isaac Holloway (1735-c.1809) and Mary Haines (died before 1793). He married Anna Katherine Bethel. In 1812 Nathan bought from Joseph Stone and wife Elizabeth all their interest in a tract adjoining what Nathan already owned, Enoch Mason, Rawleigh Downman, and Benjamin Ficklen (Stafford Deed Book AA, p. 365). This was in the vicinity of Tackett's Mill.

[264] In 1812 William Primm paid tax on 1 horse in Stafford.

[265] John Holloway (1762-1831) was a Quaker and the son of John Holloway (1732-before 1799) and Margaret Buck (born 1733). He married Mary Shinn (1764-after 1831) and ran a mill on Potomac Run on what is now Abel Reservoir.

1802

William Stark's Company:
William Brahan	Robert Holloday[268]	William Payne
William Bronaugh	George Hansbrough[269]	Rhoadham Sims[270]
Ezekiel Cummins	Peter Horton	James Stark[271]
James Garrison	Hezron Horton	Jeremiah Stark
John Gough	Moses Kendall[272]	Francis Sudduth
John Heifornon	Christopher Knight[273]	William Templeman
William Heifornon	Baily Knight[274]	
James Heifornon	Peter Knight	

Thomas Fristoe's Company:
John Ashby	William Combs	John Mitchel
Elijah Bowling	Charles Dodson[275]	Lawson Robertson
Samuel Bridwell, Jr.	John Dodson	William Williams
Seth Combs[276]	Jacob Gun[277]	

---

[266] Aaron Holloway (1778-after 1824) was the son of Quaker Asa Holloway (1744-1819) and Abigail Wright. By 1818 he had moved to Loudoun County. At some time prior to his removal from Stafford, he had been deputy sheriff. Aaron moved to Stark County, Ohio, then to Belmont County, Ohio. In 1812 he paid taxes on 1 slave, 2 horses, and 217 acres in Stafford.

[267] Joseph Wright was a Quaker.

[268] Robert Holloday (died c.1837).

[269] George Hansbrough (born 1768) was the son of Peter Hansbrough (c.1724-1781) and Lydia Smith. In 1785 he was apprenticed to James Stigler, blacksmith and wheelwright of Fauquier. The following year he was apprenticed to Charles Ralls (died 1806) of Stafford to learn the coach making trade. In 1804 he paid tax on 35 acres in Stafford.

[270] Rodham Simms (1756-1853) was born in Stafford and died in Ralls County, Missouri. He was the son of Richard Simms, Sr. (c.1720-c.1812) and Elizabeth Bridwell (died c.1816) of Stafford. Elizabeth was the daughter of Abraham Bridwell of Stafford. Rodham married Mary Stark (born 1758).

[271] James Stark (1774-1866) was born in Stafford. Around 1808 he removed to what is now West Virginia and died at Jones Run, Harrison County, West Virginia. He married Nancy Knight (1786-1854), the daughter of Peter Knight (1760-c.1840) and Elizabeth Kendall (1758-c.1840) of Stafford. In 1807 he was overseer for Lewis Bridwell (Stafford County Personal Property Tax Records).

[272] Moses Kendall (1752-c.1825) was the son of John Kendall and Catherine Key. In 1812 Moses paid taxes on 23 slaves, 17 horses, and 3,215 acres on Aquia Run 10 miles northwest of the courthouse.

[273] Christopher Knight moved to Harrison County, Virginia and was witness to Peter Knight's Revolutionary War pension application.

[274] Baily Knight (c.1761-1839) was born in Stafford and died in Harrison County, Virginia, now West Virginia. He may have been the son of Peter Knight, Sr. and Rachel Abbot of Stafford. Baily's brother, Peter Knight, was a veteran of the Revolution. Around 1815 Baily married Elizabeth Kendall (c.1794-c.1828), the daughter of Daniel and Sarah Kendall. He married secondly c.1829 Frances Ann Green (c.1803-1878), the daughter of George Green and Agnes Stark.

[275] In 1819 Charles Dodson paid tax on 240 acres adjoining Shelkett and on Cannon Run, putting his property near Ruby Post Office and on the Quantico reservation. In 1812 Charles paid taxes on 1 slave and 1 horse.

[276] Seth Combs (died before 1812) was the son of Ennis Combs (c.1752-c.1828) and Margaret Rousseau (born 1754) of Fauquier. In 1812 Seth's widow paid taxes on 7 slaves and 4 horses in Stafford.

[277] Relatively little is known about this family. Jacob may be related to the John Gunn who married Martha Shamblin/Chamblin in Overwharton Parish in 1753. A John Gunn was listed in the Stafford tax records until 1794. Jacob was listed in 1803, but disappeared after that.

1803

Colonel—Enoch Mason
Majors—Samuel H. Peyton
    Benjamin Ficklen
Captains— Garnett Peyton
    James M. Robertson
    John Hore
    Daniel Mason
    Thomas C. Alexander
    William A. Withers
    Benjamin Tolson
    Robert Crutcher
    William Stark
    Thomas Fristoe
    John Stern
1st Lieutenant—William Hill
Lieutenants—Charles Bell
    Benjamin D. Pettit[278]
Ensigns—Claiborne Fox
    James Stewart
    John Sharp
    Lewis Bridwell
    William Seddon[279]

Fined for failure to appear at muster:

Capt. Thomas C. Alexander's Company:

Francis Brown	Peter Jett[280]	Thomas Owens[281]
William Brown	Francis Jett	James Peyton
William Brown, Jr.	William Jones	George Robertson
John Brown	Benjamin Kenneday	James Robertson
Henry Boarn	Poarch Limbrick	Jonus Smith
William Chilton	John McCarty	James Spilman
George Cox	James McCarty	Derby Sulliven[282]
James Curtis	Daniel McCarty	Thomas Sulliven
William Fletcher	Phillip Mannin	Meryweather Taliaferro
William Fugate	Isaac Newton	George Thornton
Joseph Horton	Benjamin Newton	Richard J. Tutt
Walker Johnston	Thomas Newton	

Capt. William A. Withers Company:

William Adam	Henry Bloxton	John Wallace
William Burton, Jr.[283]	George Carter	Charles West
Edward Barber[284]	Thomas Holloway	Pozey Whaling[285]

---

[278] Benjamin D. Pettit was the son of Isaac Pettit.
[279] William Seddon was the son of Thomas Seddon (c.1737-1810) of Stafford. Little is known about him other than he lived on Potomac Run.
[280] Peter Jett was the likely son of Francis Jett (c.1735-1791) and Barsheba Porch (c.1741-1817). Peter married Lucretia "Lucy" Maddox, the daughter of Basil and Margaret Maddox.
[281] Thomas Owens was the son of Reuben Owens and Sarah Kenney. He married his first cousin, Leah Owens Monteith.
[282] May be Derby Sullivan (c.1761-1841) who was born in King George and died in Fredericksburg.
[283] William Burton, Jr. was the brother of James Burton.
[284] Edward Barber (died c.1843) owned land near Deep Run on the west side of Stafford.

1803

Abraham Bloxton[286]
William Burton, Sr.

William Horton
William Lakenan

Capt. Benjamin Tolson's Company:
Benjamin Adie
Jessey Bails
George Brent
Jessey Cooper, Sr.
John Dent

Knight Dorson
Jessey Fristoe[288]
Rhoadham Hord[290]
Sollomon Littleton
John Lunsford

Moses Lunsford[287]
William Shacklet[289]
Vintson Taylor
Bladen Walters

Capt. John Hore's Company:
Lewis Alexander
Charles Brimer
Isaac Burton
Alexander Bell[293]
John F. Brimer[295]
Richard Beckwith[296]

Hazelwood Farish[291]
George Forgerson
Thomas Frost
Robert Fisher[294]
Thomas Garnet
Bazel Gordon[297]

Alexander Morson[292]
Shadrick McDermont
Merryman Payne
William Richards
Hugh Riley
Thomas Seddon[298]

---

[285] Pozey Whaling (born c.1777) was born in Charles County, Maryland and was the son of Jeremiah Whaling (born c.1750) and Mary Posey (c.1750-c.1788) of Charles County. Posey Whaling married Sarah Jones (born c.1780) of Charles County. In 1812 he paid taxes on 1 slave, 3 horses, and 1 gig in Stafford. In 1817 Pozey rented part of the Bell's Hill tract to the north and west of the courthouse (Lee, VHS).

[286] Abraham Bloxton was the son of Samuel Bloxton of Charles County, Maryland.

[287] Moses Lunsford (born 1780). By 1810 he was a resident of Mason County, Kentucky. In 1818 he married Mildred Vermillion in Kentucky.

[288] Jesse Fristoe (before 1780-1833) was the son of Richard Fristoe (1742-c.1791). In 1812 he paid taxes on 1 slave and 1 horse in Stafford. In 1812 Jesse was baptized at Chappawamsic Baptist Church and was dismissed in 1816. He moved to Mason County, Kentucky where he died.

[289] In 1812 William Shacklett paid taxes on 3 slaves and 4 horses.

[290] Rodham Hord (1777-1822) was the son of Rodham Hord (1740-1811). He was born in Stafford and died in Mason County, Kentucky. He married Catherine Fristoe (1774-c.1822).

[291] Hazelwood Farish (1771-1859) was the son of Robert Farish (1735-c.1783) of Caroline County and Ann Dudley (born 1736). He was born in Caroline and married Frances Elizabeth Tilghman (born c.1775), also of that county. In 1819 he paid tax on 572 acres on Aquia Creek, but for some years was a grocer in Fredericksburg.

[292] Alexander Morson (1761-1822) was the son of Arthur Morson (1735-1798) and Marion Andrew (c.1724-1808). In 1818 Alexander married Ann Casson Alexander (1781-1833), the daughter of William Pearson Alexander (1758-1804) of Snowden. Alexander resided at Hollywood in the southeast corner of Stafford. He served as a justice in Stafford from 1788 until at least 1810.

[293] Alexander Bell married Virginia Kiger, daughter of George Kiger, Jr. (c.1767-1857) and Ann/Nancy Lucas of Falmouth. In March 1827 William S. Stone and wife Milly (Richards) Stone sold Alexander the 150-acre Prospect or Richards' Hill adjoining Falmouth (Stafford Deed Book GG, pp. 372, 374). Alexander later moved to Culpeper where he lived at Fleetwood, later the site of the Battle of Brandy Station.

[294] In 1809 Robert Fisher was listed on the Falmouth land tax rolls.

[295] John F. Brimer lived near Falmouth.

[296] In 1798 Richard Marmaduke Beckwith (1774-1820) married Elizabeth Scott Buchanan of Clearview. Richard was born in Richmond County and practiced law in Falmouth where he died.

[297] Basil Gordon (1766-1847) was a wealthy Scottish merchant in Falmouth. He was the son of Samuel Gordon (1722-1799) of Scotland. Basil married Anna Campbell Knox (1784-1867).

[298] Thomas Seddon (1779-1831) was the son of John Seddon (c.1735-c.1812). He was a merchant and banker in Falmouth and Fredericksburg. For a number of years he resided at Oaklands on Potomac Run. He operated a store in Falmouth called "Seddon & Alexander" in partnership with Philip Alexander (died

1803

Thomas Brigs[299]	Samuel Gordon, Sr.[300]	James Spilman[301]
Michael Bower[302]	Samuel Gordon, Jr.	Benjamin Thomas[303]
Burket Bowen	Henry Graves	James Templeman
Charles Crouton[304]	John Graves[305]	Robert Tombs[306]
Reuben Crump[307]	William Hooms	James Vass[308]
Alexander Dade	Thomas Harwood[309]	George Vowles[310]
John M. Daniel[311]	Samuel Johnston	Zachariah Vowles[312]

1840). Thomas married Susan Pearson Alexander (died 1845) and eventually moved to Fredericksburg where he was a banker. When Thomas died in 1831, his body was brought back to Oaklands for burial. The Seddon graves remain, but the beautiful stones have been nearly destroyed.

[299] Thomas Briggs (1782-1855) was the son of David Briggs (1730-1813) and Jane McDonald (1750-1810) of Stony Hill and Falmouth. Thomas was a merchant. He married Lucinda B. Short (1792-1863), the daughter of John Short (1763-1794) and Judith Ball (c.1770-1843) of Carlton near Falmouth. Much of Thomas' adult life was spent in Winchester where he kept a store. During the War of 1812, Thomas served in the 19th regiment of the Virginia militia. In 1812 he paid taxes on 4 slaves in Stafford. He died at his home, Air Hill, in Clarke County, Virginia.

[300] Samuel Gordon (1759-1843) was the son of Samuel Gordon (1722-1799) of Scotland. He and his brother Basil were merchants in Falmouth and Fredericksburg. Samuel lived first at Gordon Terrace in Falmouth and then moved to Kenmore in Fredericksburg. In 1798 he married Susannah Fitzhugh Knox (1775-1869).

[301] James Spilman was a merchant in business with Thomas Briggs under the firm name of Spilman & Briggs.

[302] Michael Bowers (died 1827) married Elizabeth Withers and died in Scott County, Kentucky. In 1790 he was a resident of Falmouth. In 1812 he paid taxes on 4 slaves and 8 horses and the following year he paid taxes on 240 acres in Stafford.

[303] Benjamin Thomas (died after 1827) was the son of John Thomas. In 1814 he was accused of unlawful gaming at James Young's tavern in Fredericksburg (Fredericksburg "Grand" 1814). Benjamin seems to have resided in or near Falmouth.

[304] Charles Croughton (c.1760-1819) married Margaret Hudson (died 1804). For some years Charles owned Woodend near Greenbank. He was a merchant.

[305] John Graves (died c.1813) had a brother George W. Graves and sister Fanny Catlett. His estate included 1 slave, 2 horses, 1 looking glass, a small amount of household and kitchen furniture, 1 ox, 1 barrel of fish, cooper's tools, 108 pounds of bacon, 371 pounds of pork "Injured for the want of salt," and 2,860 barrel staves (Stafford Deed Book AA, p. 414). John lived in or near Falmouth.

[306] Robert B. Tombs (c.1764-after 1850). By 1850 Robert was a resident of the poor farm in the northern end of the county.

[307] In 1809 Reuben Crump married Mary Green in Fredericksburg.

[308] James Vass (c.1769-1837) was a Scottish merchant in Falmouth. He lived next door to Bazil Gordon. In 1799 he married Susan Brooke of Prince William County.

[309] Thomas Harwood (1769-1832) may have been the son of John Harwood (died c.1787) of Harwood Branch, Stafford. Thomas was a millwright and worked at Hunter's Iron Works near Falmouth. John and Thomas also kept an ordinary very near the modern junction of Sanford Road (Route 670) and U. S. Route 17. Thomas' first wife was Bessie Bussell (born 1784). He married secondly Elizabeth Upshaw (c.1785-1832) by whom he had five daughters.

[310] George Frazier Vowles (1780-1825) was the son of Henry Vowles (1752-1803) and Mary Frazier of Fredericksburg. In 1822 George insured a counting house, lumber (storage) house, and dwelling he owned on Lot #3 in Falmouth. This is where the Falmouth Bridge now abuts on the Stafford side of the Rappahannock. In 1811 George was granted a business license in Stafford. He died in Falmouth.

[311] Dr. John Moncure Daniel (1769-1813) was the son of Travers Daniel, Sr. (1741-1824) of Crow's Nest. John's first wife was Maria Niven (died 1792). He married secondly Margaret Eleanor Stone (1771-1809), the daughter of the Hon. Thomas Stone and Margaret Brown of Maryland. His third wife was Maria

1803

Thomas Dobing
Thomas Dogget[314]
Joel Elington[315]
Joseph Enniver

William Ker
William Mills
John Moss
James Moss[316]

Benjamin Weaks[313]
John Weaks

Capt. Daniel Mason's Company:
John Beagle
Enoch Cox
Newton Cox
Jessey Cooper
George Hedgman

Henry Jones
Benjamin Knight
Fielding Knight
William Limbrick
Enos Monteith

William Payne
Gerard Puzey[317]
Thomas Turner

Capt. William Stark's Company:
Major Fog
George Hansbrough
Hesron Horton

James Horton, Jr.
Peter Horton
Baily Knight

Peter Knight
Bartlet Mason[318]

Capt. Robert Crutcher's Company:
John Bloxton[319]
Joseph Black
Samuel Bloxton[320]
Martin Bronaugh
Baily Bell
Charles Colvin[321]
Rawleigh Colvin[322]
Thomas Cooper[324]

Samuel R. Filer
Nathaniel Fog
John Fog, Jr.
James Gough
John Garrison
Joseph Graves
Joseph Guye
Joel Harding[325]

James Knight
Thomas Knight
Ozborn McDaniel
William Mountjoy
Mathew Norman
Fielding Readish
Silas Walters[323]
Joseph Wormsly

Vowles (1786-before 1855), the daughter of Henry Vowles (1752-1803) and Mary Frazier of Fredericksburg and Falmouth. John served in the war of 1812. He studied medicine in Scotland.
[312] Zachariah Vowles (1749-1825) was the son of Thomas Vowles (before 1727-1800) and Susannah Chunn (born c.1730). For a number of years he worked in partnership with Robert Dunbar of Falmouth. Zachariah died unmarried.
[313] By 1815 Benjamin Weeks was a resident of Orange County, Virginia.
[314] Thomas Doggett was the son of Reuben Doggett, Sr. and Mary Browne.
[315] In 1804 Joel Ellington was granted a license to run an ordinary (Eby, Men 270).
[316] In 1812 James Moss paid taxes on himself only.
[317] Gerrard Puzey (died 1845) was a laborer. Most of the Puzeys lived in or near Falmouth.
[318] Bartlet Mason was the son of Lewis Mason (1757-c.1834) and Mary Bethel (died 1831).
[319] This may be John Bloxton, the son of Samuel Bloxton (died 1817). In 1802 John Bloxton rented a small farm near Chestnut Hill in central Stafford (Fredericksburg Land Causes).
[320] Samuel Bloxton (died 1817) of Maryland married Benedicta Maddox. In 1813 he bought 300 acres in Stafford that included what later became Aquia Town Center and Aquia Episcopal Church. In December 1810 Samuel conveyed to nephews Samuel Bloxton, Jr. and Thompson Bloxton 2 horses and 3 cattle (Stafford Deed Book AA, p. 193). In 1816 Samuel was granted a license to keep an ordinary (Eby, Men 271).
[321] May be Charles Colvin, Jr. (born 1770), the son of Charles Colvin, Sr. (born c.1748) of Stafford. Charles Jr. was born in Fauquier. By 1840 he was a resident of Monroe County, Ohio.
[322] Rawleigh Colvin (1776-1860) was born in Stafford and died in Harrison County, Kentucky. He may have been the son of Charles Colvin and Susannah Day of Fauquier. He married Agnes Miflin (1778-1857) and moved west between 1808 and 1810.
[323] In 1812 Silas Walters paid taxes on 1 horse in Stafford.
[324] May be Thomas Cooper (born 1756) who was the son of Joseph and Elizabeth Cooper of Stafford.
[325] Joel Harding lived on Aquia Run.

1803

John M. Conway[326]
Joseph Davis

Baily Jordin
John Knight

Henry Woodroe

Capt. Thomas Fristoe's Company:
William P. Baily[327]
Sollomon Beagle
Samuel Bridwell[328]
James Cloe

Jacob Gun
Charles Humphry
John H. Peyton
Lawson Robertson

William Ross
William Williams

Capt. James McRobertson's Company:
John Ashby
Elijah Abbot[331]
John Bridges[332]
William Bronaugh
Fielding Combs
William Combs
John Carter
Jessey Carney
Richard Crop

Thomas B. Conway[329]
Ezekiel Cummens
Richard Dilley
Henry Jones
Isaac Jones
Thomas Jones
Jessey Pettit[333]
Garnet Peyton
Benjamin Shacklet

Daniel Sims[330]
James Sinclare
John Suttle
Lewis Templeman
William Wats
James Waugh
John West

Capt. John Stern's Company:
Isaac Branson
William Barber[335]

Nathan Holloway
Daniel Humphry[336]

Rowland T. Turner[334]
Rhoadham Wood

---

[326] John Moncure Conway (1779-1864) was the son of Walker Conway (died 1786) and Ann Moncure (born 1748). He married Catherine Storke Peyton (1786-1865) and for many years was clerk of the court for Stafford.
[327] William Pierce Bayly (1773-c.1835) was the son of Pierce Bayly (1742-1800) and Mary Payne (1754-1826). Pierce was an inn keeper at Colchester and later served as sheriff of Fairfax. William P. Bayly married Mary Lester. In 1798 the Stafford court granted him a retail license and he kept a store in the village of Aquia (Eby, Men 252). He was also in partnership with his father in a store in Alexandria. In 1799 William bought Auburn, a farm that is now part of the Quantico Marine Corps base and was directly north of modern Apple Grove subdivision. In 1837 William P. Bayly's estate paid taxes on 8 slaves, 6 horses, and a carryall (a type of wheeled vehicle) in Stafford.
[328] May be Samuel Bridwell (born 1756), the son of Jacob and Elizabeth Bridwell.
[329] Thomas Barret Conway (1779-1825) owned the Mt. Pleasant/Rock Rimmon freestone quarry on Aquia Creek. He was the son of Katherine Ketura Barret (1746-1794) and married Eliza Newton (1797-1814).
[330] Daniel Simms may be the son of James Simms (born 1753) of Stafford. His name last appeared in the Stafford land tax records in 1816.
[331] Elijah Abbot (c.1759-after 1824) served in the Revolution under Lafayette. He was discharged at Cumberland Courthouse and returned to Stafford. In 1787 Elijah paid taxes on 3 horses and 10 cattle in Stafford. He owned no slaves. By 1824 he was a resident of Bourbon County, Kentucky.
[332] John Bridges (c.1756-1838) later moved to Boone County, Kentucky. During the Revolution, he served under Capt. William Washington of Stafford (National Archives, Revolutionary War Pensions, #W.4904). According to the Stafford personal property tax records, John was a blacksmith.
[333] Jesse Pettit was the son of Benjamin Pettit and Mary Banks.
[334] Rowland T. Turner married Elizabeth, the daughter of Benjamin Edge.
[335] William Barber (1787-1881) was the son of Edward Barber (died c.1843) who owned land on Deep Run. William married Sarah Roy Mason, the daughter of Enoch Mason of Clover Hill. His farm, which he called Wyoming, is now part of the Quantico Marine Corps reservation. He held many public offices in Stafford. In 1870 William submitted his Homestead Exemption. This included 367 acres, 3 cows, 1 yoke of oxen, 1 horse, 14 sheep, 4 beds, 2 "single beds (chicken feathers)," 1 dining table, 1 sofa, 1 sideboard, 1 wardrobe, 1 old buggy, 1 ox wagon (Stafford Loose Papers, Homestead Exemptions).

1803

Thomas Brock[337]
John Branson
John Fant
Aaron Holloway

Thomas Nichols
Caleb Rogers
Robert Rose
Daniel Shoemate[339]

John Wort[338]
Joseph Wright

1804

Adjutant—Thomas Fristoe
Lt. Colonel Commandant—Enoch Mason
Major—Benjamin Ficklen
Captains—John Seddon[340]—in room John Hore, resigned
    William Waller—"in room of himself who resigned in consequence of indisposition" (Governor, Folder 16)
    Thomas Mountjoy[341]—in room of William Waller who refused to serve
    Elijah Harding—in room of William Starke, resigned
    Gervis C. Davis
    Robert Crutcher
    James McRobertson
    Benjamin Tolson
    William A. Withers
    Thomas Fristoe
    Thomas C. Alexander
    Daniel Mason
Lieutenants—John Allison—in Capt. Davis' company
    William Stewart
    Thomas Mountjoy—in room of Rawleigh T. Browne, dec.
    Fielding Reddish
    Benjamin Sharp—in room of William West, resigned
    Richard J. Tutt—in room of Charles Bell, resigned
    Henry Williams
    Enoch Harding
Ensigns—Benjamin Withers—Capt. Tolson's company
    William Primm
    Thomas B. Conway
    John A. Ratcliff[342]—in Elijah Harding's company
    Benjamin Tolson—in John Seddon's company
    William Stewart—in room of William Seddon, resigned
    John Crop, Jr.—in room of Fielding Fant, resigned
    Robert Briggs[343]

---

[336] Daniel Humphrey was the son of William Humphrey (died c.1799).
[337] In 1803 Thomas Brock was accused of unlawful gaming in Fredericksburg (Fredericksburg "Grand" 1803).
[338] May be John Wirt (1783-1860), the son of George Wirt (1750-1812) of Berks County, Pennsylvania. John was born in Stafford and married Mary Simms. By 1810 he was a resident of Scott County, Kentucky.
[339] This may be Daniel Shumate (1769-1851) who was the son of William Shumate (1728-c.1787) and Ann McCormick of Stafford and Fauquier counties. Daniel married Millender Skinner and died in Garrard County, Kentucky.
[340] John Seddon (1781-1808) was the son of John Seddon (c.1735-c.1812). He was killed in a duel with Peter V. Daniel over a difference of opinion on U. S.-British relations.
[341] There were several Thomas Mountjoys in Stafford during this time and it's unclear which one this was.
[342] John A. Ratcliff (died c.1810) was the son of Richard Ratcliff (1765-1819) and Margaret Gaddess (died 1837).
[343] Robert Briggs (1785-1838) was the son of David Briggs (1730-1813) and Jane McDonald (1750-1810) of Stony Hill and Falmouth. His first married his cousin, Eleanor Atwell (died before 1828), daughter of

1804

Robert Fisher—in room of Samuel Marquess, resigned
Provost Marshall—Richard Morton
Clerk of the Court Martial—William Mountjoy
Men fined for failure to appear at muster:

Robert Crutcher's Company:

Isaac Branson	Charles Guye	John H. Peyton
Thomas Brewen	James Heifornon, Jr.	Thomas Shelton[344]
Thomas Bridwell	Peter Horton	Silas Walters
John M. Conway	Baily Knight	George West
John H. Combs	Thomas Knight	James Wilson
Barnard Cooper	William Mountjoy	Henry Woodroe
Samuel R. Filer	Edwin C. Moncure[345]	
John Fog, Jr.	William Payne	

Benjamin Tolson's Company:

Benjamin Adie	Knight Dorson	William Melion
Robert Ashby	John Dunbar	Edward Mountjoy
George Brent	Jessey Fristoe	William Mountjoy
John Bronaugh, Jr.[346]	Richard Fristoe	William Shacklet
John Bridwell	Robert Garrison[347]	William Slade
Thomas Burroughs[348]	Baily Jordin	Benjamin Tarrier
Presly Bridwell	John Scot Jordin	Vintson Taylor
Jessey Bobo[349]	George Lane	Benjamin Wells
Jessey Cooper, Jr.	Edward Loe[350]	Henry Woodroe
Thomas Cooper	John Lunsford	Rhoadham Young
William Dent	Sollomon Littleton	
John Dent	Robert Lyle	

Gervis C. Davis' Company:

Thomas L. Alison[351]	Edmund Graves	Thomas Poarch[352]

Capt. Francis Atwell. His second wife was Helen Buckner (c.1815-1871) who was 13 when she eloped with Robert and was a widow at age 20 and had two children. Robert was a physician and began his medical practice near Madison Courthouse. In 1835 he petitioned the Virginia General Assembly to incorporate a medical college in Richmond.

[344] Thomas Shelton may be the son of John Shelton and Susan Hord. He married his cousin Sarah Hord (1742-1799).

[345] Edwin Conway Moncure (1787-1816) was the son of John Moncure (1747-1784) and Anne Conway (born c.1750). In 1808 Edwin married Eleanor Edrington.

[346] John Bronaugh, Jr. (1775-1821) was the son of Dr. John Bronaugh (1743-1777) and Mary Anne Carter (1747-1825). John, Jr. married first Rosa Bronaugh (born 1777). His second wife was Frances Graham.

[347] Robert Garrison (died c.1854) lived near Garrisonville and to the north and west of Anne E. Moncure Elementary School.

[348] Thomas Burroughs (died c.1808) died in Fauquier County.

[349] Jesse Boboe (died c.1825) lived near what is now Garrisonville. His estate included 1 horse, 4 cattle, 1 shotgun, farm tools, and a small quantity of household and kitchen furniture (Stafford Deed Book GG, p. 218).

[350] In 1812 Edward Lowe paid taxes on himself only.

[351] Thomas Lawson Allison (c.1763-1808). In 1785 he married Mary Dorothea Stadler, the only known child of John Jasper/Casper Stadler (died 1796) and Mary Elizabeth Scarisbrook (1764-1795) who had been married in Pennsylvania. In 1825 Mary D. Allison was one of the founding members of Yellow Chapel, now Hartwood Presbyterian Church. John and Mary Stadler later moved to Spotsylvania County.

1804

Thomas Bettys
Robert Briggs
George Cowgill[354]
James Crop, Jr.[356]
James Fouracres

John Gollahorn
James Jett
William McCoy
Benjamin Newton
Merryman Payne

Alexander Rose
Jessey Rose[353]
William Sharp[355]
Mourning Smith

Thomas Fristoe's Company:
William Beagle
Moses Bridwell

Jacob Gun
Charles Humphry

Lawson Robertson

James McRobertson's Company;
Elijah Abbot
Lewis Bridwell
John Bridges
Samuel Botts[357]
Enoch J. Brown[358]
William Bronaugh
John Carter
Seth Combs
Thomas B. Conway

Richard Crop
Jessey Carney
Joseph Graves
Henry Jones
Isaac Jones
Zachariah Jones[359]
Jessey Pettit
Garnet Peyton
Benjamin Shacklet

James Sinclare
John Smith
William Smith
William Stark
Robert Steaphens
Lewis Templeman
William Watts
John West

Capt. Elijah Harding's Company:
George Green[360]
Robert Gollohorn[361]
George Hansbrough

Peter Horton
Peter Knight
William Mason

John Sinclare

Lt. Enoch Harding's Company:
Daniel Beach
William Bethel

John Harding
Bennet Harding

Alexander McGee
Samuel Skinker

---

[352] Thomas Porch (died after 1809) was the son of Esom Porch (c.1745-1826) who lived on the Rappahannock River southeast of Richlands Baptist Church. Much of this property was later mined for gold.
[353] In 1790 Jesse Rose (c.1750-1830) paid taxes on 1 slave and 2 horses. He died in Harrison County, Kentucky.
[354] In 1792 George Cowgill married Phebe Wait in Orange County.
[355] William Sharp was the son of Linsfield Sharpe, Jr. and the grandson of Linsfield Sharpe, Sr. (1685-1759). The Stafford Sharpes owned land off Rt. 17 near Deep Run.
[356] In 1812 James Cropp, Jr. paid taxes on 16 slaves and 8 horses in Stafford.
[357] Samuel Botts (c.1781-1835) lived on the middle branch of Chappawamsic Run. He was the son of Aaron Botts (1746-1790) and Ann Parks (c.1746-1827). Samuel's first wife was Susannah Stone (born c.1783), the daughter of Josias Stone (born 1747). He married secondly Mary Gains (born c.1794), the daughter of William Gains (died 1818) and Jane Botts (1757-c.1824). In May 1809 Bernard Botts of Prince William County sold to Samuel all Bernard's interest in the lands of his father Aaron Botts. This land was in Stafford and Culpeper counties (Stafford Deed Book AA, p. 17).
[358] Enoch J. Brown (died c.1810) was the son of Joseph Brown (died 1806) and Ann Innis. He married Elizabeth Harrison (1773-1852), the widow of George Dent (died 1801). Enoch left an estate in Fauquier.
[359] Zachariah Jones was a carpenter and the son of Henry Jones (died 1806) who owned what is now known as Bellmeade just north of Falmouth. In 1812 Zachariah paid taxes on 1 slave and 1 horse.
[360] In 1827 George Green paid taxes on 315 acres on Aquia Run 12 miles northwest of Stafford Courthouse. His wife, Catherine Green (c.1785-1815) died in the epidemic of the winter of 1814-1815 and is buried in the King cemetery on the north side of Aquia Creek.
[361] Robert Gollohorn (died 1814).

1804

Isaac Branson
John Branson
John Fant
Aaron Holloway

Daniel Holloway[362]
George Holloway[364]
Nathan Holloway
William Jones

John Wright[363]
Joseph Wright

Capt. Daniel Mason's Company:
Richard Anderson
John Beagle
Richard Brooks
Henry Bradley
Nimrod Byram[365]
George Cheshire

Enoch Cox
Edmund Graves
Daniel Grigsby
Robert Holloday
Robert Stark
John Sullivan

William Sullivan
Charles Thornton
John Thornton
Thomas Turner
John Watson
James Waugh

Capt. William A. Withers' Company:
James Adam
Henry Bloxham
Reuben Ball
William Burton, Jr.
George Carter[368]
George Clemmons
Charles Croton
James Curtis
Thomas Dogget

Jacob England[366]
Thomas Harwood
Francis Hooe
Robert H. Hooe
Vintson Limbrick[369]
John Latham, Jr.
Francis Martin[371]
John McCaulay
James Nelson

William Payne
Isaac Pierce
Moses Pilcher[367]
James Sullaven
James Templeman
Edward Tison[370]
John Wallace
Charles West

Capt. Thomas C. Alexander's Company:
Charles Bruce
James Bates
William Brown

Thomas Fox
Francis Jett
Berryman Jett[372]

Thomas Owens
Chandler Pates
Elijah Payne

---

[362] Daniel Holloway (1777-1836) was a Quaker and the son of James Holloway (1749-before 1811). Daniel removed to Belmont County, Ohio.
[363] May be John S. Wright who in 1807 was listed as a blacksmith (Stafford County Personal Property Tax Records).
[364] George Holloway (born 1784) was a Quaker and the son of John Holloway, Jr. (1762-1831) and Mary Shinn (1764-after 1831) of Stafford.
[365] Nimrod Byram (born 1776) was the son of George Byram (born 1752) and Elizabeth Fielding. He married Catherine Jones, the daughter of William Jones (died c.1812) and died in Culpeper.
[366] Jacob England (1783-1857) was the son of John England (1755-1851) and Ann Musselman (c.1760-1823) of Stafford. He married Lavinia (last name unknown) (c.1782-1851). Jacob was a blacksmith and lived some years in Richmond, though he and his wife and grown children were included on the 1850 Orange County census.
[367] There were at least two and possibly three Moses Pilchers associated with Stafford County. This one may be Moses Pilcher (1771-1806), the son of Joshua Pilcher (1749-1810) and Nancy Fielding of Culpeper. Moses married Elizabeth Collins and died in Nashville, Tennessee. In 1807 Moses was overseer for Travers Daniel, Sr. (Stafford County Personal Property Tax Records). While a resident of Stafford, he was a member of Hartwood Baptist Church (Hartwood).
[368] "George Carter—his musket in bad order at Regt. muster fined $1."
[369] Vincent Limbrick (1790-1849) was the son of John Limbrick (1740-1826) and Sarah Snipe.
[370] Edward Tyson. This branch of the Tyson family came from King George and settled in and near Falmouth. Edward was a brother of John and Joseph Tyson, also listed in the militia records.
[371] Francis Martin was a member of Hartwood Baptist Church (Hartwood).
[372] Berryman Jett (c.1780-1805) was the son of Francis Jett (c.1735-1791) and Barsheba Porch (c.1741-1817). He married Sallie Carter who married secondly James Butler.

1804

William Brown, Jr.	Peter Jett	Daniel Pilcher[373]
William Chilton	George Jones	Richard Pilcher[374]
Fielding Clift[375]	George Limbrick	George Robertson
John Cox	Poarch Limbrick	Richard Rowley
George Cox	Thomas Limbrick	Jonas Smith
Benjamin Cox	Daniel McCarty	Joseph Stewart
Thomas Curtis[376]	John McGuire	Thomas Sullaven
Henry Dillon	Enos Monteith	William Sullivan
William Fletcher	Thomas Newton	Mariweather Taliaferro

John Seddon's Company:

Lewis Alexander	Samuel Gordon, Jr.	William Roberts
Charles Bell	Bazel Gordon	Thomas Seddon, Jr.
Alexander Bell	Thomas W. Garnett[377]	Benjamin Sneling[378]
Burket Bowen	John Graves	James Spilman
Thomas Briggs	John Hall	Benjamin Thomas
Richard M. Beckwith	William Hooms	George Thornton
William Brooke[379]	Samuel Johnston	Joseph Tison[380]
Charles Brimmer	Lewis Jones[381]	James Vass
Daniel Degarnet	George Kenneday	George Vowles
Robert Dunbar[382]	Robert Lewis[383]	Zachariah Vowles

---

[373] May be Daniel Pilcher (c.1759-1819) who fell off the schooner *Miranda* and drowned in the Potomac River in 1819 (*Virginia Herald*, Sept. 18, 1819 and *Alexandria Gazette*, Sept. 8, 1819). In 1812 Daniel paid tax on himself only.

[374] Richard Pilcher was the brother of Frederick Pilcher. In 1805 Richard was convicted in the Madison County court of raping Jane Sullivant. He was sentenced to 13 years and 9 months in the Virginia State Penitentiary. It's unclear what became of him after his release or if he died in prison.

[375] Fielding Clift (c.1774-1856) married Elizabeth Elkins.

[376] In 1810 Thomas Curtis was listed as living in the Poplar Settlement (Stafford County Personal Property Tax Records).

[377] Thomas W. Garnett (died c.1826) was the son of Thomas Garnett (died before 1809) and lived in or near Falmouth. Thomas married Elizabeth C. Short, the daughter of John Short (1763-1794) of Carlton, just above Falmouth. Based upon his estate inventory, Thomas may have been a doctor (Stafford Deed Book GG, p. 128). In 1812 he paid taxes on 6 slaves and 5 horses in Stafford.

[378] May be Benjamin Snellings (c.1785-1859) who was born in England and lived in Stafford. His wife, Catherine (last name unknown) (1795-after 1860) was from Maryland and died in Stafford.

[379] William Brooke, Jr. was the son of William Brooke (1750-1799) and Mary Beale of Fredericksburg. At this 1804 muster he "refuse[d] to fall in ranks at Octr. Muster" and was fined $4. From around 1812 until at least 1830 William was a trustee for the town of Falmouth. In 1820 he bought a vacant lot in Falmouth and built a combination store and residence. This was later called the Temperance Tavern. In 1838 he was an officer in the Falmouth Manufacturing Company and from at least 1826-1834 was an officer in the Farmer's Bank in Fredericksburg. William became involved in the Horsepen and Franklin gold mines in Stafford and by 1838 was hopelessly in debt.

[380] Joseph Tyson (born c.1790) was born in King George County.

[381] Lewis Jones was the son of Henry Jones (died 1806) who owned what is now called Bellmeade just north of Falmouth.

[382] Robert Dunbar (c.1745-1831) was a Scottish merchant in Falmouth. He married Elizabeth Gregory Thornton (c.1767-1851) of Fall Hill. Robert owned several flour mills in Falmouth and built the first bridge across the Rappahannock from Falmouth to Fredericksburg. He also ran a store in Falmouth and was part owner of a sandstone quarry on Aquia Creek.

[383] Robert Lewis (1769-1829) was the son of Col. Fielding Lewis (1725-1781) and his second wife Betty Washington (1733-1797) of Fredericksburg. Robert married Judith Walker Browne (died 1830). He had

1804

Joel Ellington[384]	William Lunsford	Benjamin Weaks
Joseph Ennever	Shadrick McDermott	John Weaks
Johnston Farish	James Moss	William Wine
George C. Forgerson[385]	John Moss	
Almond Fortune	Benjamin Newton	
Thomas Frost	Isaac Newton	
Steaphen Fox	Theodcious [sic] Payne[386]	
William Gollohorn	William Richards	
Samuel Gordon, Sr.	Hugh Riley	

Thomas Mountjoy's Company:

Joseph Boteler	John Gollohorn[387]	James Mitchell
John T. Brooke	James Gollohorn	John W. Payne
George Cheshire	Alexander Hay	William Randoll
Peter V. Daniel[388]	William Hay	Allen Sudduth
Jeremiah Day	John G. Hedgman	
John B. S. Fitzhugh	Benjamin James	

1805

Captains—Enoch Harding—in room of John Sterne, resigned
    Daniel Mason
    Gervis C. Davis
    Thomas C. Alexander
    Benjamin Tolson
    John Seddon
    Robert Crutcher
    Thomas Fristoe
    James McRobertson
    Elijah Harding
    William A. Withers
    Thomas Mountjoy
Lieutenants—John Crop, Jr.
    William Shelton—in Daniel Mason's company—in room of Innis Browne, removed
    William Primm—in Gervis C. Davis' company—in room of John S. Allison,[389] resigned

---

been a private secretary to his uncle, George Washington, and had accompanied his aunt Martha to New York for her husband's first inauguration. Robert was chief magistrate of Fredericksburg and gave the speech welcoming Lafayette to that town. For some years he resided at Pine Grove, located between the present Chatham Bridge and Ferry Farm. He also owned Mantua on Potomac Run, which he used as a summer retreat. By 1817 Lewis owned some 730 acres on both sides of Potomac Run.

[384] Joel Ellington "refuse[d] to fall in ranks at Regt. Muster" and was fined $4.

[385] George C. Forgerson was the son of Samuel Forgerson. In 1809 George bought from John Yates and wife Julia lot #42 in Falmouth which he had been renting (Stafford Deed Book AA, p. 60).

[386] Theodocious Payne (c.1781-after 1850). In 1839 he paid taxes on 31 acres located north of Falmouth on Rt. 17.

[387] This may be the same John Gollohorn who in 1813 and 1814 rented part of the Bell's Hill tract on the north and west side of the courthouse (Lee, VHS).

[388] Peter Vivian Daniel (1784-1860) was the son of Travers Daniel, Jr. (1763-1813) and Mildred Stone (1772-1837). He married Lucy Nelson Randolph (1788-1847). Peter was admitted to the Virginia bar in 1808 and was only 25 years old when he was elected to the General Assembly. In 1812 he was elected to the Privy Council of Virginia where he served until 1835. Six years later he was elected Lieutenant Governor. Peter sat on the bench of the District Court for Eastern Virginia and in 1841 was appointed to the United States Supreme Court, the fourth Associate Justice from Virginia. He held this position for 18 years. Peter lived in Richmond for much of his life.

Thomas Pilcher—in Thomas C. Alexander's company—in room of Claiborne Fox, removed Innis Browne

Ensigns—Thornton Fant
Matthew Norman
Alexander Hord[390]
Robert Finnall
John Cooke, Jr.[391]—in Benjamin Tolson's company—in room of Benjamin Williams[392] who refused to serve
Thomas Vowles[393]—in John Seddon's company—in room of Benjamin Thomas who refused to serve

Clerk of the Court Martial—William Mountjoy

Men fined for failure to appear at muster:[394]

Benjamin Tolson's Company:

Waller S. Bell	John Cooke	George Nicholson
Thomas Burroughs	Alexander Gaddes[395]	James Pursley
William Brent	Baily Jorden	William Shacklet
Sanford Carter[396]	Edward Low	Rodham Young

Robert Crutcher's Company:

Isaac Branson	Barnet Cooper	Edwin C. Moncure
Baily Bell	Aaron Holloway	Thomas Shelton
John Bloxton	Peter Horton	Silas Walters
Thomas Bridwell	William Lunceford	James Wilson
Joseph Carter		

---

[389] John Stadler Allison was the son of Thomas Lawson Allison (c.1763-1808) and Mary Dorothea Stadler. In 1790 John was living in Spotsylvania. In 1822 he married Emily Richard Taylor (1801-1842).
[390] Alexander Hord (died after 1836) was the son of Kellis Hord (c.1744-1815) and was a carpenter. He later moved to Missouri.
[391] John Travers Cooke, Jr. (born 1787) was the son of Col. John Travers Cooke (1755-1819) and Mary Thomson Mason (1762-1806) of West Farm. He helped his brother, George M. Cooke, with the settlement of their father's estate, but little more is known of him.
[392] In 1812 Benjamin Williams paid taxes on 3 slaves and 2 horses. From 1806-1808 he was postmaster at Aquia.
[393] Thomas Vowles (died after 1830) seems to have been the son of Henry Vowles (1752-1803) and Mary Frazier of Fredericksburg and Falmouth. In 1794 he married Mary Harper, daughter of John Harper. In 1782 he paid taxes on Lot #25 in Falmouth upon which stood Vowles' Ordinary. Thomas may have been a carpenter as in 1771 he was paid for building a new ferry house in Falmouth (Town 10). During the 1790s he became overwhelmed by debt and the Fredericksburg court records contain many suits against him. By 1830 he had been declared a lunatic (Fredericksburg "Cox").
[394] These names were compiled from lists of men court-martialed and fined for failing to appear at monthly musters. They do not include those who did muster as required by law.
[395] Alexander Gaddess, Jr. (c.1767-1815) lived at Palace Green in Wide Water. He was involved in the sandstone business and from at least 1796-1804 was one of the tobacco inspectors at the Aquia Warehouse. Alexander married Catherine Kendall, the daughter of Joshua Kendall (1723-1797) and Catherine Smith (born c.1727). Alexander and his family are buried at Palace Green.
[396] Sanford Carter (c.1785-c.1872) married Hannah Read, the daughter of John Read (died c.1812) of Stafford and lived at Rock Hill Farm. He was the son of James Carter (1751-1793) and was a descendant of Capt. Thomas Carter (c.1630-1700) of Lancaster County. In 1807 Sanford was running Brent's Mill in Wide Water (Stafford County Personal Property Tax Records).

Thomas Fristoe's Company:
Learken Care	Yelverton Mason[397]	John Thompson
Aaron Garrison[398]	William Melion	William Willis
Robert Garrison	Perry Payne	
Samueld Harreld	Shelah Smithson	

Enoch Harding's Company:
Thomas L. Alison	Thomas Briggs	Samuel Skinker
Daniel Beach	Alexander Hord	John Wright
William Beach	James Jett	Joseph Wright
John Branson	Enos Monteith	

James McRobertson's Company:
Christopher Blackbourn[399]	William P. Fant	Jessey Petet
Thomas Brock	Joseph Graves	John H. Peyton
William Bronaugh	Jessey Haney	Thomas White
John Carter	Henry Jones	
Jessey Carney	William Mason	

Elijah Harding's Company:
Fielding Abbot[400]	Thomas Harding	James Loury
James Bethel	Jessey Holloway[401]	Lewis Martin
Harbison Bradshaw	George Holloway	Alexander McGee
Joseph Cooper	Bartimus Jewel	John Sinclare
Thomas Cooper	Peter Jewel	William Stadlow
Charles Dodson	Anthony Latham[402]	Thomas Tharp[403]

Gervis C. Davis' Company:
David Bradly	Frank Hill[404]	John Nelson[405]
Henry Bradly	James Latham	Richard Ratliff[406]

---

[397] Yelverton Mason (c.1776-1854) was the son of Daniel Mason (c.1725-c.1810) and Elizabeth Nelson. By 1809 he was residing in Hawkins County, Tennessee and was in Nelson County, Kentucky by 1812.

[398] Aaron Garrison, Jr. (born 1749) was the son of Aaron Garrison, Sr. and the grandson of John C. Garrison and Bell Evelyn McKnight (born c.1720).

[399] Christopher Blackburn (died c.1819) kept an ordinary in Falmouth. In 1785 he was apprenticed to William Grymes of Fredericksburg to learn the trade of a tailor. In 1812 he paid taxes on 3 slaves and 2 horses in Stafford.

[400] Fielding Abbot (died c.1813) died in Pendleton County, Kentucky. Based upon the 1810 census, he resided in the northern end of the county in what is now the Marine Corps reservation.

[401] Jesse Holloway (born 1786) was a Quaker and the son of John Holloway, Jr. (1762-1831) and Mary Shinn (1764-after 1831). He was disowned in 1815 owing to his military service.

[402] Anthony Latham (1765:80-c.1807) was the son of John Latham (c.1730-1834). He married Elizabeth Barber, the daughter of Thomas Barber of Fauquier.

[403] Thomas Tharp (c.1761-1841). In 1807 he was overseer for George Lane on a farm that is now part of the Quantico Marine Corps reservation. Thomas was the brother of John Tharp (c.1757-1838) of Spotsylvania. He married Margaret Braham and also served in the Revolution. Thomas' family later moved on to Page County, Virginia.

[404] This may be Francis Hill (died c.1809) who left an estate in Stafford. This included 2 slaves, 2 horses, 1 "Powdering tub," "4 Setting Chairs," 4 cattle, 1 spinning wheel, a small quantity of household and kitchen furniture, and farm tools valued at £185 (Stafford Deed Book AA, p. 84).

[405] In 1812 John Nelson paid taxes on 2 slaves and 3 horses in Stafford. The Nelsons owned land near the fork of Aquia and Cannon runs.

1805

Isaac Burton	William Latham	William Rose
John Byrum	Charles Lewis	John Sharp
James Crop, Jr.	Weadon Latham	William Sharp
Adonijah Delany[407]	Lewis Martin	John Shelton
William Edrington[408]	John Mills	John West[409]
Lewis Edmunson	Edward More, Jr.[410]	Woodford Yeastis

Capt. Daniel Mason's Company:

Henry Bradly	Charles Guy	Jessey Turner[411]
William Enzor	Gustavus Knight[412]	Thomas Turner
James Ford[413]	Abner Schooler[414]	
Edmund Graves	John Sullivant	

Capt. William A. Withers' Company:

Nathaniel Burton	Robert H. Hooe	Moses Pilcher
William Burton, Jr.	William Horton	John Rodgers
Reuben Ball	Thomas Harwood	Andrew Ross[415]
Charles Croughton	Francis Martin	Neri Sweatman[416]
Thomas Dogget	Theodosius Payne	John Wallace
Jacob England	George Payne	

Capt. Thomas C. Alexander's Company:

James Adam	Robert Finnel	William Proctor
John Burton	John Fennel	Thomas Prichard[417]
Henry Bourn	Berryman Jett	George Robison
William Brown, Sr.	Peter Jett	James Robison
William Brown, Jr.	Porch Limbrick	James Roe
John Cox	Vintson Limbrick	Jonas Smith
Jessey Curtis[418]	Elijah Payne	Alexander Sorrel[419]

---

[406] Richard Ratcliff (1765-1819) was born in Charles County, Maryland and moved to Stafford around 1782. He married Margaret, the daughter of Alexander Gaddess (died 1786) of Palace Green.
[407] Adonijah Dulany married Judith Barnes (born c.1768), the daughter of Leonard Barnes (c.1740-1810) of Culpeper.
[408] In 1804 William Edrington paid tax on 207 acres in Stafford.
[409] John West "refuse[d] to fall in the rank at Battn. Muster" for which he was fined $4.
[410] The son of Edward Moor (died 1806) and Ellen MacDonald. Edward, Sr. was a merchant in Falmouth.
[411] In 1829 Jesse Turner rented property from Mark Harding on Potomac Run.
[412] According to family history, Gustavus Knight (born c.1792) was born in Loudoun County. He married ___ Riley and moved to what is now Clarksburg, West Virginia.
[413] James Ford (1768-1863) was the son of James Ford (died 1794). The younger James married Elizabeth Taylor, the daughter of William and Hannah Taylor of Stafford.
[414] Abner Schooler (1775-after 1850) was the son of Thomas Schooler (born c.1723) and Mary Fant (born 1750) of Stafford. Around 1818 Abner married Margaret Kirk (born 1785). In 1832 Abner was overseer of the road "from Holloway's Mill road near Thornton Taylors, to Lewis" (Eby, Men 149). He died in Autauga, Alabama.
[415] Andrew Ross (died 1836). In 1812 he paid taxes on 1 slave and 1 horse in Stafford.
[416] Neri Swetnam (1777-1861) was the son of John Swetnam (c.1747-c.1815) and Sarah Ficklen (born before 1751). He was born in Culpeper and in 1803 married Mildred Cross (1778-1860). Neri died in Lawrence County, Kentucky.
[417] Thomas Prichard was the son of Daniel Prichard. In 1812 Thomas paid tax on himself only.
[418] In 1812 Jesse Curtis paid taxes on 3 slaves and 5 horses in Stafford.

Henry Dillon	James Peyton	Marmion Sullivant[420]
Benjamin Dillon	Perry Patterson[421]	William Wine
Robert Ellis[422]	Thomas Proctor	

Capt. John Seddon's Company:

Lewis Alexander	Bazel Gordon	John F. Slaughter[423]
David Brigs[424]	William Homes	John Settle
John F. Brimer	Robert Lewis	John Spencer
William Brooke	Shadrack McDormot	Benjamin Thomas
Richard M. Beckwith	Robert Martin	George Thornton
George Cannady	James Moss	Robert Toombs
Reuben Crump	John Moss	Joseph Tyson
Daniel Degarnet	William Mills	James Vass
Joel Ellington[425]	Joseph Martin	George Vowels
Jacob England	James Murray	Zachariah Vowels
Thomas Frost	Theodosius Payne	Thomas Ware
George C. Forgusan	Frederick Pilcher[426]	John Weeks
Robert Fisher	William Richards	Robert Weir
Thomas Garnet	Hugh Reiley	William Wiggenton[427]
Henry Graves	Thomas Seddon, Jr.	
John Graves	James Spilman	

Capt. Thomas Mountjoy's Company:

John T. Brooke	Benjamin James	Thomas Limbrick
Fielding Clift	Archibald Jett[428]	James Mitchell
Newton Cox	Allen Jones[429]	John Randol

---

[419] By 1829 Alexander Sorrel was a resident of Fredericksburg though he was still paying taxes on 136 acres in White Oak.

[420] Marmion Sullivan's name was actually Merriman Sullivan (1792-1863) though he went by Marmion for much of his life. He was the son of Benjamin Sullivan, Sr. Merryman's first wife was Virginia "Jane" Payne of Orange County. He married secondly Susan Howard (died 1889) and moved to Spotsylvania.

[421] Perry Patterson (c.1776-after 1850) married Winifred Shackelford (c.1782-1858). Perry was buried at Mt. Ida, King George County.

[422] Robert Ellis was a carpenter and operated a sawmill (Stafford County Estate Accounts, 1823-1834, p. 165).

[423] John Field Slaughter (c.1765-after 1805) was the son of Lawrence Slaughter (died 1806) and Elizabeth Field. He married Jane Alexander (1771-1804) of Prince William County.

[424] David Briggs, Jr. (1779-1837) was the son of David Briggs (1730-1813) and Jane McDonald (1750-1810) of Stony Hill and Falmouth. Like his father, David, Jr. was an attorney and spent his early legal career at Madison Courthouse where his brother, Thomas, was a physician. From 1820-1821 he served as mayor of Fredericksburg. He was also a member of the Virginia legislature and Secretary of the Constitutional Convention that framed the Virginia Constitution of 1829-1830. David married Mary Frazier Vowles (1784-1853), the daughter of Henry Vowles (1752-1803) and Mary Frazier of Falmouth.

[425] Joel Ellington "refuse[d] to fall in the ranks at Regt. Muster" for which he was fined $4.

[426] Frederick Pilcher (1769-1832) was the son of Richard Pilcher (died 1798) of Stafford. Frederick was a barrel manufacturer in Falmouth and Fredericksburg. During the early 1800s, he occupied the cooper's shop in James Hunter's old forge complex (Fredericksburg, "Dunbar vs Swan"). He married Margaret Alsop.

[427] William Wigginton (born 1775) was the son of William Wigginton (1749-1829) and his wife Elizabeth of Stafford.

[428] Archibald Jett was the son of James Jett (born c.1756) and Rosa Ann Gregory. He married Hannah Tate (born 1766) and moved to DeKalb County, Georgia.

1805

Jeremiah Day
John Fletcher
John Fox
John B. S. Fitzhugh
John G. Hedgman

Francis Jett
Robert Jacobs
Pearson King[431]
James Lance
James Leich[432]

Edward Shacklet[430]
Allen Sudduth
Thomas Sullivant

1806[433]

Lt. Colonel—Enoch Mason
Majors—Benjamin Ficklen
       Samuel H. Peyton
Captains—Thomas Fristoe
       Gervis C. Davis
       Daniel Mason
       James McRobertson
       Robert Crutcher
       William A. Withers
       Thomas C. Alexander
       John Seddon
       Benjamin Tolson
       Elijah Harding
       Enoch Harding
       Thomas Mountjoy
Lieutenants—John A. Ratcliff—in room of Fielding Reddish, resigned
              William Stewart
              William Hill
              John C. Edrington
              William Primm
Ensigns—Samuel Botts—in Thomas Fristoe's company—in room of George H. Tolson, resigned
       Willis Benson[434]—in Gervis C. Davis' company—in room of Alexander Hord, resigned
       James Crop, Jr.—in room of Thornton Fant, resigned
       Jesse Curtis—in room of Robert Finnall, resigned
       William McInteer[435]
       Armistead Alexander[436]—in Daniel Mason's company—in room of Matthew Norman, resigned

---

[429] In 1804 Allen Jones paid tax on 50 acres acquired from William Mauzy. This was probably on Accokeek or Potomac Run.

[430] Edward Shacklett (born 1787) was the son of Edward Shacklett (1758-1826) and Elizabeth Rector (1766-1839) of Rectortown, Virginia.

[431] Pearson King (died 1844) married Sarah Burroughs. For some period prior to 1824 he worked at Cossom Horton's fishery at Hope plantation on Aquia Creek (Stafford County Estate, 1823, p. 233). Pearson's widow married secondly Pearson's brother, Peter King (c.1806-1862) who lived at Coal Trips on the south side of Aquia Creek. Pearson's mother, Mary (died 1845) married secondly William Roles (died 1832). Peter and Pearson King and Mary and William Roles are buried on the north side of Aquia Creek.

[432] James Leach/Leitch "refuse[d] to receive a Musket at Apl. Muster" for which he was fined $1. In 1804 he paid tax on 200 acres in Stafford.

[433] On May 19, 1806 Lt. Col. Enoch Mason wrote to the governor informing him that an inspection of arms found "several of the guns bursted and a number of the locks unfit for use" (Auditor, Box 148, Folder 18).

[434] This may be William Willis/Wilson Lewis Benson (died 1815) was the son of Robert Benson (1762-1825) and Nancy Stringfellow (born 1771). He married Eleanor Bullard (1786-1846). Willis lived near Richlands Church in the lower part of Stafford. In 1812 he paid taxes on 11 slaves and 11 horses.

[435] William McInteer (1786-1834) was the son of Henry McInteer (born 1765) and Margaret Hansbrough (born 1768) of Stafford. He married Adah Harding (1790-1856), the daughter of Cuthbert Harding (died 1842). William, Adah, and Cuthbert all moved to Barren County, Kentucky and are buried in what is now Metcalfe County, Kentucky. The McInteers lived in the upper end of Stafford on what is now the Marine Corps reservation.

1806

Clerk of the Court Martial—William Mountjoy

Men fined for failure to appear at muster:

Capt. Benjamin Tolson's Company:
William Brent	Led W. Payne	Roadham Young
Charles Bridges[437]	James Pursley	

Capt. Robert Crutcher's Company:
Aaron Holloway	Silas Walters

Capt. Thomas Fristoe's Company:
Lawrence Botts[438]	John Burroughs[439]	Moses Rauls[440]
Charles Botts	William Bridwell	Henry Riley
William Bridges[441]	John Dorson	James Woodyard

Capt. Enoch Harding's Company:
John S. Allison	John Branson	Henry Turner
William Beach	Reuben Janens	
Daniel Beach	Nelson Mason[442]	

Capt. Elijah Harding's Company:
James Butler[443]	Haden English	John Sinclare
Zachariah Bradshaw	George Holloway	Baily Washington, Jr.
Thomas Cooper	Jesse Holloway	

Capt. Gervis C. Davis' Company:
David Bradly	John Cristy[444]	Elishea Powel
Henry Bradly	Lewis Edmundson	John Wiat
George Banks[445]	William Edrington	

---

[436] Armistead Alexander (died 1810) was the son of William Alexander (c.1736-1810). He married Sarah Hore (c.1776-1846), the daughter of Elias Hore (1749-1832) and Theodosia Waller (1753-1820). Armistead's daughter, Aliza Alexander, married Richard Marshall Scott (1807-1847).

[437] Charles Bridges (c.1785-after 1850). In 1833 he paid tax on 50 acres on Accokeek Run three miles west of the courthouse.

[438] Lawrence Botts (1786-1833) may be the son of Joseph Botts (1748-1814) and Catherine Butler (1755-1834). In 1810 he married Margaret Henderson in Kentucky and died in Jackson County, Missouri.

[439] John Burroughs (before 1775-c.1836) married Margaret Riley, the daughter of Bailey Riley of Stafford. He also married Margaret Elizabeth Vaughn (died after 1869). In October 1809 George Dawson and wife Mary (late Mary Riley, widow of Bailey Riley), William Riley and wife Margaret, Elijah Wigginton and wife Ann, and George Riley conveyed 109 acres to John Burroughs. This was land that Bailey had bought from William Fitzhugh in 1786 and was in what is now the Quantico reservation. John also operated a sandstone quarry on Aquia Creek.

[440] Moses Ralls was the son of Achsa Ralls (died c.1791). The Ralls family lived in northern Stafford and part of their property is now included in the Marine Corps reservation. Another parcel was near what is now Hampton Oaks subdivision on the south side of Garrisonville Road (Rt. 610).

[441] William Bridges lived on Potomac Run. In 1804 he paid tax on 251 acres "for Gavin Lawson."

[442] Nelson Mason (born 1753) was the son of John Mason (born c.1722) and Mary Nelson and was the brother of Col. Enoch Mason. Nelson married Lucy Benson.

[443] James Butler (c.1774-1854). In 1809 he married Sally Jett, the widow of Berryman Jett

[444] John Cristy (died c.1827).

1806

Capt. James McRobertson's Company:
John Carter	Zachariah Jones	John West
Jesse Hany	John Peyton	Thomas White

Capt. William A. Withers' Company:
Nathaniel Burton	Robert Martin	William Payne
Sira Collins	Francis Martin	Theodosius Payne
Charles Croten	George Martin	John Reamy
Thomas Harwood	George Payne	Jesse Rose
William Horton	John Payne	James Templeman
Robert H. Hooe	Jesse Payne, Jr.	Benjamin Withers[446]

Capt. Daniel Mason's Company:
William Cash	Charles Price[447]	William Taulmarsh[448]
Edmund Graves	John Sudduth[449]	Jesse Turner
Benjamin Knight	Gabrel Sullaven	
Elijah Knight[450]	John Sullaven	

Capt. Thomas C. Alexander's Company:
William Brown[451]	Benjamin Jett	George Robeson
Robert Finnel	Peter Jett	Martin Sullavin[452]
Joseph Garnet[453]	Poarch Limbrick	

Capt. Thomas Mountjoy's Company:
John T. Brooke	John B. S. Fitzhugh	James Lunsford
Jeremiah W. Bronaugh[454]	John G. Hedgman	Robert Lowry[455]
John W. Bronaugh[456]	Archabald Jett	James Mitchel
Newton Cox	John Kenney	Richard Randol

---

[445] George Banks (1779-1837) was the son of Gerard Banks (c.1725-1787) and Frances Bruce (c.1736-1818) of Greenbank. He married Jemima Anne Overton (1789-1863) and resided at Greenbank.
[446] Benjamin Withers was fined 75 cents "for returning a Musket in bad order."
[447] Charles Price, Jr. (1783-1851) was the son of Charles Price (1754-1790) and Betsy Haskins and the grandson of Pugh Price (c.1700-1775) and Jerusha Penick (died 1808) of Prince Edward County, Virginia. Charles lived some years in Stafford and married Elizabeth Fulcher (1785-1862).
[448] In 1806 William Taulmarsh (died c.1826) was listed as "suspended." He lived near the Aquia Run/Courthouse area. He was sometimes listed in county records as William Talmadge or William Talmark.
[449] This may be John Suddoth (died c.1834) who served in the Revolution and was granted a bounty land warrant (National Archives. Revolutionary War Pensions, #B.L.Wt. 2112-100).
[450] In 1812 Elijah Knight paid taxes on 1 slave and 2 horses in Stafford.
[451] The militia ledger lists William Brown as "Son of James."
[452] Martin Sullivan (c.1775-c.1827) was the son of Benjamin Sullivan (c.1760-1803) and Susannah Kitchen(?). He was included in the 1800 census of King George County (Deyo 18).
[453] Joseph Garnett was the son of Thomas Garnett (died before 1809) who lived near Falmouth.
[454] Jeremiah William Bronaugh (1779-1856) was the son of William Bronaugh (1730-1800) and Mary Doniphan (1737-1781). He married Elizabeth Hope Mitchell (1792-1849) of Maryland. In 1812 Jeremiah paid taxes on 4 slaves, 9 horses, and 950 acres on Aquia Creek adjoining John Cooke.
[455] This may be the same Robert Lowry who was listed in the 1800 census of king George County (Deyo 18). He married Margaret "Peggy" Edwards, the daughter of Andrew Edwards (1725-1788) of Potomac Creek (Fredericksburg, Land Causes, "Mountjoy," p. 180).
[456] John William Bronaugh (1772-1834) was the son of William Bronaugh (1730-1800) and Mary Doniphan (1737-1781). John married Ann Eilbeck Mason McCarty.

1806

Jeremiah Day Thomas Limbrick Sarsfield Snoxall

Capt. John Seddon's Company:
Charles Brimer	James Hobs	George W. Thornton[457]
John F. Brimer	Robert Lewis	Joseph Tison, Jr.[458]
Alexander Bell	John Lewis	James Vass
William Brooke	James Moss	Samuel Vinyard
Joel Elington	William McDaniel	George Frazier Vowels
George C. Forgerson	Isaac Newton	Zachariah Vowels
Johnson Farish	Thomas Seddon, Jr.	Robert Ware
John Gibs	James Spilman	Joseph Wharton[459]
Bazel Gordon	Benjamin Thomas	

1807

Colonel—Samuel H. Peyton—in room of Enoch Mason, resigned
Major—Benjamin Tolson
Captains—Henry Williams
         Thomas Mountjoy
         Robert Crutcher
Lieutenants—George Williams, Jr.—in Henry Williams' company
               Thomas B. Conway—in room of William Stewart, removed
Ensigns—George G. Hedgman[460]—in Thomas Mountjoy's company
         William Fitzhugh—in Thomas Mountjoy's company
         Charles Hill—in Enoch Harding's company—in room of James Crop, Jr., resigned
         George Waller[461]—in Robert Crutcher's company

1808

Lt. Colonel—Samuel H. Peyton
1st Major—Benjamin Ficklen
2nd Major—Benjamin Tolson
Captains—Allen W. Withers
         Robert Crutcher—Light Infantry
         Gervis C. Davis
         Thomas Fristoe
         Daniel Mason—Light Infantry
         Thomas C. Alexander
         John Seddon
         Elijah Harding
         Thomas Mountjoy
         Enoch Harding
         Henry Williams

---

[457] George Washington Thornton (c.1761-1816) was the son of Maj. George Thornton (1743-1781) and Mary Alexander (born 1756). He owned Rumford Farm and married Mary Goode Randolph (1785-1865). She married secondly James F. Maury. Rumford is located on Route 3 east of Fredericksburg and, at one time, included what is now Tylerton subdivision in lower Stafford.

[458] Joseph Tyson, Jr. (born c.1790) was the Joseph Tyson, Sr. (born c.1750). The elder Joseph moved around quite a bit. In 1796 he was in Stafford. From 1785-1795 he was in King George and was back in Stafford from 1800-1821. He then moved to Culpeper.

[459] Joseph Wharton married Sarah, the daughter of Benjamin Edge.

[460] George Grayson Hedgman (1785-c.1827) was the son of John Hedgman (1758-1796) and Catherine Grayson (1760-1795). He married Nancy Morton, the daughter of George Morton of King George County.

[461] George Waller (1787-c.1855) was the son of William Waller (1740-1817) and Elizabeth Allen (1746-1768) of Concord on Aquia Creek. He married Harriet C. Alexander (c.1802-1856), the daughter of Lewis Alexander of Falmouth. He was the last Waller to live at Concord.

1808

Captain of Cavalry—James M. Robertson
1st Lieutenant—Joel Mason
2nd Lieutenants of Cavalry—Thomas Hill[462]
    Joel Mason
Lieutenants—John C. Edrington—Light Infantry
    Coleman R. Browne
    Benjamin D. Pettit
    Richard J. Tutt
    John Crop
    Thomas Pilcher
    William Shelton—Light Infantry
    William Primm
    John A. Ratcliff
    George Williams, Jr.
    Thomas B. Conway
    Thomas Hill
    Rhodham Hord
Cornet of Cavalry—Rhodin Hord
Ensigns—Joseph Reddish[463]
    Barton S. Stone[464]
    Thomas Vowles
    Samuel Botts
    Jesse Curtis
    William McInteer
    Willis Benson
    Armistead Alexander—Light Infantry
    Thomas Burroughs
    George Waller—Light Infantry
    George G. Hedgman
    Joseph Reddish

1809

Major—William Allen Withers—in room of Benjamin Ficklen, resigned
Captains—Benjamin D. Pettit
    Thomas Fristoe
    Lewis Alexander—in room of Richard J. Fant, resigned
    Enoch Harding
    Thomas Mountjoy
    Richard J. Tutt—in room of John Seddon, dec.
    Willis Benson—in room of Gervis C. Davis, resigned
Lieutenants—Barton S. Stone
    John Bell, Jr.
    Lewis Alexander

---

[462] Thomas Hill (c.1781-c.1870) was the son of Leonard Hill (died c.1814) who was overseer for Landon Carter. Leonard purchased a tract in Stafford called Oak Grove, which Thomas later inherited. Thomas married his cousin, Mary Hill (c.1782-after 1870). He was a deputy sheriff in Stafford from 1818-1823 and various other years, as well. He served as a justice in Stafford from at least 1833-1848.

[463] Joseph Reddish (1787-1873) was the son of Joel Reddish (1748-c.1826). He was born in Stafford and died in Franklin County, Kentucky. Joseph married Lucy Lee Templeman. In 1812 he paid taxes on 1 slave and 5 horses in Stafford.

[464] Barton Speake Stone was the son of Hawkins Stone (1748-1810) who lived at Dipple on Chappawamsic Creek. Barton inherited his father's fishing shore above Swan Point in Maryland. In 1812 he paid taxes on 8 slaves, 4 horses, and 281 acres on Accokeek Run 2 miles south of the courthouse. In 1817 he rented part of the Bell's Hill tract to the north and west of the courthouse (Lee, VHS).

1809

Peter V. Daniel—in Enoch Harding's company
Joseph Reddish—in room of Peter V. Daniel who refused to qualify
Ensigns—Jeremiah B. Templeman[465]
John Botts[466]—in Thomas Fristoe's company—in room of Samuel Botts, resigned
Francis Sterne[467]—Enoch Harding's company in room of Abednego Adams who refused to serve
Archibald Rollow[468]—in Thomas Mountjoy's company
John S. Allison
John Bell, Jr.—in room of Thomas Vowles, resigned
John G. Hedgman—in room of George G. Hedgman, resigned
Abendigo Adams[469]

1810

Captains—Barton S. Stone—in room of Benjamin D. Pettit who refused to qualify
Henry Williams
Lewis Alexander
Daniel Mason
Lieutenants—Jeremiah B. Templeman
Thomas Burroughs—in Henry Williams' company in room of George Williams, removed from county
Ensigns—John H. Wallace[470]
John Hord
Benjamin Thomas—in Lewis Alexander's company—in room of John Lewis
Allen W. Markham[471] —in Daniel Mason's company
George Billingsley[472]—in Enoch Harding's company

1811

Major—Robert Crutcher—in room of William A. Withers, resigned
Captains—Thomas Hill—in room of James M. Robertson, resigned
Barton S. Stone
Willis Benson
Thomas Fristoe
Henry Williams
John C. Edrington
Thomas C. Alexander
Robert Crutcher

---

[465] Jeremiah Bridwell Templeman (1787-1839) was the son of James Templeman (1758-1814) and Cavey Bridwell (1768-1845).
[466] John Botts was the son of Aaron Botts. In 1812 he paid taxes on 3 slaves and 3 horses in Stafford.
[467] In 1812 Francis Stern paid taxes on 3 slaves and 3 horses in Stafford. In 1819 he paid tax on 350 acres adjoining Mason and Mathews.
[468] Archibald Rollow (1755-1820) was born in Scotland and settled in Falmouth where he was employed at the Falmouth tobacco warehouse under inspector Francis Jett. Archibald married Jett's daughter, Ann (1757-1830). In 1829 Archibald placed a notice in the local newspaper informing the public that he was running Robert Lewis' Rappahannock River ferry between Fredericksburg and Pine Grove and also advertised his services as a blacksmith (*Virginia Herald*, Jan. 14, 1829).
[469] Abednego Adams (died before 1827). In 1827 his heirs paid taxes on 103 acres on Aquia Run.
[470] Dr. John Hooe Wallace (1793-1872) was the son of John Wallace (1761-1829) and Elizabeth Hooe (c.1766-1850) of Liberty Hall. He married Mary Nicholas Gordon (1800-1879) and inherited Liberty Hall.
[471] Allen Waller Markham was the son of John Markham (1732-1804) and Jane Waller (1746-1815). In 1812 he paid taxes on 104 acres near Holloway's Mill (on or near what is now Abel Reservoir on Potomac Run).
[472] May be George Washington Billingsley (1787-after 1870), the son of Clement Billingsley (1754-1844) and Cynthia Turner (1764-1844). Around 1833 he moved to Alabama, then to Winston County, Mississippi.

Lewis Alexander
Joseph Reddish—in room of Enoch Harding, resigned
Elijah Harding
1st Lieutenant of Cavalry—Thomas Jones
2nd Lieutenant of Cavalry—Robert Beaty[473]
Lieutenants—John Botts—in Thomas Fristoe's company—in room of Coleman R. Browne, resigned
   Alexander S. H. Stone[474]—in Henry Williams' company—in room of Thomas Burroughs, removed
   Bernard Peyton[475]
   Jesse Curtis—in Thomas C. Alexander's company in room of Thomas Pilcher, resigned
   George Billingsley
Cornet—Christopher Blackburn
Ensigns—William Marquess[476]—in Barton S. Stone's company
   Levi Swetnam[477]—in Willis Benson's company
   Samuel Cole[478]
   Abner R. Alcock[479]
   John Ross[480]—in Elijah Harding's company in room of John A. Ratcliff, dec.
   Matthew Norman
   James Waller[481]
   Nathaniel P. Williams—in Thomas Fristoe's company
   Hibbard Ball[482]

---

[473] In August 1810 Basil Gordon of Falmouth sold Robert Beaty (died 1826), then of Prince William, 130 acres formerly conveyed by Samuel H. Peyton and wife Nancy to Thomas Washington. This was on Aquia Run adjoining the land of Robert Taylor (Stafford Deed Book AA, p. 236). In 1819 Robert paid taxes on 690 acres on Aquia Creek and Aquia Run. His estate included 29 hogs, 14 cattle, 31 sheep, 7 horses, 1 gig, 12 Windsor chairs, household and kitchen furniture, 1 flax wheel, 1 cotton wheel, and 6 slaves valued at $2,082.77 (Stafford Deed Book GG, p. 198). Prior to 1806 Robert was a member of Hartwood Baptist Church. That year he was dismissed to join the Baptist Church at Rock Hill (Hartwood).

[474] Alexander Smith Hawkins Stone (c.1767-1823) was the son of William Barton Stone (1757-1793) and Jemima Smith. In 1812 Alexander paid taxes on 7 slaves, 6 horses, and 100 acres on Aquia Creek adjoining John Edrington's land. In 1821 he rented Cossom Horton's fishery at Hope plantation on the south side of Aquia Creek. Alexander was buried in the Edrington/Stone cemetery in what is now Aquia Overlook subdivision in Wide Water.

[475] Bernard Peyton (1792-1854) was the son of John Rowzee Peyton and Ann Hooe. Bernard served in the 20th Infantry, U. S. Army and from 1823-1841 served as adjutant General of the Virginia Militia. He married Julia Amanda Green, daughter of Gen. Moses Green. He was also postmaster of Richmond. Bernard died at Farmington, Albemarle County and was buried in Shockoe Cemetery, Richmond.

[476] William Marquess was the son of Anthony Marquess (1752-1821) of Stafford.

[477] Levi Swetnam (1785-1838) was the son of John Swetnam (c.1747-c.1815) and Sarah Ficklen. He married Fanny Buckner Roane (1792-1858). Levis' estate inventory included 12 slaves, 12 plows, farm implements, 7 horses, 4 mules, 2 oxen, 13 cattle, 42 sheep, 33 hogs, blacksmith's tools, 1 loom, 1 spinning wheel, household and kitchen furniture, 1 sideboard, 1 walnut table, 1 settee, 17 chairs, 1 writing chair, 2 wagons, 3 table cloths, 1 shot gun, 1 silver watch, 5 beds, 1 trundle bed, and 6 counterpanes, all valued at $5,804.75 (Stafford Deed Book LL, p. 292).

[478] In 1812 Samuel Cole paid taxes on 3 slaves and 2 horses in Stafford.

[479] Abner Roane Alcock (died c.1831) was the son of Thomas Alcock (1744-1834) who owned Spotted Tavern in the Hartwood area of Stafford. Abner married Elizabeth Hazelgrove in Spotsylvania.

[480] In 1812 John Ross paid taxes on 2 slaves and 4 horses in Stafford.

[481] James E. Waller (1789-1824) married Ann Adie (1792-1870). He was the son of William Waller (1740-1817) and his third wife, Ursula Withers (1752-1818).

[482] This may be Aaron Hubbard Ball (1792-1839), the son of William Ball (born 1762) and Sarah Ann Keas (born 1769). This William Ball was born in Pennsylvania and moved to Virginia prior to 1788. In 1839

Burditt Clifton[483]—in Henry Williams' company
James Mountjoy[484]—in Thomas Mountjoy's company—in room of A. Rollow, removed from county
Bernard Peyton—in Robert Crutcher's company—in room of George Waller "moved away"
William Langfitt[485]—in Lewis Alexander's company—in room of Benjamin Thomas who refused to qualify
George Shelkett—in Barton S. Stone's company

1812

Lt. Colonel—Samuel Heath Peyton
Majors—Benjamin Tolson
   Robert Crutcher
Captains—Thomas Mountjoy
   Lewis Alexander
   Thomas C. Alexander
   Elijah Harding
   Willis Benson
   John C. Edrington
   Joseph Reddish
   Levi Swetnam
   Barton S. Stone
   William H. Fitzhugh[486]
   Thomas Hill
   Thomas Fristoe
   Daniel Mason
   Henry Williams
Lieutenants—William H. Fitzhugh—in Thomas Mountjoy's company—in room of Thomas B. Conway removed from county
   William McInteer—in Elijah Harding's company
   William Shelton
   James Waller—in J. C. Edrington's company in room of Bernard Peyton, resigned
   Levi Swetnam—in Willis Benson's company—in room of William Primm resigned
   Samuel Willcocks[487]—in Lewis Alexander's company—in room of John Ball, Jr., removed
Ensigns—William Stringfellow[488]
   Edward Templeman[489]—in Willis Benson's company

Aaron's estate paid tax on 340 acres in White Oak and near Muddy Creek. He married Elizabeth Bowen, the daughter of John Pratt Bowen (died c.1838).

[483] Burdit H. Clifton (died 1821) was the son of Henry Clifton (born 1746) and Elizabeth Hore (1751-1792). In 1812 he paid taxes on 5 slaves, 3 horses, and 453 acres on the Potomac River (Clifton). In 1816 Burdit married Hannah Waller (born 1793), the daughter of William Waller (1740-1817) of Concord. They had no children.

[484] James Mountjoy (c.1785-c.1834) was the son of William Mountjoy (1737-1820) of Locust Hill near Brooke. From his father he inherited Locust Hill and 200 acres. In 1828 he married Catherine Owens (c.1807-1874), the daughter of Thomas Owens and Leah Monteith of Stafford.

[485] In 1819 William Langfitt paid tax on 102 acres on Claiborne's Run, probably the present Glencairne, which had belonged to his father, John Langfitt. By 1841 William was a resident of Ohio (Stafford Deed Book MM, p. 199).

[486] William Henry Fitzhugh (1788-1859) was the son of Thomas Fitzhugh (1760-1820) of Boscobel. William lived at Chappawamsic Farm and married Eliza Churchill Darby (born 1795).

[487] Samuel Willcocks lived in Falmouth. In 1812 he paid taxes on 1 slave and 1 horse in Stafford.

[488] William Stringfellow (died 1831). In 1810 the Stafford court granted him a business license. In 1815 and 1816 he held a license to operate an ordinary (most likely located in Falmouth); from 1830-1831 he served as a flour inspector in Falmouth and died while holding that position. He also worked as bridge keeper on Robert Dunbar's bridge between Falmouth and Fredericksburg.

1812

Samuel Wilcocks—in Lewis Alexander's company
George M. Cooke[490]—in J. C. Edrington's company
Quartermaster—Coleman R. Browne
Drummer—Presley Cox
Fifer—Peter Cox

Men fined for failure to appear at muster:

Name	Company	Note
William Abbot[491]	Elijah Harding	No property
M. Bauer	Elijah Harding	Removed
George Bisset(?)	Alexander	No property
William Brimmer	Alexander	No property
William Brown	Alexander	No property
Robert Bowler	Barton S. Stone	No property
Alexander Brawner[492]	Thomas Fristoe	Not found
William Brimmer	Willis Benson	No property
John F. Brimmer	Willis Benson	No property
William Burgess	Alexander	Moved to Fredericksburg
John Busel	Daniel Mason	No property
Randal Busel[493]	Daniel Mason	No property
Walter Chandler	Barton S. Stone	No property
Walter Chandler	Daniel Mason	No property
Henry Colvert	Alexander	No property
Austin Cowne[494]	Alexander	Moved to Fredericksburg
Cary Cox	Thomas Mountjoy	No property
James Curtis	Willis Benson	Not found
Richard Clark	Alexander	No property
James Curtis	Alexander	No property
Madison Dillard	Alexander	Not found
Anthony Ensor	Alexander	No property
George Fergison	Alexander	No property
Martin Fishback[495]	Alexander	No inhabitant
John Fletcher	Thomas Mountjoy	No inhabitant

---

[489] Edward Templeman was a member of Hartwood Baptist Church (Hartwood).

[490] George Mason Cooke (1792-1866) was the son of Col. John Cooke (1755-1819) and Mary Thomson Mason (1762-1806) of West Farm in Wide Water. For part of his life he lived at Chelsea on Wide Water Road (Route 611). Later, he resided at Woodford on the north side of Garrisonville Road (Route 610). He and his father shared business interests in farming, timbering, quarrying, and fishing. George's first wife was Agatha Eliza Eustace (1796-1833), by whom he acquired an interest in the Woodford property. He married secondly Ann Jane Carter (1806-1864).

[491] William Abbot (c.1786-after 1850).

[492] In 1810 Alexander Brawner was granted a business license in Stafford (Eby, Men 254).

[493] Randall Bussell (c.1776-c.1820) was the son of George Bussell (born 1733) and Catherine Randall (born c.1737) of Stafford. Around 1797 he married Frances Black (born c.1780).

[494] During the Revolution, Austin Cowne served as a first lieutenant in the 2nd Regiment Virginia Artillery (Creel 5).

[495] May be Martin Fishback (1791-1815) who was the son of Martin Fishback (1763-1842) and Lucy Amiss (1763-1843) of Culpeper. The younger Martin died unmarried.

James Fouracers	Willis Benson	No property
Benjamin Gilbert	Alexander	No inhabitant
Washington Gill	Alexander	No property
Robert Gollahorn	Daniel Mason	No property
William Gordon	Alexander	No inhabitant
John Hefling	John C. Edrington	No property
Brooke Hill	Alexander	No inhabitant
Francis H. Hooe[496]	Alexander	No inhabitant
John Holladay	Alexander	Not found
Samuel Jackson	Alexander	No property
Jesse Jordan	Willis Benson	Removed
B. B. Kendall[497]	Thomas Hill	Moved to Fauquier
Benjamin Lowe	Alexander	No property
John Lewis	Alexander	No property
William Langfit	Alexander	No property
Porch Limbrick	Alexander	No property
Vincent Limbrick	Alexander	No property
Vincent Limbrick	Barton S. Stone	No property
John Martin	Willis Benson	No property
Robert W. Massey	Alexander	No inhabitant
James F. Maury[498]	Alexander	No inhabitant
Daniel McCoy[499]	Thomas Hill	Moved to Kentucky
Joshua Miller	Joseph Reddish	No inhabitant
Thomas Mozingo[500]	Alexander	Not found
Rhodam Myers	Alexander	No property
John Pates	Alexander	No property
Richard Patton[501]	Daniel Mason	Not found
William Payne	Barton S. Stone	No property
William Payne	Daniel Mason	Not found
John Payton	Thomas Mountjoy	Not found
Yelverton Porch[502]	Alexander	No inhabitant
Samuel Porter	Alexander	No property
John Powel	Joseph Reddish	No property
William Red	Alexander	Moved to Fredericksburg
John Redder	Alexander	No property
John Rodgers	Alexander	No property
Jesse Roach	Joseph Reddish	No inhabitant

---

[496] In 1819 Francis H. Hooe paid tax on 800 acres near Falmouth.

[497] Bird Braxton Kendall's (1782-1822) parentage is uncertain. He was born in Stafford and died in Fauquier. Bird married Mary Snape (1782-1854), the daughter of Robert Snape (before 1759-after 1820) of Stafford. The 1810 and 1811 Stafford personal property tax records list him as Braxton B. Kendall and the author has also seen a reference to him as Bloxton B. Kendall.

[498] James Francis Maury (born 1786) was the son of Abraham Maury (1758-1834) and Mildred Washington Thornton (1751-1806) of Spotsylvania. He married Mary Goode (Randolph) Thornton (1785-1865), the widow of George W. Thornton of Rumford.

[499] This may be Daniel McCoy (born 1790) who was born in Virginia and married Margaret Taylor. He had a brother named Samuel who was born in Maryland in 1782.

[500] Thomas Mozingo was also listed in the 1812 Richmond County militia records. This may be the same Thomas Mozingo who married Betsy Williams in Fauquier in 1817.

[501] In 1812 Richard Patton paid taxes on himself only.

[502] Yelverton B. Porch (c.1785-before 1850) was the son of Esom Porch (c.1745-1826). In 1826 he married Letitia Lee Corbin, daughter of Gavin Corbin of Caroline County.

1812

Richard Sharp	John C. Edrington	No property
Thomas Sharp[503]	Elijah Harding	Removed
William Skidmore	Alexander	No property
Sarsfield Snoxall	Thomas C. Alexander	Not found
George Stribling	Alexander	No property
Lewis Sullivan	Alexander	Not found
William Thompson[504]	Thomas Mountjoy	No inhabitant
Lewis Tiltcomb(?)	Alexander	No property
Z. Truslow	Alexander	Not found
Thomas Trussel	Joseph Reddish	No property
John Trussel	Joseph Reddish	No property
Henry Turner	Joseph Reddish	No property
William Timberlake[505]	Willis Benson	No property
John Tut	Alexander	No property
Sepleman(?) Tyler	Thomas Mountjoy	Not found
Joseph Tyson	Willis Benson	No property
Joseph Wormsley	Elijah Harding	No property
Joseph West	Thomas C. Alexander	Not found
Joseph Wealch	Alexander	No property
William Young	Lewis Alexander	No property
Richard Young	Alexander	No property

1813[506]

Adjutant—Thomas Fristoe[507]
Major—Benjamin Tolson
Captains—Levi Swetnam—in room of Willis Benson
        Lewis Alexander
        William H. Fitzhugh—in room of Thomas Mountjoy
        Daniel Mason
        Thomas C. Alexander
        John C. Edrington
        Henry Williams
        Thomas Fristoe
        Thomas Hill
        Elijah Harding
        Joseph Reddish
        Barton S. Stone
Lieutenants—Innis Browne
        George Waller
        Jeremiah B. Templeman
        William Shelton

---

[503] In 1804 Thomas Sharp paid taxes on 107 acres in Stafford.
[504] William Thompson was the son of Mary Thompson.
[505] William Timberlake (died c.1840).
[506] In this year Charles B. Robinson of Falmouth wrote to Peter V. Daniel stating that the legislature had just passed an act for raising and equipping 1,000 men for the defense of the Commonwealth and volunteering his services as Regimental Surgeon.
[507] In 1813 Thomas Fristoe submitted a claim to be paid for "two days rideing [sic] over Staffd. County for the purpose of Summoning the Officers of the same to Carry the Draft into affact [sic] the second time, agreeable to Brigade Orders" (Auditor #478).

Ensigns—John S. Knox[508]—in Lewis Alexander's company
　　　　　Archibald Rollow, Jr.[509]—in Capt. Fitzhugh's company
Quartermaster—Coleman R. Browne
Quartermaster Sergeant—John Fant
Sergeant Major—William Seddon
Paymaster—John Moncure, Jr.[510]
Forage Master—Elijah McIntire
Commissary—William P. Bayly[511]
Surgeon—Benjamin H. Hall[512]
Surgeon's Mate—Alexander Fitzhugh[513]
Clerk of the Court Martial—William Mountjoy
Provost Marshals—Amos Fristoe[514]
　　　　　　　　　John M. Conway
Drummers—James Bowling
　　　　　　Presley Cox
　　　　　　John Garner
　　　　　　George G. Shelton[515]
　　　　　　William Edwards[516]
Fifers—John Cox
　　　　　Peter Cox

---

[508] John Somerville Knox (1786-1873) was the son of William A. Knox (1729-1805) and Susanna Stuart Fitzhugh (1751-1823). He married Elizabeth Ann Selden.

[509] In 1813 either Archibald Rollow, Jr. or Sr. was paid £3.17.6 "for repairing publich arms." Archibald, Jr. married Mary Bullard, the daughter of Reuben Bullard and Fannie Davis. The younger Archibald removed to Mason County, Kentucky.

[510] John Moncure (1793-1876) was the son of John Moncure (1772-1822) and Alice Peachy Gaskins (1774-1860) of Clermont. John's primary residence was at Woodbourne. In addition to timbering, John also served as an agent for the Mutual Assurance Society. His first wife was Esther Vowles (1795-1833) of Falmouth. He married secondly Frances Daniel (1797-1871).

[511] William Pierce Bayly (1773-1842) was the son of Pierce Bayly (1742-1800) of Fairfax and Loudoun counties and Mary Payne (1754-1826). William was in partnership with his father in a store in Alexandria. He also operated a store in Aquia. In 1799 William bought Auburn in Stafford. This was near modern Apple Grove subdivision on Route 610 and is now part of the Marine Corps reservation.

[512] Dr. Benjamin Harrison Hall (1781-1852) was the son of Dr. Elisha Hall (1754-1814) and Caroliana Carter (1756-1799) of Fredericksburg. Prior to settling in Falmouth in 1806, Benjamin practiced medicine in Fredericksburg. In 1811 Stephen Bowen and wife Sarah of Fauquier sold Benjamin their interest in lots 30 and 36 in Falmouth (Stafford Deed Book AA, p. 239). In 1812 he paid taxes on 4 slaves and 1 horse in Stafford. Benjamin married Lucy Fitzhugh (born c.1789) and removed to St. Louis, Missouri where he died.

[513] This may be Alexander Fitzhugh, the son of Thomas Fitzhugh (1754-1820) and Anne Rose of Boscobel. Little is known about him.

[514] Amos Fristoe (1792-1872) was the son of Thomas Fristoe (1767-1815) and Lydia Wells (died 1830). In 1816 he served as deputy sheriff in Stafford. In 1821 he paid taxes on 320 acres on Falls Run 9 miles southwest of Stafford Courthouse. Amos married Susan Waller Withers (1798-1862) and moved to Pettis County, Missouri.

[515] George G. Shelton married Lucinda Pates.

[516] William Edwards. From 1799-1806 he was postmaster at Aquia. From 1799-1804 he held a retail license.

Men fined for failure to appear at muster:

Name	Company	Note
Charles Bridges	Henry Williams	Not found
William Bridwell		No property
William Brimmer		No property
David Bradley		No property
William Brown		Not found
John Conyers, Jr.[517]		Removed
Joseph Curry		No property
Edward Davis	Thomas Mountjoy	Not found
Lewis Dickenson[518]		
John England[519]		No property
George C. Ferguson		No property
Edward Flurry[520]	Thomas Mountjoy	No property
George Franklin		
John Franklin		Not found
James Garrison[521]		
Moses Garrison[522]		
Yelverton Garrison[523]		
John Gollahorn	John C. Edrington	No property

---

[517] John Conyers, Jr. (died after 1830) was the son of John Conyers (1754-1819) and his first wife, Mary Davis. The elder John was a millwright. The younger John married Ann Blackburn, the widow of Christopher Blackburn of Stafford. By 1826 the younger John had bankrupted. The Conyers family owned considerable property in lower Stafford and were involved in the goldmines there. Their home place was Cedar Hedge on the south side of Rt. 17.

[518] Lewis Dickenson (died before 1829) ran a spa at Stafford Springs where people flocked to "take the waters." It was believed that mineral springs were beneficial in the treatment of many ailments. Lewis operated this from the late 1700s until 1828 when he sold it to Barnaby Cannon (died 1833). Elias and Nancy King bought in 1840 and the King family remained there for the next 102 years. In 1942 the U. S. Government condemned this as part of the Marine Corps expansion.

In 1826 Lewis Dickenson bought 61 acres partly in Prince William and partly in Stafford. It was located near Dickenson's Shop (Stafford Deed Book GG, p. 360). From about 1813-1820 Lewis held licenses to run an ordinary in Stafford. In 1829 Lewis' heirs paid tax on 428 acres near Stafford Springs in what is now the Quantico reservation.

[519] In 1812 John England paid taxes on 5 slaves and 4 horses in Stafford.

[520] Edward Fleurry/Floury was from Charles County, Maryland. He came to Stafford and married Benedicta (Maddox) Bloxton, widow of Capt. Samuel Bloxton (died 1816). Samuel had bought a part of the old Peyton/Harrison property on the south side of Aquia Church. Although Edward Fleurry never actually owned the farm, it came to be known as The Fleurry's and retained the name until it was destroyed to make way for Aquia Town Center.

[521] James Garrison (1771-after 1850) was the son of Moses Garrison, Sr. (born 1755) and Nancy Atchison. James was a wheelwright and blacksmith.

[522] Moses Garrison, Jr. (1776-after 1850) was the son of Moses Garrison, Sr. (born 1755) and Nancy Atchison. Moses, Jr. married Mary Peyton (died after 1850). In 1821 he paid taxes on 243 acres on Aquia Run.

[523] Yelverton Garrison (1795-c.1867) was the son of Moses Garrison, Jr. (1776-after 1850) and Mary Peyton (died after 1850). He was a blacksmith and wheelwright and lived in Garrisonville. Yelverton married Mary "Polly" Garrison (1798-before 1860). His estate inventory included carpenter's tools, 1 clock, 1 paint grinder, and household and kitchen furniture valued at $49.00 (Stafford Deed Book 26A, p. 480).

Joel Gray	Elijah Harding	No property
James Green		No property
John Griffin		Not found
John Harry(?)	John C. Edrington	Not found
John Holeda (Holladay)	Barton S. Stone	No property
Samuel Holloway		No property
Moore F. Hooe[524]		
Edward Homes[525]		
George Homes		
Peter Jett		No property
Samuel Kemper	Elijah Harding	Removed
John Kendall	Elijah Harding	No property
William Leach		Removed
Porch Limbrick		No property
Gerard Lomax[526]		No property
John Markam[527]	Thomas Mountjoy	Kentucky
George Martin		Removed
John Martin		No property
Thornton Martin		No property
Daniel Mason		Died
Horace Mitchell[528]	Elijah Harding	No property
Samuel Mitchell		No property
William McCoy	Thomas Hill	Kentucky
Thomas M. Morton[529]		
William B. Mountjoy		No property
William Murphy[530]		Removed
Reuben Payne[531]		
Watson Pearson[532]		Removed
James Presley(?)		No property
George Roberson		No property
John Roles		No property
Gustavus Rye		
Arthur Sharp	Elijah Harding	No property
Elias Smith		Not found
Benjamin Snellings		No property

[524] Moore Fauntleroy Hooe. He moved to Louisiana and little is known of him.
[525] Edward Homes married a daughter of Isaac Bridwell (died 1833) of Prince William County.
[526] Gerard Lomax (born c.1789). In 1813 he married Sarah Simms (died 1823), the daughter of Richard Simms (1752-1850) of Stafford.
[527] This may be John Markham, Jr. (c.1781-after 1809), the son of John Markham (1732-1804) and Jane "Jenny" Waller (1746-1815). In 1812 John paid taxes on 1 slave and 1 horse in Stafford.
[528] Horace Mitchell was a member of Hartwood Baptist Church but was excommunicated in 1816 (Hartwood).
[529] Thomas Mountjoy Morton (1787-1859) was the son of Robert Baylor Morton (1761-1807) and Mary Mountjoy (1769-1804). In 1812 he married his first cousin, Ann Baylor Morton (1792-c.1825). That same year he paid taxes on 6 slaves, 5 horses, and 200 acres on Accokeek Creek 5 miles east of the courthouse. Thomas moved to Mason County, Kentucky.
[530] In 1821 William Murphy paid taxes on 62 acres on Chappawamsic Run 12 miles north of Stafford Courthouse.
[531] Reuben Payne (c.1795-1866) married Frances Sullivan.
[532] Watson Pearson was the son of William George Pearson (1750-c.1801) of Prince William and Fauquier counties.

1813

William S. Stevens			
William Strullow(?)	Barton S. Stone	Not found	
William Sullivan			
Silas Walters		Removed	
Joseph Wealch		No property	
Lawson Wheatly[533]	Elijah Harding	No property	
Wesley Wilson	Elijah Harding	Removed	
Jenings Withers[534]		Removed	
John Watson	Thomas Mountjoy	No property	

Men in John C. Edrington's Company:[535]

Benjamin Ashby	William Ford[536]	George Paulding
Robert Ashby	Thomas Franklin[537]	George Payne
Moses Batley	Ephraim Fritter	Humphrey Pope
Peter Beach[538]	Samuel Geter	Daniel Ralls[539]
David Benton	William Gollahorn	Peter Rankins
Thompson Bethel[540]	Thomas Graves	Alexander G. Ratcliff[541]
Joseph Bryant	George Green	Noah Reed
Francis Brown	John Gregory	Rossall Rollow[542]
Wallis Brown	Ralph Griffith	John Rolls
James Brummett[543]	Philip Harding[544]	Lawrence Sanford[545]

---

[533] In the mid-1820s Lawson Wheatly was in the quarry business with his brother Landon. They were the sons of James Wheatley (died c.1795) of Fauquier. Lawson married Mary Peyton, the daughter of Dr. Valentine Peyton (1856-1815) of Tusculum.

[534] Jenings Withers (1784-1857) was the son of James Withers (1752-c.1828) and Chloe Jennings (1755-1837). He married Matilda Williams. In 1819 Jennings paid tax on 219 acres on Potomac Creek.

[535] These men served in Edrington's company and were NOT fined for failure to appear at the required musters.

[536] Capt. William Ford (1788-1834) was the son of James Ford (1768-1863) and Elizabeth Taylor. By late 1813 William was a lieutenant in the 38th regiment of U. S. Infantry and in charge of the distribution of rations and other supplies to soldiers at the town of Aquia (Kendall, private). William's first wife was Deborah Thompson Duncan (died 1813) of Baltimore. He married secondly Elizabeth Allen Hore (1791-1822), the daughter of Elias Hore (1749-1832) and Theodosia Waller (1753-1829) of Stafford. From at least 1817-1828 he held a license to operate a retail store in Stafford (Eby, Men 255-257).

[537] Thomas Franklin (died before 1850). In 1850 his heirs paid taxes on 262 acres near the town of Aquia.

[538] May be the same Peter Beach that in 1827 leased 150 acres on Aquia Run 14 miles northwest of Stafford Courthouse (Stafford Land Tax Records).

[539] Daniel Stone Ralls (1785-1820) was the son of Nathaniel William Ralls and Susannah Stone of Stafford. He married Mary Stone (born c.1786), the daughter of Valentine Stone and Keziah French (born 1761). Daniel was born in Prince William and died in St. Louis, Missouri. Ralls County, Missouri was named for him.

[540] Thompson Bethel was the son of Edward of Stafford.

[541] Alexander G. Ratcliff may be the son of Richard Ratcliff (1765-1819) and Margaret Gaddess (died 1837) of Stafford. She was the daughter of Alexander Gaddess, Sr. (died 1785) and Ann Jenkins (died 1810) of Palace Green, Stafford. This may also be the same Alexander G. Ratcliff who left a will in McCracken County, Kentucky.

[542] Rossall Rollow was the son of Archibald Rollow (c.1755-1829) and Nancy Jett. He later moved to Tennessee.

[543] In 1812 James Brummett paid taxes on 1 horse in Stafford. He was a member of Hartwood Baptist Church (Hartwood).

[544] Philip Harding (c.1791-1869) died in Stafford.

[545] Lawrence Sanford (1778-1858) was born in Westmoreland County. He married Aphia Farmer (1784-1864), the daughter of David Farmer of Culpeper. In 1811 Lawrence bought 104 acres from James

1813

Reuben B. Bullard	Willis Harrel	Solomon Shackelford[546]
William R. Butler	Thomas P. Harrison[547]	John H. Simms
Fielding Byram[548]	Robert Holoday	John Stark
James Carpenter[549]	Elias Hore[550]	Charles Stewart
Jeremiah Carter[551]	William Jett[552]	Stephen Stewart
William Carter[553]	Bayly Knight	Rodney Sullivant
Briant Chadwell[554]	Elijah Knight	John Tharp[555]
John Colvin	John Knight	Charles Thornton
William Coram[556]	Uriah Knight	John C. Tyler[557]
Lemuel Cox	Thomas Lewis	James Tyson
Lewis Cropp	John McFee[558]	Sanford Walters
George Curtice[559]	Charles Miflin[560]	Hezekiah Waple
Richard Curtice[561]	James Miflin	James White[562]

Hunter's estate. In 1842 he purchased an adjoining 160 acres, all of which was near the old Greenbank farm. The remains of his house survive.

[546] Solomon A. Shackelford (c.1780-before 1850) was born in Culpeper. He married Clarissa Heflin, the daughter of John Heflin (1741-1823) and Sarah Champion (1750-1798).

[547] Thomas P. Harrison was the son of John Peyton Harrison (1750-1807) and Frances Peyton (1754-1795).

[548] Fielding Byram (born 1779) was the son of George Byram (born 1752) and Elizabeth Fielding.

[549] James Carpenter (died 1820). In 1819 he was a tenant on John Dunbar's property on Aquia Creek.

[550] Elias Hore (1790-1820) was the son of Elias Hore (1749-1832) and Theodosia Waller (1753-1820). Little is known of him.

[551] Jeremiah Carter (c.1784-after 1828) was the son of Joseph Carter (born 1759) and Sally Edwards (born 1763). He lived very near Stafford Courthouse.

[552] William Jett. From at least 1788-1791 he was one of the inspectors at the Falmouth Tobacco Warehouse. In 1790 he was deputy sheriff in Stafford.

[553] This may be William Carter (c.1765-1858), the son of Jeremiah Carter (1720-1781) and Elizabeth Anne Harrison (1728-1778). William married Catherine Stark and owned Fristoe's Mill in what is now the Quantico reservation.

[554] Bryant Chadwell married Mary Murphy, daughter of Peter Murphy and Elizabeth Mauzy. Around 1784 he married his second wife, Hannah Gough, the widow of Thomas Gough (died c.1783) of Stafford. In 1790 he paid taxes on 3 slaves and 4 horses in Stafford. In 1798 this or another Bryant Chadwell married Precy Gray of Fauquier County.

[555] During the Revolution, John Tharp served with Capt. Alexander Parker's company. He was wounded at the Battle of Savannah and so badly hurt that he was incapable of earning a livelihood (Virginia Legislative Petitions, "John Tharp," Dec. 21, 1813, Reel 187, Box 238, Folder 98. Library of Virginia).

[556] William Coram (c.1787-1844) was the son of Richard Coram. He married Elizabeth Allen and removed to Granger, Tennessee.

[557] John Cooke Tyler (born 1791) was the son of Thomas G. S. Tyler (c.1740-1816) and Anne Fisher Adie.

[558] John McFee (born 1795) was the son of John McFee (1760-c.1847) who lived in Stafford and later moved to Tuscarawas County, Ohio. John, Jr. was a carpenter (Stafford County Estate, 1823, p. 287). He married Lucinda Hudson.

[559] George Curtis, Jr. (1767-1844) was the son of George Curtis (1730:35-c.1806) and Elizabeth Jett. His first wife was probably Mary McIlhaney, whom he married c.1792. He married secondly in 1804 Jemima Payne (died c.1869), the daughter of Francis Payne and Susannah Jett. George and Jemima were both buried at their home, Green Meadows, located between Poplar Road (Rt. 616) and Stefaniga Road (Rt. 648). Part of George's extensive land holdings in this part of Stafford became Seven Lakes subdivision and had once been part of the old Carter plantation, Ludlow.

[560] Charles Miflin lived near the Stafford/Fauquier line and in 1821 paid taxes on 78 ½ acres on Aquia Run. In 1786 he paid taxes on 2 horses and 5 cattle in Stafford

[561] Richard Curtis was the son of John Curtis (died c.1812) of Stafford. In 1786 he paid taxes on 1 horse, and 1 cow in Stafford.

1813

John Dozier
Elias Fant[563]
George B. Fant[565]
Joel Fant[566]
Richard L. Fant[568]
Arthur Fitzhugh

John Miflin
Sanford Miflin
Edwin C. Moncure
John J. Musselman[567]
John Oliver
Thomas Patison[569]

John Williams
Walter Williams[564]
Joseph Winlock

Men in unknown companies:
Hugh Adie[570]
Isaac Bridwell[573]

Charles Bussell[571]
Elliott Patton[574]

Francis Rollow[572]
Patrick G. Wardell

---

[562] James White (died 1814).
[563] Elias Fant (1771-1842) was the son of John W. Fant (born c.1737) and lived near Deep Run. He married first Lucy Berry. His second wife was Margaret Brahan, widow of John Atwood.
[564] Walter Williams was the son of Pearson Williams (c.1743-c.1824) of Stafford.
[565] George Buckner Fant (1790-1843) was the son of George Fant (died c.1814) of Stafford. By 1836 George was a resident of Rappahannock County. His first wife was Nancy Strother Ficklen; he married secondly Elizabeth Deatherage.
[566] Joel Fant was the son of John W. Fant (born c.1737). In 1812 he paid taxes on 3 slaves and 2 horses in Stafford. Joel lived near Enoch Mason.
[567] John Jacob Musselman (born c.1795) was the son of Henry Musselman (c.1765-c.1815) of Stafford.
[568] Richard Lovell Fant (c.1789-after 1845) was the son of George Fant (died c.1814) and his second wife, Elizabeth Sewell. Richard married Rachel Blackburn by whom he had four children. From Stafford he moved to Salem, Virginia where he was a carriage maker. In 1836 he removed to Missouri and ended up in Jefferson City where he ran a hotel.
[569] Thomas Patterson (died 1824) lived in Hartwood. A member of Hartwood Baptist Church, his death was recorded in that church's minutes (Hartwood).
[570] Hugh Adie (c.1788-1872) lived on the north side of what is now Garrisonville Road (Rt. 610) nearly across from the Meadows Farms Nursery. He was the son of Benjamin Adie (1762-c.1825) and Margaret Gibson Gillison (born c.1770) of Bloomington, Wide Water, Stafford County. Hugh married Elizabeth Waller (c.1795-1871), the daughter of Edward Waller (1768-1818) and Elizabeth Chadwell of Concord. Like many of the Adies, Hugh was a carpenter, but in the 1820s also had some involvement in one of the county fisheries (Stafford County Estate, 1823, p. 159).
[571] Charles Bussell (1799-1875) was the son of Randall Bussell (born c.1776) and Frances Black (born c.1780). He enlisted in Fredericksburg in 1815 and, during the War of 1812, was sent to Florida and Mexico. Charles was in and out of military service from 1815-1848 and attained the rank of sergeant. In October 1848 he was discharged after having been injured and re-injured in service. After about 1873 he was largely confined to his bed. For much of his life Charles lived in the Mountain View area of Stafford. According to his pension records, he was about 5' 11" tall with dark complexion, blue eyes, and dark hair (National Archives, Invalid Pension #20660). Charles' first wife is thought to have been Lucinda English. He married secondly Mary Black (c.1800-before 1850) and thirdly, Lucy Ann Wine (born c.1838). Lucy applied for a widow's pension at which time she was described as a lunatic (National Archives, Widow's Pension #10506).
[572] Francis Rollow (died c.1841). His estate inventory included household and kitchen furniture, 1 straw bed, 1 saddle, 1 shuck mattress, 9 curtains and a table cloth, 1 buffet, 10 chairs, 3 bedsteads, 1 side saddle, and a pair of steelyards all valued at $58.70 (Stafford Deed Book MM, p. 462).
[573] Isaac Bridwell (c.1782-1867) married Mary Bradshaw (born c.1800). In 1812 he paid taxes on 2 slaves, 5 horses, and 100 acres on South Run of Chappawamsic. Isaac was born in Prince William County. He later lived in Stafford and his farm is now part of the Marine Corps reservation.
[574] Elliott Patton, Sr. (c.1793-1882) was the son of George and Sarah Patton. He lived his entire life in Hartwood. Elliott married Maria E. Aulman (c.1801-1883) of Orange County. During the War Between the States, he was a Unionist. He had one son in the Minnesota Regiment who died in service. Another

1813

William Bronaugh   James Patton

1814

Units stationed at Camp Hope,[575] Camp Potomac Church, White Oak Meeting House, and Camp Drummond's Old Field.[576]

Adjutant—Thomas Fristoe
Lt. Colonel—Samuel H. Peyton
Majors—Benjamin Tolson—1st Battalion
         Robert Crutcher—2nd Battalion
2nd Major—William Buchanan[577] (stationed at Potomac Church)
Captains—Rowzee Peyton[578]—in room of Daniel Mason, deceased
         Vincent Shackelford—artillery
         Thomas C. Alexander—stationed in the Northern Neck
         Daniel Mason—light infantry
         Joseph R. Lynn[579]
         Joseph Reddish
         Henry Williams
         Barton S. Stone—stationed at Hope
         William H. Fitzhugh
         Thomas Hill—cavalry
         Robert W. Carter[580]—cavalry
         John Brawner
         Benjamin Thomas—stationed at Mattox Bridge
         Levi Swetnam
         John C. Edrington
         Lewis Alexander
         Elijah Harding
1st Lieutenant of Cavalry—Robert Beaty—in room of Thomas Jones, resigned
2nd Lieutenants—John E. Hewitt[581]

---

son joined the Confederate service, but deserted and joined the Quartermaster Department in Washington (Southern Claims Commission. Approved. Claim #57532).

[575] This was likely on the south side of Aquia Creek near the present railroad bridge.

[576] This was near the old Earl's Store, Deacon Road, and White Oak Road.

[577] Dr. William Buchanan (died c.1842) was the brother of Andrew Buchanan (died 1804) of Clearview. William inherited that farm from his brother and lived there until 1815. He died unmarried. William's estate included 1 mahogany bedstead, 1 refrigerator, 1 brass clock, 4 carpets, 1 set of dinner china, 1 dozen silver spoons, 12 bedspreads, 2 cows, 1 map, 1 set of blacksmith's tools, and 1 turning lathe all valued at $9,058 (Stafford Deed Book NN, p. 86).

[578] Rowzee Peyton (1789-1867) was the son of John Rowzee Peyton (1754-1798) and Anne Hooe (1754-1833) of Stony Hill, Stafford County. His first wife was Eliza Strother Galleher (1791-1822). He married secondly Eliza Murray (1791-1878). After his second marriage, Rowzee removed to Geneva, New York.

[579] Joseph Reid Lynn (1777-1844) was the son of William Lynn (before 1744-1795) and Elizabeth Reid of Prince William County. His first wife was Sarah Ashford Nelson. He married secondly Pamelia C. Humphrey. By 1820 Joseph was a resident of Prince William and lived on Quantico Creek. He later moved to Loudoun where he died.

[580] Robert Wormley Carter (1792-1861) was the son of Landon Carter (1757-1820) of Sabine Hall and Catherine Griffin Tayloe (1761-1798) of Mt. Airy. Robert married Elizabeth M. Tayloe (died 1832) and inherited Parke Quarter in Stafford. Robert also inherited Sabine Hall where he spent much of his life.

[581] John E. Hewitt (c.1795-1843) was the son of William Hewitt (1740-1795) and Catherine Edmonds (1756-1823). He married Margaret Markham (c.1795-c.1842) and moved to De Soto County, Louisiana where he later died. In 1812 John paid taxes on 8 slaves and 1 horse in Stafford. In 1825 John bought from Moses Pilcher a quarry and ½ acre (Stafford Deed Book GG, p. 96). This location of the quarry is unknown.

1814

        Thomas Jones
Cornets—Thomas Garner
        Christopher Blackburn
        Thomas Yarby
Lieutenants—Aaron H. Ball—in Thomas C. Alexander's company
        John S. Knox—in room of Samuel Wilcocks, deceased
        Innis Browne
        Jeremiah B. Templeman
        Jesse Curtis
        George Billingsley
        Thomas Jones—cavalry
        William McInteer
        Alexander S. H. Stone—in Capt. Henry Williams' company
        Innis Browne—in Capt. Joseph Reddish's company
1st Lieutenant—James Waller
Cornet—Christopher Blackburn
Ensigns—William Hewitt
        Boswell Alsop[582]
        John Mason—in Daniel Mason's company
        Archibald Rollow
        George T. Shelkett
        Burditt H. Clifton
        Edward Templeman
        John S. Knox
        Allen W. Markham
        John Ross
        George M. Cooke
        Richard Gaines[583]
        Aaron H. Ball
        Abner R. Alcock
Sergeant Major—William Seddon
Sergeants—John G. Rowe[584]—in Thomas C. Alexander's company
        William Walker
2nd Sergeant—William Burton, Sr.—in Capt. Levi Swetnam's company
Quartermaster—Coleman R. Browne
Deputy Quartermaster—John McIntere[585]
Assistant Quartermaster—John Moncure, Jr.
Quartermaster Sergeant—James E. Hewitt
Forage Masters—Frederick Cline
        William Peyton
Clerk—George M. Parsons[586] (stationed at Potomac Church)

---

[582] Boswell Alsop (c.1788-1836) was the son of John Alsop and Lucy Spindle. He lived much of his life in Fredericksburg where he and Strother Harding ran a hotel. Boswell was probably unmarried.

[583] May be Richard Henry Gaines, Jr. (1788-1854) who was the son of William Henry Gaines (1754-c.1818) and Jane Botts (1757-1826) of Culpeper and Prince William. Richard's first wife was Elizabeth Brady (born c.1793). He married secondly Mary C. Shumate.

[584] John Gasking Rowe (1788-1862) was the son of John Rowe (1762-1799) and Sarah Peyton (1767-1856). He married Nancy McGuire (1800-1858), the daughter of Thomas McGuire (1773-1821). John was a minister.

[585] This may be the John McInteer (born 1791) who was the son of Henry McInteer (1765-1834) and Margaret Hansbrough (born 1768) of Stafford.

Paymaster—Samuel H. Skinker[587]
Surgeon—Alexander H. Fitzhugh[588]
Surgeon's 1st Mate—Thomas F. Knox[589]
Surgeon's 2nd Mate—Benjamin H. Hall
Surgeon's Mate—William Buchanan[590]
Corporals—James P. Rowe[591]—in Thomas C. Alexander's company
　　　　　　Ellis Gravatt[592]—in Thomas C. Alexander's company

Militiamen:[593]

Name	Company	Note
William Abbot	John C. Edrington	
Philip Alexander[594]	William H. Fitzhugh	Served in Northern Neck
Joseph Ashby	Henry Williams	
James Atchison[595]	Elijah Harding	Served at Camp Mattox
John Ashby		
John Ball[596]		Served in Northern Neck
John Bowling		Served on the Potomac

---

[586] George M. Parsons was a merchant in Hartwood, though from 1818-1820 he operated a tavern in Falmouth.. George married Fanny Green, sister of Duff Green of Falmouth. In 1812 George paid taxes on 3 slaves and 5 horses and in 1819 he was taxed on 275 acres near Yellow Chapel (Hartwood). George moved to Louisville, Kentucky.

[587] Samuel Hampson Skinker (1785-1856) was the son of William Skinker and Mary (Sells) Powlett (c.1745-1798) and resided at Oakley on the west side of Poplar Road (Route 616). He married Margaret Wilson Julian (died 1863), the only daughter of Dr. John Julian of Fredericksburg. From at least 1814-1827 Samuel served as a justice in Stafford.

[588] Alexander H. Fitzhugh (1786-1847) was the son of Thomas Fitzhugh (1754-1820) and Ann Rose of Boscobel. In 1810 he graduated from the University of Pennsylvania with a degree in medicine. In 1815 he married Eliza Gibbs Clare of Clarke County, Virginia. From 1838-1840 he represented Stafford in the Virginia House of Delegates.

[589] Dr. Thomas F. Knox (1772-1835) was the son of William Knox (1729-1805) and Susanna Stuart Fitzhugh (1751-1823). He bought Belmont for his widowed mother. Thomas owned land on Potomac Run that in 1839 his son, also Thomas F. Knox, sold to the president and directors of the Potomac Silk and Agricultural Company. This tract included the old Potomac Church site (Stafford Deed Book LL, p. 517).

[590] Dr. William Buchanan (died 1842) was the brother of Andrew Buchanan (died 1804) of Clearview. William inherited that farm from his brother and lived there until 1815. He died unmarried. William's estate included 1 mahogany bedstead, 1 refrigerator, 1 brass clock, 4 carpets, 1 set of dinner china, 1 dozen silver spoons, 12 bedspreads, 2 cows, 1 map, 1 set of blacksmith's tools, and 1 turning lathe all valued at $9,058 (Stafford Deed Book NN, p. 86).

[591] James Peyton Rowe (1787-after 1850) was the son of John Rowe (1762-1797) and Sarah Peyton (1767-1856). James married Elizabeth Leitch, daughter of Benjamin Leitch and died in Stafford.

[592] Ellis Gravatt may have been the son of Ellis Gravatt (c.1725-c.1782) and Elizabeth Wren (born c.1735) of Caroline County.

[593] These names were compiled from hand-written notes authorizing someone other than the actual militiaman to collect his pay. Some of these notes named parents, siblings, or wives.

[594] This may be Philip Thornton Alexander (1783-1817) who was the son of Philip Thornton Alexander (1760-1783) and Lucy Brockenbrough. He married his cousin Lucy Brooke (c.1783-after 1850). In 1812 Philip paid taxes on 13 slaves and 5 horses in Stafford.

[595] James Atchison was the son of Arnold Atchison. He married the daughter of J. Beagle (Stafford County Personal Property Tax Records). In 1812 James paid taxes on 1 horse in Stafford.

[596] In 1819 John Ball paid tax on 44 ½ acres on Muddy Creek. By that time he was a resident of Spotsylvania County.

1814

John Burton		
Bailey F. Ball	Henry Williams	
Richard M. Beckwith		
Robert Benson[597]		
John Berry	Barton S. Stone	
James Boling		
John Bridwell	Henry Williams	
Richard Bridwell[598]		
George Burroughs	Henry Williams	
William Burton, Jr.	Lewis Alexander	Served at Falmouth
Joseph Beagle	Daniel Mason	
Abijah Boling[599]	Levi Swetnam	
George Boling[600]	Levi Swetnam	
Brook Barker[601]		Served at camps Mattox & Drummond
William Brent	Joseph Reddish	
William Bryant[602]	Levi Swetnam	Served on Potomac
Joseph Burnham (private)	Levi Swetnam	
Randol Busle	Daniel Mason	
James Bernard (?)	Henry Williams	Served in Northern Neck
Thomas Berry[603]	Elijah Harding	
William Billingsley[604]		
Elijah Barby[605]	William H. Fitzhugh	
Lameth Barbee[606] (private)	Elijah Harding	
John Bell, Jr.		Served in Northern Neck
William Bettis		Served in Northern Neck
Clement Billingsley[607]		
John A. Bohannon		
Charles Bowling		

---

[597] Robert Benson (1762-1825) served in the Revolution and later became a Baptist preacher. In 1771 he married Nancy Stringfellow (born 1771), the daughter of Robert Stringfellow and Catherine Stigler of King George. Robert moved to Greenville, South Carolina.

[598] Richard Bridwell (c.1785-1853) was born at Onville in northern Stafford. He married Elizabeth Jacobs (born c.1797).

[599] Abijah Boling (1775:94-1858) was the son of Frances Boling. Around 1819 he married Frances Guy (c.1790-1879).

[600] George Boling was the son of Frances Boling.

[601] Brooke Barker was a member of Chappawamsic Baptist Church. The church minutes of 1822 note he had "been absent several years, and is supposed to be in the western country…[he] left the Church without asking a letter of the Church…it being reported that he was some times in a state of Intoxication and did use profane language" (Chappawamsic Baptist Church Minutes).

[602] In 1812 William Bryant was running Conyers' Mill on the western side of the county (Stafford County Personal Property Tax Records).

[603] Thomas Berry married Margaret Newton, the daughter of William Newton, Sr.

[604] William Billingsley (born 1789) was the son of Clement Billingsley and Cynthia Turner.

[605] In 1812 Elijah Barbee paid tax on only 1 horse. He later moved to Kentucky.

[606] Lameth Barbee (born c.1785) was born in either Stafford or Prince William. He was the son of John Barbee and Patty Gaines of Stafford and Mercer counties and was the grandson of John Barbee and Elizabeth Welch. In 1811 Lameth married Clarky Wigginton (1791-1851), the daughter of Seth Wigginton and Elizabeth Clarke of Stafford. By 1816 Lameth was in Bullitt County, Kentucky.

[607] Clement Billingsley (1754-1841) married Cynthia Turner (1764-1844). In 1812 Clement paid taxes on 4 slaves and 7 horses in Stafford. They removed to Autauga County, Alabama and founded the town of Billingsley.

William Bowlin		
James Brown	Elijah Harding	
Isaac Burton		
Samuel Bloxton	Barton S. Stone	Served in Northern Neck
William Brown		Not found
Joseph Bryan		Not found
Thomas S. Burton	Thomas C. Alexander	
James Butler	Elijah Harding	
Baily Byram[608]	Daniel Mason	
Loyal Carter[609]	Henry Williams	Served at Camp Mattox
William Chadwick	Daniel Mason	
John Cloe[610]		
Peter P. Cox[611]		
John Christy[612]	Joseph Reddish	Served in Northern Neck
John Combs	Henry Williams	Served in Northern Neck
George Coakley		
Joseph A. Carter		
James P. Carter		
Sanford Carter (private)	John C. Edrington	Camp Selden
Robert Childs	Levi Swetnam	
Lewis Courtney[613]		
Berryman Cox[614]	Thomas C. Alexander	
Charnock Cox[615]	Thomas C. Alexander	
George Cox	William H. Fitzhugh	
John Cooper	Thomas Hill	
William Cox	Elijah Harding	
John Cooke, Jr.		
Champ Coram[616]	Elijah Harding	Served on the Potomac & at Camp Mattox
Mason Corbin[617] (private)	Elijah Harding	
Frederick Cline		No property
Joseph Curry		No property
James Curtis		Not found
William Curtis		
Presley Cropp[618]		

[608] Baily Byram lived near Ramoth Church.

[609] Loyal Carter (c.1781-c.1847) was the son of James Carter (1751-1793) of Aquia Creek and was a descendant of Capt. Thomas Carter (c.1630-1700) of Lancaster County. He lived near what is now the Home Depot store on Garrisonville Road and was a carpenter. In 1820 and 1822 he was granted licenses to run an ordinary and in 1827 a retail license (Eby, Men 257, 272).

[610] John Cloe (born 1780:90) is thought to have been the son of James Cloe, Jr. (1763-c.1806) and is believed to have married Elizabeth Mason. By 1820 he was living in Bourbon County, Kentucky.

[611] In 1823 Peter P. Cox married Margarette Bryan in Fredericksburg.

[612] Sometime prior to 1806 John Christy joined Hartwood Baptist Church (Hartwood).

[613] Lewis Courtney (died 1825).

[614] Berryman Cox (c.1787-after 1850) married Delila Payne.

[615] Charnock Cox (born 1783) lived on Accokeek Run. He married Leah (Monteith) Owens, widow of Thomas Owens.

[616] Champ Coram (born c.1775) was the son of Champ Corum, Sr. (died 1787) and Catherine Lutterell of Fauquier. In 1804 he paid tax on 109 acres in Stafford.

[617] Mason Corbin (died before 1840) was the son of John Corbin and Mary Tapp. In 1826 he married Elizabeth Ennis in Fauquier. She married secondly William Fugit.

1814

John H. Cochran		
Cadwallader Dade[619]		
Walter R. Daniel[620]	William H. Fitzhugh	
John Dasher(?)		Served in Northern Neck
George Davis		
Barton Dawson[621]		Camp Mattox & Camp Drummond
Barnet Dawson[622]	Elijah Harding	Camp Mattox & Camp Drummond
William P. Dunnington[623]		Baltimore
William Edwards		
Cylas Edwards		
James Edwards		
John England, Jr.[624]		Served in Northern Neck
Lovel Fant[625]		
James Finnall		Served in Northern Neck
Robert Finnall (private)	Joseph Reddish	Served in Northern Neck
Arnold Fritter[626]	Daniel Mason	
James Ford		Served at Mattox Bridge & Camp Drummond
John Fritter[627]	Daniel Mason	
Barnet Fritter[628]	Daniel Mason	
Travis Fritter[629]		Served in Northern Neck
William Gaines[630]		Served in Northern Neck

[618] Presley Cropp (born 1796) was the son of John Cropp (1753-1830) and Rosie Thomas and brother of Thornton Cropp (born 1792). Presley moved to Culpeper and then to Harrison County (now West Virginia). In the 1830s he also owned land in Fauquier County. Presley married Sarah Green.

[619] Cadwallader was probably Cadwallader Jones Dade (died 1817) who lived at Albion on the Rappahannock. He was the son of Townshend Dade (1743-1807) and Susannah Fitzhugh (1757-1817).

[620] Walter Raleigh Daniel (1783-1818) was the son of Travers Daniel, Sr. (1741-1824) and Frances Moncure (born 1745) of Crow's Nest. He married Elizabeth Lewis, the daughter of Dr. Richmond Lewis (1774-1831) of Bel-Air, Spotsylvania County. From 1822-1824 Walter represented Stafford in the Virginia House of Delegates.

[621] Barton Dawson (died c.1815) was the son of John Dawson (1751-1839) and Elizabeth Bridwell. He was a Revolutionary War pensioner and died in Prince William County.

[622] This was actually Bernard Dawson (1788-1853), the son of John Dawson (1751-1839) and Elizabeth Bridwell. Bernard was born near Dumfries and married Elizabeth Lowe (1789-1852). He was in Washington when the British burned that city. He, his father, and two brothers moved to Shelby County, Kentucky in 1817. Bernard moved on to Oldham County, Kentucky, then to Morgan County, Illinois where he died.

[623] William P. Dunnington was a merchant. In 1808 he married Malenda Wyatt in Prince William County.

[624] John England, Jr. (1794-1878) was the son of John England (1755-1851) and Ann Musselman (c.1760-1823). It was around 1814 that John removed to Richmond. In 1840 he was appointed a flour inspector, a position he held until 1851. John never married and died near Atlee's Station. He was buried at Hollywood Cemetery in Richmond (*Virginia Star*, Feb. 15, 1878).

[625] Lovel Fant was the son of Samuel Fant (1741-1821) and Mary Throne (born c.1745). Lovel moved with his parents to South Carolina.

[626] Arnold Fritter was the brother of Ephraim Fritter.

[627] John Fritter (c.1786-before 1860) was the son of John Fritter (born 1752).

[628] Barnett Fritter (1792-1872) was the likely son of John Fritter (born 1752). In 1820 he married Betsy Fant (born c.1773), probably the daughter of Joseph Fant. Around 1828 he married his second wife, Mary L. Fant, the daughter of John W. Fant.

[629] Travis Fritter (1787-after 1850) was the son of John Fritter (born 1752). He is listed in some records as being blind and may have lost his sight in the service.

Alexander Garrison		
L___ Garrison	John C. Edrington	
George Garrison		
Thomas Gollohorn	Daniel Mason	
William Gordon	Elijah Harding	
James Garrison		
Amos Garrison		Served at camps Mattox & Drummond
Benjamin Gilbert		
Joel Gray		No property
Peter Grigsby	William H. Fitzhugh	
Rodham Graves[631]		
Charles Gollyhorn		
John Gollyhorn		
Joseph Graves		Served in Northern Neck
William Gregory	Barton S. Stone	Served at Hope
Benjamin Guy[632]	Henry Williams	Served in Northern Neck
Joel Gray (private)	William H. Fitzhugh	Served in Northern Neck
James Gunn[633]		
William Guy[634]	Daniel Mason	
Robert Gallagher (private)	John C. Edrington	
Daniel Grinnan[635]		
George G. Hedgman		
William Hefflin (private)	Elijah Harding	Served in Northern Neck
Daniel Hall[636]	Barton S. Stone	
William Harding[637]	Henry Williams	Served at Mattox Bridge
Jeremiah Homes[638]	Henry Williams	Served at Mattox Bridge
James Heflin (private)	William H. Fitzhugh	Served in Northern Neck
Thomas Hensey (?)		Served at camps Mattox & Drummond
William Holowday	William H. Fitzhugh	
Edmund Homes[639]	Elijah Harding	

[630] May be William Gaines (died 1818) who married Jane Botts (1757-c.1824). William was a member of Chappawamsic Baptist Church.

[631] This may be Rodham Graves (c.1775-after 1850) who was born in Virginia and died in Franklin County, Ohio. While a resident of Stafford, he was a member of Hartwood Baptist Church (Hartwood).

[632] Benjamin Guy was the brother of William Guy.

[633] James Gunn was listed in the Stafford tax records from 1811-1814, then disappeared. He may be the same James Gunn who was born in Maryland and later moved to Kentucky to join other Gunn relatives there.

[634] William Guy (born c.1795) was the son of John Guy (c.1755-c.1817).

[635] Early members of the Grinnan family were Scottish merchants who worked in Falmouth and Fredericksburg. By 1815 Daniel Grinnan owned land near the Rappahannock River and what is now Richlands Baptist Church. Several generations of his descendants remained on that land. Daniel was buried in the Masonic Cemetery in Fredericksburg.

[636] Daniel Hall (born 1787) was the son of Benjamin Hall (1759-1845) and Jemima Thacker (1758-1830). In 1813 he was baptized at Chappawamsic Baptist Church and dismissed that same year. He married Nancy Curtis, the daughter of George Curtis (c.1767-1844) of Stafford. From her father Nancy inherited land in Culpeper. Daniel purchased additional property across the Rapidan River in Orange County.

[637] William Harding (c.1776-after 1850).

[638] Jeremiah Homes (1786-1865) married Lydia McInteer (1786-1867) and lived on or near Aquia Run.

[639] Edmund Holmes, Jr. (1745-1805) married Sarah Ann Stark (1749-c.1813), the daughter of James Stark of Stafford. Edmund was born in Prince William and died in Fauquier.

1814

Joseph Homes	Elijah Harding	
John Horton	Barton S. Stone	
Fielding Hudson[640]		
James S. Homes[641]	Henry Williams	
James Hawkins[642]	Elijah Harding	
Harrison Harding[643]	Thomas Hill	
William Harding	Joseph Reddish	
James Hefling (private)		
William Horton		
Francis Jackson[644]	Henry Williams	
William Jackson[645]		
James Jackson		No property
John Jackson, Jr.		No property
Peter Jett		No property
George Jenkins		
Peter Jett, Jr.	William H. Fitzhugh	Served at Mattox Bridge
Thomas Jones	Elijah Harding	
Barton Johnson	Daniel Mason	
Zachariah Jones	Barton S. Stone	
Allen Jones	William H. Fitzhugh	
Henry Jones	Henry Williams	
Noah Jones[646]	Elijah Harding	
Barnet Kendall[647]	John C. Edrington	
Travis Kendall[648]	John C. Edrington	
Joshua Kendall[649]		

---

[640] Fielding Hudson (1800-1855) was the son of Samuel Hudson (c.1750-1813) and Susannah Rogers (born 1765). In 1835 he married Parthenia Monteith (c.1812-1848), the daughter of Enos Monteith and Eleanor Thorne. Fielding's employer, George M. Hooe, placed a newspaper notice that said of him, "On Thursday last, I lent one Fielding Hudson, who at that time lived on my land in the pretended capacity of Overseer, an animal to ride to Fredericksburg on—since which time I have heard nothing of it. His story is that he left it tied in the street and that some person took it and rode off. He is, however, such a liar and withal so infamous a scoundrel that I should not be surprised if he had sold it…I take this occasion to warn the public against employing Fielding Hudson, or in any manner trusting him, on the faith of a note of recommendation given him by me some time since. If I had said that he was worthless and not to be trusted I should only have said the truth" (*Political Arena*, Jan. 1, 1836).

[641] James S. Holmes (c.1794-1857) was the son of Edmund Holmes, Jr. (1745-1805) and Sarah Ann Stark (1749-c.1813). She was the daughter of James Stark of Stafford. Edmund was born in Prince William and died in Fauquier. James left an estate in Fauquier County.

[642] James Hawkins was the son of James Hawkins.

[643] Harrison Harding (died c.1824).

[644] In 1809 Francis Jackson bought from Jesse Evans and wife Sarah of Prince William 182 acres on Beaverdam Run (Stafford Deed Book AA, p. 4). In 1813 he paid taxes on this tract described as adjoining Bridwell, Tebbs, and French. This is now part of the Quantico reservation.

[645] William Jackson was the brother of James Jackson.

[646] Noah Jones owned land in the southwest corner of Stafford on the Rappahannock River and Deep Run.

[647] Barnet Kendall was the son of Daniel Kendall.

[648] Travis Kendall (1773-1843) married Susannah Horton and died in Tazewell County, Virginia. In 1812 Travis paid tax on himself only (Stafford County Personal Property Tax Records).

[649] Joshua Kendall (1796-1852) was the son of Henry Kendall (1749-1810) and lived on Aquia Run near what is now Ruby. He also bought property on Accokeek Run, formerly part of Edward Mountjoy's patent (Stafford Deed Book S, pp. 108, 370). In 1812 Joshua paid taxes on 2 slaves and 4 horses, and two tracts of 245 and 61 acres respectively, these being located 10 miles northwest of the courthouse. His estate included 2 oxen, 10 cattle, 1 wagon, farm implements and tools, 9 pewter plates, 216 acres in Stafford, and 1 Bible (Stafford Deed Book OO, p. 126). His will ordered that his slaves be freed and all his property sold

John King (private)	Daniel Mason	
John Kendall (private)	Thomas Hill	
James Knight	J. Reddish & L. Swetnam	
Allen Lakenan	Daniel Mason	
Robert Lang[650]	John C. Edrington	
Thornton Latham	Joseph Reddish	
Rawleigh Latham[651] (private)	Levi Swetnam	Served in Northern Neck
Lewis Lawless[652]	Daniel Mason	
George Lewis[653]		Served in Northern Neck
John Leach		No property
John Lewis		Served in Northern Neck
James Limbrick[654]	Joseph Reddish	
William Limbrick		
William Lowry		
Abner Leitch[655]	Joseph Reddish	
Richard Lomax		
John Limbrick (private)		Served at Mattox Bridge
Benjamin McCoy	Lewis Alexander	Served in Northern Neck
Robert Maccaboy[656]		Served in Northern Neck
Thomas Masters[657]		
John McCartey	Joseph Reddish	
Lewis G. Martin[658]		
Nelson Mason (private)	Elijah Harding	Served on the Potomac
William McInteer		
Daniel Monroe[659]		
James Mills	Lewis Alexander	
John More		Served in the Northern Neck
James Mountjoy		
Jesse Musselman[660]	Levi Swetnam	
John G. Musselman	Levi Swetnam	
William Murray	Daniel Mason	

and the proceeds divided between the slaves (Stafford Deed Book OO, p. 104). Joshua and his father were buried off Choptank Road in Vista Woods subdivision in Stafford.

[650] Robert Lang/Laing married Lucy Bruce (died 1831), the daughter of William Bruce (c.1724-1792) and Elizabeth Grant of King George.

[651] Rawleigh Latham (c.1795-1868) was the son of John Latham (c.1730-1834) and lived near Spotted Tavern. He never married.

[652] Lewis Lawless is listed in the 1817 Stafford personal property tax records as a mulatto.

[653] George Lewis was the son of Conrad Lewis of Falmouth. By 1826 George was a resident of Fredericksburg (Stafford Deed Book GG, p. 239).

[654] James Limbrick was the son of William Limbrick.

[655] Abner Leitch (1790-before 1870) married Sarah Rowe (1797-after 1870), the daughter of John Rowe (1762-1799) and Sarah Peyton (1767-1856). He owned land on Muddy Creek, but by 1829 was a resident of Fredericksburg. This may be the same Abner Leitch listed in the 1850 census of Edgar County, Illinois.

[656] In 1817 Robert Maccaboy married Susan "Sukey" Magee (born c.1800) in Fredericksburg.

[657] Thomas Masters (c.1775-after 1850).

[658] In 1812 Lewis G. Martin paid tax on 1 horse in Stafford.

[659] Daniel Monroe was the brother of James Monroe. Most of the Monroes lived near what is now Richlands Baptist Church.

[660] Jesse Musselman (c.1793-1863) was the son of Henry Musselman (c.1765-1811:19) and lived near Mountain View. In 1816 he married Rosa Stone (c.1801-1822). In 1826 he married his second wife, Delilah Ann Black (1806-1901).

1814

Ebanezer Murray		Port Royal
Rhodham Myers		Removed
James S. Norman[661]	Henry Williams	
Thomas Norman[662]	John C. Edrington	
Alexander Obyrhim[663]		
W. Pemberton (private)	Levi Swetnam	
Aaron Pates		Served in Northern Neck
William Patten[664] (private)	Thomas Hill	
William Pain	Henry Williams	Served in Northern Neck
John Pain	Henry Williams	Served in Northern Neck
John Payne		Removed
Rubin Pain	Henry Williams	Served in Northern Neck
Eli Patterson[665]	Elijah Harding	
John Payne	Lewis Alexander	
Lewis Paine	Barton S. Stone	
John Patten[666]	Thomas Hill	
Valentine Potes[667]	Henry Williams	
John S. Phillips[668]	William H. Fitzhugh	
Silem G. F. Phillips[669]	Elijah Harding	
Stephen Pratt[670]		Served in Northern Neck
Richard Randall	William H. Fitzhugh	
Archibald Rollow		Served at Hope
John Richardson		
Valentine Roles[671]	Henry Williams	
Andrew Ross		
Jesse Rowe[672] (private)	Thomas C. Alexander	Served at Mattox Bridge
Jesse Rowe (private)	John C. Edrington	
Henry Rose	William H. Fitzhugh	
Archibald Rye[673]	Daniel Mason	

---

[661] James S. Norman (c.1777-1814) was the son of Edward Norman (1752-1814) and Jane Stewart (c.1756-1814) of Edge Hill. James, his brother Matthew, and both of his parents died in the epidemic of 1814/15.

[662] Thomas Norman (c.1790-1846) was the son of Edward Norman (1752-1814) and Jane Stewart (c.1756-1814) of Edge Hill in Wide Water. Thomas' first wife was Paulina Ficklen (c.1800-1830). He married secondly Mildred Ficklen Hill (1804-1886). All are buried at Edge Hill.

[663] Alexander Obryham (1788-1854) was born in Ireland. He married Mary Timmons (1798-1860), the daughter of Thomas Timmons (c.1775-1842) of Stafford. Later generations of this family modified the last name to "OBrien."

[664] May be William Patton (1785-1814), son of George Patton (c.1757-c.1813) and Sarah Stringfellow (1766-1848) of Stafford. William married Lydia McInteer (1786-1867).

[665] Eli Patterson was a member of Hartwood Baptist Church (Hartwood).

[666] May be John Patton (born c.1789), the son of George Patton (c.1757-c.1813) and Sarah Stringfellow (1766-1848) of Stafford.

[667] Valentine Potes lived in the Wide Water area near Edge Hill. He married Nancy ___ and buried two year old son, William Potes (1818-1820) at Macedonia Church Cemetery. This is located very near the game station on the Marine Corps reservation. The surname Potes also appears as Potts.

[668] John Sidenham Phillips (born 1777) was the son of Col. William Phillips (1744-1797) and Elizabeth Ann Fowke (died c.1830) of Traveler's Rest, Stafford County.

[669] Silem Frederick Gustavus Phillips (1790-c.1871) was the son of Col. William Phillips (1744-1797) and Elizabeth Ann Fowke (died c.1830) of Traveler's Rest, Stafford County.

[670] Also went by the name Stephen Pratt Bowen.

[671] Valentine Roles was the son of Jesse Roles.

[672] Jesse Rowe (born 1795) was the son of John Rowe (1762-1797) and Sarah Peyton (1767-1856). He married Atsey Humphries.

Presly Simms[674]	Henry Mason	
John Smith		Served at Mattox Bridge
Abner Schooler	Thomas Hill	Served on the Potomac
Harris Smith (private)	Elijah Harding	
Thomas Storke[675]		Served at Camp Drummond
Jonas Swillavant[676]	Joseph Reddish	Served at Potomac Church & Camp Drummond
William Sidebottom[677]		
Richard Sharp (private)	Elijah Harding	
James B. Starke[678]	Henry Williams	
Thomas Stewart[679]		
Benjamin Sims[680] (private)	Levi Swetnam	
Thomson Sincler		
Benjamin Snellings (private)	Barton S. Stone	
William Stadler		Not found
Bailey W. Storke[681]		No property
Gustavus Sullivan[682]		No property
James Sullivan		No property
Thornton Skidmore		No property
Marmion Sullivan	Lewis Alexander	Served at Mattox Bridge
James Taylor	Daniel Mason	
Thornton Taylor[683]		
James Tharp[684]	Elijah Harding	
James Thompson	Daniel Mason	
William Thompson	Daniel Mason	
John Truslow[685]	William H. Fitzhugh	
William Trussell		

[673] In 1818 Archibald Rye married Elizabeth Condiffe in Fredericksburg.

[674] Presley George Simms (1754-1852) was born in Stafford. He was the son of Richard Simms, Sr. (c.1720-c.1812) and Elizabeth Bridwell (c.1730-c.1816). Presley married Nancy Bridwell (died 1845) and died in Montgomery County, Indiana.

[675] Thomas Storke lived on Cannon Run in northern Stafford. His farm was later owned by William Barber (1787-1881) who called it Wyoming.

[676] Jonas Swillavant was the son of Daniel Swillavant. This surname gradually changed to Sullivan.

[677] In 1812 William Sidebottom, Jr. paid taxes on 1 horse in Stafford.

[678] James Barton Stark (c.1790-c.1825) was the son of William Stark (1754-1838) and Mary Kendall. In 1810 he married Ann Caroline Million, the daughter of Cuthbert Million. They later moved to Madison, Kentucky.

[679] Thomas Stewart (died c.1833) was the son of Charles Stewart (1781-1819) and Eleanor V. McIntosh.

[680] Benjamin Simms (c.1800-1854) was the son of Richard Simms, Jr. (c.1752-1850) and Elizabeth Ashby, the daughter of John Ashby and Sarah McCullough of Stafford. He died in Clay County, Missouri.

[681] Bailey Washington Storke married Elizabeth Townshend Dade (born 1786), the daughter of Townshend Dade (1760-1808) who resided at Studley on the Stafford side of Chappawamsic Run. In 1812 Bailey paid taxes on 5 slaves, 2 horses, and 1 gig in Stafford.

[682] Gustavus Sullivan (1785-after 1850) was the son of Daniel Sullivan and Mary Jett.

[683] Thornton A. Taylor (born c.1796) married Elizabeth Kirk (born c.1796), the daughter of Jeremiah Kirk (died c.1817) and Ann Monroe. For a few years he and Elizabeth resided on her father's farm near what is now Abel Reservoir. Thornton was a farmer and Methodist minister and moved to Alabama and then to Noxubee County, Mississippi.

[684] This may be James Tharp (born 1795), the son of Thomas Tharp and Margaret Brahan. He married Nancy Skelton and removed to Page County, Virginia.

[685] John Truslow was the son of Benjamin Truslow.

1814

William Turner	Thomas Hill	
Crede True[686]		No property
James Tison		No property
John Tison[687]		No property
Thomas Walker		Served at Mattox Bridge
Thomas Waters[688]	Elijah Harding	Served at Camp Drummond
Baily Watson	Daniel Mason	
Landon Walters[689]		Removed
James Williams		Not found
John Way		No property
James Watson		Removed
Samuel Wharton		Removed
Joseph Welch (private)		Served in Northern Neck
George White (private)		Served at Mattox Bridge
George White	Thomas C. Alexander	Served at Mattox Bridge
Jessee Williams	Joseph Reddish	
Allen Wray		
Linsfield Young[690]		Removed

1815

Colonel—Samuel H. Peyton
Majors—William H. Fitzhugh—in room of Robert Crutcher
       George M. Cooke—in room of Benjamin Tolson, resigned
Captains—George Waller
       William McInteer—in room of Elijah Harding, deceased
       William Shelton
       John S. Knox—in room of Lewis Alexander, removed
       Aaron H. Ball—in room of Thomas C. Alexander, removed
       George M. Cooke—in room of John C. Edrington, resigned
       Thornton Alexander[691]—in room of Jeremiah Templeman, resigned
       John Moncure, Jr.—in room of James Waller who refused to qualify
       Abner R. Alcock—in room of Joseph Reddish, removed
       Jeremiah B. Templeman—in room of B. S. Stone, resigned
       Alexander S. H. Stone—in room of Henry Williams, resigned
       James Briggs[692]—in room of Rowzee Peyton, resigned
       James Waller—in room of George M. Cooke, promoted
       Thomas Hill—cavalry—stationed at Camp Selden
1ˢᵗ Lieutenant of Cavalry—Thomas James[693]

---

[686] By 1846 Crede True was an insolvent pauper in Fredericksburg.
[687] John Tyson (born c.1794) was born in King George.
[688] Thomas Waters was the son of William Waters.
[689] In 1820 Landon Walters married Sophia Patterson in Dumfries.
[690] Linsfield Young was the son of William Young.
[691] Thornton Alexander's (1790-1842) exact parentage is unclear, but he is seems to have been from the Stafford branch of the Alexander family. In 1816 he married Frances A. Waller. In 1819 he took over Moses Phillips' old ordinary near the courthouse and also worked as a slave trader. Around 1837 he removed to Natchez, Mississippi and became manager of the Steamboat Hotel there. Thornton is buried in Natchez.
[692] James McDonald Briggs (1787-1845) was the son of David Briggs (1730-1813), a Scots merchant in Falmouth and Jean McDonald (c.1750-1810). James inherited his father's Stony Hill plantation in Hartwood. He married Charlotte Ashmore Keith (1782-1866), the daughter of Isham Keith of Fauquier. She was a niece of Chief Justice John Marshall.
[693] In 1812 Thomas James paid taxes on 6 slaves and 5 horses in Stafford.

1815

2ⁿᵈ Lieutenant of Cavalry—Thomas P. Harrison—in room of Robert Beaty, resigned
Cornet—Thomas Wilson[694]
Lieutenants—Walter R. Daniel
    John Tackett[695]
    Allen W. Markham
    John B. Taylor[696]
    Boswell Alsop
    William Hewitt
    Thomas Tutt[697]
    Thornton W. Cropp[698]—in room of Amos Fristoe who refused to qualify
    George T. Shelkett[699]
    Thornton Alexander
    John L./D. Tolson
    John Moncure, Jr.
    Amos Fristoe—in room of William Shelton, resigned
    Edwin C. Moncure
Ensigns—James Hewitt[700]—in room of John Ross, removed
    James Homes
    William W. McNeil[701]
    Joseph A. Carter
    Thomas W. Conyers[702]
    Philip Leitch—in room of Thomas Wallace[703] who refused to qualify
    Richard Cropp
    Allen W. Norman[704]—in room of Archibald Rollow, resigned
    William Langford—in room of Thomas Tutt
    John P. Williams[705]—in room of Benjamin Williams who refused to qualify—in John

---

[694] In 1819 Thomas Wilson paid tax on 23 acres above Falmouth.

[695] John Tackett (1788-1850) was probably born in Prince William County. He was the son of William Tackett, Jr. (c.1751-after 1830) and Frances Reno (c.1750-1796:99). John married Enfield Mason (1796-1836), the daughter of Joel Mason (died 1817) and Sarah Bourne (c.1771-1835) of Stafford. From 1813-1814 he was post master at Tackett's Mills. John died in Shelby County, Illinois.

[696] In 1819 John B. Taylor paid tax on part of a lot in Falmouth and 10 ½ acres near Yellow Chapel (Hartwood). He was a carpenter (Stafford Estate Accounts, 1823, p. 207).

[697] Thomas Tutt (born c.1794) was the son of Archibald Tutt and Catherine Pendleton. Thomas was probably born in either Orange or Culpeper County.

[698] Thornton W. Cropp (born 1792) was the son of James Cropp (1755-1833) and Susan Thomas (1760-1833).

[699] In 1792 George Shelkett (c.1771-after 1816) was a resident of King George. He married Mary D. Owens of King George.

[700] James Hewitt. From about 1813-1819 he was granted licenses to operate an ordinary in Stafford (Eby, Men 270-271). In 1812 James paid taxes on 7 slaves and 3 horses in Stafford.

[701] William Walker McNeil (died 1822) married Fanny R. Seddon (c.1795-1868), the daughter of Thomas Seddon (c.1737-1810). William later moved to Warrenton where he was a merchant.

[702] Thomas W. Conyers (1795-1879) was the son of John Conyers (1754-1819) and Mary Davis. He married Eliza Wall and died in Monroe County, Missouri.

[703] May be Thomas Wallace (1761-1818), the son of Dr. Michael Wallace (1719-1767) of Ellerslie. Thomas married Mary "Polly" Hooe (born 1772) and resided for a time at Chestnut Hill in Stafford. He later removed to Clover Hill, Culpeper where he spent the remainder of his life.

[704] Allen Waller Norman was the likely son of George Norman (1743-1807) and Elizabeth Stewart (1749-1822). He was buried in the Norman/Stewart cemetery between Hope Road and Hidden Spring Lane in northeastern Stafford.

Moncure, Jr.'s company
John Ball
Bailey W. Dawson[706]
Thornton Cropp
Thomas Tutt—in room of William McNeil, resigned
Henry Washington[707]—in room of Burdett Clifton, resigned
Benjamin Williams, Sr.—in room of Thomas Conyers, resigned
Thomas Wallace
Alexander Obryham—in room of George T. Shelkett
Thomas Norman

Quartermaster—Coleman R. Browne
Provost Marshall Pro Tem—Daniel P. Harrison[708]
Trumpeter—Mason G. McCoy[709]—in Capt. Thomas Hill's troop

In May 1815 Drum Major Allen Duffey and Fife Major William Purnell of the Prince William County militia attended the training of officers of the 45th regiment at Stafford Courthouse.

Men fined for failure to appear at muster:

Name	Note
William Abbett	No property found.
Boswell Alsop	No inhabitant
James Allen	Not found
William Anderson[710]	Removed
Jeremiah Atchison[711]	Removed
James Armstrong[712]	No property found.
Robert Allen	No property found.
Charles Bridwell[713]	No property found.
Henry Booton(?)	Removed
Servis(?) Bowling	Removed
Charles D. Bridwell	Remitted
John Bridwell	Not found

---

[705] John Pope/Polk Williams (c.1800-before 1850) was the son of Pearson Williams (c.1743-c.1824). This branch of the Williams family came to Stafford in the mid 18th century to work at Accokeek Iron Furnace. John married Charlotte ___ (c.1798-1850:52). Both died prior to mid-1852 leaving children Hannah (born c.1830), James (born c.1833), Elizabeth Ann (born c.1838), and William (born c.1835). All except Hannah were underage and Martha Ann Roles agreed to serve as their guardian (Stafford Circuit 438).

[706] Bailey Dawson (c.1776-1856) was the son of John Dawson (1751-1839) who also moved to Shelby County, Kentucky in 1817. In 1818 Bailey was dismissed from Chappawamsic Baptist Church. By 1840 he and his wife were in Shelby County. Bailey died in Jefferson County, Kentucky.

[707] This may be Henry Washington who was the son of Bailey Washington, Jr. (1753-1814) and Euphan Wallace (1765-1845) of Windsor Forest.

[708] In 1819 Daniel Peyton Harrison paid tax on 100 acres on Aquia Creek adjoining Mason.

[709] Mason G. McCoy (c.1789-1870) died of old age at Nash's Hill in Stafford.

[710] William Anderson (c.1795-after 1850).

[711] Possibly Jeremiah Atchison (c.1776-1859) who was born in Hampshire County, Virginia and died in Fleming County, Kentucky. He married Adah Wright.

[712] James Armstrong (c.1790-after 1850). In 1829 the Stafford court granted him a license to run an ordinary (Eby, Men 273).

[713] May be the same Charles Bridwell who married Ruth ___ and buried his eight-year old son, Yelverton Wimsted Bridwell at Macedonia Church cemetery in 1797. This cemetery is located very near the game station on the Marine Corps reservation.

William Bridwell	Removed
William Bridwell	No property found.
William Brimmer	No inhabitant
William Brown	No property found.
William Button	Removed
Thomas Bloxton	Not found
John Bussel	Not found
Thomas Carback	Removed
William Chissom	No property found.
Burdit Clifton	Remitted
Daniel Cole	Removed
John Combs	Removed
Alexander Cooper	Not found
James Curry	No property found.
George Coakley	No property found.
Benjamin S. Corbin[714]	No property found.
James Chapman	Not found
William Dickinson	Not found
Thomas Doggett	Removed
Lemuel Dorson	Not found
Barton Dawson	No property found.
Lewis Dickerson	Remitted
Lewis Edmonson	No property found.
George Ensor[715]	Removed
William R. Ensor[716]	Remitted
Daniel Fines[717]	No property found.
John Franklin	Removed
James Ford	Removed
Philip A. Foxworthy[718]	Not found
Barnett Fritter	Remitted
Fielding George	Not found
Richard Ganes	Removed
John Gollehorn	Not found
Thomas Gill	No property found.
Benjamin Groves	No property found.
William Guy	No property found.
Jesse Gray[719]	No property found.
Philip Harmage	Not found

---

[714] In 1819 Benjamin S. Corbin (c.1790-after 1856) married Sarah Preston, the daughter of William Preston. Benjamin removed to Clay County, Missouri.

[715] In 1804 George Ensor paid taxes on 100 acres in Stafford.

[716] William R. Ensor (1788-1867) was the son of George Ensor (before 1760-1810) and Docia Stephens (c.1766-1848) of Fauquier. In 1812 he married Ann Hickerson. In 1813 William bought from John Ross and wife Mary of Stafford 45 acres on Deep Run, formerly belonging to George Ensor, deceased (Stafford Deed Book AA, p. 415). In 1819 William paid tax on 90 acres on Deep Run.

[717] Daniel Fines was the son of James Fines and Rachel Curtis.

[718] Philip Alexander Foxworthy (1797-1875) was the son of Vincent Foxworthy (1758-1820). He was born in Stafford and died in Morgan County, Indiana. He married first Katherine T. Fredericks (c.1801-1840). He married secondly Martha Evans (c.1801-1843) and thirdly Martha's sister, Phoebe Evans (1819-1882). All of his marriages occurred after he left Virginia. In the mid-1820s Philip leased land from Willoughby Tebbs. This property is now part of the Quantico Marine Corps base.

[719] Jesse Gray (born 1790:1800) may have been the son of James Gray. He lived much of his life in Fauquier. In 1818 he married Rhoda Brown, the daughter of Thaddeus Brown, in Fauquier.

1815

John W. Harris[720]	Removed
Francis H. Hooe	No property found.
John Harding	Not found
Charles Haslip	Remitted
Thomas P. Harrison	Remitted
William Hollady	Removed
John Herndon[721]	No property found.
Isom Jordan	Not found
George Jones	Not found
Jeremiah Jordan[722]	No property found.
William Jones	No property found.
Peter Jett	No property found.
John Jackson, Jr.	No property found.
Francis Jackson	Remitted
Thomas Johnson	No property found.
William Kendall[723]	No property found.
John F. Kemper[724]	Removed
Bailey Knight	No property found.
Elijah Knight	No property found.
James Limbrick, Jr.	No property found.
James Leach	No property found.
John Limbrick	No property found.
Vincent Limbrick	No property found.
William Latham	Removed
John Lewis	No property found.
Fulsom Langfit[725]	No property found.
Robert Mcoboy	Removed
Thornton Martin	Removed
Thomas M. Morton	Removed
Jesse Musselman	No property found.
James Newton	Remitted
Led G. Payne[726]	No property found.
Lemuel Potes[727]	No property found.

---

[720] John W. Harris married Marthew Portch, the daughter of Esom Porch (c.1745-1826). In 1843 John paid tax on 49 acres of Esom Porch's old farm near Horsepen Run.

[721] May be John Herndon (c.1794-1882). He married Lucinda Combs (c.1796-c.1867). John was born in Fauquier and died near Stafford Store. From 1812-1814 he served in Capt. William Dulin's company, having mustered in at Elk Run Church in Fauquier.

[722] In 1812 Jeremiah Jordan paid taxes on himself only; he owned no slaves or livestock.

[723] This may be William Kendall (1792-1851), the son of Henry Kendall (1749-1810) of Stafford. William and other family members are buried off Choptank Road in northern Stafford.

[724] In 1812 John F. Kemper paid taxes only on himself.

[725] Israel Folsom Langfitt was the son of John Langfitt (died c.1824) and Sarah Folsom (died after 1844), daughter of Israel Folsom (died 1772) who was buried in Dumfries, Prince William County. Early on, the Langfitts had settled in Westmoreland County, Virginia, but a branch of this family moved to the Pittsburgh region of Pennsylvania. John Langfitt seems to have been descended from this branch. He kept a store in Falmouth and resided at Glencairne just north of the town. In 1825 the Langfitts sold their farm to Richard C. L. Moncure (Stafford Deed Book GG, p. 73). In 1822 Israel was "arrested by a warrant from Mr. Thomas Seddon, of Stafford, on chrg. of being the person who, in Nov last, shot at the mail driver bet[ween] Falmouth & Stafford Crt-Hse, Va." (*National Intelligencer*, Mar. 4, 1822).

[726] Ledmus/Ledman Godfrey Payne (1780-1881) lived in the northern part of the county very near Stafford Store. He married Melvina S. ___ (c.1793-1867) of Stafford.

1815

William C. Potes[728]	Not found
Yelverton B. Poarch	No property found.
John Rodgers	No property found.
Keilding Roe[729]	Removed
William Rose	No property found.
Andrew Ross	No property found.
Archibald Rye	Not found
George Reeves	Not found
James Richerson	Not found
George Servis(?)	Not found
Joseph Silmon	Not found
Bailey W. Storke	No property found.
Thomas Storke	No property found.
Augustin Sullivan	No property found.
Carson Sullivan[730]	No property found.
William Sullivan	No property found.
Marmian Sullivan	No property found.
William D. Simmons	Removed
John Sorrell	Not found
Robert Tooms	No property found.
Joseph Tyson	No property found.
Rodney Thompson	No property found.
William Tharp	No property found.
James Tharp	No property found.
Richard Tharp	Not found
James Thompson	Removed
Landon Walters	No property found.
Mason Walters	Removed
Joseph Wamsley[731]	No property found.
Allen Way	No property found.
Linsfield Young	No property found.

1816

Colonel—Samuel H. Peyton
Major—George Waller—in room of William H. Fitzhugh, resigned
Captains—Walter R. Daniel
        John N. Tolson[732]
        Thomas Hill
        Henry Williams
        Daniel Mason

---

[727] During the War of 1812, Lemuel Potts served with the 25th regiment of the Virginia militia (King George County).

[728] May be the William C. Potts (c.1786-after 1850) who was included on the King George County census of 1850.

[729] Keeling Row (1785-1869) was the son of Thomas Row (1754-1840) and Rachel Keeling (1754-1827) of Orange County. Keeling's first wife was Rebecca Dillard; he married secondly Fanny Brumley and thirdly Fanny Bates. He died in Caroline County.

[730] Possibly Casson Sullivan (died before 1821), the sun of Benjamin Sullivan (c.1760-1803) and Susannah Kitchen(?).

[731] Joseph Wamsley (died before 1850) was from Maryland. He married Victoria ___ (c.1774-1854) and left a family in Stafford.

[732] John Nelson Tolson (1796-1851) was the son of Benjamin Tolson (c.1763-1836). He married Margaret E. Shacklett (1809-1866) and was buried at Locust Shade in Prince William County.

Joseph Reddish
Lewis Alexander
John C. Edrington
William H. Fitzhugh
Barton S. Stone
Elijah Harding
Levi Swetnam
Lieutenants—William Waller
James Morton[733]
George L. Brent[734]
John Taylor
James Homes—in room of Allen W. Markham, resigned
Lieutenant of Cavalry—Mark Harding[735]—in room of Thomas P. Harrison, resigned
Cornet—William Marquess—in room of Thomas Wilson, resigned
Ensigns—John Marquess[736]
Stephen P. Bowen[737]
James Morton—in room of Allen W. Norman, deceased
John H. S. Potts[738]—in John N. Tolson's company
Silas F. Cropp[739]—in room of William Leitch, resigned
Joseph Armstrong[740]
1st Captain of Flying Artillery—Abner R. Alcock—in room of Thomas Green of Fauquier, removed from state
2nd Captain of Flying Artillery—Thomas Norman
1st Lieutenant of Flying Artillery—Lawson Wheatley
2nd Lieutenant of Flying Artillery—John Oglevy
Paymaster—Samuel H. Skinker

---

[733] James Morton (1793-1859) was the son of Richard Morton (1771-1812) and Margaret Ursula Waller (1771-1821). He married Lucy Brown Horton (c.1818-1898) and lived at Spring Hill (now Vestavia Woods subdivision just east of the courthouse). James was in the timber business and left numerous children in Stafford. As a young man he was in the shipping business with his cousin, Withers Waller (1785-1827) and hauled some, if not all, of the stone columns from Brent's (Government) Island to Washington for use in the U. S. Capitol. From at least 1835 until his death in 1859 James served as a justice in Stafford. Other official posts in the county included overseer of the road and overseer of the poor. From at least 1832-1833 James held a license to operate an ordinary.

[734] George Lee Brent (1793-1818) was the son of Daniel Carroll Brent of Richland.

[735] Mark Harding (c.1788-1873) was the son of Mark Harding, Sr. and Nancy Young. He operated a grist mill at Loch Lomond on Potomac Run. Mark's first wife was Agnes Hord (c.1795-after 1850), the daughter of Peter Hord (c.1749-after 1790). He married secondly Ann Sharp.

[736] John Marquess was the son of Anthony Marquess (1752-1821) and was a saddler. In 1829 he paid tax on 159 acres on Horsepen Run. By 1827 John had bankrupted and the sheriff sold his property. This consisted of one tract inherited from his father, a second tract purchased from David Briggs and John G. Beale, and a third purchased from Thomas Wilson (Stafford Deed Book GG, p. 458).

[737] Stephen P. Bowen (c.1813-1854) was probably the son of John Pratt Bowen and Elizabeth Curtis. He married Lucy Went. By 1825 he was living in King George though he still owned land in the White Oak area of Stafford (Stafford Deed Book GG, p. 55). In June 1825 Charles and Elizabeth Peyton sold Stephen 50 acres on which Margaret Mattox then lived (Stafford Deed Book GG, p. 58).

[738] John H. S. Potts (died 1847) was a merchant.

[739] Silas Flavius Cropp (1795-1871) was born in Stafford and died in DeWitt, Missouri. He was the son of James Cropp (1755-1833) and Susan Thomas (1760-1833) and married Sarah A. C. Noel of Spotsylvania. Silas was the brother of Warner L. Cropp (c.1785-1879). In the 1830s he owned land in Fauquier County.

[740] In 1819 Joseph Armstrong paid tax on 125 acres on Austin Run.

In May 1816 Gustavus Shelton[741] of Stafford served as drum major at the officers' training at Stafford Courthouse. William Purnell of Prince William was fife major. After drumming at Stafford Courthouse, Gustavus then performed the same duty for the 89th regiment near Haymarket.

Men fined for failure to appear at muster:

Name	Note
James Armstrong	Not found
James Bowling	Remitted
James S. Bowling	Remitted
William Brimmer	Removed
William Brown	No property found.
John Conyers, Jr.	Not found
James Curry	No property found.
Fantlyroy Hooe	Remitted
Leonard Horton	Removed
John Jackson, Jr.	Not found
Peter Jett	No property found.
William T. Jones	Removed
Thornton Latham	No property found.
George Lewis	Removed
William Limbrick	No property found.
Thornton Martin	No property found.
Daniel Monroe, Jr.	No property found.
James F. Murray	Remitted
Amos A. Parker	Removed
George Payne	No property found.
William S. Payne	Remitted
Yelverton B. Porch	No property found.
James Puller	Not found
Thomas Roberson	No property found.
Gustavus Sullivan	No property found.
Triplett Shumate[742]	Removed
Joseph Stilman	Removed
Robert Tooms	No property found.
Joseph Tison	No property found.
James Tison	No property found.
John Weeks	Removed
Martin Wilhite[743]	Removed

---

[741] George Gustavus Shelton (born 1793) was the son of Edward Shelton and Nancy Seddon. He is believed to be buried near Bethel Church in White Oak. George was the brother of Rodney Seddon Jefferson Shelton. George married Lucinda Pates (1805-1873).

[742] May be Triplett Shumate (c.1796-c.1850), the son of Lewis Shumate (1773-1861) and Mary Chadwell of Fauquier County.

[743] May be Martin Wilhite (born 1781), the son of Joel Wilhite (c.1743-1825:30) and Miry Wilhoit. Martin was born in Culpeper.

1817

Colonel—Samuel H. Peyton
Captain—William Hewitt
Captain of Light Infantry—William Ford—1st battalion—in room of John Moncure, Jr., resigned
　　　　　　　Alexander
Lieutenants—George T. Shelkett
　　　　James Morton—in room of John Williams, resigned
　　　　Burkett Pratt[744]
Ensigns—Thomas Payne—in room of Allen W. Norman, deceased
　　　　Alexander Obryhim—in Capt. Alexander's company

In May 1817 Gustavus Shelton acted as "Brigade Drummer" for officers' training and regimental muster. That same year Peter P. Cox served as "Brigade Fife" at the same events.

Men fined for failure to appear at muster:

Name	Note
James Anderson	Removed
William Abbitt	Not found
James Allison	Not found
Benjamin Alsop	Not found
Charles Beach[745]	Not found
Bailey Byram	No property found.
William Bridwell	Not found
James S. Bowling	No property found.
William Brown	No property found.
Ira Burton	Removed
John Burton	No property found.
John Bell, Jr.	No property found.
James Bowling	Remitted
Abijah Bowling	No property found.
Whitfield Brooke[746]	Removed
Robert Brooke	Removed
Fielding Baker[747]	Not found
John Bustle	Remitted
George Bowling	Remitted
Lewis Bowling	Not found
Jesse Brooks	No property found.
Thomas Brooks[748]	No property found.
Augustus Butler[749]	Not found
William Burton	Removed
William Butler	No property found.
Washington Cliff	Not found

---

[744] Burket Pratt was supposedly the father of an illegitimate son, John Pratt Bowen, by Susannah Bowen.
[745] In 1817 Charles Beach was granted a license to keep an ordinary (Eby, Men 271).
[746] Whitfield Brooke was the son of William Brooke (1750-1799) and Mary Beale of Fredericksburg. He married Sarah Newton.
[747] Fielding Baker (1799-c.1879) was born in Fauquier and died in Stafford. In 1830 he worked as a constable in Stafford (Eby, Men 146). His estate included 2 feather beds, 1 carpet, 2 flax wheels, 1 shot gun, 1 lounge, 3 bee hives, and 10 barrels of corn all valued at $64.70 (Stafford Deed Book 1, p.11).
[748] Thomas Brooks (c.1795-after 1850).
[749] This may have been Augustine Butler who married Nancy Crews in 1803 in Louisa County. He was the son of Nathaniel Butler and Pricilla Anthony.

James Coakley[750]	Removed
Richard Cunninghame	Not found
James Curry	No property found.
Joseph Curry	No property found.
James Curtis	Removed
George Cox	Removed
John Conyers, Jr.	No property found.
Harris S. Corbin	No property found.
William Chissom	No property found.
John P. Clanton	Not found
Rawleigh Cooper[751]	Remitted
Lewis Dickinson	Remitted
Hiram Davis	No property found.
William Doyal	No property found.
John Dagins	Not found
Jacob England	Removed
Lewis Edmondson	Not found
Samuel French	Not found
George Farish	Not found
Alexander Foxworthy[752]	Not found
Ephraim Fritter	Not found
Barnett Fritter	Not found
John Fritter	No property found.
Travers Fritter	No property found.
John Fines	No property found.
Daniel Fines	No property found.
Thomas Fines[753]	No property found.
John Garner	No property found.
James Graves[754]	No property found.
Seth Gains[755]	No property found.
William P. Gaines[756]	Remitted
John Gollohorn	
Jeremiah Gordon	Not found
Perry Griffis	No property found.
Thomas Groves[757]	Not found

[750] In 1812 James Coakley paid taxes on 8 slaves and 9 horses in Stafford.

[751] Rawleigh Cooper was originally from Fauquier. He lived near Chappawamsic Run in which is now the Quantico reservation. In September 1826 Gustavus Ashby of Orange County and wife Julia sold Rawleigh 131 acres adjoining the lands of Joseph Combs, Robert Ashby, and the Brentown Road (Stafford Deed Book GG, p. 423). In 1813 he served as deputy sheriff of Stafford.

[752] Alexander Foxworthy (1798-1856) was the son of William Foxworthy and Clarissa Calvert of Prince William County. Alexander married Nancy Glascock.

[753] Thomas Fines (born 1795) was the son of James Fines (c.1769-1812) and Rachel Curtis. He married Emily Bates (born c.1812), the daughter of James Bates and Mary Limbrick.

[754] James Graves (c.1795-after 1850) was a carpenter.

[755] Seth Gaines (1800-1834) was the son of William Henry Gaines (1754-c.1818) and Jane Botts (1757-1826). His parents resided in Culpeper for many years and then moved to Prince William County. Seth was born in Culpeper and left an estate in Fauquier.

[756] William Pendleton Gaines (1791-1822) was the son of William Henry Gaines (1754-c.1818) and Jane Botts (1757-1826) of Culpeper and Prince William. He married Euphema Holliday (1805-1881) and died in Loudoun County. In 1812 William paid taxes on 8 slaves, 9 horses, and 466 acres on North Run of Chappawamsic.

William Green	No property found.
James Hawkins, Jr.	No property found.
James Hefflin	No property found.
Charles B. Hines	Removed
Lemuel Ingalls	Not found
Thomas Jenkins[758]	Removed
Jacob Johnston	Not found
Jeremiah Jordan	No property found.
Isom Jordan	No property found.
John F. Kemper	Not found
Elijah Knight	No property found.
Alexander Kendall[759]	Not found
Amos Keys	Not found
Thornton Latham	Removed
Syrus Lee	Not found
George Lewis	No property found.
John Lewis	No property found.
Allen Lakenan	Remitted
John Limbrick	No property found.
John Mozingo[760]	Removed
John McFee	Removed
Thornton Martin	No property found.
Horace Mitchell	No property found.
William Murphy	Remitted
Steven Moody	No property found.
Enos Monteith	No property found.
Thomas Newton	No property found.
Eli Patterson	Removed
Perry Patterson	Removed
William S. Payne	No property found.
Coleman Perks	Removed
Yelverton B. Porch	No property found.
James Powel	Removed
Amos H. Parker	Removed
William Patterson	No property found.
John Pates	Not found
Sidney Pilcher[761]	Not found
William C. Potes	Not found
George Rankins	Not found
Henry Rose	Not found
George A. Rucker	Not found
Archibald Rye	Not found

[757] In 1807 Thomas Groves was overseer for Nathaniel P. Williams (Stafford County Personal Property Tax Records).
[758] In 1812 Thomas Jenkins paid taxes on 1 slave and 2 horses in Stafford.
[759] Alexander Kendall (1785-1821) married Elizabeth Tungett (1795-1861) and died in New Orleans.
[760] This may be the John Mozingo (c.1783-1870:80) who from 1826-1828 owned 50 acres near Hartwood. From at least 1830 until sometime after 1860, he was in King George County. By 1870 he was in Westmoreland County. His second wife was Catherine Inscoe (c.1811-after 1880).
[761] Sidney A. Pilcher (1794-1863) may have been the son of Frederick Pilcher (1769-1827) and Margaret Alsop (born c.1772). In 1818 he married Susan Roberson (c.1798-1856) in Shepardstown, now West Virginia. Sidney worked as a cooper in Frederick County, Virginia and both he and Susan died at Harper's Ferry.

Henry W. Richarson	Removed
Alfred S. Sam	Not found
John Smith	No property found.
Elias Stone[762]	No property found.
Thomas C. Scott[763]	Remitted
Gustavus Sullivan	No property found.
James Sullivan	No property found.
John A. Stork	Not found
Joseph Smith	Not found
Richard Tharp	Not found
John Tackett	Not found
Ephraim Templeman[764]	Not found
Joseph Tison	No property found.
Hezekiah Waple	No property found.
Bailey Watson	No property found.
Joseph Welch	Not found
Samuel Withers	Not found
Richard Willers(?)	No property found.
Jesse Williams	Not found

1818

Colonel—George M. Cooke
Lt. Colonel—George Waller—in room of Samuel H. Peyton, resigned
Major—James Briggs
Captains—Thornton Cropp
    Thomas Hill
    Abner R. Alcock
    John N. Tolson
    William Hewitt
Lieutenants—Silas F. Cropp
    Jones Green[765]—in Capt. Tolson's company—in room of George Brent, deceased
    John A. Starke[766]
    William W. Peyton[767]—in Thomas Hill's troop of horse
1ˢᵗ Lieutenant of Cavalry—Mark Harding—in Thomas Hill's Troop of Cavalry
Cornet—John Stevens—in Thomas Hill's Troop of Horse

---

[762] Around 1837 Elias Stone married Rose Anna Musselman (c.1805-after 1850), the daughter of Henry Musselman (c.1765-c.1815) (Stafford Deed Book LL, p. 29).

[763] Thomas Cropper Scott (1791-1858) was a merchant in Falmouth and was listed in the 1850 King George census. Thomas' first wife was Mary Lucinda Seddon (died c.1847), the daughter of Thomas Seddon (c.1737-1810) of Stafford; they lived at Clearview in Falmouth. He married secondly in 1849 Sarah Rust (died 1856), the daughter of John Skinker and Elizabeth Bowie and widow of Benjamin Rust of King George. In 1830 Thomas was elected a trustee of Falmouth and served as such until at least 1842.

[764] Ephraim Templeman (c.1777-after 1850) was born in Stafford and moved to Bath County, Kentucky.

[765] Originally from Culpeper, Jones Green (c.1794-1858) came to Falmouth with his brother, Duff Green, and was a merchant. Jones was the son of Capt. James Green (c.1734-after 1809) and Elizabeth Jones. He didn't remain in Falmouth very long, returning to his farm Greenock in Culpeper. Jones married Susan Elizabeth Margaret Scott (1800-1844), the daughter of John Scott (died 1848) of Fredericksburg.

[766] John A. Starke (c.1794-c.1865) was the son of William Stark (1754-1838) and Mary Kendall (1760-1858). He never married. John's modest estate inventory consisted of 1 bed and bedding, 1 corn sheller, 1 wheat fan, and a shot gun (Stafford Deed Book 26A, p. 316).

[767] William Washington Peyton (1799-1847) was the son of Dr. Valentine Peyton (1756-1815) and Mary Butler Washington (1760-1822) of Tusculum. He married Mary Lucy Mason (1801-1838), daughter of Col. Enoch Mason. William inherited his father's Tusculum plantation, but lost it to debt.

1st Lieutenant—Joseph Johnson—in Abner Alcock's company in 2nd regiment of artillery
Ensigns—William L. Cleveland
    John Starke—in Capt. Tolson's company
    Daniel F. Payne[768]—in Thomas Hill's Troop of Cavalry
    Richard Cropp
    Benjamin Combs[769]—in John N. Tolson's company
    Samuel S. Brooke[770]—in William Hewitt's company of infantry
    Joseph Billingsley—in Capt. Tolson's company of infantry

In May 1818 Gustavus Shelton served as Brigade Drummer at officers' training and muster. He performed the same duty for the 89th and 36th regiments (Prince William), and the 44th and 85th (Fauquier). That same year Peter Cox was Brigade Fife for the 45th, 44th and 85th, 89th and 36th, and the 25th (King George) regiments.

Men fined for failure to appear at muster:

Name	Note
William Black	Remitted
William Brown	No property
James Bowling	No property
John Bowling	No property
James S. Bowling	No property
William Beckwith	Removed
John Boucher	No property
Nelson Bridwell	No property
Benjamin Burges	No property
Williamson Barnes	Removed
Robert Carrol	No property
Alexander Cloe[771]	No property
John Conyers, Jr.	No property
James Carter	No property
James Curry	No property
Thornton Coakley	Removed
Chandler Clift	No property
Benjamin S. Corbin	No property
George Doggett	No property
William Dunbar[772]	Remitted

---

[768] Daniel Floweree Payne (c.1772-c.1855) was the son of John Payne (c.1736-1811) of King George. He married Elizabeth Johnson and lived much of his life in Fauquier.

[769] In 1819 Benjamin Combs paid tax on 500 acres in the north end of Stafford adjoining Hore and Overall in what is now the Quantico reservation. In July 1825 Ishmael Pritchett leased Benjamin 76 acres near Plumfield, also in the northern part of the county (Stafford Deed Book GG, p. 39).

[770] Samuel Selden Brooke (1800-1861) lived in Brooke and owned and operated the old Mountjoy's Mill there. He was the son of John Taliaferro Brooke (1763-1821) and Ann Mason Mercer Selden (1770-1812). Samuel married Angelina Edrington (c.1803-1862). From at least 1831-1845 he served as a justice in Stafford. From at least 1831-1846 he was a school commissioner; in 1855 he became superintendent of schools for Stafford.

[771] Alexander Cloe (c.1799-1865) was the son of James Cloe (1763-c.1814). He married Drucilla Burroughs (c.1798-1883), the daughter of John Burroughs and Margaret Elizabeth Vaughn of Stafford. Alexander died in Stafford of consumption.

John Dickinson	Removed
Joseph Dunaway	Removed
Robert Farish	No property
Solomon Gollohorn[773]	No property
William Graves	No property
James Graves	No property
James Haney	No property
Thomas P. Harrison	No property
Jesse Hewitt	No property
Moor F. Hooe	Remitted
William Jones	No property
William Jackson	No property
Cornelius Jewel[774]	No property
Daniel Jones	Removed
Isham Jordan	No property
Elijah Knight	No property
John King	No property
Enoch Ker	Not found
Daniel Latham	No property
John Limbrick	No property
Francis Martin	No property
Stephen Moody	No property
Thornton Martin	No property
Enos Monteith	No property
Thomas Newton	No property
Mercena Newton[775]	No property
William S. Payne	No property
Strother Purvis[776]	No property
Colman Perks	Removed
George Payne	No property
Yelverton B. Porch	No property
William Rose, Jr.	No property
James Richerson	No property
Alexander Snelling[777]	No property
Thomas Smith	No property
Gustavus Sullivan	No property
James Sullivan	No property
Martin Sullivan	No property
Elias Stone	No property
William Smith	No property
Benjamin Tolson, Jr.	Removed
Benjamin Truslow[778]	No property

---

[772] William Dunbar (1805-1861) was the son of Robert Dunbar (c.1745-1831) and Elizabeth Gregory Thornton (c.1767-1851) of Falmouth. William was an attorney and moved to New Orleans in the 1820s.

[773] Solomon Gollohorn (1791-1874). In 1812 he lived near Aquia Church (Stafford County Personal Property Tax Records).

[774] In 1812 Cornelius Jewel paid tax on himself only. He owned no slaves or livestock.

[775] Marsena Newton was the son of Benjamin Newton (born 1769) and Nancy Butler and the grandson of John Newton and Mary Thomas. He married Clarissa Lee.

[776] Nicholas Strother Purvis (1800-1848) was the son of John Purvis (c.1765-1835) and Margaret Strother. He was born in Spotsylvania and married Elizabeth E. Stern (1802-1884) of Port Royal, Caroline County. Strother later moved to Montgomery County, Missouri where he and his wife are buried.

[777] Alexander Snellings (1800:05-before 1850) married Annis Mannin(g) (1806-1853).

1818

William Truslow	No property
William Tharp	No property
Joseph Tyson	No property
George Wilson	No property

1819[779]
Colonel—George M. Cooke
Lt. Colonels—George Waller
             Samuel H. Peyton
Major—James Briggs
Captains—Abner R. Alcock
           William Hewitt
           Duff Green[780]
           Thomas Hill
           John N. Tolson
           Thornton Crop
           William Ford
           Thornton Alexander
           Walter R. Daniel
Lieutenants—George Brent, Joseph M. Johnson[781]
Ensigns—William B. Stone,[782] Robert Croughton[783]

Brigade Drummer—George G. Shelton—drummed for the 36th and 89th regiments (Prince William), 45th regiment (Stafford), 25th regiment (King George), and the 85th and 44th regiments (Fauquier).

Brigade Fifer—Peter P. Cox—fifed for the 36th and 89th regiments (Prince William), 45th regiment (Stafford), 25th regiment (King George), and the 85th and 44th regiments (Fauquier).

Men fined for failure to appear at muster:

Name	Note
William Abbitt	No property found.
Robert Alan	No property found.
Stephen Armstrong	No property found.
William Bell	No property found.

---

[778] Benjamin Truslow (c.1792-1869) married Nancy Dicken(s) and died in Stafford.

[779] On June 26, 1819 the Falmouth Volunteers were formed. Duff Green (1792-1854) was unanimously chosen captain; George Brent was lieutenant, and Robert Croughton (1791-1872) and William B. Stone (died 1845) were ensigns. In 1819 there were about 70 members in the company, which was comprised of "respectable, and well informed gentlemen in the Town of Falmouth and its vicinity, who are desirous to organize an effective Uniform Company to be denominated Riflemen, or Light Infantry" (Box 148, Folder 31).

[780] Duff Green (1792-1854) was the son of Maj. James Green (c.1734-after 1809) and Elizabeth Jones of Culpeper. In 1824 Duff married Eliza Ann Payne (1806-1876), the daughter of Capt. William Payne (1755-1837) of Fauquier. He settled in Falmouth around 1817 and became a wealthy industrialist there. Duff owned cotton and flour mills in the town as well as a store and hotel.

[781] Joseph M. Johnson married Sarah C. Franklin whose parents lived in or near the town of Aquia (Stafford Deed Book GG, p.200).

[782] May be William Barton Stone, the son of Richard Stone (died 1825) and Hannah Withers (c.1774-1857) of Mt. Olive, now part of the Marine Corps reservation.

[783] Robert Croughton (1791-1872) was the son of Charles Croughton (c.1761-1819) and Elizabeth Hudson (died c.1791). For several years Robert kept a grocery and dry goods store in Falmouth. He married his mother's first cousin, Thomas Reveley's widow, Elizabeth Stubberfield (died 1872) of Spotsylvania. Around 1835 Robert and Elizabeth moved to La Grange, Missouri.

George Bowling	No property found.
Charles Bridwell	Not found
Burdit Bridges	No property found.
Jesse Brooks	No property found.
William Bates	No property found.
John Bowling	No property found.
Rolly Butler	No property found.
William Browne	No property found.
Edward M. Buckner	No inhabitant
William Butler	No property found.
John Burton	No property found.
Richard Berry[784]	Fine reld. by Ct. Marl.
A. H. Bull	
Egery(?) Burton	No property found.
George Cox	Released by Ct Martl.
William Cox	No property found.
William Charters	No property found.
Henry Crump	No inhabitant
Henry Calender	No property found.
John W. Coalman[785]	Fredericksburg
Robert Carrol	No property found.
William Doyle	Not found
Jameson Ellington[786]	Not found
John Ellison[787]	Not a citizen of the U. States
John Fugate[788]	No property found.
John Fines	No property found.
Ralph Flory	No property found.
Solomon Gollohorn	No property found.
Thomas Gill	No property found.
James Graves	No property found.
Atchison Gray[789]	Westmoreland
William Gray	No property found.
George Green	No property found.
James Haney	No inhabitant
Harrison Harding	Spotsylvania
Alfred C. Hays[790]	Dumfries

---

[784] Richard Berry (died c.1826) left a will in Stafford. He had children Jemima, Susan, Richard, Jr., John, and Elizabeth Gollihorn and grand daughter Catherine Puzey (Stafford Deed Book GG, p. 391). Richard married Catherine Curtis, the daughter of John Curtis (died before 1815).

[785] May be John Wyatt Coleman (1788-1857), the son of William J. Coleman (c.1757-1806) and Nancy Jobson (born c.1759). In 1809 John married Ann Woolfolk. He married secondly Eliza Wigginton Templeman (1801-1885). John lived at Loch Lomond near Mt. Olive Road (Route 650).

[786] In 1820 Jameson Ellington married Elizabeth Heflin in Fauquier.

[787] The Stafford court granted John Ellison retail licenses from 1819-1822.

[788] John Fugate (c.1797-after 1850).

[789] Atchison Gray (1798-1822) was the son of John Gray (1769-1848) and Lucy Robb (born 1773) of Traveler's Rest in lower Stafford. He married Catherine Dangerfield Willis, the daughter of Col. Byrd C. Willis of Fredericksburg and Mary Willis Lewis. Less than a year after his marriage, Atchison died at Wakefield and was buried at Traveler's Rest. Catherine went with her parents to Florida where she met Achille Murat, former prince of Naples and nephew of Napoleon Bonaparte. They were married and traveled between Europe and America.

[790] Alfred C. Hayes (c.1795-after 1850) was a merchant in Falmouth. From about 1834-1850 he held licenses to operate a store and sell liquor.

Moore F. Hooe	New Orleans
Joseph Hewitt	No property found.
Thomas B. Hay[791]	No property found.
Philip Harding	No property found.
Thomas P. Harrison	No property found.
James Heffling	Fauquier County
Zacheus Holliday	Remitted
Fielding Hudson	No property found.
Lewis Jenkins	Removed
Isom Jordan	No property found.
William Jackson	No property found.
George Jett	No property found.
William Jett	No property found.
Henry Jones	No property found.
William Kellogg[792]	No property found.
Abel E. Kinner	No inhabitant
Elijah Knight	No property found.
John Knight	No property found.
John Lang	No property found.
John Leitch[793]	No property found.
William Martin[794]	No property found.
Thornton Martin	No inhabitant
Alexander Munroe	No property found.
Christopher Musselman[795]	Not found
Francis Martin	No property found.
Henry Mills	No property found.
Thomas K. Newton[796]	No property found.
Fielding Patterson	Not found
Asa Pearson[797]	No property found.
Henley Potes[798]	No property found.

---

[791] Thomas Battle Hay (1801-1868) was the son of William H. Hay (died c.1818) and Margaret Bruce of Stafford. He married Sarah Mason Bruce (1810-1848), the daughter of Charles Cary Bruce (1768-1845) and Sarah Jane Mason (1787-1839). Thomas resided on Springfield in lower Stafford, which he bought from the heirs of his father-in-law. The Stafford death records list him as a laborer.

[792] William Kellogg (1784-1848) was born in Stillwater, New York, the son of Ozias Kellogg (1760-c.1789). He was reared by his grandfather in Egremont, Massachusetts. William came to Stafford sometime prior to 1819 and later bought a small tract of land he called Egremont. He married Mary Stadler Allison (1790-1873), the daughter of Thomas Lawson Allison (1763-1808) of Stafford. William was a merchant in Fredericksburg and Richmond. He later bought Bellview on Potomac Creek, but lost it to debt.

[793] John Leitch was captain of Cossom Horton's schooner *Betsey* (Stafford Estate Accounts, 1823, p. 279).

[794] This may be the same William Martin who in 1791 was bound by the overseers of the poor to John England to learn the trade of carpentry (Stafford Scheme Book 1790-1793, p. 92).

[795] Christopher Musselman (c.1781-after 1850) may have been a Quaker and was likely employed at Rappahannock Forge near Falmouth. He owned property off Sanford Road near the Rappahannock River.

[796] Thomas K. Newton (dead by 1845) was the son of Thomas Newton and his middle name may have been Kenyon. Thomas had children by Mary Frances Dillon/Dillion. In 1839 he paid tax on 250 acres near the Rappahannock in White Oak. In 1844 Thomas owed various debts amounting to $124.91 and secured this with three slaves and the 250-acre farm on which he lived (Stafford County Deed Book NN, p. 421). He died before satisfying the debt and his land was sold to Richard Berry of Fredericksburg. Thomas had inherited this land from his father and it adjoined the lands of Bruce, Fitzhugh, and Pollock (Stafford Deed Book NN, p. 512).

[797] Asa Pearson (born 1780) was the son of William George Pearson (1750-c.1801) of Prince William County.

William Payne	No property found.
William Peyton	No property found.
Yelverton B. Portch	No property found.
Strother Purvis	No property found.
Gustavus Read[799]	No property found.
Peter J. Rollow[800]	Fredericksburg
Peter Rolly	Fredericksburg
John Roles	No property found.
John Shakleford	Not found
James Shelkett[801]	No property found.
John Skidmore	Not found
William Smith	No property found.
William Sullivan	No property found.
John Sudduth	Remitted
Francis Stern	Remitted
James Sullivant	No property found.
Martin Sullivant	Fine relsd. by Ct. Marl.
Gustavus Sullivant	No property found.
William Talmarsh	No property found.
James Tharp	No property found.
Joseph Tyson	Fined in Cap: Crops company
Benjamin Watson[802]	No property found.
Hezekiah Waple	No property found.
Lawson Wheatley	Removed
Joseph Wormsley	No property found.
Landon Walters	Removed
Posey Whaling	Remitted
Abner Wine	No property found.

Capt. Thomas Hill's Company:

John Conyers	Joel Gray	Newman B. Stark[803]
Travis Dodd[804]	Thomas James	John Stephens
William R. Endsor	Daniel Latham	Sennet Tackett[805]

---

[798] In 1810 Henley Potes/Potts paid taxes on 65 acres that he seems to have been leasing from George Harding. This was near Chappawamsic Run and in what is now the Quantico reservation. By 1826 he was a resident of Campbell County, Virginia. That year he sold to Joseph Grayson 65 acres in the north end of Stafford (Stafford Deed Book GG, p. 160).

[799] Gustavus Read (c.1786-after 1850) lived near Austin Run. His first wife was Mary Gallahan (c.1776-1856). He married secondly Elizabeth Musselman (c.1788-after 1870).

[800] Peter Jett Rollow was the son of Archibald Rollow (c.1775-1829) and Ann Jett (1757-1830). Peter's second wife was Permelia Payne; he married her in Loudon County, Tennessee in 1842. Peter died in Quitman, Arkansas.

[801] James Shelkett (1793-1858). His estate inventory included 6 slaves (Stafford Deed Book MM, p. 531).

[802] Benjamin Watson (c.1795-after 1850).

[803] Newman Basil Stark (1799-1860). Around 1828 he moved to Boone County, Missouri. Newman married Priscilla Thornton.

[804] Travis Dodd (c.1790-1859) was the son of Benjamin Dodd (c.1750-1815) of Fauquier County. He was born near Bealeton and died in Stafford. In 1821 Travers Dodd paid taxes on 244 acres on Aquia Run "for Mrs. Dodd" 12 miles west of the courthouse. In 1839 he paid taxes on 214 acres on Aquia Run, 15 ½ acres on Deep Run, and 210 acres on Beaverdam Run (part of Aquia Run) where he may have lived. Travis married Elizabeth E. Humphrey (c.1790-1845), the daughter of Charles Humphrey. As a result of his military service, he was granted land in Missouri.

1819

Lovel Fant	Rowsy Latham[806]	Joel Vant
Townson Graves	John Marquis	

Capt. Abner Alcock's Company:
Henry Bloxton	William Graves	Absalom King[807]
Thomas B____	Benjamin Groves	John King
Charles D. Bridwell	Moses Gui[808]	Rawleigh Latham

Capt. John N. Tolson's Company:
Samuel Botts	John Loga	Scarlet Renno[809]
Travis Dickenson	Thomas Murphy[810]	John D. Simms[811]
William Groves	William W. Peyton	George Tolson, Jr.
Strother Heflin[812]	John Potes	
Thomas James	Ishmael Prichett[813]	

Capt. Thornton Crop's Company:
Alexander Boling	Hansford Garner[814]	James Tyson
Harris W. Burton[815]	Ezekiel Garner	Edward Templeman

---

[805] Senate Tackett (1770:80-1836) spent much of his life in Prince William County. In 1819 he was granted a retail license in Stafford. In 1819 and 1823 he also held licenses to run an ordinary here. Senate married Elizabeth, the daughter of George Burroughs (c.1750-c.1827) and widow of an unknown Stone.

[806] Rowzee Latham (1785-1881) was the son of John Latham, Sr. (c.1730-1834) and his second wife, Nancy Kendall. During the War of 1812, Rowzee served in Capt. Thomas Hill's company. In November 1817 he married Nancy Turner, the daughter of Eleanor (Maines) (Turner) Robertson (1778-1855). Eleanor's husband, William W. Robertson (1774-1842) owned Robertson's Quarry on Rocky Run in Stafford. By 1830 Rowzee had taken his family to Ohio, though in 1855 Nancy returned to Stafford to nurse her dying mother. William W. Robertson had willed Nancy a house, warehouse, and several lots in the town of Aquia, though she did not come into possession of them until after her mother's death (Stafford Deed Book OO, p. 60). Eleanor left Nancy a life estate in all her property. Upon the latter's death the property was to pass in fee simple to her Latham children, free from Rowzee's debts (Lombus 65-69).

[807] Absalom King (c.1791-1853) was a cooper and owned several lots in Falmouth (Stafford Deed Book NN, p. 34). He served as a town trustee from at least 1836-1849.

[808] Moses Guy (born c.1800) may be the son of William Guy (born c.1780).

[809] Scarlet Reno (1783-after 1850). His parentage is unclear, but he may have been the son of David Reno (c.1750-1821) and Nancy Ann Suttle. In 1810 he was a resident of Prince William County.

[810] In 1821 Thomas Murphy paid taxes on 350 ½ acres in the "Ragged and Tough" area of Stafford 8 miles west of the courthouse. This area is in the vicinity of Hull's Memorial Chapel.

[811] John Douglas Simms (1786-1843) married Eleanor Carroll Brent (1787-1846), the daughter of Daniel Carroll Brent of Richland. The lower part of the Richland peninsula is sometimes referred to as Simms' Point and was named after John D. Simms.

[812] May be Strother Heflin (1798-before 1860) who lived in the upper part of the county near Rock Hill Church.

[813] Ishmael Prichett married Margaret A. Burroughs, daughter of George Burroughs (c.1750-c.1827) of Stafford.

[814] John Henceford/Hansford Garner (c.1811-1886) was the son of Henceford Garner and Elizabeth Conyers (1798-1843), the daughter of John Conyers (1754-1819). He married Ann Elizabeth Littrell (c.1825-1886), the daughter of Thomas and Leithia Littrell of Stafford. Both John and Ann contracted pneumonia and died within a week of each other.

[815] Harris W. Burton (c.1796-c.1883). During the War Between the States, Harris was a Unionist. In 1874 he submitted a claim to the Southern Claims Commission. Then 78 years of age, he was described as a "harmless, feeble, old man, who never went two miles from home during the whole war, except, when he went to see the Provost Marshal to take the oath of allegiance to the U. S., which he did Aug. 28, 1863."

| Strother Burton | William Marquis | William Young |
| James Conner | Alexander F. Rose[816] | |

Capt. William Forde's Company:

Hugh Adie	Weeden Grigsby	Thornton Shackleford[817]
Atchison H. Armstrong	Walter Hore[818]	Robert Spibyvide(?)
William Anderson	James Hewitt	James Waller
Charles Bussel	George Homes	William Whorton
William Dent	John Linch	Charles Williams[819]
Kenas Fritter	John D. Miller	John P. Williams
Gustavus Fritter[820]	John Moncure, Jr.	Nathaniel P. Williams
Enoch Fritter	William Murphy	
Reubin Fritter[821]	John H. S. Potes	
George Franklin	Frederick Purley[822]	

Capt. Thornton Alexander's Company:

| James Armstrong | Joseph B. Ficklen[823] | Lewis Potes |
| William C. Beale[824] | Murray Forbes[825] | Thomas Peyton |

During the war, he and his family cooked and washed for the Union soldiers. He had a son who opposed his wishes and fought for the Confederacy. Harris was a wheelwright and had a shop where he repaired wagons. Burnside's troops camped near his shop and used it and, he claimed, took all his tools (Southern Claims Commission. Approved. Claim #55229). Harris left a will in Stafford and mentioned his wife Elizabeth and son Selden W. Burton (Stafford Will Book R, p. 131).

[816] Alexander Fontaine Rose (1780-1831) was the son of Charles Rose (1747-1802) and Sarah Elizabeth Fontaine (1755-1788). He lived at Hampstead off Poplar Road (Route 616) and married Sarah Rose Fontaine (c.1796-1863).

[817] Thornton Shackleford (c.1806-before 1840) was the son of Solomon A. Shackelford (c.1780-before 1850) and Clarissa Heflin (born c.1785).

[818] Walter Hore (1781-1858) was the son of Elias Hore (1749-1832) and Theodosia Waller (1753-1829). He married Margaret E. Combs (c.1784-1859) and lived in the northern part of Stafford on what is now the Quantico Marine Corps reservation. In 1812 Walter paid taxes on 5 slaves and 3 horses in Stafford.

[819] Charles Williams was the son of Pearson Williams (c.1743-c.1824).

[820] Gustavus Fritter (c.1798-1874) lived near Aquia Run in what is now Quantico. He was the son of Enoch Fritter (born c.1765) and ___ Grigsby.

[821] Reuben T. Fritter (c.1795-1874) was the son of Enoch Fritter (born c.1765). He married Anna Litterel (c.1804-1892).

[822] Frederick Purley/Perley was in partnership with Cossom Horton (c.1735-1821) in the stone quarrying business. They also owned a schooner called Betsey on which they hauled their stone to Washington (Stafford County estate Accounts, 1823-1834, p.280).

[823] Joseph Burwell Ficklen (1800-1874) was the son of Fielding Ficklen (died 1809) and Elizabeth Fant (died 1814) of Culpeper. Joseph lived first at Belmont just above Falmouth, then later in Fredericksburg. His first wife was Ellen McGehee. He married secondly Anne Eliza Fitzhugh (died 1907). Joseph owned several large flour mills in Falmouth and Fredericksburg.

[824] William Churchill Beale (1791-1850) was the son of William Beale and Hannah Gordon of Fauquier. His first wife was Susan C. Vowles (1772-before 1855), the daughter of Henry Vowles (1752-1803) and Mary Frazier of Fredericksburg. William married secondly Jane Briggs Howison (1815-1882). They spent their first five years of married life in the Conway house in Falmouth before moving to Fredericksburg. William C. Beale was heavily involved in flour milling in Falmouth and also had interests in several of the local gold mines. He died deeply in debt.

[825] Murray Forbes (1782-1863) was the son of Dr. David Forbes (1751-1789) and Margaret Sterling (1754-1806). Murray was born in Dumfries, Prince William County, but spent most of his life in Falmouth. In 1815 he married Sallie Innes Thornton (1776-1807), the widow of Col. Francis Thornton (1767-1836).

1819

James Beale
William Bettis
William Brooke
Charnoc Cox
James Curkman
John Curry

William Hiks
Robert S. Hoe
Robert Jackson
George Leach
William McDaniel
James F. Murry

Ezelburton D. Porch
Thomas H. Ratliff
George Seddon[826]
Dawson Sullivant[827]
John H. Weeks[828]

Capt. Walter R. Daniel's Company:
William Brimley
John Cooke
John B. S. Fitzhugh
John Gallohorn

Edmund Hogans
Francis Jett
William Jones
John Leach

James Mountjoy
Travers P____
James Robinson
James Templeman[829]

Capt. William Hewitt's Company:
William Brown
Chandler Clift
David G. Coit
John Cox

James S. Cole[830]
Daniel Fines
Thomas Fines
Jonathan Finnal

Thomas Horton
Peter Jett, Jr.
Samuel Monteith[831]
John Pates

Capt. Duff Green's Company:
Alexander Bell
Oliver Fixx
William K. Gordon[834]

William Limbrick
George Payne
William Philips

Ezekiel Skinner[832]
Thomas A. Smith[833]

1821
Colonel—George M. Cooke
Lt. Colonels—George Waller
Major—James Briggs
Captains—William Ford
        Abner R. Alcock
        Thornton Alexander
        Thomas Hill
        John N. Tolson

Murray was a merchant in Falmouth, but was also involved with the flour and cotton mills in that town as well as with the gold mines on the Rappahannock River.

[826] George Seddon (died 1822) was the son of Thomas Seddon (c.1737-1810) of Stafford. George lived in Falmouth but owned a large tract on Potomac Run that included what later became known as Carmora.

[827] In 1817 Dawson Sullivan married Lucy Payne in Spotsylvania.

[828] John H(olliday?) Weeks was the son of Benjamin Weeks (died 1815) and Agnes Holladay (died 1817) of Falmouth. John's father operated a dry goods store in that town.

[829] James Templeman married Julietta Coakley. He was a brother of Jeremiah Bridwell Templeman.

[830] In 1821 James S. Cole was granted a license to keep an ordinary (Eby, Men 272).

[831] Samuel Owens Monteith (1785-1862) was the son of James Monteith (c.1740-1804) and Leah Owens who resided in Fauquier prior to moving to Stafford. Samuel married Mildred Fines (born c.1787) and lived in White Oak. In 1870 his estate paid taxes on 244 acres in White Oak.

[832] This may be Ezekiel Ludwell Skinner (1765-1823) who lived in or near Falmouth. In 1812 he paid taxes on 4 horses in Stafford.

[833] This may be the Thomas A. Smith who in 1810 was a resident of Dumfries, Prince William County. That year he married Priscilla T. Short of Carlton, Falmouth.

[834] William Knox Gordon (1799-1886) was the son of Samuel Gordon (1759-1843) and Susannah Fitzhugh Knox (1775-1869). He married Eliza Stith Fitzhugh (1810-1872), daughter of John Bolling Stith Fitzhugh (1778-1825) of Bellair, Stafford County. William was buried at Kenmore in Fredericksburg.

Silas F. Crop
Walter R. Daniel
William Hewitt
Lieutenants—William B. Stone—in William Ford's company
John A. Starke
Robert Croughton
1ˢᵗ Lieutenants—Mark Harding
James W. Stone[835]—in Abner Alcock's artillery unit
2ⁿᵈ Lieutenant—John Stephens
Sergeant Major—William H. Tyler[836]
Ensigns—Valentine Y. Conway[837]—in William Ford's company
Thomas Payne
Provost Marshall—Rawleigh Cooper
Clerk of the Court Martial—James Alexander

Brigade Drummer—Augustin Shelton—drummed for the 85ᵗʰ regiment (Germantown, Fauquier), 44ᵗʰ (Salem, Fauquier), 25ᵗʰ regiment (King George), 45ᵗʰ regiment (Stafford Courthouse), and the 36ᵗʰ regiment (Maddux's Tavern and "Randolph's old field).

Men fined for failure to appear at muster:

Capt. Abner R. Alcock's Company:

James Byram	Robert Guy[838]	Mason G. McCoy
James Chadwell[839]	Charles Holly	George S. Miflin[840]
Thomas Cooper[841]	John Jackson	John A. Payne
Robert Carrol	Elijah Knight	Daniel Rolls
Ralph Florey	John King	Benjamin H. Shackleford[842]
Benjamin Groves	Joshua Kendal	Solomon Shackleford
Moses Guy	Rawleigh Latham	Thomas Wilson

---

[835] James Withers Stone (1796-1869) was the son of Richard Stone (died 1825) and Hannah Withers c.1774-1857) of Mt. Olive in northern Stafford. James died of "cholera morbus."

[836] William H. Tyler was the son of Thomas G. S. Tyler (c.1740-1816) and Anne Fisher Adie (1756-1818) of northern Stafford.

[837] Dr. Valentine Yelverton Conway (1803-1881) was the son of John Moncure Conway (1779-1864) and Catherine Storke Peyton (1786-1865). In 1824 Valentine married his first cousin, Mary Catherine Washington Henry (1806-1890), the daughter of Edward Hugh Henry (died 1815) and Elizabeth Washington Peyton. They resided at Cabin Hill in Stafford and Dr. Conway provided medical care to Stafford residents for many years. In 1866 he was chosen one of the trustees of Andrew Chapel in Brooke.

[838] Robert Guy (born c.1802) was the son of Joseph Guy (born c.1790) of Stafford.

[839] James Chadwell owned land near Aquia Run and Garrisonville Road (Route 610) (Stafford Deed Book GG, p. 290).

[840] In 1827 George S. Miflin worked as overseer for Withers Waller (1785-1827) (Stafford County Estate Accounts, 1823, p. 351).

[841] This may be the Thomas Cooper who married Susannah S. Shelkett, the daughter of John Shelkett (died 1825) of Stafford.

[842] Benjamin Howard Shackelford (1819-1870) married Rebecca B. Green.

1821

Capt. William Ford's Company
James Alexander[843]	Walter Hore	William Simms
Stephen H. Armstrong	James Morton	William Stuart
George Homes	John H. S. Potes	John P. Williams

Capt. Thomas Hill's Company:
John Conyers	Thomas Jones	Newman B. Starke
Travers Dodd	Daniel Latham	Thomas Turner
Richard Hill[844]	John Marquis	Senit Tackett
George Jones	Nelson Mason	
Gerrard Jones	William W. Payton	

Capt. John N. Tolson's Company:
Ferdinand Arrington[845]	Thomas P. Harrison	John D. Simms
Timothy Bridwell[846]	Elijah Jewell	Ellis Suttle
Richard Burroughs	John Loga	Benjamin Tolson
Harrison Combs[847]	Benjamin Murphy	George Tolson, Jr.
Lewis Dickenson	Asa Pearson	Joseph Wamsley
Meredith Estredge[848]	Hiram Reaves	Nathaniel P. Williams, Jr.
Seth Gains	Scarlet Rennoe	Moses Wilson[849]
Zacheus Holada	John Rolls	Robert Zatum(?)

Capt. Silas F. Crop's Company:
John Boling	Benjamin S. Corbin	Alexander F. Rose
James S. Boling	William Gough	William Timberlake
George Banks	James S. Homes	William Tyson
Strother Burton	Willis Mills[850]	

Capt. Thornton Alexander's Company:
James Armstrong	Thomas W. Cowne[851]	William McDaniel, Jr.
William C. Beale	James Dickens[852]	William McDaniel

---

[843] James Alexander may be the brother of Thornton Alexander, also mentioned in these records. In July 1826 William Dunbar of Falmouth sold James the old Accokeek Furnace Tract near Ramoth Church (Stafford Deed Book GG, p. 187).

[844] In 1819 Richard Hill paid tax on 34 acres near Deep Run.

[845] Ferdinand Arrington (1801-1875) was born in Stafford and died in Grandville, Ohio.

[846] Timothy Bridwell (c.1798-after 1860). In 1822 he married Sythia C. Holmes in Prince William County.

[847] Joseph Harrison Combs was the son of Joseph Combs (c.1750-1810).

[848] Meredith Eskridge was the son of John Eskridge (born c.1743) and Elizabeth Moxley of Westmoreland County. Meredith lived in Fauquier County and married Sophia Smith Bridwell. In 1858 Meredith still owned 166 acres on Chappawamsic Run. He left a large estate in Fauquier County and at his death was part owner of the Tump Fishery in Stafford.

[849] Moses Wilson (c.1800-1870) was a carpenter. He owned land on Mountain View Road (Route 627) near Salem Meeting House (Stafford Deed Book LL, p. 247). Moses' will, recorded in Stafford, mentioned children Alexander, Sally, Caroline, Jane, and William Wilson (Stafford Will Book R, p. 51).

[850] Willis Franklin Mills (c.1803-1883) was the son of John Mills (born c.1783) and Phoebe Stevens (born c.1780). Around 1828 he married Ann D. Lewis (born c.1814), the daughter of John Lewis and Rachel Porch. Willis lived in Fredericksburg for many years and died there.

[851] Thomas Whiting Cowne (1784-1857) was the son of Robert Cowne (c.1756-1829) and Sarah Whiting of Culpeper. Thomas' first wife was Martha H. Buchanan (Died 1818) whom he married in 1809. In 1820 he married his second wife, Susan Latham (born 1787), of Fauquier. Thomas was a merchant in Falmouth.

[852] James Dickens (c.1803-after 1850) was a ship carpenter and lived in Falmouth.

1821

Jessey B___den
Thomas D. Beard(?)
Abijah Boling
George Boling
Bartlet Browne
Westly Bridwell
William Brooke
Alexander Cloe
James Corbin

William Daffin[853]
James W. Ford[854]
Murry Forbes
Thomas Gill
George Gollohorn[855]
James R. Hewitt[856]
James Hockman
Elijah Jones
George Leatch

James F. Murry
Gerrard Newton
Thomas Peyton
George Seddon
William Smith
James Thompson
Bayley Watson
John H. Weeks

Capt Walter R. Daniel's Company:

John Berry
Samuel S. Brooke
John Cooke
Joseph Collat[857]
James Curry
Archibald Douglas[858]
John R. Fitzhugh[859]
John B. S. Fitzhugh
John Gollohorn
Thomas Gollohorn
Robert Hepborn
Cossom Horton[861]

Alexander Lane
John Lang
William Leach
James Limbrick
James Mountjoy
Hezekiah Reder(?)
James Robinson
Archibald Rye
William Snelling[860]
Benjamin Snelling
George Scott
David Slaughter

William Tallmarsh
James Templeman
Benjamin Truslow
Mark Talmarsh

---

[853] William Daffan (1777-1855) lived on part of the old Bellair tract near Potomac Run. He was the son of Vincent Daffan (c.1750-1813) and Betty M. Wilson (died after 1800). The portion of Bellair that William bought was on Potomac Run and the area where Brooke Road (Rt. 608) crosses the run is still known as Daffan's Crossing. In addition to this farm, William also owned several lots in Falmouth. In 1818 he rented the "lower Ferry to Fredericksburg" (*Virginia Herald*, Dec. 5, 1818). His second wife was Nancy Davis (c.1795-1870). William was buried on his farm near Leeland Road in Stafford.

[854] James Walter Ford (1791-1865) was probably the son of James Ford (1768-1863) and Elizabeth Taylor. He was a lawyer in Falmouth and a partner in the firm of Kelly, Tackett and Ford that made fabric before and during the War Between the States. He married Clarissa Ellen Taylor. In 1860 James was living at Clearview with the Scott sisters.

[855] George Gollahorn (c.1794-after 1850).

[856] James R. Hewitt lived in the town of Falmouth. From c.1808 until sometime after 1818 he resided on the upper floor of the old Swan Tavern and used the lower floor as a cooper's shop. In 1818 he was jailed for beating Murray Forbes (Fredericksburg "Morson"). In 1816 James married Eleanor Swan, the daughter of Robert Swan, Falmouth miller.

[857] This may actually be Joseph Golatt.

[858] Archibald Douglas (1804-1852) was the son of Mourning Douglas (1771-1823) of Virginia. Mourning died in Stafford and Archibald was born there. Archibald married Eliza Frances Moore (1811-1886) of North Carolina. Both are buried in Lowndes County, Alabama.

[859] John Rose Fitzhugh (1795-1879) was the son of Thomas Fitzhugh (1760-1820) of Boscobel and Anne Rose (born 1763).

[860] William Snelling (1785-1855) married Elizabeth Jett (c.1781-1881), the daughter of John and Nancy Jett. William froze to death.

[861] This may be Cossom W(estern?) Horton, the son of Cossom Horton (c.1735-c.1821) and Lucy Rye who lived on the Hope plantation on Aquia Creek. In 1805 the younger Cossom married Malvina Dumas and moved to Wilcox, Alabama.

Unknown Companies:
James Armstrong
John Butler
Rawleigh Chinn
John Fugate
Martin Fugate[863]
James Green
Peter Jett, Jr.

Elijah Leatch
George Limbrick
Samuel Monteith
James F. Murray
John Newton
Marsina Newton
Thomas T. Newton

John S. Pates
Ely P. Perry[862]
Alexander Peyton
Thomas Sullivant
Thomas Williams

Name	Note	Company
William Anderson	Not found	
Atchison H. Armstrong	No property	
Robert Allen	No property	
Burdit Bridges	No property	Abner R. Alcock
Charles D. Bridwell	No property	Abner R. Alcock
Henry Bloxton	No property	
William Bettice	No property	Thornton Alexander
William Butler	No property	
William Brown	No property	William Hewitt
Alexander Bowling	No property	
Jesse Brooks	No property	William Ford
Harris W. Burton	No property	Silas F. Cropp
Charles Bustle	No property	Thornton Alexander
Chandler Clift	No property	William Hewitt
John Conner	No property	
George Cox	No property	William Hewitt
John Cox	No property	William Hewitt
John Curry	No property	Thornton Alexander
George Franklin	Removed	
Enoch Fritter	No property	William Ford
Gustavus Fritter	No property	
Reubin Fritter	No property	
Kenaz Fritter	No property	
Joel Fant	Remitted	
Oliver Finks	Remitted	
Daniel Fines	No property	William Hewitt
John Fines	No property	
Thomas Fines	No property	
Ezekiel Garner	No property	
Townson Graves	No property	
Joel Gray	Dead & insolvent	
George Green	No property	
William Groves	Not found	
William Graves	Not found	
William Grigsby	No property	
Strother Heflin	No property	
Philip Harding	No property	
George Henderson	King George	

[862] Elijah P. Perry married Ann, the daughter of Richard C. Webb.
[863] Martin Fugate (c.1800-after 1850) married Elizabeth Smith, the daughter of Nancy Combs and minister Richard Smith.

William Hite	No property	
Thomas Horton	Not found	
William Horton	No property	
Robert Jackson	No property	Silas F. Cropp
William Jackson	Not found	
Thomas James		
George Jett	No property	
Peter Jett	No property	
Isham Jordan	No property	Walter R. Daniel
William Jett	Not found	Walter R. Daniel
William Jones	Not found	
John Leach	Not found	Walter R. Daniel
James Maury	Remitted	
Thornton Martin	No property	Silas F. Cropp
Travis Martin	Not found	
William Marquess	Remitted	
John Miller	No property	
Alexander Monroe[864]	No property	
Thomas Murphy	No property	
William Murphy	No property	
Alexander O'Bryhim	No property	
John Pates	No property	
William Perry	King George	
George Payne	Miller—exempt from fine	
William Phillips	Fauquier	
John Potes	Remitted	
Lewis Potes	Remitted	
Yelverton D. Porch	Remitted	Thornton Alexander
Travis Purvis	No property	
Thomas H. Ratcliff	Removed	
Ezekiel Skinner	Ohio	
James Shelkett	No property	
Dawson Sullivant	King George	
Gustavus Sullivant	No property	
James Sullivant	No property	
Marmion Sullivant	No property	
Martin Sullivant	No property	
William Sullivant	No property	
James Tyson	No property	
Lovel Vant	Removed	
Hezekiah Waple	No property	Walter R. Daniel
Charles Williams	No property	
William Young	No property	Walter R. Daniel

---

[864] Alexander Monroe (c.1800-c.1873) married Delila Littrall (born c.1805) and lived near the gold mines on U. S. Route 17.

1822

Lt. Colonel—George Waller
Captains—Duff Green—45th regiment, 5th brigade, 2nd division
    Burkett P. Bowen[865]—in room of William Hewitt, resigned
    Silas F. Cropp—in room of Thornton Cropp, resigned
    Thornton Alexander
Lieutenants—William Dunbar—in Duff Green's company
    Presley Cropp
    Samuel S. Brooke
Cornets—Joseph M. Johnson
    John M. Stephens
Ensigns—Enoch Mason, Jr.[866]—in room of Charles T. Hay—in Duff Green's company
    James Templeman
    Philemon M. Leitch[867]
    Jameson Corbin[868]—in Thornton Alexander's company
    _____ Billingsley
    Thomas Payne
Clerk of the 45th Regiment—James Alexander
Brigade Drummer—George G. Shelton
Brigade Fifer—Peter P. Cox

Men fined for failure to appear at muster:

Name	Name	Name
James Alexander	William Bayly[869]	Landon N. Carter[870]
Walker Adie[871]	Charles D. Bridwell	Philip Chapman[872]

---

[865] Burkett Pratt Bowen (c.1802-1852) was the son of John Pratt Bowen (died c.1838) and Elizabeth Curtis. He lived at the old Brunswick Glebe near Muddy Creek. In 1848 (and likely other years as well) he was one of the overseers of the poor for Stafford. Burkett's estate included 26 slaves, 7 horses, 9 oxen, 21 cattle, 46 sheep, 50 hogs, farm implements, blacksmith's tools, "6 Ottoman seats," 3 paintings, 13 silver teaspoons, 1 map of the United States, and 1 carpet (Stafford Deed Book RR, p. 45).

[866] Enoch Mason, Jr. (1797-c.1835) was the son of Enoch Mason (1769-1828) and Lucy Wiley Roy (1798-1835) of Clover Hill. He married Mary Eliza Mason (1810-1885).

[867] Philemon M. Leitch (born c.1798) was the son of James Leach (died c.1823), deputy surveyor of Stafford. He married Mary "Polly" Curtis (1799-1880), the daughter of George Curtis (c.1767-1844) of Stafford and lived on part of the Richlands tract near Warrenton Road. George Curtis, a very wealthy man, didn't care much for Philemon who borrowed money from his father-in-law but didn't repay it. George Curtis' will named administrators to manage Polly's share of his estate in order to prevent its falling into Phil's hands (Stafford Deed Book NN, p. 530). In 1825 Philemon and Mary were founding members of Yellow Chapel, now Hartwood Presbyterian Church. In 1837 Phil moved to Spotsylvania and, about four years later, to Brokensword, Crawford County, Ohio. In 1839 Philemon paid taxes on 393 acres of the Richlands tract near the Rappahannock River.

[868] Jameson Corbin (1790-1862) was the son of William Corbin (1749-1815) and Sally Hill (died 1815) of Rappahannock County. Jameson's first wife was Mary Nelson Mason (born 1786) of Stafford. He married secondly Judith Cooke (Terrier) Taylor of Stafford and thirdly Priscilla Peters (died c.1855) of Fauquier. From the mid to late 1830s Jameson was a trustee for Falmouth. In 1840 he was appointed tax collector for the town.

[869] A sheriff's margin notation reads, "Remitted."

[870] A sheriff's margin notation reads, "Removed." Landon N. Carter moved from Stafford to King George, but in 1849 paid tax on 111 acres of Parke in Stafford.

[871] Walker Adie (died 1827) was the son of William Adie (1729-1797) and Elizabeth Parrender (1729-c.1842) of Bloomington.

1822

Stephen Armstrong	Westly Bridwell	Turner Chapman[873]
William Alexander	William C. Beale	Thornton Chilton[874]
Gustavus Ashby[875]	Jonathan Beckwith[876]	John Conyers
William Bettis	Joseph Billingsley (ensign)[877]	Rawleigh Chinn
William Brooke	Thornton Browne	John Cooke
Whitfield Brooke[878]	William Brown	Mitchell Carney[879]
Jesse Brooks	Thomas Browne	James Curtis
Peter Bowler[880]	Joshua Burton	Fielding Curtis[881]
Reubin Bowler[882]	William Burton	John M. Corbin[883]
John Bowling	George Banks	Thomas W. Cowne[884]
Alexander W. Bowling	Robert Burroughs[885]	Thomas Cooper
Thomas Bowling	James L. Bowling	Berryman Cox
George Bowling	Richard Botts	William Cox
Abijah Bowling	Bartlett Brown	John Chinn
William Butler[886]	Harris W. Burton	Chandler Clift[887]
Silas Bryant[888]	Charles Bussle	James S. Cole[889]
James Byram	Baily Byram	Benjamin S. Corbin
John Curtis	James Curry	Robert Croughton[890]
James Dekins	Travers Dodd	William Dent[891]
Joel T. Doniphan[892]	Daniel Fines	James Finnel

[872] In 1785 Philip Chapman leased from Thomas Strother of Stafford a grist and saw mill (Stafford Deed Book S, p. 246). The location of this mill is unclear. A margin notation on this page of the militia records says Philip was "Removed." He moved to Caroline County.
[873] A margin notation says Turner Chapman was "Removed." He moved to Caroline County.
[874] William George Thornton Chilton was the son of Thomas Chilton and Charlotty Limbrick. He married Susan Roberson, the daughter of John Roberson and Mary Labraun Rogers.
[875] Gustavus Ashby (born c.1800). In 1828 he was granted a license to keep an ordinary. In 1830 he held a license for "private entertainment" (gambling) (Eby, Men 273, 274).
[876] Jonathan Beckwith (1799-1856) was a doctor and was born in Stafford. A note in the militia records states that he "removed to Alabama." He married Dolly Winston, the daughter of Isaac Winston of Virginia and moved to Lauderdale County, Alabama.
[877] A sheriff's margin notation reads, "Removed."
[878] Whitfield Brooke was exempt from fine.
[879] A sheriff's margin notation reads, "Removed."
[880] Peter Bowler (1803-1883) was born in Caroline County and died in Spotsylvania. In 1828 he married Lucinda Bowling (died 1876).
[881] Fielding Curtis (1798-after 1850) worked as a millwright in Hartwood. Around 1821 he bought part of Robert Lewis' Mantua tract on which he constructed a new building, presumably a house. This modest building was assessed at just $100. Fielding resided just a short distance north of Mt. Olive Church. In 1839 Fielding paid tax on 300 acres on Potomac Run.
[882] Reuben Bowler (1800-1856) was the son of Charles Bowler (born 1752) of Newport, Rhode Island and Elizabeth Donahoe (born c.1778) of Caroline County. He was born in Caroline County and died in Stafford. Reuben married Mildred Jones (c.1802-c.1834).
[883] A sheriff's margin notation reads, "Not found."
[884] A sheriff's margin notation reads, "Remitted."
[885] Robert G. Burroughs was the son of George Burroughs (c.1750-c.1827) of Stafford.
[886] A sheriff's margin notation reads, "Removed."
[887] A sheriff's margin notation reads, "King George."
[888] Silas Bryant married Jane Payne in Fauquier County in 1825.
[889] A sheriff's margin notation indicated that James S. Cole had removed to Richmond.
[890] A sheriff's margin notation indicated that Robert Croughton had removed to Spotsylvania.
[891] A sheriff's margin notation reads, "Remitted."
[892] Joel T. Doniphan (c.1776-1826) was the son of Alexander Doniphan (1750-1817) and Mary Davis (born 1750). Joel was born in King George County. In 1812 he married Alice Savage (born c.1785) in Caroline

1822

John B. S. Fitzhugh	Murray Forbes	James W. Ford
John Fugate	Martin Fugate	Philip Foushee[893]
William P. Gains	Benjamin Groves	Charles T. Hay[894]
William Gill	James Green	John G. Hedgman
Thomas Gill, Jr.	Thomas Gill, Sr.	William Heflin
William K. Gordon[895]	Solloman Gollahorn	James R. Hewitt
Alexander Gordon[896]	William Gollahorn	Richard Hill
Benjamin Guy	Mason Guy	Francis H. Hooe
Luke Guy	Moses Guy	Robert Hebron
Robert Guy	James S. Holmes	William Hore[897]
Peter J. Jett	Noah Jones	Robert Hepburn
George Johnson[898]	George Jett[899]	George Leach[900]
George Jones	William Jett	Philimon Leach[901]
Elisia Jones	Robert Jackson	John Leitch
Isham Jordan	Thomas Jones	Daniel Latham
Branson Knight	Elijah Leitch[902]	Rawleigh Latham
John Lewis	George Lewis	Joseph Lakenan[903]
James Limbrick[904]	George Limbrick	William Limbrick
William Limbrick, Jr.	John Limbrick	William McDaniel, Sr.
Thornton Martin	James F. Maury	John Marquess[905]
Alexander W. Massey[906]	William McDaniel, Jr.	Gerrard Newton
Henry Mills[907]	John Moncure, Jr.	Alexander Peyton
James Mountjoy	John A. Payne[908]	Thomas J. Payne[909] (ensign)
Willis Mills	Alexander O'Bryhim	John Pates
Samuel Monteith	Eli P. Perry	William Payne

County. Joel died in Stafford and in 1833 his heirs paid tax on 44 acres on Accokeek Run about five miles southeast of the courthouse.

[893] Philip Foushee (c.1780-1861) was the son of Elijah T. Foushee (1763-1838) and Anna Stewart (1765-1841). Philip married Mary "Polly" Ficklen (born 1794), the daughter of Charles Ficklen (c.1755-1816) and Mary Strother (1757-after 1836). He died in Chatham County, North Carolina. A sheriff's margin notation reads, "Remitted."

[894] In 1819 Charles T. Hay paid tax on 58 ½ acres on Accokeek Run adjoining Daniel. He acquired this from William Hay.

[895] A sheriff's margin notation indicates that William K. Gordon had gone to New York.

[896] Alexander Gordon (1798-1832) was the son of John Gordon (1752-1812) of Scotland. He married his first cousin, Susan Gordon. Alexander was buried at Kenmore in Fredericksburg.

[897] A sheriff's margin notation reads, "Remitted." This may be William Waller Hore (born 1782), the son of Elias Hore (1749-1832) and Theodosia Waller (1753-1829). In 1812 William paid taxes on 9 slaves, 7 horses, and 240 acres 7 miles north of the courthouse.

[898] A sheriff's margin notation reads, "Not found."

[899] A sheriff's margin notation reads, "Remitted."

[900] A sheriff's margin notation reads, "Remitted."

[901] A sheriff's margin notation reads, "Remitted."

[902] The sheriff's margin notation said that Elijah was "Dead." This may be the Elijah Leitch who married Sarah White in 1809 in Fauquier County. If so, he was the son of Enoch Leach/Leitch of Fauquier.

[903] A sheriff's margin notation reads, "Remitted."

[904] A sheriff's margin notation reads, "Remitted."

[905] A sheriff's margin notation reads, "Remitted."

[906] Alexander W. Massey (died c.1837) later lived in Spotsylvania. He left children Eliza (Massey) Ballard, William B. Massey, and Edmund W. Massey (Stafford Deed Book LL, p. 513).

[907] A sheriff's margin notation reads, "Remitted."

[908] A sheriff's margin notation reads, "Remitted."

[909] Thomas J. Payne (c.1796-after 1850) was a merchant.

1822

John Newton	John H. Peyton	Daniel Peyton
Marcena Newton[910]	Rowzee Peyton	Richard Potts[911]
Valentine Peyton[912]	Yelverton B. Porch	Frederick Perry
John N. Peyton	James Rye	William Randoll
William Rolls[913]	John Roe	James Roberson
Hezekiah Ruder[914]	James P. Roe	Archibald Rye
Robert Sanders	Robert Saunders[915]	Benjamin Snelling
John M. Stevens[916]	Joshua Skidmore	Thomas Stanly[917]
John D. Simms	John Suthard	James Sorrell[918]
Benjamin H. Shacklett[919]	William Stringfellow	John C. Shelton[920]
John Shackelford[921]	James Shelkett[922]	William Snellings
Thomas Smith	Thomas Stewart	Charles Stewart
William Smith	William Stewart	Mark Talmarsh
Gustavus Sullivant	Martin Sullivant	William Talmarsh
Daniel Sullivant[923]	Dawson Sullivant	Jeremiah Templeman
Marmion Sullivant	Benjamin Truslow	Dolphin True[924]
Alexander Turner	William Tyson	John Walker
Joseph Wormsley	John H. Weaks	Robert Voss[925]
Nathaniel P. Williams, Jr.	William White	William Young

---

[910] A sheriff's margin notation reads, "Remitted."

[911] This may be the same Richard Potts who served with the 25th regiment of the Virginia militia (King George County) during the War of 1812.

[912] May be Valentine Peyton (c.1805-c.1852), the son of Charles Peyton (1756:61-1845) of Woodlawn in White Oak. In 1849 Valentine's wife, Nancy (maiden name unknown) sued for divorce, claiming he had been insane and dangerous since 1820. In the 1850 census Valentine was listed as living with his aunt or cousin, Atsey Rowe (c.1810-after 1850). Soon thereafter, he was committed to the lunatic hospital in Williamsburg (Virginia, "Nancy Payton").

[913] William Rolls (died 1832). Following Cossom Horton's death in 1821, William rented Cossom's Hope plantation on the south side of Aquia Creek. The year he died William was granted a license to keep an ordinary. He and his wife, Mary Rolls (died 1845), were buried in the King cemetery on the north side of Aquia Creek.

[914] A sheriff's margin notation reads, "Removed."

[915] A sheriff's margin notation reads, "Removed."

[916] A sheriff's margin notation reads, "Removed." John M. Stephens (c.1800-1840) married Louisa V. Atchison, daughter of Hugh and Sarah Atchison of Stafford.

[917] A sheriff's margin notation reads, "Remitted."

[918] James Sorrell (1799-before 1860). In 1819 he married Emily Lewis in Spotsylvania.

[919] A sheriff's margin notation reads, "Remitted." Benjamin H. Shacklett owned land in Fauquier County.

[920] John Conyers Shelton (c.1803-1883) was the son of John Shelton, Jr. (1774-1818) and Lethe Conyers (1780-c.1867) and the grandson of John Shelton, Sr. (1740-1805) and Susanna Hord (1742-1799). John served as a magistrate in Stafford and in 1865 was appointed to the Committee to Care for Citizens Made Needy by the War."

[921] A sheriff's margin notation reads, "Remitted."

[922] A sheriff's margin notation reads, "Remitted."

[923] Daniel Sullivan (c.1799-1867) married Maria ___. He died of pneumonia.

[924] Dolphin True (c.1800-after 1860). By 1840 he was living in Spotsylvania. He married Mahala ___ (c.1802-after 1860) and was a carpenter. In 1842 he was accused of unlawful gambling in Fredericksburg. By 1849 he was insolvent (Fredericksburg, "Commonwealth vs Hore" and "Insolvent Whites").

[925] May be Robert Somerville Voss (1803-1861) who was born in Culpeper and died in Rappahannock County. He married Mary Frances Gallego Thornton (born 1816).

1823

Commandant—Thornton Alexander
Captain—Samuel S. Brooke—in room of Walter R. Daniel, resigned
Lieutenants—Walker P. Conway[926]—in room of George Shelkett, deceased
    Walter H. Finnall[927]—in Capt. Burkett P. Bowen's company
Ensign—Joseph Billingsley
Clerk of the 45th Regiment—James Alexander
Brigade Drummer—George G. Shelton
Brigade Fifer—Peter P. Cox

Men fined for failure to appear at muster:

Name	Name	Name
Robert Allen	William C. Beale	Jesse Burton[928]
James Armstrong, Jr.	John Berry	Strother Burton
Stephen H. Armstrong	John Beach	William Bloxham[929]
Gustavus Ashby	George Banks	William Butler
Ephraim Brown[930]	Joseph H. Ball	Charles Bussle
Fielding Brown	William Ball	Burdit Bridges
Thornton Brown	Alexander Bell[931]	Baily Byram
Bartlett Brown	James Bell	Loyal Carter
William Brooke	James Beagle	Alexander Cloe
Abijah Bowling	George W. Billingsley[932]	John Cooke
Alexander Bowling	Charles D. Bridwell	Harrison Combs
George Bowling	Westly Bridwell	Thomas Cooper
Peter Bowler	Elias Elliot	Howard Cooper[933]
John Davis	John English	George Cox
William Dickinson	William R. Ensor	Samuel Cox[934]
James Fines[935]	Seth Ganes	William Cox

---

[926] Walker Peyton Conway (1805-1884) was the son of John Moncure Conway (1779-1864) and Catherine Storke Peyton (1786-1865). For many years Walker was chief justice in Stafford. He married Margaret Eleanor Daniel (1807-1891) and lived at Inglewood, now the site of Drew Middle School. Walker was noted for his integrity and willingness to be a public servant.

[927] Walter Henry Finnall (c.1800-1861) was the son of Richard Monteith Finnall (1776-1847) and Mary Rollow (born c.1780) and was the grandson of Jonathan Finnall, Sr. Walter operated a fishery at Tump between Thorny Point and Marlborough Point. He married Elizabeth F. Bridwell (1805-1875), the daughter of Lewis Bridwell (died c.1824) and Elizabeth Stark (c.1780-1854).

[928] In September 1826 William Foushee of Stafford leased to Jesse Burton 75 acres including the house and 25 acres where William West formerly lived. This was described as being located on the right hand side of the road leading from the courthouse to Edward Burrage's tavern (Stafford Deed Book GG, p. 296).

[929] William Bloxham (c.1794-1864) lived near present Abel Reservoir on Potomac Run. In June 1845 John McDermott of Washington sold William 310 acres on Potomac Run described as adjoining Michael Wallace, John R. Fitzhugh, and John Moncure. It was the land upon which McDermott "lately resided" and purchased by him under a decree of the county court from John Moncure, commissioner, who had been appointed to sell the lands of Fielding Alexander, deceased. The other part of the tract was purchased from the trustee of Daniel Coakley (Stafford Deed Book NN, p. 478).

[930] In 1827 Ephraim Brown paid taxes on 89 acres on Potomac Run 9 miles southwest of the courthouse.

[931] By the time this militia list was made, Alexander Bell had removed to Spotsylvania.

[932] By the time this militia list was made, George Billingsley had removed to Spotsylvania.

[933] Howard Cooper (c.1802-1868) married Elizabeth Guy (c.1809-1854), the daughter of Luke Guy. Howard left a will in Stafford in which he devised all his estate to his children by Sally Jackson. Howard lived in the northern part of Stafford (Stafford Will Book R, p. 33).

[934] In 1839 Samuel Cox (died 1844) paid taxes on 315 acres in White Oak. In August 1837 Thomas Shelton and wife Charlotte sold Samuel 5 acres in White Oak (Stafford Deed Book LL, p. 244).

1823

John Fines	Thomas Gill, Jr.	John Craig
Thomas Fines	Thomas Gill, Sr.	James Curtis
Joseph B. Ficklen	Alexander Gordon	Robert Haborn
John B. S. Fitzhugh	Samuel Gordon, Jr.	James H. Harwood
Murray Forbes	John Gollihorn	Alfred C. Hayes
James W. Ford	William Gollihorn	Strother Heflin
Barnett Fritter	James Green	William Hewitt
Martin Fuget	Robert Gaddis	Joseph Hewitt
Leroy Jenkins	William Graves	James N. Hord
Isome Jordan	Benjamin Groves	William Hunt
Azariah Jones[936]	Absalom King	Alexander Lanz(?)
Charles Jones	John Kirk	John Lang
George Jones	John Knight	Israel F. Lankfit
Edward Jones	William Limbrick	Rawleigh Latham
Elisha Jones[937]	James Limbrick	Thornton Latham
Thomas Jones	George Limbrick	George Leitch
William Jones	John Marquis	George Lewis
William Limbrick, Jr.	Henry Mills	John Lewis
William Limbrick, Sr.	Nathaniel McCarty	William McDaniel
Cornelius Manon[938]	Thomas G. Moncure[939]	Burwell Million
James Newton	James Mountjoy	Alexander Morson
Jerrard Newton	Alexander O'Bryhim	Perry Patterson, Jr.
John Pates	Alexander Peyton	John H. S. Potes
William Payne	Rowsey Peyton	William W. Peyton
Edmund R. Payne	Thomas Peyton	Ishmaiel Pritchard
George Payne	William Peyton	Gustavus Reid
John Payne	Reubin Payne	Zelia Renoe
John Rogers	James Robinson	Thomas M. Robinson
Henry L. Rogers[940]	Archibald Rye	James Rye
Daniel Rolls	John Rolls	William Rolls
Joseph Santford[941]	John C. Shelton	Benjamin H. Shacklett

[935] James Fines (c.1799-1865) married Rachel Curtis, the daughter of John Curtis (died before 1815).

[936] In 1839 Azariah Jones paid taxes on 10 acres on Deep Run in the southwest corner of the county. He lived very near Noah Jones and they may have been related.

[937] In 1829 Elisha Jones (c.1805-after 1850) paid tax on 10 acres on Deep Run. He lived very near Noah and Azariah Jones and they may have been related.

[938] Cornelius Manning was most likely the son of either John or Robert Mannin/Manning and Ann Limbrick. She was the daughter of John Limbrick (died 1826) and had two sisters who also married Mannings. Between 1830 and 1836 Cornelius married Elizabeth Stone. In November 1826 Cornelius' mother, Ann Manning, gave him a mare, 2 cows with their calves, a feather bed and furniture, a pine chest, a pine table, and six chairs (Stafford Deed Book GG, p. 269). Cornelius lived between Leeland and Potomac Run.

[939] Thomas Gaskins Moncure (1799-1836) was the son of John Moncure (1772-1822) and Alice Peachy Gaskins (1774-1860). He married first in 1823 Clarissa Bernard Hooe (1800-1829) and secondly Mary Bell Haxall. Thomas represented Stafford in the Virginia House of Delegates and was a vestryman of Aquia Episcopal Church in Stafford.

[940] Around 1826 Henry L. Rogers married Patsy Potes who already owned 4 slaves and $800. They signed a marriage agreement in which Patsy's assets were placed in trust with Elzey Carter who was to invest the money "in some one of the Banks of the District of Columbia in good credit" and in Patsy's name. The assets were to remain in her control and not subject to her future husband (Stafford Deed Book GG, p. 241). In 1833 Henry was renting and residing on part of Crow's Nest (*Virginia Herald*, Aug. 7, 1833).

[941] Joseph Sanford (died c.1871). His estate inventory included 1 mahogany mohair sofa, 1 cane seat rocker, 1 mahogany dining table, 1 mahogany card table, 1 clock, 1 mirror, 1 carpet, 1 water cooler, 1 side

1823

John D. Simms	Able Skinner	William Shacklett
David C. Slaughter[942]	Thomas Smith	Thomas A. Smith
William Smith	William Snellings	James Stevens
Barnett Stewart[943]	Charles Stewart	Thomas Stewart
William Stewart	George Stone[944]	Elias Stone
Dawson Sullivant	Gustavus Sullivant	Martin Sullivant, Sr.
William Sullivant	Josias Suell(?)	William Tallmarsh
Ezekiel Taylor[945]	Dolphin True	Thomas Trussle
Alexander Turner	Michael Wallace[946]	Robert Warren
Charles Warren[947]	George West	Oliver West
John H. Weeks	William White	Nathaniel P. Williams, Jr.
Joseph Wormsley	William Woodward	George Young

1824

Lt. Colonel—James Briggs—in room of George Waller, resigned
Major—Thornton Alexander
Captains—Jameson Corbin
    Presley Cropp—in room of Silas F. Cropp, resigned
    Samuel S. Brooke
    Thornton Alexander
    Burkett P. Bowen
    Silas F. Cropp
    Abner R. Alcock—captain of Flying Artillery—he resigned and Thomas Norman was elected captain in his stead (Folder 35)
Lieutenants—Charles E. S. Fitzhugh[948] —in Samuel S. Brooke's company—in room of Walker P. Conway who failed to qualify
    William J. Whaling—in Burkett P. Bowen's company
    James M. Hord—in Silas F. Cropp's company
Brigade Drummer—Augustin Shelton[949]

---

board, 1 tureen, matting on the parlor and dining room floors, 1 mahogany wardrobe, 1 china tea service, 1 freezer, 7 hogs, 2 oxen, 4 cattle, 1 wagon, and farm implements (Stafford Deed Book TT, p. 256). Joseph lived in White Oak.

[942] David C. Slaughter married Frances Alexander.

[943] Barnett Stewart (1788-c.1845) was the likely son of James Stewart (c.1740-1822) and Mary Barnett (born c.1750). In 1839 Barnett was listed in the personal property tax records as living on Stony Hill (now part of Aquia Harbour subdivision). That year he paid taxes on 4 slaves and 13 horses. He also paid taxes on slaves and horses on Accokeek Creek.

[944] May be George Stone (c.1784-after 1850) who lived near Falmouth.

[945] Ezekiel Taylor married Jane W. Shelkett, daughter of John Shelkett (died 1825) of Stafford.

[946] Michael Wallace (1800-1877) was the son of John Wallace (1761-1877) and Elizabeth Hooe (c.1766-1850) of Liberty Hall. Michael paid taxes on Chestnut Hill from 1830 until after the War Between the States. He married Hannah Hull Moncure (1801-1866), the daughter of John Moncure (1772-1822) and Alice Peachy Gaskins (1774-1860) of Clermont.

[947] Charles Warren came to Stafford from either Washington, DC or Delaware and bought a large farm on the Wide Water Peninsula. He died intestate leaving eleven children. Jacob Harrison married Charles' daughter, Rachel H. Warren. They lived on the Warren farm from c.1856-c.1870. Rachel died in 1873 and Jacob filed a claim with the Southern Claims Commission to try and obtain her portion of any money due her father's estate. One deponent in the SCC claim stated that he had been responsible for collecting "all Forage that I could upon the Peninsula lying between the Potomac River and the Acquia Creek, and through Mr. Charles Warren, I was enabled to collect large quantities that were secreted" (Southern Claims Commission. Approved. Claim # 36524, pp. 6-10).

[948] Charles Edward Stuart Fitzhugh was the son of Thomas Fitzhugh (1754-1820) and Ann Rose (born 1763) of Boscobel. He died unmarried.

[949] Thornton Alexander noted this year that Augustin lived near Stafford Courthouse.

1824

Brigade Fifer—Peter P. Cox

Men fined for failure to appear at muster:

Gustavus Ashby	Abner R. Allcock	Barney Barker
George Banks	Robert Beaty	Thornton Brown
Rawleigh Brown[950]	Thomas S. Burton	Harris Burton
William Bayley	Reuben Bowler	James S. Bowling
John Combs	Benjamin Cox	William Cox, Jr.
William Cox	George Cox	Alexander Cloe
James Curtis	Walker P. Conway	Lewis Dickinson
William Dickinson	Henry Dawson	Gerard Dunaway
Walter R. Daniel	William R. Ensor	David Elkins
William Eustace[951]	William H. Fitzhugh	Strother Ficklen[952]
Joseph B. Ficklen	Walter H. Finnall	James Finnall
John Franklin	Alexander Fitzhugh	Nicholas Follis
Martin Fugate	Gerard Fugate[953]	John Fugate
Thomas Fines	James Fines	John Fines
Elijah Fines[954]	Nathaniel Gaines[955]	Seth Gaines
William P. Gaines	James Graves	Benjamin Groves
Thomas Gill	William Gill	Thomas Gollyhon
Duff Green	Corbin Hale	William Harding
William Hewitt	John E. Hewitt	John G. Hedgman
John Hedgman	Peter D. G Hedgman[956]	Robert Hebron
Alfred C. Hayes	William Hunt	Chares T. Hay
Esra Jones	Thomas Jones, Jr.	James Jones
Charles Jones	William Jones	George Jett
Isom Jordan	William Kirk	James Latham
William Limbrick	William Limbrick, Jr.	George Limbrick
James Limbrick	John Limbrick	Alexander Lang
George Lunsford	Burrel Million[957]	William Murphy
Thomas G. Moncure	John Marquess	Samuel Monteith

---

[950] By 1850 Raleigh Travers Brown (1792-after 1850) was a resident of Fredericksburg, but he paid taxes on 486 acres of Belle Plains.

[951] William Eustace, Jr. was the son of William Eustace, Sr. (died before 1823).

[952] Anthony Strother Ficklen (c.1785-1831) was the son of Charles Ficklen (died c.1816) and Mary Strother (?) of Fauquier. He married but died childless. Anthony held various public offices in Stafford.

[953] Gerard Fugate (c.1806-1841) married Orpha Sullivan, the daughter of Martin Sullivan. From about 1836-1839 Gerard held licenses to operate a store in Stafford (Eby, Men 259-260).

[954] Elijah was the son of James Fines (c.1769-1812) and Rachel Curtis. In 1845 Isaac Fines conveyed to Elijah half of a 78-acre tract Isaac had bought from John Moncure. Excluded from this conveyance were the White Oak Meeting House and its one acre (Stafford Deed Book OO, p. 102). Elijah married Lucretia Shackelford (died c.1868), the daughter of Dudley Shackelford.

[955] May be Nathaniel P. Gaines (1798-1855) who was the son of William Henry Gaines (1754-c.1818) and Jane Botts (1757-1826) of Culpeper and Prince William. Nathaniel was born in Culpeper and died in Hardin County, Kentucky.

[956] Peter Daniel Grayson Hedgman (c.1801-after 1885) lived on Accokeek Run. He was the son of George Grayson Hedgman (1785-c.1827) and Nancy Morton, the daughter of George Morton of King George. Peter married first Louisa Mitchell of Charles County, Maryland. His second wife was Frances C. Hedgman (born c.1813), the daughter of his uncle, John G. Hedgman (1782-c.1845).

[957] Burrel Million moved to Madison County, Kentucky.

1824

James Mountjoy	John McDaniel	Henry Mills
Thomas Norman	James Newton	John Newton
James Nash	John Oliver, Jr.[958]	Ishmael Pritchard
John Pumfrey[959]	George Purvis[960]	George Payne
John Pates	William W. Peyton	William Peyton
Valentine Peyton	Alexander Peyton	John Rolls
Zele Renoe	Charles C. Randolph[961]	James P. Rowe
Thomas M. Robinson	James Robinson	Charles Randall
Thompson Randall	John D. Simms	Abel Skinner
Thomas Stewart	Barnett Stewart	Thornton Shelton[962]
John Shelton	Gustavus Sullivant	William Sullivant
Martin Sullivant	Thomas Sullivant	Samuel H. Skinker
Nathaniel Snipe[963]	Elias Stone	James W. Stone
William B. Stone	William Snelling	David C. Slaughter
Joshua Skidmore	Joseph Sanford	James Tyson
Thomas Trussel	Jeremiah B. Templeman	Henry N. Templeman
William D. Timmons[964]	William Talmarsh	William Truslow
John Thompson	Dolphin True	Edwin B. Vass[965]
James C. Vass[966]	Landon Walters	Anthony Watts
Nathaniel P. Williams	Charles Williams	James Williams
William White	Henry White[967]	William Wolfe
George Waller		

1825

Commandant of Troop of Stafford—William Barber
Major—Thornton Alexander
Captains—James M. Hord—in room of Presley Cropp, resigned
          John C. Edrington[968]—formerly Capt. William Ford

---

[958] In 1826 John Oliver executed a deed of trust using a small schooner called *Fly*, 1 bed, 2 tables, and all his household and kitchen furniture to secure a debt of $60 due Joseph Gilbert of Dumfries (Stafford Deed Book GG, p. 264).
[959] John Pumfrey (c.1805-after 1850) married Mariah Porch (1800-1856), the daughter of Esom Porch (c.1745-1826). He lived off Warrenton Road (U. S. Route 17).
[960] George Purvis (died c.1834) was the son of John Purvis (died 1834).
[961] Charles Carter Randolph (1788-1863) was the son of Robert Randolph (1760-1825) of Eastern View, Fauquier County and Elizabeth Hill Carter (1764-1832). In 1825 he married Mary Anne Fauntleroy Mortimer in Spotsylvania County. In 1832 and 1834 he served as a school commissioner in Stafford.
[962] Thornton Shelton (1805-1851) was the son of Thomas Shelton (1776-1870) and Elizabeth Stark (born 1777) of Stafford. Thornton married Elizabeth Leechman in Adams County, Ohio.
[963] This may be the son of Nathaniel Snipe (c.1757-after 1824) and Frances Kidwell of Stafford and Spotsylvania.
[964] William D. Timmons (born c.1805) was the son of Thomas Timmons (c.1777-1842) of Stafford. From at least 1839-1850 he was incarcerated in the penitentiary in Richmond having been convicted of murder.
[965] Edmund Brooke Vass (died 1839) was the son of James Vass (1770-1837) and Susannah Brooke (died 1816). He married Charlotte J. McRae.
[966] James Cumming Vass (1800-1870) was the son of James Vass (1770-1837) and Susannah Brooke (died 1816). He married Elizabeth Eleanor Hawkins Smith (born 1806) of Fredericksburg.
[967] Henry White (c.1799-1867) died in Stafford of "apoplectic fits." He was unmarried.
[968] John Catesby Edrington (1800-1879) was the son of John Catesby Edrington (1775-1820) and Sarah Porter Stone (1769-1816). He lived at Myrtle Grove on Aquia Creek where he ran a fishery, quarry, and store. He also had a ship that he used to haul sandstone up to Washington (Stafford Estate Accounts, 1823, p.281). John married Elizabeth Hawkins Stone (1810-1891), the daughter of Hawkins Stone and Elizabeth Burroughs (died before 1833).

1st Lieutenant—William W. Peyton
2nd Lieutenant—Nathaniel Barber[969]
2nd Lieutenant of Flying Artillery—James Alexander
                                  Edward Waller[970]
Cornet—Ransom M. Hickerson[971]
Lieutenants—John McFee
       Benjamin Tolson, Jr.—in Capt. Tolson's company
       Samuel H. Adie[972]
Ensigns—Philip E. Gill[973]
       James Edrington
Brigade Drummer—Augustin Shelton
Brigade Fifer—Peter Cox

Men fined for failure to appear at muster:

Stephen Armstrong	John Ashby	John Atchison[974]
John Anderson	Thornton Brown	William Brown
Reuben Bowler	Thomas Bowler[975]	Burdit Bridges
Elijah Bell[976]	Joseph H. Bell[977]	John Bates
Uriah Bradshaw	William Brooke	William C. Beale
John Bowling	James S. Bowling	George Bowling
James Beagle	Thomas Brooks	Henry Barker
George Bussel[978]	Charles Bussel	Benjamin Ball
John W. Byram[979]	Ezra Burr[980]	Charles D. Bridwell

---

[969] Nathaniel Barber (c.1795-after 1850). In 1827 Nathaniel bankrupted and was "in custody by virtue of two executions which have been levied on the body of the said Nathl. Barber." He conveyed all his interest in land in Fauquier and Stafford acquired from his father, William Barber (Stafford Deed Book GG, p. 487).

[970] Edward Waller (1805-1883) was the son of Edward Waller (1768-1818) of Concord and Elizabeth Chadwell. Edward married Susan Newton Conway (1814-1864), the daughter of Thomas B. Conway (1779-1825) and Eliza Newton (1797-1814). He resided at Grafton, part of which is now Anne E. Moncure Elementary School on Garrisonville Road (Rt. 610). Edward operated the Mt. Pleasant and Rock Rimmon sandstone quarries on Aquia Creek.

[971] Ransom M. Hickerson (c.1794-1844) was the son of Charles Hickerson of Fauquier County. He married Mary Mason Kendall (born 1799) of Fauquier. Ransom resided at Apple Grove, part of which is now on the Marine Corps reservation and part (including the house site) now Apple Grove subdivision.

[972] May actually be Samuel F. Adie (1806-1860), the son of Benjamin Adie (1762-c.1825) and Margaret Gibson Gillison (born c.1770). Samuel moved to Nevada where he was secretary of the Phoenix Copper Mining Company. He was buried at Hollywood Cemetery in Richmond.

[973] Philip E. Gill (1805-1870) was the son of Presley Gill (1778-1827) and Sarah S. Phillips (1786-1872) of Fauquier. Some of the family moved to Logan County, Kentucky where Sarah and three of her sons died.

[974] John Atchison was a teacher. He married Rosanna Horton.

[975] Thomas Bowler (1804-1887) was born in Caroline County and died in Falmouth. He was a brother of Reuben Bowler (1800-1856) and married Anna M. Payne.

[976] In 1826 Elijah Bell worked as postmaster at the Stafford Courthouse Post Office (Eby, Men 245).

[977] In 1823 and 1825 Joseph H. Bell (died c.1838) was granted licenses to keep an ordinary in Stafford and seems to have done so in Falmouth (Eby, Men 273). In 1838 he married Lucy Starke.

[978] In 1812 George Bussel paid rent on an unnamed mill and was listed as a millwright (Stafford County Personal Property Tax Records).

[979] John William Byram (born 1804) was the son of Nimrod Byram (born 1776) and Catherine Jones of Stafford.

1825

Harris Burton	William Bettis	William Bryant
John Cox	William Cox	Walker Cropp[981]
Thornton P. Cropp	Thomas Cooper	John Cooper, Sr.
Benjamin S. Corbin	James Curtis	Esom Coppage[982]
James Conner[983]	John Conyers	William Chinn
Walker P. Conway	Thomas Curtis[984]	Walter R. Daniel
William Dillon	John Daffin	Henry Dawson
John Davis	William Dickinson	John Ervin[985]
James Edrington[986]	William English	William Edwards
John Franklin	James Farnham	James W. Ford
John Farnham	John Fugate	Martin Fugate
Isaac Fines[987]	James Fines	Thomas Fines
James Finnall	John Finnall[988]	Murray Forbes
Strother Ficklen	Temple Fouche[989]	William H. Fitzhugh
William Garner	Thomas Gill	Samuel Gordon
Solomon Gollahon	William Gollahon	William K. Gordon
Sidney Graves	Townsend Graves	William Graves
Robert O. Grayson[990]	Robert Green	James Green
Benjamin Groves	Benjamin Guy	Branson Guy[991]
Moses Guy	Robert Guy	Boswell Harding[992]
Thomas Harding	William Harding	William Harding, Jr.
Joseph Hall[993]	Alfred C. Hayes	John T. Hedgman[994]

---

[980] Ezra Burr (c.1781-after 1850) was born in Connecticut. In 1823 he was granted a license to keep an ordinary in Stafford. He also kept a dry goods store and was a member of the Yellow Chapel Temperance Society. From at least 1826-1830 he was a constable in Stafford. In 1825 Ezra and his wife were founding members of Yellow Chapel, now Hartwood Presbyterian Church.

[981] Walker L. Cropp was the son of John Cropp (1753-1830) and Rosie Thomas. Walker bankrupted and his 242-acre farm near Spotted Tavern was auctioned (*Political Arena*, May 5, 1840).

[982] Esom/Eastham Coppage (c.1790-after 1850) lived in Hartwood. Around 1824 he married Marian Curtis (born 1808).

[983] A sheriff's margin notation reads, "No Inhabitant."

[984] Thomas Curtis was the son of John Curtis (died before 1815). He married Emily Bates and left numerous children in Stafford. Emily held the reputation of being the meanest woman in White Oak. Eventually, Thomas moved in with one of his daughters because he could no longer tolerate living with Emily.

[985] A sheriff's margin notation indicated that John Ervin moved to Fauquier County.

[986] In 1826 James Edrington (1798-1860) bought from Thornton Alexander 495 acres of the old Accokeek Furnace tract (Stafford Deed Book GG, p. 139). Around 1840 James married Sarah A. Withers, the daughter of Thomas Withers of Stafford (Stafford Deed Book MM, p. 66).

[987] Isaac Fines (1805-1886) was the son of James Fines (c.1769-1812) and Rachel Curtis. Isaac married Delilah Brown. In 1840 he bought from John Moncure 79 acres adjoining the White Oak Meeting House (Stafford Deed Book MM, p. 61). During the War Between the States, Isaac was a spy for the Union.

[988] May be John Finnall (born 1808). Most of this family lived in White Oak.

[989] Temple Fouch (1797-1834) was the son of Thomas Fouch (1755-1828) and Sarah Combs of Loudoun County. In 1823 he was employed as an "agent" for William H. Fitzhugh of Stafford (*National Intelligencer*, Jan. 11, 1823).

[990] Dr. Robert Osborne Grayson (1789-1841) was the son of Benjamin Grayson (1763-1829) of Loudoun County and Ann Bronaugh. He married first Susan Margaret Peyton (1787-1824) and secondly Sarah Mason Cooke (1791-1861), the daughter of Col. John Cooke (1755-1828) and Mary Thomson Mason (born 1762) of West Farm, Stafford County.

[991] Branson Guy (c.1808-c.1848) married Eliza Sciford and died in Winchester. He may have been the son of William Guy (born c.1780).

[992] Boswell Harding was the son of Henry Wildy Harding (1800-1878) and Nancy Hansbrough. He left Stafford and moved to the border between Tennessee and Kentucky.

1825

John G. Hedgman	Joseph Hewitt	William Hewitt
Francis Hill	Edwin C. Hooe[995]	Robert S. Hooe
Walter Hore	William Hore	Roy W. Horton[996]
Daniel R. Huffman	John Humphrey	William Hunt
Thomas Jackson[997]	Elisha Jones	Ezekiel Jones
George Jones	Thomas Jones, Jr.	Thomas Kerns
Alexander Kelly	Joshua Kendall	Toliver S. Kendall[998]
Absalom King	Israel F. Langfitt	Alexander Lang
Thornton Latham	Rawley Latham	John Lang
John Lewis[999]	George Lewis[1000]	George Limbrick
William Limbrick	Thomas Limbrick	John Limbrick
James Limbrick	Alexander W. Massey	John Masters
John Marquess	William McDaniel	Michael McKenny
John Meizings	Henry Mills	James Mills
Burrel Million	Fielding Monroe	Alexander Morson
Branson Mountjoy	James F. Murray	Jesse Musselman
James Newton	William Nicholson	Alexander Obryhim
Sandford Payne[1001]	Thomas Payne	Eli P. Perry
Alexander Peyton[1002]	John N. Peyton	Thomas Peyton
Valentine Peyton	Ishmael Pritchard	John Pumfrey
George Purvis	William Randall[1003]	Charles C. Randolph
John Roberson	Thomas N. Roberson	John Rogers
Daniel Rolls	John Rolls	William Rolls
Jesse Rowe	Perry Rowe	Alfred Rye
Archibald Rye	James Rye	Toliver Shackleford
Thornton Shelton	John C. Shelton	Abel E. Skinner[1004]
John D. Simms	Hanson Simms	David C. Slaughter
James Smith	Thomas Smith	Thomas A. Smith

[993] This may be Joseph Hall (born 1797), the son of Benjamin Hall (1759-1845) and Jemima Thacker (1758-1830).

[994] John T. Hedgman (c.1804-1857) was the son of George Grayson Hedgman (1785-c.1827) and Nancy Morton. He married Mary M. Horton (died before 1850), the daughter of Cossom Horton (c.1735-1821) who lived on the Hope plantation on Aquia Creek. In 1843 John paid tax on 430 acres on Accokeek Run.

[995] Edwin Carter Hooe (died 1827) was the son of Robert H. Hooe (1748-1834).

[996] Roy W. Horton (c.1803-after 1856). By 1849 he was a resident of Prince William County. He married Mary Bridwell.

[997] A sheriff's margin notation reads, "Removed."

[998] Taliaferro S. Kendall (c.1801-1868) is thought to have been the son of Henry Kendall (1749-1810) and Lucy Travers and was a brother of Joshua Kendall (1796-1852). He was born in Stafford and died in Clinton County, Missouri. He married Lauretta Wamsley (c.1795-1839:50) of Stafford.

[999] A sheriff's margin notation reads, "No Inhabitant."

[1000] A sheriff's margin notation reads, "No Inhabitant."

[1001] Sanford Payne (born c.1795) was born in Fauquier, moved to Prince William, and then to Stafford. In 1822 he was indicted for stealing clothes from William Gordon, a slave belonging to John Shelkett and working for Hazelwood Farish as a stage driver (Fredericksburg Court Records, "Commonwealth vs Payne").

[1002] A sheriff's margin notation reads, "No Inhabitant."

[1003] William Randall (died before 1850). In 1850 his estate paid tax on land on Accokeek Run.

[1004] Abel E. Skinner (c.1802-after 1860) was born in Virginia and died in Dubuque County, Iowa. In the 1820s he rented a lot in Falmouth from Robert Dunbar and in 1825 Abel was one of the founding members of Yellow Chapel, now Hartwood Presbyterian Church. In 1827 he rented 8 ¾ acres on Poplar Road (Route 616) 15 miles west of the courthouse. The very high rate of assessment makes it possible there was a mill on the property. In 1847 he married Mary Marshall in Linn County, Iowa.

1825

John H. Smoote[1005]	John Snelling[1006]	Jesse Snelling
Thomas Snelling	William Snelling	Barnett Stewart
Charles B. Stewart[1007]	Thomas Stewart	Elias Stone
George Strother	Martin Sullivan	Thomas Sullivan
William Sullivan	William Talmarsh	James Templeman
Moses Templeman[1008]	Lewis Timmons[1009]	William D. Timmons
Henry R. Thornton[1010]	Dolphin True	William Trussel
John Walker	Landon Walters	George Waller
Withers Waller[1011]	Anthony Watts	William Went
William West	Henry White	William White
Horace Wilder	Nathaniel P. Williams	

1826

Lt. Colonel—James Briggs
2nd Lieutenant Flying Artillery—James Garrison
Brigade Drummer—Gustavus Shelton
Brigade Fifer—Peter Cox
Regimental Clerk—Daniel Bell

Men fined for failure to attend muster:

Hugh Adie	Stephen Armstrong	John Anderson
William Anderson	Albert Anderson	Luke Anderson[1012]
John Abbott	Rodney Atchison[1013]	James Armstrong
Benjamin Ashby, Jr.	William Anderson	Henry Atchison[1014]
Martin Atchison	John Atchison	Elijah Bell[1015]

[1005] In 1825 John H. Smoot was granted a retail license in Stafford (Eby, Men 257).
[1006] John Snellings (born 1808) was the son of William Snellings (1785-1855) and Elizabeth Jett (1790:95-1881). He married Sarah Bates/Yates (c.1803-1885), the daughter of William and Nancy Bates/Yates of Stafford.
[1007] Charles Bruce Stewart was the son of James N. Stewart (died 1825) and Elizabeth Ficklen of Coal Landing. Charles removed to Randolph County, Missouri where he served as a judge. He married Fannie Hill.
[1008] Moses Templeman (born 1807) was born in Stafford. He married Catherine Nigh in Lancaster, Ohio. While a resident of Stafford, Moses was a member of Hartwood Baptist Church (Hartwood).
[1009] Lewis Timmons (c.1797-after 1850) was the son of Thomas Timmons, Sr. (c.1777-1842). In 1843 Lewis paid tax on 244 acres on Deep Run that he had received from his father.
[1010] Henry Randolph Thornton (1807-1862) was the son of George Washington Thornton (1776-1815) and Mary Goode Randolph (1785-1865) of Rumford Farm in lower Stafford. Henry's first wife was Maria Agnes Bradford (1810-1849). He married secondly Ellen Thom (1823-1903), the daughter of George Slaughter Thom.
[1011] Withers Waller (1785-1827) was the son of William Waller (1740-1817) and his third wife, Ursula Withers (1752-1815) of Concord. During the late 18th century, Withers was in business with his cousin, James Morton (1793-1859) of Spring Hill. They owned at least one sailing vessel that carried freestone from the Aquia Creek quarries to the new city of Washington. This included some, if not all, of the columns for the Capitol. Withers was buried at Mt. Pleasant near Aquia Creek.
[1012] In 1835 Luke Anderson served as an overseer of the road in Stafford.
[1013] Rodney Atchison (1806-1881) married Cynthia Ashby (1802-1881), daughter of Robert Ashby. They moved from Stafford to Linville Creek, Rockingham County, Virginia.
[1014] Henry Atchison (c.1799-1858) was the son of Hugh and Sarah Atchison. Hugh owned land on both sides of Jumping Branch Road (Route 742) about two miles south of the courthouse. At least part of this property conveyed to Henry Atchison and part to Henry's sister, Louisa V., who married John M. Stevens (c.1800-1840). Henry died in Stafford.
[1015] A sheriff's margin notation reads, "Removed."

1826

Laurence Alexander	Charles D. Bridwell	Thomas Bowler
Peter Bowler	Reuben Bowler	Uriah Bradshaw
Bartlet Brown	Thornton Brown	Sinclear Barber[1016]
Cuthbert Byram[1017]	John W. Byram	William Ball
Abijah Bowling	Samuel Beavers[1018]	John Beavers
Jesse Brooks	Alfred Burroughs[1019]	Aaron H. Ball
Rawley Browne	Fielding Browne	Richard Berry, Jr.[1020]
Benjamin Ball	George Black[1021]	Edward Burrage[1022]
Strother M. Burton	Joseph Burton	John Burton
William B. Burton	John Bowling	James S. Bowling
George Bowling	William Baxter	William Bettice
William Brooke	William Bryant	James Bradley, Jr.
Bailey Byram	William C. Beale	Joseph H. Bell
William Browne	George Bryant[1023]	George Billingsley
Jesse Burton	Dixon Brown[1024]	William Bloxham
Burdit Bridges	Deacon Brown	Elias Butchard[1025]
Joseph Carpenter	Joseph Conns	James Chadwell
James Carter	John Cooper, Sr.[1026]	James Cave[1027]
John Combs	Thomas Chinn	William Chinn
Thornton W. Cropp	Robert Cropp[1028]	Thomas Curtis
Harris S. Corbin	Benjamin Corbin	John Conyers
Cary Cox	John Craig	James Curtis

[1016] Sinclair Barber and wife Margaret owned land in Hartwood (Stafford Deed Book GG, p. 273).

[1017] Cuthbert Byram (c.1796-1854) married Sarah H. Kendall (c.1784-1854), the daughter of Daniel and Sarah Kendall. Cuthbert's estate included 3 slaves, farm implements, household and kitchen furniture, 4 bee gums and bees, 23 hogs, 4 horses, and 11 cattle (Stafford Deed Book RR, p. 47).

[1018] Samuel Beavers (born c.1801) later lived in Brentsville, Prince William County.

[1019] Alfred Burroughs (c.1802-c.1867) was the son of John Burroughs (c.1748-c.1836) and Margaret Elizabeth Vaughn (died after 1869). He married Martha Ellen Herndon and died childless in Stafford. Alfred owned 346 acres on Beaverdam Run in what is now the Quantico reservation.

[1020] Richard Berry, Jr. was the son of Richard Berry (died c.1826). In October 1845 Richard Berry, then of Fredericksburg, bought 250 acres in White Oak formerly belonging to Thomas K. Newton (Stafford Deed Book NN, p. 512). The younger Richard worked as a toll collector on the Chatham Bridge. He married a Curtis and died in the 1850s or 1860s.

[1021] May be George Washington Black, Sr. (c.1801-after 1880), the son of William Black (born c.1775). He married Rachel Honey (born c.1815) and was a merchant.

[1022] Edward Burrage was from Charles County, Maryland. He moved to Stafford sometime prior to 1817 when he rented a building from Quaker John Holloway (1762-1831). This stood in the Mountain View area of Stafford and Edward ran an ordinary there. His name last appeared in the Stafford land records in 1836 when he sold his land to Joseph W. Honey (1810-1879).

[1023] George Bryant (c.1800-after 1850) was a miller and lived in or near Falmouth.

[1024] Dixon Brown was the son of John Brown, Sr. and employed himself as a blacksmith and wheelwright (Stafford Deed Book GG, p. 413 and Stafford County Estate, 1823, p. 289). In 1816 the Stafford court granted him a license to keep a house of "private entertainment" (gambling). In 1833 he worked as a constable in Stafford (Eby, Men 150, 271).

[1025] Elias Butchard (c.1808-after 1850) lived off Warrenton Road (U. S. Route 17).

[1026] A sheriff's margin notation reads, "Not an Inhabitant."

[1027] In 1833 James Cave paid tax on 214 acres in Hartwood. From 1835-1836 he worked as postmaster at Hartwood. From around 1828-1836 he held licenses to run a retail store, which may have been at Hartwood, though he also occupied a building in Falmouth. This structure is now gone, but stood between the Barnes House and Belmont. In 1828 and 1829 he had licenses to run an ordinary and in 1832 advertised his fishery on the Maryland shore. Fish from there were sent to Belle Plains (*Virginia Herald*, Mar. 17, 1832). From around 1830-1835 he also held licenses to sell liquor.

[1028] Robert Cropp (c.1800-1885).

1826

George Cox	William Cox	John M. Daniel[1029]
Moncure Daniel	John Dillon	James Dickens
Henry Dawson	William Dickinson, Sr.	Wishart Dogget[1030]
Bailis Davis[1031]	William Dickinson	Columbus Dickens
Seamor Dobson	Richard Dykes[1032]	William Edwards
Patrick H. England[1033]	William R. Ensor	Leonard H. Ficklen[1034]
Chares E. S. Fitzhugh	Strother Ficklen	William H. Ficklen[1035]
John Finnall, Jr.	Charles Franklin[1036]	John Franklin
Daniel Fines	Thomas Fines	Ewel Fisher
Elijah Fines	Nicholas J. Follis[1037]	Reuben Fritter
James Fines	Temple Fouche	James W. Ford
Martin Fugate	William Garner	Thomas Gill
James Graves	John Graves	Thomas Gollahon
Solomon Gollahon	Robert O. Grayson	Townsend Graves
Duff Green	James Green	Robert Green
Ralph Griffis	Robert Guy	Mark Harding
Robert Hebbron	Joshua Hudson[1038]	Alfred C. Hayes
Jarvis Hayden	William Harding, Jr.	George F. G. Hedgman[1039]
Richard Hill	Thomas Harding	Francis H. Hooe
Gustavus Hefflin[1040]	William Hewitt	John Henderson
John E. Hewitt	Peter D. G. Hedgman	Robert S. Hooe
Joseph Hewitt	John Holloway	William Jackson
Peter Jett, Jr.	Littleton Johnson	Charles Jones
Joseph M. Johnson	Thomas Jones, Jr.	Azariah Jones

[1029] Dr. John Moncure Daniel, Jr. (c.1800-c.1845) was the son of Dr. John M. Daniel (1769-1813) and Margaret Eleanor Stone (1771-1809). His first wife was Eliza Mitchell (died c.1835). He married secondly Euphemia Tolson, the daughter of James Tolson of Stafford. The younger Dr. Daniel graduated from the University of Maryland with a degree in medicine.

[1030] More commonly known as Wishard Doggett. He was the son of Reuben Doggett, Jr. and Ann Bussell. In 1828 Wishart married Harriet Courtney in Fredericksburg.

[1031] Bailis Davis (c.1809-1857) was the son of Thomas Davis. He married Susan King (c.1804-after 1850), the sister of Peter and Pearson King of Stafford. Bailis and Susan lived on the south side of Aquia Creek. In 1850 he paid taxes on 254 acres (in which he had a life estate) conveyed from Peter King to Susan Davis. From 1856-1857 he served as one of the overseers of the poor in Stafford. Bailis died in Stafford.

[1032] In 1829 Richard Dykes paid tax on 55 acres on Aquia Run. He married Pina Ann Harding, the daughter of Clarkey (Million) Harding (1745-1826). In 1826 Richard repaired Stafford's old stone jail (Fredericksburg, "Dickinson's Admr vs Tyler's Admr").

[1033] Patrick Henry England (1804-1882) was the son of John England (1755-1851) and Ann Musselman (c.1760-1823). His first wife was Ann Truslow. He married secondly Emily Baker (born c.1824).

[1034] Leonard H. Ficklen (c.1803-after 1850) was a carpenter. He married Terissa F. Hill of Fauquier (Stafford Deed Book NN, p. 285).

[1035] William H. Ficklen (1805-1874) was the son of William Ficklen (died c.1826) and Paulina Hill. He married Jane Dickerson (died 1866) of Stafford Springs and in 1839 moved to Randolph County, Missouri where he died.

[1036] Charles C. Franklin was the son of William Franklin (died before 1841). In 1839 he paid taxes on 260 acres on Accokeek Run.

[1037] Nicholas was the son of Job Fallis/Follis (born c.1765) of Fauquier and the grandson of Quaker George Fallis (born c.1747) and Mary Ridgeway (born c.1748).

[1038] Joshua Hudson (died 1869). A margin notation this year states, "No Inhabitant."

[1039] George F. G. Hedgman was the likely son of George Grayson Hedgman (1785-c.1827) and Nancy Morton.

[1040] Gustavus Heflin (born c.1799) was Augustus M. Heflin. He was the son of Asa Holloway (c.1765-c.1804) and Rachel Heflin and the grandson of Quaker Isaac Holloway (1735-c.1809). Also known as Gusty or Gustavus, he married Linda "Kitty" Black (c.1804-before 1850).

1826

Edward Jones	Noah Jones	Alexander D. Kelly[1041]
Absalom King	Toliver S. Kendall	John Knight
Alexander Lang	Thornton Latham	Rawley Latham
William Latham	John Limbrick, Jr.	Thomas Limbrick
James Limbrick	Daniel Limbrick	John Limbrick
Vincent Limbrick	George Limbrick	John Marquess
Michael McCarney	William McDaniel	James Mountjoy
John Mills	Alexander W. Massey	John Mozingo[1042]
James Monroe	John Masters	Thomas G. Moncure
Thomas Mountjoy	Ransom Mountjoy	Alexander Morson
Lemuel S. Mountjoy	James Monteith[1043]	James Moxley
Gustavus Newton[1044]	James Newton	Jarrard Newton
Thomas J. Payne	James L. Payne	Reuben Payne
Sanford Payne	Jesse Patterson[1045]	Jesse Payne[1046]
George Payne	Alexander Patton[1047]	Thomas Payne
Rowzey Peyton	John Pates	Eli P. Perry
William Payne	Thomas Peyton	Thomas Pollard
John H. S. Potts	John Pumfrey	Gustavus Reed
Benjamin Rose	John Roberson	James P. Rowe
Alfred Rye	Thornley E. Schooler[1048]	Yelverton Shelton[1049]
John D. Simms	Hanson Simms	John Sudduth
Martin Sullivan	Thomas Stewart	William Snelling
William Sullivan	Daniel Sullivan	Elias Stone[1050]
Joseph Stone	George Stone	Robert Styers
William Talmash	Sidney H. Taylor[1051]	Thornton Taylor
Jeremiah B. Templeman	William Trussell	William Thomas[1052]
James Templeman	William D. Timmons	Lewis Timmons
Edmund B. Vass[1053]	Penrose Vass[1054]	James C. Vass

[1041] Alexander D. Kelly (died 1829). By 1825 he was a resident of Fauquier and served there as a justice.

[1042] A sheriff's margin notation reads, "No inhabitant."

[1043] James Monteith (c.1804-before 1850) was the son of Enos Monteith (born c.1780) and Eleanor Thorn (c.1778-1870).

[1044] A sheriff's margin notation reads, "No Inhabitant."

[1045] In 1843 Jesse Patterson (c.1802-1881) paid tax on 137 acres on Long Branch of Potomac Run. He was the son of Perry Patterson (1776-after 1850) and died in Stafford.

[1046] Jesse Payne was the son of Francis Payne (died c.1815). In 1835 Jesse was overseer of the road "from Accakeek run to Potomac Church" (Eby, Men 153).

[1047] Alexander Patton (c.1804-1875) may have been the son of George Gordon Patton and Sarah Stringfellow. Alexander died in Gibson County, Tennessee. In 1830 he married Anne Oakley in Madison County, Virginia.

[1048] Thornley E. Schooler (1818-1899) was the son of Henry E. Schooler (1772-1847) and Susan Bettis (1793-c.1855) of Stafford and the grandson of Thomas Schooler (born c.1723) and Mary Fant (born 1750), also of Stafford. In 1837 he tried to purchase Chelsea in Wide Water, but was unable to pay for it. Thornley died at Pleasant Home, Owen County, Kentucky.

[1049] Yelverton Shelton (c.1801-1876) was the son of William Shelton (born c.1776). Yelverton was born in Culpeper. In 1812 he married Mary Ann Cunningham in Spotsylvania. In 1842 Yelverton was accused of unlawful gambling in Fredericksburg (Fredericksburg "Commonwealth vs Hore").

[1050] A sheriff's margin notation reads, "Not an Inhabitant."

[1051] In 1825 Sidney H. Taylor was one of the founding members of Yellow Chapel, now Hartwood Presbyterian Church.

[1052] In 1829 William Thomas paid tax on 163 acres on Aquia Run. He married Sarah ___ and buried their young daughter, Mary P. (1816-1820,) and son, William (died 1826), at Macedonia Church cemetery near what is now the game station on the Quantico reservation.

1826

Seamor Walters[1055]	Juniper Walters[1056]	Daniel F. Withers[1057]
George Waller	Withers Waller	William Watson[1058]
Oliver West	William White	Henry White
John Walker	Horace Wilder	Nathaniel P. Williams
Landon Walters		

1827

Colonel—James Briggs
Captain—Benjamin Tolson, Jr. in room of John N. Tolson, resigned
Captain—"Old Artillery Company"—James W. Stone
1st Lieutenant—"Old Artillery Company"—Robert Bronaugh[1059]
2nd Lieutenant—"Old Artillery Company"—Lemuel Chadwell[1060]
Lieutenant—Levi Swetnam—in Capt. Hord's company—in room of John McFee, resigned
Regimental Clerk—Daniel Bell

Men fined for failure to appear at muster:

John Atchison	Martin Atchison	Albert Anderson
Lawrence Alexander	Luke Anderson	William Anderson
John Anderson	Edward Burrage	Thornton Browne
William Ball	Benjamin Ball	George Black
George Bowling	James Bradley	Burditt Bridges
Strother M. Burton	John Bowling	James S. Bowling
John Burton	William Bettis	William B. Burton
Reubin Bowler	Uriah Bradshaw	Peter Bowler
William Browne	Thomas Bowler	William Bloxton[1061]
John W. Byram	Bartlett Browne	Charles D. Bridwell
Elias Butchard	James Carter	Harris S. Corbin
Thomas Curtis	Benjamin Corbin	William Cox
John Craig	George Cox	Cary Cox
William Chinn	Joseph Conns	John Conyers
Thornton W. Cropp	Bailis Davis	Columbus Dickins

[1053] A sheriff's margin notation reads, "Not an Inhabitant."
[1054] A sheriff's margin notation reads, "Not an Inhabitant." Horatio Penrose Vass (c.1806-1837) was the son of James Vass (1770-1837) and Susannah Brooke (died 1816) of Falmouth. He died in Baltimore.
[1055] In 1849 Seymour Walters (died before 1870) paid tax on 103 acres on Chappawamsic Run in what is now the Quantico reservation. He was the son of Mark Walters and brother of Juniper Walters.
[1056] Juniper Walters was the son of Mark Walters of northern Stafford. In 1839 Juniper paid tax on 27 acres on Chappawamsic Run in what is now the Quantico reservation. This was part of his father's farm, which straddled the Stafford/Prince William County line (Stafford Deed Book NN, p. 225).
[1057] Daniel F. Withers was the son of Thomas Withers (1766:70-c.1826) and Grace F. Allen (1780-1855) of Stafford.
[1058] William Watson (c.1797-after 1850).
[1059] In 1828 Robert Bronaugh was granted a retail license in Stafford.
[1060] Lemuel Chadwell (c.1800-after 1850) was involved in a number of ventures. In 1830 he paid taxes on 30 slaves and 1 horse and seems to have had either business dealings or family connections with the Waller family of Clifton. In 1832 and 1835 he was one of the overseers of the road in Stafford (Eby, Men 150, 153). Exactly what brought about his turn of fortune is unknown, but by 1850 he was a resident of one of Stafford's poor farms. Most of this family lived in the vicinity of Aquia Creek and the Potomac River. There were also Chadwells in Fauquier County.
[1061] William Bloxton (c.1808-1864) left a will in Stafford and named sons Thomas, William, Jr., and Alexander by his "present" wife Mary Elizabeth. He also had son Albert by a former marriage (Stafford Deed Book TT, p. 38).

1827

James Deakins	John Dillon	Seymour Dodson
William R. Ensor	John Finnall	John Franklin
Ewel Fisher	James Fines	Thomas Fines
Martin Fugate	William Garner	Hansford Garner
Robert Green	James Graves	John Graves
Robert O. Grayson	James Green	Thomas Gill
William Green	William Gollahorn	Solomon Gollahorn
Ralph Griffis	Rosall Harding	Townsend Graves
William Harding, Jr.	Strother Harding[1062]	George Hill
Ambrose Hayden[1063]	Rawley Humphries[1064]	William Hunt
Robert S. Hooe	Joseph Hewitt	John Holloway
Bazil Holliday	Robert Hebron	Richard Hill
Marshall W. Horton	William Jackson	George Jett
Edward Jones	Noah Jones	Ambrose Jackson[1065]
Joseph M. Johnston	Azariah Jones	Isham Jordan
Elisha Jones	William Jones	John Knight
Westley Knight	John Lang	Daniel Limbrick
William Limbrick	George Lunsford	Thomas Lymbrick
Thomas Lymbrick, Jr.	John G. Masters	Willis Mills
James Monett(?)	Wiley R. Mason[1066]	James Moxley[1067]
James Monteith	John Marquiss	James Mills
William Nicholas	William P. Napier[1068]	James Newton
Alexander Obryhim	John Pates	Alexander Patton
John Pumfrey	Robert M. Patton[1069]	Richard Patterson
Sandford Payne	James L. Payne	William Payne
Harris Payne	Thomas Pollard	Robert Payne
George Payne	Rowzee Peyton	Thomas Payne
Valentine Peyton	Eli P. Perry	Richard Puzey
Alfred Rye	Archibald Rye	William Roberson
James A. Rye	John Scott	Thomas Shackleford[1070]
John Scrivner	Robert Skidmore	William Shacklett
Hanson Simms	William Snelling	Gustavus Sullivan
Jesse Snelling	Barnett Stewart	Thomas Stewart
William Stone	William Talmarsh	Lewis Timmons
Benjamin Truslow	Dolphin True	Landon Walters
Walter West	Charles Williams	William Walters[1071]
Oliver West	James White	Henry White

[1062] From about 1856-1865 Strother Harding (c.1808-1868) was a justice in Stafford.

[1063] Ambrose Hayden (1793-before 1839) was the son of William Hayden (1754-1802) and Catherine Ensey (1754-1837) of St. Mary's County, Maryland.

[1064] Rawleigh Humphrey (c.1768-c.1860) was the son of William Humphrey (died c.1799). He lived near Deep Run and between Spotted Tavern and Tackett's Mill. In 1804 he paid taxes on 125 acres in Stafford.

[1065] Ambrose Jackson (c.1806-after 1870) was a cooper and lived in Hartwood.

[1066] Wiley Roy Mason (1804-1865) was the son of Enoch Mason (1769-1828) and Lucy Wiley Roy (1798-1835) of Clover Hill. Wiley married Susan Taylor Smith (1806-1873) and died in King George County.

[1067] A margin notation stated that he was "No Inht. [Inhabitant] of Stafford."

[1068] William Parsons Napier (died c.1844) married Elizabeth Cooke and died in Caroline County.

[1069] Robert M. Patton (born 1806) was the son of George Gordon Patton and Sarah Stringfellow. He was born in Stafford and died in Ohio.

[1070] Thomas Shackelford (c.1804-before 1840) was the son of Solomon A. Shackelford (born c.1780) and Clarissa Heflin (born c.1785).

[1071] William Walters was the son of Charles Walters who owned land on the waters of Deep Run and Aquia Run (Stafford Deed Book AA, p. 162).

| Nathaniel P. Williams, Jr. | George Wilson | |

1828

Colonel—James Briggs
Captains—William Barber—2nd Regiment, 2nd Division—in room of Thomas Hill
    Robert Cropp—in room of James M. Hord, removed
    Joseph D. Withers[1072]—in room of Burkett P. Bowen, resigned
1st Lieutenant—2nd Regiment, 2nd Division—Joel J. Jameson[1073]—in room of William W.
    Peyton, resigned
2nd Lieutenant—2nd Regiment, 2nd Division—Richard M. Scott[1074]—in room of Nathaniel Barber, resigned
Regimental Clerk—Daniel Bell
Enlisted—Richard Patton

Men fined for failure to appear at muster:

Henry Atchison	William Atchison	Hugh Adie
Lewis Adie[1075]	John Atchison	John Anderson
Jesse Butler	George Bowling	John Bowling
Abijah Bowling	William Bloxham	Burdit Bridges
Elias Butchard	George Billingsley	Richard Berry
Reubin Bowler	Thomas Bowler	William Beagle[1076]
John Beagle	James Beagle	Aaron H. Ball
William Ball	Thornton Brown	Rawley Brown
William Brown	Ambros Brown[1077]	Alexander Bell
William Backster	William Bettice	James W. Byram
George Black	Charles D. Bridwell	Lewis Courtney[1078]
Elias Courtney[1079]	John Cox	Cary Cox
William Cox	George Cox[1080]	William Colbert
Zachariah Carpenter[1081]	Francis Chisom	John Cash[1082]

[1072] Joseph D. Withers (1803-after 1834) married Eliza Elzira Gatewood (born c.1803) of Caroline County. Joseph operated a store in "the Woodcutting" in the central part of the county. In 1833 he was also granted a license to keep an ordinary. In 1826 Joseph served as a constable in Stafford.

[1073] Joel James Jameson (1801-1860) was the son of John Jameson (1763-1842) and was a teacher. He lived in the northern end of Stafford County. He married Ann Morton, daughter of Richard Morton (1771-1812) and Margaret Ursula Waller (1771-1821).

[1074] Richard Marshall Scott (1807-1847) was the son of Gustavus Hall Scott (1753--1800) and Margaret Hall Caile (born 1759) of Fairfax. Richard married Eliza Alexander (born 1805) of Fredericksburg. He was buried at Dipple; later, those graves were moved to Aquia Episcopal Church.

[1075] Lewis Adie (born 1800) was the son of Benjamin Adie (1762-c.1846) and Margaret Gibson Gillison (born c.1770). Like many of the early Adies, Lewis was a carpenter, though he also served as a preacher (Stafford County Estate, 1823, p. 231, 357). Lewis later removed to Missouri.

[1076] William Beagle (c.1810-after 1860).

[1077] By 1842 Ambrose Brown and wife Elizabeth C. were living in Mercer County, Kentucky. While living in Stafford, they had owned property near Enoch Mason in Roseville. Elizabeth's maiden name may have been Kendall (Stafford Deed Book NN, p. 239).

[1078] A sheriff's margin notation reads, "No inhabitant."

[1079] Elias Courtney (c.1812-after 1850) was the son of Daniel Courtney (born c.1766) and Lucy Jones of Stafford and Fauquier. Elias' name was listed on the Fauquier censuses of 1840 and 1850 and he seems to have been unmarried.

[1080] A sheriff's margin notation reads, "No inhabitant."

[1081] Zachariah Carpenter (1775:85-after 1880) may have been the son of William Carpenter. In 1810 he was a resident of Loudoun County. In 1832 he married Catherine (Carper) Bowen (c.1800-after 1880). From 1840 until at least 1880 he lived in Frederick County, Virginia.

[1082] A sheriff's margin notation reads, "Removed."

1828

Laurence Clift[1083]	Thomas Curtis	Francis Curtis[1084]
John Craig	Benjamin Corbin	Thornton Cropp
John Conyers	William R. Combs[1085]	John Daffin
William Dunbar	Wishart Dogget[1086]	Seamour Dodson
Scott Dent	John J. Dermot[1087]	James Davis
John Davis	John Dillon	Walter R. Daniel
John M. Daniel	Patrick England	William Edwards
George Fulcher	Jarred Fugate	Martin Fugate[1088]
Thomas Fines	Walter H. Finnall	Joseph Graves
Willis Graves[1089]	James Graves	Townsend Graves
Hansford Garner	Robert O. Grayson	Elisha Green
George Green	James Green	William Gill
Thomas Gill	John Golahon	Thomas Golahon
Ralph Griffis	Robert Griffis[1090]	Richard Griffis, Jr.
Joseph Hewitt	John E. Hewitt	Robert S. Hooe[1091]
Francis H. Hooe	John Holloway	George F. G. Hedgman
Peter D. G. Hedgman	John T. Hedgman	Rosall Harding
Fielding Hudson	William Horton	Joseph Homes
George Jett	Francis Jett	Isom Jordan
Edward Jones	Noah Jones	George Jones
Ezra Jones	Elisha Jones	William Jackson
Westley Knight	John Knight[1092]	Branson Knight

[1083] Lawrence Clift (c.1807-1901) lived near Stafford Courthouse. At the time of his death, he was the oldest man in Stafford.

[1084] Francis Curtis (1806-1891) was the son of George Curtis, Jr. (c.1767-1844) and Jemima Payne (c.1774-c.1869) and he inherited his father's Ludlow farm in Hartwood. He was quite wealthy by Stafford standards and owned land in several counties. At one point, Francis owned nearly 1,000 acres in Stafford. Francis married first in Fauquier County Mary M. Stone (c.1809-1865), the daughter of William Stone. She died of typhoid fever on Mar. 23, 1865. In 1869 he married Maria A. Duffy (born 1828). Francis was killed in a wagon accident and buried at Green Meadows, part of Ludlow.

[1085] William Rousseau Combs (1784-1836) was the son of Ennis Combs (c.1752-c.1828) and Margaret Rousseau (born 1754). He married Sallie Wickliffe. In 1833 William was appointed an overseer of the poor. William's estate inventory included a parcel of china and earthenware, 1 buffet, 1 bureau, 1 clock, 3 tables, 6 large silver spoons, 12 silver teaspoons, 10 knives and forks and a box, 1 desk, 1 looking glass, 1 candle stand, 5 beds, bedsteads, and furniture, 9 Windsor chairs, 7 flag bottom chairs, and 2 old trunks (Stafford Deed Book LL, p. 412).

[1086] A sheriff's margin notation reads, "No inhabitant."

[1087] John James Dermott (c.1797-1844) was the son of James Reed Dermott (1755-1803) and Alice James (c.1770-c.1860). John was an attorney and later resided in Washington. His father taught surveying in Alexandria and was one of the assistant surveyors for the new city of Washington. John's mother, Alice James, was the daughter of John James (c.1732-c.1794) of Stafford. After James' death, Alice married a "Mr. Bird." He died and she and her children returned to Stafford where they resided with Alice's sister, Mary James (c.1773-1833) who lived just southwest of the courthouse. A margin notation in this year's militia records says that John had "Removed."

[1088] A sheriff's margin notation reads, "No inhabitant."

[1089] Willis Graves (c.1810-after 1850) was a carpenter and lived in Hartwood. On May 28, 1860 he bought 35 acres of Ariel Foote's farm in Hartwood. This was part of the property now known as Hartwood Manor on Hartwood Road (Rt. 612).

[1090] The estate of Robert Griffis (died c.1869) included 1 clock, 1 carbine, 1 pistol, household and kitchen furniture, 1 quilting frame, ½ barrel of herrings, 28 cords of wood "in the woods," 40 cords "on Landing," livestock, and farming implements valued at $965.77. Robert lived in or near Wide Water (Stafford Deed Book 26A, p. 789).

[1091] A sheriff's margin notation reads, "No inhabitant."

[1092] A sheriff's margin notation reads, "Removed."

1828

William Kendall	Robert Kendall[1093]	John Knoxville[1094]
Thornton Latham	Alexander Lang	John Lang
George Lunsford	John Limbrick	George Limbrick
Gustavus Limbrick[1095]	Thomas Limbrick	Thomas Limbrick, Jr.
William Limbrick	George Lewis	John Lewis
John Moncure	Richard C. L. Moncure[1096]	Thomas G. Moncure
Cornelius Manning	Alexander Morson	William Morson[1097]
Ransom Mountjoy	James Mountjoy	Thomas Mountjoy
Lemuel Mountjoy[1098]	Thomas Marquess	Joseph Marquess
Peter Musselman[1099]	Jesse Musselman	Fielding Monroe
John Mickie	Alexander W. Massey	James F. Murray[1100]
Sanford Mifflin	Amos Murphy	James Newton
Jarred Newton	Samuel Nicholas	Manuel Ogden
Alexander Obryhim	Harris Payne	John Payne
Robert Payne	Thomas Payne	William Payne
James L. Payne	William Pollock	Thomas Peyton
Absalom Peyton	William Peyton	Valentine Peyton
William W. Peyton	John Pates	George Purvis
Jesse Patterson	Alexander Patton	Hezekiah Pettit
Washington Queen	John Queen	Jesse Rowe
Charles Randall	William Randall	Thomas Roberson
Barcelius Roberson[1101]	Jackson Rolls[1102]	Zele Rennoe
Daniel Rolls	Gustavus Rye[1103]	James Rye
Archibald Rye	John Rogers	Francis Rollow
John Randolph	Gustavus Reed	Uriah Shackleford[1104]

[1093] Robert Kendall (1805-1827) was the son of Bird Braxton Kendall (1782-1822) of Stafford and Margaret Snape (1782-1854). In 1843 Robert paid taxes on 136 acres near Aquia Run and near what is now Ruby Post Office. He also paid tax on another 334 acres on Aquia Run that did not adjoin the first. Robert died in Fauquier.

[1094] A sheriff's margin notation reads, "Removed."

[1095] Gustavus Limbrick (1797-1867) married Ann Peyton (c.1802-1866), the daughter of Charles Peyton/Payton and Elizabeth Roberson. In 1866 John T. Roberson was accused of murdering Gustavus and his wife, Ann Limbrick. John's family claimed he was simple-minded and wouldn't have committed such a crime. Despite their arguments, John was convicted and hung for the crime. Gustavus' estate inventory consisted of farm implements, 2 shoats, 1 stack of fodder, 1 cow, 1 horse, 26 barrels of corn, and 20 acres of land ($5 per acre) all valued at $337.00 (Stafford Deed Book 26A, p. 183).

[1096] Richard Cassius Lee Moncure (1805-1882) was the son of John Moncure (1772-1822) of Clermont on Chappawamsic Creek. Richard married Mary Butler Washington Conway (born 1807), the daughter of John Moncure Conway (1779-1864) and Catherine Storke Peyton (1786-1865). R. C. L. bought Glencairne on the west side of U. S. Route 1 just to the north of Falmouth. For some 40 years he was a vestryman of St. George's Parish, Fredericksburg. From 1852-1864 he served as presiding judge of the Virginia Court of Appeals. He also represented Stafford in the Virginia House of Delegates.

[1097] William Morson (1806-c.1851) was the son of Alexander Morson (1761-1822) and Ann Casson Alexander (1781-1833).

[1098] Lemuel Mountjoy (born c.1807) was the son of William B. Mountjoy (c.1782-before 1840). It's believed that Lemuel married Mary Arrington and resided in Prince William County.

[1099] Peter Musselman (1792-1870) lived in Hartwood and died in Stafford.

[1100] A sheriff's margin notation reads, "No inhabitant."

[1101] Barcelus Roberson (c.1811-1888) was the son of George and Nancy Roberson. He was a minister and died in Stafford.

[1102] Jackson Roles/Rolls (c.1800-1882) was the son of Jesse and Rosanna Rolls. The Stafford court granted Jackson a retail license in 1828 (Eby, Men 273). He died in Stafford unmarried.

[1103] Gustavus Rye (born c.1810) married Elizabeth Garrison of Stafford. They moved to Mason County, Kentucky and raised a large family.

1828

Strother Shackleford[1105]	Thornton Shackleford	Elias Stone
James Stone	Joseph Stone	William Stone
Absalom Smith[1106]	Thomas A. Smith	John Shelton
Thornton Shelton	Worthington G. Smithers	Robert Stewart[1107]
John F. Strother[1108]	Thomas Snelling	Jesse Snelling
William Snelling	Alexander Snelling	John Scott
William Sidebottom	Gustavus Sullivan	Claibourn Simms
William Talmarsh	John A. Starke	William Tyson
John Truslow	James Thompson	Benjamin Truslow
James E. Towson[1109]	Jeremiah B. Templeman	William Trussel
James Templeman	Alexander Turner	William Walters
Nathaniel Williams	William Watts	Michael Wallace
Thomas Wallace	William Wilson[1110]	Edward Waller
George Waller	William Went	Henry White
James White	William White	Sandy Walters
Charles Warren	Charles Williams	

1829

Brigadier General—George M. Cooke
Colonel—James Briggs—in room of George M. Cooke, promoted
Lt. Colonel—Thornton Alexander—in room of James Briggs, promoted
Major—Samuel S. Brooke
Captains—Charles E. S. Fitzhugh
　　　　　___ Norman
　　　　　Robert Cropp
　　　　　William H. Hayes—in room of Joseph D. Withers, resigned
Lieutenants—John L. Alexander[1111]
　　　　　Levi Swetnam—Capt. Norman's company
　　　　　William T. Cropp[1112]—Capt. Robert Cropp's company

[1104] Uriah W. Shackelford married Diadema Hilman.
[1105] This may be Strother Henry Shackelford (born 1803) who married Anne Edwards.
[1106] Absalom Smith (1808-1841:50) was the son of Mourning Smith, Sr. (c.1777-1853) and Sally Ann Stewart (died before 1840). This family was heavily involved in the gold mines in the lower part of the county. In 1839 Absalom paid tax on 274 acres on the Rappahannock.
[1107] Robert Stewart (c.1811-1889).
[1108] John F. Strother (c.1797-c.1840) was the son of George Strother (c.1765-1811) and Sarah Kenyon (c.1770-1825) of Albion in lower Stafford. In 1839 John paid tax on 550 acres on the Rappahannock, having acquired all the interest of his sister, Mildred F. Strother (died c.1837), in the property. John's estate inventory included 8 oxen, about 20 cattle, 48 hogs, 44 sheep, 1 carriage horse, 8 other horses, 1 hay wagon, 2 ox carts, 1 turning lathe, farm and garden tools, carpenter's tools, sleigh bells, blacksmith's tools, 330 barrels of corn, 1 hair sofa, 12 drawing room chairs, a drawing room carpet, a map of the U. S., 2 pictures in frames, a rocking chair, 2 mahogany tea caddies, 21 wine glasses, 2 wine decanters, 1 china tea set, 36 yards "Double servants cloth," 2 dozen ivory handled knives and forks, 2 fowling pieces, a fishing boat and net, a carriage and harness, and 27 slaves all valued at $13,793.70 (Stafford Deed Book MM, p. 222).
[1109] James Edward Towson (1808-1888) was the son of Thomas Towson (1780-1861) and Eleanor Norman (1782-1848) of Rockdale. His first wife was Frances Isabella Hening (c.1808-1841) who is buried in the Norman cemetery at Edge Hill. James married secondly Agnes Ann Suttle (c.1811-1865), the daughter of John H. Suttle, Sr. (died c.1830) and Susan Barret Conway (died c.1838). James was buried at Mt. Paran Presbyterian Church in Randallstown, Maryland.
[1110] William Wilson was the son of Moses Wilson (c.1800-1870) of Stafford (Stafford Will Book R, p. 51).
[1111] John L. Alexander (c.1802-1854) was the son of Philip Thornton Alexander (1783-1817) of Stafford and Lucy Brooke (c.1783-after 1850).

1829

James Edrington—in Capt. John C. Edrington's company of light infantry
1st Lieutenant—Lemuel Chadwell—in James W. Stone's company of Flying Artillery
2nd Lieutenant—Thomas L. Brent[1113]—in Capt. James W. Stone's company of Flying Artillery
Ensigns—Joseph Marquess
    Charles Jones
    Lawrence B. Alexander[1114]—in Capt. John C. Edrington's company of light infantry

Men fined for failure to appear at muster:

Hugh Adie	Lewis Adie	William Adie
Laurence B. Alexander	Benjamin Ashby	Gustavus Ashby
Henry Atchison	Rodney Atchison	Ferdinand Arrington
John Butchard	Abijah Bowling	Joseph H. Bell
Francis Bell[1115]	William Backster	Rawley Brown
James Brown	James Bruce	William C. Beale
William Brooke	Timothy Bridwell	Peyton Bridwell[1116]
James Bridwell	Peter Bowler	John N. Byram
Nathaniel Barber	James W. Byram	Bernard Barber[1117]
Jesse Butler	William Bettice	John Banks
William Ball	William Beagle	James Beagle
William B. Burton	Joseph Burton	James Burton
Richard Berry	James Berry	William Bradshaw
William Bussell[1118]	George Bryant	Samuel Beavers
Thomas Burrage[1119]	Taliaferro Chadwell	Richard Coakley
John Craig	James Cave	John Combs
William R. Combs	Francis Chisom	John Conyers
Henry Camper	William Cox	Cary Cox

[1112] William T. Cropp (1804-1864) was the youngest son of James Cropp (1755-1833) and Susan Thomas (1761-1833). William married Juliet Ann James (born 1817) and lived near Spotted Tavern in Hartwood. In the 1830s William owned Cropp's Mill on Deep Run. In 1848 (and possibly other years as well) he was one of the overseers of the poor for Stafford.
[1113] Thomas Ludwell Lee Brent (1784-1847) was the son of Daniel Carroll Brent 1759-1815) and Anne Fenton Lee (born 1754) of Richland. In 1810 he traveled around Europe and returned to America with a Spanish bride. In Washington he accepted a job with State Department. In 1814 he was appointed Secretary of Legation in Spain. He worked as charge d'affaires in Spain and Portugal until 1834, though the presence of his name in the militia records proves he spent at least part of these years home in Virginia. In 1834 he returned to Virginia but decided to try the lumber business in Michigan. He invested most of his fortune buying 70,000 acres and building two sawmills and a grand house. A poor businessman, he was unable to keep up with his bills and died heavily in debt.
[1114] The son of Philip Thornton Alexander (1783-1817) and Lucy Brooke (c.1783-after 1850).
[1115] In September 1827 Joseph Grayson and wife Winney sold Francis Bell 52 acres on Silver Mine Branch in the northern part of Stafford (Stafford Deed Book GG, p. 482).
[1116] Peyton Bridwell (born c.1800) was the son of Lewis Bridwell (c.1776-c.1824) and Elizabeth Stark (born c.1780). Peyton died unmarried.
[1117] Bernard Barber (c.1808-after 1854) was the son of Edward Barber (died c.1843) of Stafford. He lived in the north end of Stafford in or near what is now the Marine Corps reservation. Around 1854 he bought Clover Hill, the old Enoch Mason farm.
[1118] William Bussell (born c.1802) was the son of Randall Bussell (born c.1776) and Frances Black (born c.1780) of Stafford. He married Amanda Acres (born c.1814) of Stafford and was a ditch digger.
[1119] Thomas Burrage was the son of Edward Burrage who came to Stafford c.1817. Thomas was a carpenter.

1829

Howard Cooper	Benjamin S. Corbin	Thomas Curtis
Fielding Curtis	Triplet Douglas[1120]	John M. Daniel
Moncure Daniel	Hugh Davis	Columbus Dickings
Patrick H. England	John F. England	John English
John Franklin	Thomas Franklin	James W. Ford
John Frazier	Leonard H. Ficklen	William H. Ficklen
James Graves	Townsend Graves	Ralph Griffis
John Gollahon	Thomas Gollahon	Solomon Gollahon
Hansford Garner	William Garner	William Green
John E. Hewitt	Peter D. G. Hedgman	John Holloway
Gustavus Hefflin	Strother Harding	John Howerson
Francis Hill	Warner Hale	Richard Jackson
James Jackson	George Jett	Peter Jett
Francis Jett	Noah Jones	Elias Jones
Roy Jones[1121]	James Jones	William Jones
Meriwether Jones	Elisha Jones	Azariah Jones
Isom Jordan	James Johnson	Joseph M. Johnson
Thomas James	Wesley Knight	Absalom King
John King	James Knoxville	William Limbrick
Vincent Limbrick	Anthony Latham	Rawley Latham
Thornton Latham	John Lang	George Lewis
George Lunsford	Joseph Marquess	James Mountjoy
Arrington Mountjoy[1122]	Thomas Mountjoy	John Marmaduke
John Moncure	Richard C. L. Moncure	William A. Moncure[1123]
Thomas G. Moncure	Jesse Musselman	Peter Musselman
John Mills	Gustavus Mills[1124]	Edmund Massey[1125]
Alexander W. Massey	Amos Murphy	Fielding Monroe
Jared Newton	James Newton	Alexander Obryhim
John Patton	James Patton	William W. Peyton
Thomas Peyton	Valentine Peyton	William Peyton
Rowzey Peyton	John Payne	James L. Payne
Thomas Payne	William Payne	Sanford Payne
Francis Rollow	Zele Renoe	Rossall Rollow
William Richards	Thomas Roberson	William Roberson
Philip Roberson	Charles Randall	William Randall
John Randall[1126]	Absalom Smith	Harris Smith

[1120] Triplett Douglas (1805-1866) was the son of Mourning Douglas (1771-1823) of Stafford. He married Eliza Whaling (c.1823-1853), the daughter of Posey Whaling. Triplett was a member of Hartwood Baptist Church and died at his residence on Potomac Run.

[1121] In 1843 Roy Jones paid taxes on 80 acres near Potomac Church.

[1122] Arrington Mountjoy (c.1800-after 1860) was the son of John Mountjoy (c.1772-c.1844) and Aurelia Reily (died 1844) of Stafford. Sometime after 1840 Arrington and wife Nancy moved to Alexander where he worked as a "scavenger." He either oversaw the removal of trash from the streets or did it himself (Kinsey 151).

[1123] William Augustus Moncure (1803-1862) was the son of John Moncure (1772-1822) and was born at Clermont. In 1828 he married Lucy Ann Gatewood (1807-1895) of Caroline County. William was educated at William and Mary and served in both houses of the Virginia Legislature. In 1834 he was granted a license to keep an ordinary in Stafford.

[1124] Gustavus Mills (died c.1844). His estate inventory consisted of 1 bellows, 1 vise, 4 tongs, 1 sledge hammer, 2 small hammers, 2 "screw wrenches," 2 set hammers, 3 punches, 1 anvil, 2 old rasps, 1 lot of iron, 1 cart, collar, and hames, and 1 gimlet all valued at $18.56 (Stafford Deed Book NN, p. 338).

[1125] Edmund W. Massey was the son of Alexander W. Massey (died c.1837). He represented King and Queen and King William counties in the Virginia Reconstruction Convention (Lowe 358).

1829

William Smith	Thomas Smith	Robert Stewart
William Stewart	Richard M. Scott	John Scott
Alexander Snelling	Jesse Snelling	Thomas Snelling
William Snelling	Hanson Simms	Coleman Shackleford[1127]
Uriah Shackleford	John Shelton	William Sidebottom
William Shacklet	William Stone	Stephen Sullivan[1128]
John Shelket[1129]	John Suttle	Jeremiah B. Templeman
James Templeman	James Thompson	Lewis Timmons
William Trussel	Benjamin Truslow	William Talmarsh
James M. Thompson	James Tyson	George Waller
Thomas Wallace	Michael Wallace	William Watts
Charles Warren		

1830

Brigadier General—George M. Cooke
Major—Jameson Corbin—2nd Battalion, 45th Regiment—in room of Samuel S. Brooke, resigned
Captains—James Stone
      George F. G. Hedgman—in room of Charles E. S. Fitzhugh
Lieutenant—William H. Stone[1130]
Ensign—James Lunsford

Men fined for failure to appear at muster:

Hugh Adie	Enoch S. Armstrong[1131]	Gustavus Ashby
Benjamin Ashby	Lawrence B. Alexander	Rodney Atchison
William Adie	Ferdinand Arrington	Henry Atchison
John W. Arrington[1132]	William Anderson	John Anderson
Abijah Bowling	Charles D. Bridwell	Timothy Bridwell[1133]
Francis Bell	William Ball	William Beagle
William Baxter	William Bussle	James W. Byram[1134]
John W. Byram	James Burton	James Berry[1135]

[1126] John Randall (1810-1869) was the son of Abraham Randall, Sr. (1780-1855). Like his father, John was a cooper. He was born in Fauquier, raised in Stafford, and died at Independent Hill, Prince William County.
[1127] Coleman Shackleford later worked as a plantation overseer for Joseph Thomas Norman of Fairfield, Culpeper County and operated Norman's gristmill there. Coleman also worked as overseer for John S. Pendleton of Culpeper. He lived at Jeffersonton.
[1128] Stephen Sullivan (c.1805-1889) died in Stafford.
[1129] John Shelkett (1793-1857) married Nancy Stark (1786-1834), the daughter of Rodham Stark (born 1786) and Phoebe Venhook of Fauquier. John and Nancy lived in the northern end of Stafford. In 1812 John paid taxes on 5 slaves, 5 horses, and Shelkett's Mill.
[1130] William Hawkins Stone (c.1809-c.1851) was the son of Barton Speake Stone. He married Mildred ___ (c.1805-1865) and lived in the southwestern part of Stafford. In 1855 he was president of the board of the overseers of the poor for Stafford.
[1131] May be Enoch Armstrong (1810-1842) married Winifred Patterson (born 1810), the daughter of Perry Patterson (1776-after 1850). His estate was inventoried by James Homes, Barnett Stewart, and William Knight (Stafford Deed Book MM, p. 426).
[1132] In 1841 John W. Arrington (1796-1878) bought Stafford Store (Stafford Deed Book MM, p. 418). A sheriff's notation on this page of the militia records stated that John W. Arrington was no longer an inhabitant of Stafford; he had removed to Fauquier. John married Sarah Franklin (1814-1889) and was buried at Cedar Run Cemetery on the Stafford/Fauquier line.
[1133] A sheriff's margin notation reads, "Remitted."
[1134] A sheriff's margin notation reads, "Not a resident."

1830

John Banks	William C. Beale	William B. Billingsley[1136]
James Bradley[1137]	Rawleigh Browne	George Black
Richard Bowling[1138]	Samuel Beavers	Jesse Butler
Burdit Bridges	William Bradshaw	James Bruce
William Bettice	Peter Bowler	John Brown[1139]
Joseph H. Bell[1140]	William B. Burton	Nathaniel Barber
Edward Burrage	Joseph Burton	Henry Camper
Joseph Carpenter	Francis Chisum	Michael Carney
James Cave	James M. Coakley	Esom Coppage
Taliaferro Chadwell	Howard Cooper	Cary Cox[1141]
William Cox	John Craig[1142]	Fielding Curtis
Thomas Curtis	James Curtis	John Conyers
Benjamin S. Corbin	John M. Combs[1143]	Hugh Davis
Columbus Dickens	Samuel G. Daniel[1144]	Richard Dikes
Edward Dickinson	George Dye	William Edwards
John F. England[1145]	Patrick H. England	John English
William R. Ensor	William H. Ficklen[1146]	John Frazier
Strother Ficklen	Leonard H. Ficklen	Thomas Finnall[1147]
John Franklin	John Fristoe	Yelverton Garrison
John Gollahon[1148]	Solomon Gollehorne[1149]	Ralph Griffis[1150]
Robert Griffis[1151]	William Gill[1152]	Willis Graves[1153]
Townsend Graves	James Graves	Hensford Garner
Benjamin Guy, Jr.	Robert O. Grayson	Duff Green
William Garner	Thomas Gollahon[1154]	Ezekiel H. Glasscock[1155]
Sydney Green	Strother Harding	Warner Hales[1156]

[1135] A sheriff's margin notation reads, "Not found."

[1136] In 1830 William B. Billingsley was a trustee for the town of Falmouth and was appointed overseer of the streets for one year (Town 50).

[1137] A sheriff's margin notation reads, "No inhabitant."

[1138] May be Richard W. Bowling (1808-1859), the son of Lawrence Bowling (born 1772). He was born in Stafford and died in Fredericksburg. He married Eliza Lewis (born c.1817).

[1139] A sheriff's margin notation reads, "Not found."

[1140] A sheriff's margin notation reads, "No inhabitant."

[1141] A sheriff's margin notation reads, "Removed."

[1142] A sheriff's margin notation reads, "No inhabitant."

[1143] In 1823 John M. Combs married Elizabeth Million, the daughter of Cuthbert Million.

[1144] Samuel Greenhow Daniel (1810-1865) was the son of Travers Daniel (1763-1813) and Mildred Stone (1772-1837). His first wife was Margaret (Richardson) Lewis, widow of Dr. Richmond Lewis (c.1754-1831). He married secondly Maria K. Henderson (died c.1837). Samuel was trained in the law, but gave up that profession to become editor of the Fredericksburg newspaper, *The Democratic Recorder*.

[1145] A sheriff's margin notation reads, "No inhabitant."

[1146] A sheriff's margin notation reads, "No inhabitant."

[1147] Thomas Finnall was the son of Robert Monteith Finnall (1775-1847) and Mary Rollow (born c.1780). In 1830 the Stafford court granted him a liquor license (Eby, Men 279). That same year he married Ann F. Ballard.

[1148] A sheriff's margin notation reads, "No inhabitant."

[1149] A sheriff's margin notation reads, "No inhabitant."

[1150] A sheriff's margin notation reads, "No inhabitant."

[1151] A sheriff's margin notation reads, "No inhabitant."

[1152] A sheriff's margin notation reads, "No inhabitant."

[1153] A sheriff's margin notation reads, "No inhabitant."

[1154] A sheriff's margin notation reads, "No inhabitant."

[1155] Ezekiel H. Glasscock (1797-1839) was the son of Benjamin P. Glascock (1760-1827) and Peggy Floweree of Fauquier. He married Maryann Wolf.

1830

Gustavus Hefflin	Alfred Harding	Harris Hill[1157]
John Holloway[1158]	John Howison[1159]	John Hore[1160]
Alfred C. Hayes	Peter D. G. Hedgman	Joseph W. Honey[1161]
George Jett[1162]	James Johnson[1163]	Burkit Johnston[1164]
Joseph M. Johnston	Richard Jackson	Azariah Jones
Merewether Jones	Elisha Jones	Isom Jordan
Absalom King	James Knoxville	John King
Wesley Knight	George Lunsford	John Lang
William Limbrick	Anthony Latham	George Latham[1165]
Raleigh Latham	Thornton Latham	George Lewis
Lewis Lunsford[1166]	Joseph Marquess[1167]	Alexander McPherson[1168]
Cornelius Mannon	Gustavus Mills	John Mills
Christopher Musselman	Jesse Mussleman	Peter Mussleman
Fielding Monroe	John Moncure[1169]	Arrington Mountjoy
Thomas Mountjoy	Amos Murphy[1170]	Thomas G. Moncure
Henry Moncure[1171]	Richard C. L. Moncure	Jared Newton
James Newton	Alexander Obryhim	Robert Payne[1172]
Rowzey Peyton	James L. Payne[1173]	Valentine Peyton

[1156] A sheriff's margin notation reads, "Not found."

[1157] Harris Hill (1809-1908) married Mary A. Latham (c.1812-1864), the daughter of George Latham (c.1780-c.1846) of Spotted Tavern. A notation this year said "Removed." An 1855 newspaper announced the arrest of Harris for the murder of John Limerick (*Virginia Herald*, Jan. 8, 1855). In 1860 Harris was appointed tax collector and constable of Falmouth and was a trustee from then until at least 1866 (Town, 83, 84).

[1158] A sheriff's margin notation reads, "No inhabitant."

[1159] A sheriff's margin notation reads, "Remitted by the court martial."

[1160] John Hore (died c.1865) was a stone mason and in 1826 was hired to do stonework on the Stafford jail. (Fredericksburg, "Dickinson's Admr vs Tyler's Admr"). His will mentioned grand niece Martha Jeffries and nephew John Hore Hickerson and asked that all his slaves be freed (Stafford Will Book R, p. 13). His estate included farm implements, 3 cattle, 5 sheep, and household and kitchen furniture valued at $194.35 (Stafford Deed Book AA, p. 56). John lived in the vicinity of Warrenton Road (U.S. Route 17) and Poplar Road (Route 616).

[1161] Joseph Wiley Honey (1810-1879) was a merchant and kept a store in Falmouth. He served as a town trustee in 1849 and possibly during other years as well (Town 66). In 1885 he married Jane Amanda Harding (1813-1880), the daughter of Mark Harding (died c.1873).

[1162] A sheriff's margin notation reads, "No inhabitant."

[1163] A sheriff's margin notation reads, "Not found."

[1164] A sheriff's margin notation reads, "Not found." In 1829 Burkett G. Johnston paid tax on 150 acres near Hartwood. In 1824 Burkett G. Johnston advertised the Broadfield Races to be held near his tavern about six miles above Falmouth. He added the note, "Great sport expected and good accommodations furnished at my House, and on the field" (*Virginia Herald*, Aug. 25, 1824).

[1165] On May 22, 1843 George Latham executed a deed of trust to secure a debt of $8,000 due Gould Phinney. As collateral he used 11 slaves, all his household and kitchen furniture, and 906 acres, part of which was part of Parke (Stafford Deed Book NN, p. 150). In 1848 (and possibly other years as well) George was one of the overseers of the poor for Stafford.

[1166] A sheriff's margin notation reads, "Removed."

[1167] A sheriff's margin notation reads, "No inhabitant."

[1168] A sheriff's margin notation reads, "No inhabitant." Alexander McPherson (died c.1865) was born in Maryland. By 1838 was in Belmont County, Ohio.

[1169] A sheriff's margin notation reads, "Remitted by the court martial."

[1170] A sheriff's margin notation reads, "No inhabitant."

[1171] May be Henry Wood Moncure (1800-1866) who married Catherine Cary Ambler (1802-1850).

[1172] A sheriff's margin notation reads, "No inhabitant."

[1173] A sheriff's margin notation reads, "Not found in my Bailiwick."

1830

Sanford Payne[1174]	William Payne	Thomas Payne
Thomas J. Payne	Thomas Peyton	William W. Peyton
William Randall	Charles Randall	John Randall
Zele Renow	Franklin Richards[1175]	Lyburn Rogers
Thomas Roberson[1176]	William Richards	William Roberson
Francis Rollow[1177]	Philip Roberson[1178]	Jackson Rolls
Henry L. Rogers	John Scott	Richard M. Scott
John Shelton[1179]	Harris Smith	Absalom Smith[1180]
Thomas Smith	William Smith[1181]	Thomas Snelling
William Snelling	Stephen Sullivan	George G. Shelton
William Sidebottom	Hanson Simms	William Shacklett
Coleman Shackleford	Thomas Shackleford[1182]	Strother Shackleford
Robert Stewart	William Stewart	Thomas Stewart
Richard Stone[1183]	George Stone	John H. Suttle[1184]
James Templeman	James M. Thompson	William Talmarsh
James Thompson	Lewis Timmons	William D. Timmons
James E. Towson	Benjamin Truslow	William Truslow
James N. Tolson	James Tyson	Robert Tyson[1185]
William Tyson	Thomas Wallace	Sandy Watters[1186]
Charles Warren	John P. Williams	William Watts
Alexander P. Williams[1187]	Benjamin Williams, Jr.[1188]	James Wilson[1189]

[1174] A sheriff's margin notation reads, "No inhabitant."

[1175] This may be Benjamin Franklin Richards (1806-after 1879), the son of Capt. James Richards and Winifred Berry Benson (1782-1856). In 1833 Franklin was overseer of the road "from Richards' Ferry to the Yellow Chapel" (Eby, Men 151). He married Dulcibella C. Benson. A sheriff's margin notation on this page of the militia records reads, "No inhabitant."

[1176] A sheriff's margin notation reads, "Remitted by court martial."

[1177] A sheriff's margin notation reads, "No inhabitant."

[1178] A sheriff's margin notation reads, "No inhabitant."

[1179] A sheriff's margin notation reads, "No inhabitant."

[1180] A sheriff's margin notation reads, "No inhabitant."

[1181] A sheriff's margin notation reads, "No inhabitant."

[1182] A sheriff's margin notation reads, "Dead."

[1183] This may be Richard Stone who was the daughter of Richard Stone (died 1825) and Hannah Withers (c.1774-1857) of Mt. Olive, Stafford County. In 1828 Richard married Eliza Ann Evans in Fauquier County.

[1184] John H. Suttle (c.1807-1884) was the son of John H. Suttle, Sr. (died c.1830) and Susan "Sukey" Barret Conway (died c.1838). From 1883-1884 John was commonwealth's attorney for Stafford. He resided at The Fleurry's, which later became Aquia Town Center. Around 1840 he married Catherine Tolson (died 1844), the daughter of Benjamin Tolson (c.1763-1838). In October 1864 the Stafford court approved John's motion "being an application for the exemption of certain citizens of Stafford County from Military duty…Whereas the County of Stafford has been greatly wasted & destroyed by the public enemy & her Citizens from their position being unable to provide supplies unless they produce them from the soil & a very large proportion of the effective labour of the County being now in the Confederate service & another large proportion of said labour with the means of subsistence having been carried off by the enemy thereby reducing the inhabitants to a very reduced means of living and whereas There is now progressing in the County a most sweeping & undiscriminate [sic] Conscription taking the heads of families & others whose services are indispensable to supply the means of life to their families & the families of others who are now in the Confederate service—Resolved that the facts be communicated to the Governor of this Commonwealth and the Hon. Sect. War with the request that such persons only should be taken who can be spared for the public service" (Stafford Court Minute Book 1852-1867, p. 416).

[1185] By 1838 Robert Tyson was living in Culpeper.

[1186] A sheriff's margin notation reads, "No inhabitant."

Nathaniel P. Williams, Jr.	William Wilson	Walter West
James West		

1831

Brigadier General—George M. Cooke[1190]
Major—Jameson Corbin
Captains—Burkett P. Bowen—in Maj. Jameson Corbin's 2nd Battalion
    Uriah H. Bradshaw[1191]
    Joel J. Jameson—Troop of Horse
    Enoch Mason—Stafford Guards
Lieutenants—Henry W. Queen[1192]—Maj. Jameson Corbin's 2nd Battalion
    Thomas H. C. Daniel[1193]
    William Ford
1st Lieutenant—William Dickinson
2nd Lieutenant—Edward Burrage

[1187] Alexander P. Williams married Margaret E. Hore (born 1811), the daughter of Walter Hore (1781-1858) and Margaret Williams (died 1859).
[1188] Benjamin Williams, Jr. In 1832 he owned a blacksmith shop near Aquia Run.
[1189] In 1839 James Wilson paid tax on 24 acres near Ramoth Church.
[1190] On Sept. 13, 1831 George M. Cooke wrote to the governor of Virginia:
"Sir, The excitement produced in the portion of the County by the late occurrences in Southampton and its neighborhood has made it my duty to bring to your notice the defenceless [sic] condition of the white population and the danger to which they are exposed.
    The Militia are without Arms in every County of my Brigade, comprising the Counties of Fauquier, Prince William, Stafford and King George in all which there is an ___ slave population. In this County we are peculiarly situated in reference to that people.
    The Stone quarries worked in Stafford employ a large number of Negroes say 100 men, in the immediate neighborhood of which on a single estate there are as many more and in the improvement of the Rappahannock River a large number are constantly employed so that, if any design should be suggested concert would be easy.
    Since the affair of Southampton we conceive, that in the deportment of our slaves a manifest degree of imprudence is to be discovered. They have circulating amongst them a printed paper, styled the African Hymn breathing a high spirit of rebellion. We ___ are in progress to learn from whence it has sprung.
    I ask leave to suggest the propriety of immediately arming such portions of the Militia of these counties as the situation of the population may seem to require, and particularly the County of Stafford where peculiar population and location demands attention. Should it be deemed inexpedient to arm the whole Militia and I incline to that opinion the arms might be distributed at the direction of the Commandant of the Regt. in each County. It will be peculiarly proper to arm the Cavalry for the strength and description of the Militia of my Brigade I refer you to the Adjt. Genl. Having frequent and urgent calls on me upon this subject, should be pleased to hear from you as early as our attention can be brought to the subject of this letter. Very respectfully Your Obt. Srt. Geo. M. Cooke Brigr. Genl. 5th Brigade 2 Divs. Va Ml." (Gov. John Floyd).
    Shortly thereafter, Cooke wrote to Duff Green of Falmouth and informed Green that the governor had promised to send "an early supply of Arms," which Cooke expected to be shipped to Fredericksburg (Letter, George M. Cooke).
[1191] Uriah Hugh Bradshaw (1805-1865) was the son of Harberson Bradshaw. In February 1843 Joseph B. Ficklen of Falmouth sold to Uriah, then of Fredericksburg, 206 acres in Stafford adjoining the lands of Harberson Bradshaw, Moffett, and Thomas S. Harding (Stafford Deed Book NN, p. 98).
[1192] Henry Washington Queen. In 1831 and 1833 he was granted licenses to keep an ordinary in Stafford. During the War Between the States, the Queen family owned a farm near the present Stafford landfill.
[1193] Thomas H. Cushing Daniel (c.1811-1896) was the son of Dr. John Moncure Daniel (1769-1813). In 1835 he married Eliza Mason Bronaugh (1811-1889), the daughter of John W. Bronaugh, Sr. and Ann Eilbeck.

1831

Ensigns—William Bloxham—in Maj. Jameson Corbin's 2nd Battalion
Thompson M. Bloxham[1194]
John Coakley
Edward Waller

1832

Lt. Colonel—Thornton Alexander—1st Battalion
Major—Jameson Corbin—2nd Battalion
Captains—James Edrington—1st Battalion
James W. Stone—2nd Battalion
Lieutenant—Robert L. Waple—1st Battalion
Ensign—James Shackelford[1195]—1st Battalion

1833

Colonel—Enoch Mason—in room of James Briggs, resigned
Lt. Colonel—Joel J. Jameson—in room of Thornton Alexander, "removed from county"
Major—William H. Stone
Captains—James Edrington
James W. Stone
William H. Stone—in room of Jameson Corbin, resigned
John W. Queen—in room of Capt. Pratt
Lieutenants—Robert Waple
Thomas K. Newton
Surgeon—Alexander H. Fitzhugh
Quartermasters—Joseph B. Ficklen
William H. Fitzhugh
Paymaster—Samuel S. Brooke
Sergeants—John M. Daniel
John M. Conway, Jr.
Adjutant—Alexander H. Mason[1196]
Ensign—Gustavus B. Newton[1197]

1834

Captains—Henry W. Queen—in room of _____ Pratt, resigned
Sanford Cooper[1198]—in room of Joel J. Jameson, promoted
Rosel Rollow—in room of Benjamin P. Tolson,[1199] resigned

[1194] Thompson M. Bloxham married Polly Bloxham, daughter of his uncle, Samuel Bloxham (died 1817).

[1195] James H. Shackelford (c.1806-after 1850).

[1196] Dr. Alexander Hamilton Mason (1807-1858) was the son of Enoch Mason (c.1769-1828) and Lucy Wiley Roy (1798-1835) of Clover Hill. Alexander received his medical training at the University of Virginia. In 1831 he married Jane Allen Smith, the daughter of Augustine Jaqueline Smith of Fairfax County. Alexander lived in Falmouth and served as a town trustee from at least 1858-1860 (Town 77, 78, 81, 83). His estate included 250 acres near Falmouth, a house and two lots in Falmouth, 16 slaves, a set of French china, a pair of fruit stands, a tea set, 1 clock, 1 lounge, a writing desk, 3 rocking chairs, 3 wardrobes, 2 sofas, 15 counterpanes, a piano and chair, 6 mahogany chairs and 1 marble table all valued at $15,443.50 (Stafford Deed Book RR, p. 439).

[1197] Gustavus Buchanan Newton (born 1809) was the son of Benjamin Newton (born 1769) and Nancy Butler and the twin of Abraham B. Newton. His first wife was Matilda Cox. He married secondly Eleanor Monteith. Gustavus made a raid on the Union camp at Belle Plains. He and friends stole a wagon of supplies and had Temple Lomax, a local Black man, drive the wagon. The men buried the goods and dug them up later when it was safe.

[1198] In 1836 Sanford Cooper was granted a retail license for his store in the town of Aquia/Woodstock (Eby, Men 259).

1834

Thompson M. Bloxham—in room of George F. G. Hedgman, resigned
Lieutenant—John L. Alexander
1st Lieutenant—James H. Garrison[1200]—2nd Cavalry
2nd Lieutenant—John R. Queen[1201]
Cornet—Fielding L. Clift[1202]
Ensign—Alexander W. Skidmore

1836

Captains—Henry W. McInteer[1203]—in room of Rosil Rollow, resigned
  Charles F. Suttle[1204]—Capt. of Artillery company at Aquia—in room of James W. Stone, resigned
  Charles W. Stone[1205]—Militia Company at White Oak—in room of Henry W. Queen
  William T. Cropp—in room of Robert Cropp
  Dudley Shackelford[1206]—in room of James W. Stone, resigned
  Henry S. Mintern
Lieutenants—Edward Latham[1207]—in room of William T. Cropp, resigned
  John L. Alexander—in room of Henry W. Queen, removed
1st Lieutenant—James E. Towson—Artillery company at Aquia
2nd Lieutenants—James H. Shackelford[1208]—Artillery company at Aquia
  Fielding L. Clift
3rd Lieutenant—Amos Jones[1209]

1837

Commandant—Charles F. Suttle
Colonel—William H. Stone
Colonel—Joel J. Jameson—in room of Enoch Mason, deceased

[1199] Benjamin P. Tolson (1800-1879) was the son of George H. Tolson (c.1779-1832) and Sythia "Seth" Combs. He married Prudence Payne (c.1811-1855), the daughter of Ledman/Ledmus G. Payne (1780-1881). Benjamin's estate inventory included 1 English clock, 3 bedsteads, household and kitchen furniture, 1 press, 2 looking glasses, 1 flax wheel, 1 settee, and 7 chairs all valued at $60.25 (Stafford Deed Book 3, p. 453).
[1200] James H. Garrison married Mary Cooper.
[1201] In 1830 and 1832 John R. Queen was granted licenses to keep an ordinary in Stafford.
[1202] Fielding Lawrence Clift (born 1807) was the son of Fielding Clift (c.1774-1856) and Elizabeth "Sallie" Elkins. In 1859 he served as a justice in Stafford. He married Ann Rollins.
[1203] May be William Henry McInteer (born 1810), the son of William McInteer and Adah Harding (1790-1856).
[1204] Charles Francis Suttle (1807-1881) was the son of John H. Suttle, Sr. (died c.1830) and Susan Barret Conway (died c.1838). A merchant, he kept stores at Falmouth, Aquia, and Alexandria. Charles served as a trustee of Falmouth from at least 1851-1852 (Town 72, 73, 76). He married Emily L. Taliaferro (1822-1903) and died in Rocky Mount, Virginia.
[1205] Charles W. Stone (died 1842) was the son of Richard Stone (died 1825) and Hannah Withers (c.1774-1857) of Mt. Olive, Stafford County.
[1206] Dudley Shackelford (c.1799-1885) married Lucy Maddox, the daughter of Basil and Margaret Maddox and the widow of Peter Jett. In the 1830s Dudley fell deeply in debt to a long list of creditors and conveyed everything he owned to R. C. L. Moncure, trustee (Stafford Deed Book LL, p. 1).
[1207] Edward Washington Latham (1811-1851) was the son of Jesse Latham (born c.1785) and Betsy P. Horton of Fauquier. Edward was a blacksmith and died unmarried.
[1208] James H. Shackelford's estate inventory included 2 book cases, 1 poplar press, 2 bureaus, 1 looking glass, 1 pine table, 1 settee, 1 bed, household and kitchen furniture, 5 hogs, 1 bellows, 1 anvil, 1 vise, screw plates, tongs and hammers, 1 unfinished buggy body, and several cart wheels all valued at $108.93 (Stafford Deed Book MM, p. 239).
[1209] Amos Jones (c.1812-1898) was the son of Thomas Jones (died c.1807) of Ludlow, part of which is now Seven Lakes subdivision. Amos was of Quaker descent though three of his sons served in the Confederate military.

Major—William H. Stone
Captains—Richard B. Alexander[1210]—"Church Company"
    Robert L. Waple—in room of James Edrington
    James W. Stone—Riflemen
    William Cropp
1st Lieutenants—Stephen Sullivan—"Church Company"
    Amos Jones—Troop of Cavalry
    Josiah F. Bayly[1211]—Falmouth Company
    James R. Benson[1212]—William Cropp's company
    James Jones—Robert Waple's company
    Thomas A. Withers[1213]—Riflemen
2nd Lieutenants—Samuel Humphries[1214]—"Church Company"
    Robert Taylor—Troop of Cavalry
    Robert Hefling—Troop of Cavalry
    Yelverton Garrison—Artillery Company, 2nd Regiment, 2nd Div.
    Thomas Griffis[1215]—Artillery Company, 2nd Regiment, 2nd Div.
    Edward W. Latham[1216]—William Cropp's company
    Robert Flatford[1217]—Robert Waple's company
    Thomas Masters[1218]—Riflemen

[1210] Richard B. Alexander (c.1811-after 1850) was the son of Philip Thornton Alexander (1783-1817) of Salisbury, Stafford County, and Lucy Brooke (c.1783-after 1850). Richard worked as a railroad agent.

[1211] Josiah F. Bayly (1810-1862). In 1850 Josiah and his family were residents of Fredericksburg. By 1860 he and his family were included in the 1860 census of the District of Columbia where he worked as a saddler and harness maker and was living with wife Susanna (c.1820-1889) and two daughters, Esther A. (born c.1846) and Ellen Frances (born c.1851). Josiah died of smallpox in Georgetown, DC and was buried in Congressional Cemetery.

[1212] James R. Benson (1814-c.1890) was the son of William Willis Lewis Benson (died 1815) and Eleanor Bullard (1786-1846). In 1843 (and possibly other years as well) he served as a justice in Stafford.

[1213] Thomas Allen Withers (c.1814-c.1865) was the son of Thomas F. Withers (died c.1826) and Gracie F. Allen (died 1855). Thomas served as a constable in Stafford 1854-1861. He also kept a store near Poplar Road.

[1214] Samuel Humphries (c.1808-after 1850) was a shoemaker in Falmouth. He served as a town trustee from at least 1847-1849.

[1215] Thomas S. Griffis (1794-1886) was a veteran of the War of 1812. In 1857 he bought all James Stark's interest in 42 acres on Chappawamsic Run he and Thomas had bought from William Fitzhugh. In 1833 Thomas was one of the overseers of the road in Stafford. In 1866 he was overseer "from the Aquia Road near Gravelly Ridge to Telegraph Road" (Eby, Men 173). Thomas died in Stafford and was buried on the Quantico reservation just west of Interstate 95 and a short distance south of Telegraph Road (Route 637). His wife, Mary (1793-1836) was buried on the east side of Barrett Heights Road (Route 642) just off Garrisonville Road (Route 610). During the War Between the States, Thomas claimed to be a Unionist. In his Southern Claims Commission deposition he said he had been arrested by the Confederates, taken to Brook's Station and confined there for two days and nights. He was then forced to take an oath of loyalty to the Confederacy. An old man at that time, he feared being jailed at Richmond and took the oath, though on several occasions thereafter he threatened to destroy the flag of secession when it was raised (Southern Claims Commission. Approved. Claim #42997, p. 2).

[1216] Edward Washington Latham (1811-1851) was the son of Jesse Latham (died c.1826) and Betsy P. Horton. From 1839 until his death, Edward was post master at the Spottedville (Spotted Tavern) Post Office. He died unmarried.

[1217] Robert Flatford (c.1810-1892) was a Scottish immigrant and dry goods merchant in the northern part of Stafford. He married Jane Harding (died 1851). Robert resided in a log house across Garrisonville Road from what is now North Stafford High School. This old house remains standing and was later owned by Adolf Bartness. Robert's son, Robert Lawrence Flatford (1852-1898) lived on the site of the high school.

1837

3rd Lieutenants—Robert S. Mills[1219]—William Cropp's company
John F. Bell[1220]—Riflemen

1838

Lt. Colonel—Robert Cropp—in room of Joel J. Jameson, resigned
Colonel—William H. Stone
Major—Charles F. Jones[1221]—in room of William H. Stone, resigned
Captain—John L. Alexander—in room of Charles F. Jones, promoted

1839

Lt. Colonel—Charles F. Suttle—in room of Robert Cropp, promoted
Captain—James Montieth
Captain of Artillery—John F. Bell—in room of Charles Suttle, promoted
1st Lieutenants—William B. Ball[1222]
Caleb Sullivan[1223]—in room of William B. Ball
2nd Lieutenant—Robert Truslow[1224]

1840

Colonel Commandant—William H. Stone
Captains—Thomas B. Pickitt[1225]—in room of Richard B. Alexander, resigned
George S. M. Payne[1226]—in room of Henry S. McInteer,[1227] deceased
George H. Leach[1228]—in room of Dudley Shackelford, resigned
Robert L. Waple—light infantry
1st Lieutenants—Charles S. Petty[1229]—in room of Josiah F. Bailey who failed to qualify
Benjamin F. Ashby[1230]—in room of Benjamin Wamsley,[1231] resigned

---

[1218] Thomas Masters, Jr. (born c.1811) was the son of Thomas Masters (c.1775-after 1850) and lived in Hartwood.

[1219] Robert S. Mills (born c.1811) was the son of John Mills (born c.1783) and Phoebe Stevens (born c.1780). Around 1841 he married Lucy Ann Lampkin (born c.1822) of Rockingham County, Virginia. Robert was a boot and shoemaker.

[1220] John Fendall Bell (c.1802-c.1847) was the son of Ashley Bell and Susannah Southerland. He married Jane Adie (1800-1886), the daughter of William Adie (1766-c.1824).

[1221] In 1827 Charles married Sophia Stifle of Fredericksburg.

[1222] William B. Ball (died before 1849) owned land in White Oak. He was the son of Aaron H. Ball (1792-1839).

[1223] Caleb Sullivan (c.1815-after 1850).

[1224] In 1847 Robert Truslow (c.1817-after 1850) married Orpha L. Fugett of Falmouth. She was Orpha Sullivan, daughter of Martin Sullivan and widow of Jarret (Gerrard) Fugate. In 1841 the Stafford court granted her a retail license Eby, Men 261).

[1225] During the 1840s, Thomas B. Pickett was a retail merchant in Fredericksburg.

[1226] George Samuel Major Payne (1814-1892) was the son of Richard Payne (1763-1843) and Susannah Kelly (1768-1792). He was born at Bleak House, Culpeper County and married Frances Merriman Fant (born 1819) of Culpeper. She was the daughter of John Penn Fant who had family in Stafford.

[1227] Henry S. McInteer (c.1805-1839) may have married Sarah Gray. His will mentioned wife Sarah Gray McInteer (1808-after 1860) and daughter Miriam Eliza (born 1831). He ordered that the "ungovernable woman named Celia" be sold (Stafford Deed Book LL, p. 530).

[1228] George H. Leitch was the son of George Leitch of Falmouth and had sisters Harriet and Sophia T. Leitch (Stafford Deed Book MM, p. 103).

[1229] Charles S. Petty (c.1812-1877) was a tailor, probably in Falmouth. He died of consumption.

[1230] Benjamin Franklin Ashby (died 1843). His very modest estate consisted of 1 gun, 4 chairs, 1 saddle, 1 bridle, 1 martingale, 1 watch and key, 1 colt, and "3 Vols Scottish Chiefs" (Stafford Deed Book NN, p. 304).

1840

2nd *Lieutenant* (Infantry)—Joseph Golatt[1232]—in room of Robert Flatford, removed

1841

Colonel Commandant—William H. Stone
Lt. Colonel—Charles F. Suttle
Major—William T. Cropp—in room of Charles W. Jones,[1233] resigned
Captains—James R. Benson—in room of William T. Cropp, promoted
    John W. D. Ford[1234] (Artillery)—in room of John F. Bell, resigned
    James W. Stone (Riflemen)
    Charles S. Petty—in room of George Leitch, resigned
    Joseph Golatt—in room of Robert L. Waple, resigned
    William Brent[1235]—in room of Robert B. Taylor,[1236] failed to qualify
    Robert Taylor—in room of Sanford Cooper, resigned
    James Monteith
    Thomas B. Pickett
Lieutenants—Amos Jones—in room of Fielding L. Clift, resigned
    Thomas K. Newton
1st *Lieutenants*—Aquilla Randall[1237]—in room of James Jones, resigned
    Peter Wigginton[1238]—in room of Amos Jones—failed to qualify
    William Ashby—in room of Benjamin Ashby, removed
    John L. Alexander
    Stephen Sullivan
    Samuel Humphreys[1239]
    Thomas A. Withers
    Thomas Masters
    Robert Flatford
    Calep Sullivan
    Alexander B. Jones[1240]

[1231] Benjamin C. Wamsley (c.1814-1886) married Eliza F. Shelkett (c.1827-1879), the daughter of John and Nancy Shelkett of Stafford. Benjamin lived near what is now Apple Grove subdivision on the north side of Garrisonville Road. He died of "sciatic rheumatism."

[1232] Joseph Golatt (c.1816-1879) was the son of Joseph Golatt and was born in Stafford. The elder Joseph was a carpenter. The younger Golatt married Harriet E. ___ and lived on Aquia Run. In 1869 Joseph served as a magistrate in Stafford (Eby, Men 85). He died of typhoid fever.

[1233] In 1839 Charles W. Jones paid tax on 900 acres on Aquia Creek and 206 acres on Accokeek Run. He resided on part of the old Coal Trips farm on Aquia Creek.

[1234] John William Duncan Ford (1812-1876) was the son of Capt. William Ford (1788-1834) and his first wife, Deborah Thompson Duncan (died 1813). John died unmarried.

[1235] Also known as William Brent, Jr. (1783-1848), he was the son of Daniel Carroll Brent of Richland of Wide Water. He married first Winifred Beale Lee (1790-1833) and secondly Roxanna Sommers (1798-1882) about whom very little is known.

[1236] Robert Bruce Taylor (1818-1883) was the son of Robert Taylor (died c.1842) and the brother of John L. Taylor and Anne F. (Taylor) Mansfield (Stafford Deed Book OO, p.242).

[1237] Aquilla Randall (c.1816-1904) was a carpenter and moved to Stafford from Maryland. He never drank intoxicants and was a member of the Methodist Church. He died in Warrenton at the home of his daughter, Laura Robinson and was buried in Warrenton (*Free Lance*, July 2, 1904).

[1238] Peter Wigginton (1793-1862) was the son of William Wigginton (1749-1829) and owned and operated what later became known as Masters' Mill on Aquia Run. Prior to marrying Nancy Masters, Peter signed a marriage contract in which he agreed that any property that Nancy owned or acquired before or during their marriage would remain in her control free "from any liability of [Peter's] future and present creditors" (Stafford Deed Book NN, p. 325). Peter's estate included 2 cows, 1 old cart wheel, 1 old cart body, 2 saws and a bellows frame, farm implements, 2 tables, 1 desk, 2 beds, 2 lamps, 10 hogs, and some books all valued at $156.45 (Stafford Deed Book 26A, p. 55).

[1239] Samuel Humphreys (c.1808-after 1850) was a shoemaker.

1841

2nd Lieutenants—William Randall
    Rodney B. Bradshaw[1241]—in room of James R. Benson, promoted
    Gustavus S. Taliaferro[1242]—in room of Fielding L. Clift, resigned
    William F. Carter[1243]
    John F. Bell
    Robert S. Mills
Ensigns—Gustavus V. Newton[1244]
    Alexander W. Skidmore

1842

Captains—James M. Taliaferro[1245]—in room of Charles S. Petty, resigned
    Benjamin F. Ashby—in room of George S. M. Payne, removed
    John W. D. Ford
    William Brent
    James Monteith
    Joseph Golatt
    Robert L. Waple—in room of Thomas B. Pickett, removed
1st Lieutenants—George W. Conway[1246]—(Cavalry, 5th Brigade, 2nd Div.)
    John M. Edrington[1247]—in room of Charles S. Petty, promoted
    Alfred Wariner—in room of Calip Sullivan, failed to qualify
    Peter D. Lowry[1248]
2nd Lieutenants—William S. Embrey
    Charles E. Gill[1249]—in room of Yelverton Garrison, resigned

---

[1240] Alexander B. Jones (1828-after 1850) was the son of Thomas Jones (died 1842) and Ann Judd (c.1791-1856). Ann married secondly Edward Pilcher (c.1785-after 1850). In 1849 Alexander paid tax on 105 acres on Deep Run and was the son of Thomas Jones (died c.1807) of Ludlow.

[1241] Rodney B. Bradshaw was the son of Harberson Bradshaw (c.1785-1843). He was born in Stafford and died in King George. In 1850 he was working as a clerk in Fauquier. For a while he operated a store at Stafford Courthouse and in 1858 was elected lieutenant colonel of the 45th Virginia militia. During the War Between the States, he served in Cooper's Battalion.

[1242] Gustavus Sydney Taliaferro (c.1796-1877) was the son of James G. Taliaferro and Wilhelmina Wishart of King George. He died unmarried.

[1243] William Fristoe Carter (c.1818-c.1857) was the son of Sanford Carter (c.1785-c.1872) and Hannah Read. William was named for a minister at Chappawamsic Baptist Church. He removed to Ohio and married Charlotte Smith.

[1244] This was likely Gustavus B. Newton. For information see his entry in 1833.

[1245] James Monroe Taliaferro (1809-1893) was the son of James G. Taliaferro (c.1772-1840) and Wilhelmina Wishart of King George County. James resided at Loch Lomond on Potomac Run and, later, at Springfield on Aquia Run.

[1246] George Washington Conway (1818-1879) was the son of John Moncure Conway (1779-1864) and Catherine Storke Peyton (1786-1865). He died unmarried.

[1247] John Marshall Edrington (c.1817-1902).

[1248] Peter D. Lowry (c.1820-1868) was the son of Robert and Mildred Lowry and left a family in Stafford. His middle name may have been Daniel. Peter resided at Cherry Hill near Brooke. He was involved with John Schooler of nearby Orchard Field in several fishing businesses. In 1866 Peter was elected Circuit Steward for Andrew Chapel and was also chosen as one of the trustees for that property. After the War Between the States, he was unable to pay off his creditors and died after heavily mortgaging all his personal and real property. Peter's estate inventory included 2 cows, 4 oxen, 1 horse, 1 threshing machine, 1 carriage, 1 horse wagon, 1 horse cart, 1 ox wagon, 1 ox cart, farm implements, blacksmith's tools and a forge, 2 bedsteads, 1 lounge, and 1 apple mill all valued at $581.50 (Stafford Deed Book 26A, p. 487).

[1249] Charles Edward Gill (c.1818-1890) was the son of Wilsey Gill (died before 1840) and Sarah Stewart (c.1785-1860). In 1844 he married Elizabeth Virginia Homes (1822-1861). His second wife was Louisa M. Cloe (1835-after 1893). Charles was buried on his old farm, which by the time of his death, had passed by marriage to the Flatfords. This farm is now the site of North Stafford High School.

1842

Byram Harding[1250]—in room of Thomas Griffis, resigned
Leonard P. Alexander[1251]—(Artillery)—in room of James H. Shackelford, deceased
William Randall—in room of Robert Flatford, removed

1843

Lt. Colonel—Charles F. Suttle
Major—James R. Benson—in room of William T. Cropp, resigned
Captains—James R. Benson (Infantry)
    Charles E. Gill (Light Infantry)
1st Lieutenants—Wofinton Kendall[1252]—in room of Aquilla Randall, removed
    John M. Homes[1253]
    Robert Flatford
2nd Lieutenants—William S. Briggs[1254]—in room of Rodney B. Bradshaw, removed
    Austin Knight[1255]
    James H. Cloe[1256]
3rd Lieutenant—John A. Swetnam[1257]—in room of Robert S. Mills, resigned
Regimental Clerk—George Waller

Men fined for failure to appear at muster:

Benjamin T. Abbott	James T. Abbott[1258]	George A. Abbott[1259]

[1250] In 1830 Byram Harding (died c.1846) was overseer of the road "of which Richard Bridwell was overseer" (Eby, Men 147). He married Tamah ___ (c.1793-1860). Byram's estate included household and kitchen furniture, 73 barrels of corn, 84 barrels of corn shucks, 10 cows, 31 hogs, 1 side saddle, 1 coffee mortar, 20 sheep, 2 horses, and an assortment of farm implements all valued at $671.23 (Stafford Deed Book OO, p. 194). He resided in the northern part of the county, possibly on what is now the Quantico reservation.

[1251] Leonard P. Alexander (born c.1832) was the son of Lewis Alexander (died 1827) and Elizabeth Patterson (c.1783-1862). Lewis was a merchant and Leonard may also have followed that profession. In 1855 Leonard and William L. Morgan (c.1806-1873) purchased the old Garrard's Ordinary just to the northeast of the courthouse. From 1853-1856 he was post master at the Stafford Courthouse Post Office. Little else is known of him.

[1252] Woferton Kendall (c.1811-after 1880) was the son of Barnet Kendall (died before 1816). Woferton's mother married secondly Moses Pilcher who became the boy's guardian. Woferton later suffered from financial problems and Eustace Conway was appointed his administrator (Stafford Deed Book NN, p. 378). Woferton died in California.

[1253] John Marshall Homes (1817-1873) was the son of James Homes (1786-1843) and Mary Ratcliffe (1795-1867). In 1857 John married Susan Ann Peters of Fauquier. John's estate included 2 buggies and surveyor's instruments all valued at $43.10 (Stafford Deed Book UU, p. 112).

[1254] William Sheridan Briggs (1820-1892) was the son of James McDonald Briggs (1787-1845) and Charlotte Ashmore Keith (1782-1866) of Stony Hill in Hartwood. William became a minister, married Ophelia H. Riley (1818-1877) and moved to Mason County, Georgia.

[1255] Austin Knight (c.1822-before 1860) was the son of William Knight (before 1775-before 1830) and Gladys Fritter (c.1780-c.1857). Around 1844 Austin married Elizabeth Cloe (born c.1825).

[1256] James H. Cloe (1823-c.1855) was the son of Alexander Cloe and Drucilla Burroughs. He married Mary Edwards (c.1821-1887), the daughter of William and Kate Edwards and was a merchant in Falmouth.

[1257] John Alexander Swetnam (1824-1867) was the son of Levi Swetnam (1785-1838) and Fanny Buckner Roane (1792-1858). He married Elizabeth Keith Ford (c.1818-1882).

[1258] James T. Abbott (died 1873). For some years prior to the War Between the States, James was the toll keeper at Ficklen's Bridge in Falmouth. In 1857 James used "the Old Bake House lot" in Falmouth to secure a debt. That same year he used his store and dwelling house in Falmouth for the same purpose. In 1858 he bought two lots in Falmouth from George Kiger's administrator (Stafford Deed Book RR, 418 and 434). James died in Manchester, Virginia.

[1259] George A. Abbott (c.1820-after 1850) was a miller and lived in Wide Water.

1843

Walter Allen	John Anthony[1260]	James Arrington[1261]
John S. Arrington	Robert B. Alexander[1262]	Francis Aufort[1263]
Allen Abel	Luke Anderson	Daniel T. Bryant[1264]
Robert H. Bowling[1265]	James Bowling	Thomas Bowling
Peter Bloxham[1266]	John Beagle	Harrison B. Barnes[1267]
William Brown	Thornton Brown	Thomas Brown
Elias Butcher	Charles H. Bradshaw[1268]	Harris W. Burton
Thomas T. Brooks	William Bettis[1269]	Lawson Brooks[1270]
William Beagle	William Beach[1271]	Robert Beaty
Mason Byram[1272]	John Calhoun	Harris Coakley[1273]
Daniel S. Coakley[1274]	John E. Coakley[1275]	Alexander Curtis[1276]

[1260] In 1855 John Anthony (c.1809-after 1860) was overseer of the road "from the Stage road at Claibourne's Run to Potomac run at John Furneyhoughs" (Eby, Men 159).

[1261] James Arrington (born c.1828) was the son of Thomas T. Arrington (c.1796-1864) and lived on what is now the Quantico Marine Corps reservation.

[1262] Robert Brooke Alexander (c.1812-1878) was the son of Philip Thornton Alexander (1783-1817) and Lucy Brooke (c.1783-after 1850). He married Julia Anton Kale (1833-1887) and both are buried in Fredericksburg. Robert was an artist. In October 1870 James L. Taliaferro of Fredericksburg conveyed to Robert as trustee for his wife Julia 107 acres "in consideration of his esteem and regard" for Julia and for "her numerous and repeated kindnesses to him the said James L. Taliaferro" (Stafford Deed Book TT, p. 107). On May 15, 1871 Robert submitted his Homestead Exemption which included 1 wagon and harness, 1 horse, 2 cows, 1 threshing machine, 2 hogs, 2 plows, 2 harnesses, 3 hoes, 1 cultivator, 1 mowing scythe, assorted tools, kitchen furniture, 2 tables, 1 writing desk, 1 wardrobe, and 1 bureau (Stafford Loose Papers, Homestead Exemptions).

[1263] Francis Aufort (c.1805-1855) was born in Philadelphia. He lived in or near Brooke and died by drowning.

[1264] Daniel T. Bryant (died c.1890) married Mary Thomas Skinner. In April 1839 James Turner of Fauquier sold Daniel an interest in Turner's parents' property and inherited by James' brother, Jesse Turner, then deceased (Stafford Deed Book LL, p. 504). Daniel's estate included 2 oxen, 1 cow, farm implements, a small assortment of household and kitchen furniture, and come carpenter's tools all valued at $84.30 (Stafford Deed Book 4, p. 545).

[1265] Robert H. Bowling (1817-1893) was the son of Frances Bowling and Christian Musselman. He married Mary "Ann" Jackson (c.1827-1893).

[1266] Peter Bloxham (c.1814-after 1850).

[1267] Harrison Brockenbrough Barnes (born c.1813) was a merchant in Falmouth and lived in the Barnes House on Washington Street in Falmouth. From at least 1843-1852 he served as a town trustee and in 1843 was appointed tax collector for Falmouth. In 1850 he married Frances Lucy Peyton Conway (born 1822). During the War Between the States, he served in the 47th Virginia Infantry.

[1268] Charles H. Bradshaw (c.1817-after 1850) was a miller.

[1269] William Bettis (c.1812-after 1850).

[1270] Lawson Brooks (c.1795-after 1850) lived in Wide Water. He married Letisha Dickerson.

[1271] William Beach (c.1816-1889) owned 90 acres on Deep Run in Hartwood.

[1272] Mason Byram (c.1818-after 1870) was the son of Cuthbert Byram (c.1797-1854). He lived near Ramoth Church. In 1868 he bought 111 acres of the old Accokeek Furnace tract (Stafford Deed Book 26A, p. 423).

[1273] Harris B. Coakley (c.1819-1865) was a cabinet maker. He died in Stafford.

[1274] Daniel S. Coakley (c.1805-c.1866) was a merchant and cooper in Hartwood. In 1843 he paid tax on 252 acres on Potomac Run. In 1852 Willis Lucas, the son of Henry Lucas, was apprenticed to Coakley to learn the trade of cooper (Stafford Circuit 429). In 1859 Daniel was part of the old Hartwood Baptist Church congregation that met at Enon to try and re-establish that church (Hartwood).

[1275] John E. Coakley (c.1810-after 1881) was a school teacher. In 1843 he paid tax on 172 acres on Potomac Run.

1843

Presley J. Curtis[1277]	John Carrol	Austin Cox[1278]
John H. Cloe[1279]	Thornton B. Cooper[1280]	John Cooper
David Cooper	Edward Cooper	Hamilton Cooper[1281]
John M. Conway, Jr.[1282]	Walker P. Conway	Henry R. Conway[1283]
Richard Carter[1284]	William Carter	William Combs
Thomas Carrol	David W. Combs[1285]	James Davis
John Davis	Robert Dunnington	John Dillon
William Dillon	John M. Daniel	William Dent
Alfred Dent[1286]	John S. Dent[1287]	George H. Deane
William Embrey	John Edwards	William Edwards[1288]
Joseph Embrey	Joseph English	John Fugate
Edward Finnall	John Finnall	Lafayette Franklin[1289]
John H. Fritter[1290]	Noah Fritter[1291]	James Fines
Thomas Fines	John Furgason	Edwin C. Fitzhugh
John Ficklen	Leonard H. Ficklen	Samuel Gordon
John S. Graves[1292]	William Graves	William Gill
James Gollihorn	John Gollihorn	Thomas Gollihorn[1293]
Alfred Groves	William Grinnan	George Green
John Green	Robert Green	Richard Garrison

[1276] In February 1865 John W. Briggs and wife Winnie B. of King George sold Alexander M. Curtis 240 acres formerly belonging to Dr. John G. Cooke and adjoining James French, Amos Jones, William Lunsford, and Marshall Payne (Stafford Deed Book 26A, p. 7).

[1277] Presley J. Curtis (c.1811-1871) was the son of Thornton Curtis and lived near Potomac Creek. In November 1868 James M. Scott and wife Sarah T. sold Presley 17 acres of lower Salvington (Stafford Deed Book 26A, p. 522).

[1278] Austin Cox (c.1815-after 1870) was the son of Samuel Cox (died 1844) of White Oak. He married Elizabeth Brown (c.1812-1876), the daughter of Joseph and Mary Brown.

[1279] This may be John A. Cloe.

[1280] Thornton B. Cooper (c.1810-1883) lived up Garrisonville Road (Route 610). He married Frances Watson (born c.1817). In 1870 he paid taxes on 154 acres on Aquia Run. Thornton's estate included farm implements and tools, 2 horses, 2 oxen, 2 milk cows, 1 sheep, 5 hogs, 3 oars, 1 old gill net, and 1 sail all valued at $502.94 (Stafford Deed Book 2, p. 493).

[1281] Richard Hamilton Cooper (c.1815-after 1870) married c.1833 Harriet Maria Musselman.

[1282] John Moncure Conway, Jr. (1815-1848) was the son of John Moncure Conway (1779-1864) and Catherine Storke Peyton (1786-1865). He married Elizabeth Fitzhugh.

[1283] Henry Rowzee Conway (1825-1863) was the son of John Moncure Conway (1779-1864).

[1284] Richard Carter (c.1815-after 1850) lived up Garrisonville Road (Route 610).

[1285] In 1870 David W. Combs paid taxes on 238 acres on Aquia Run.

[1286] Alfred Dent (c.1820-after 1850).

[1287] John Scott Dent married Sophia Guy.

[1288] William Edwards kept a store in Falmouth.

[1289] Lafayette Franklin (1825-1911) was the son of William Franklin (c.1787-after 1850) who was a millwright. Lafayette was born in Rappahannock County, but by 1861 was living in Falmouth. In April 1862 he enlisted in the Fredericksburg Artillery, but deserted to the enemy in August 1863. He was sent to Philadelphia, but later returned to Falmouth. Lafayette served in the Mexican War, enlisting on Dec. 10, 1846. He was discharged on Apr. 2, 1847 on a surgeon's certificate due to the loss of a finger by the discharge of his own musket.

[1290] John Henry Fritter (c.1824-1896) was the son of John Fritter, Jr. (born c.1786) of Stafford. In 1870 he paid taxes on 87 acres in the Woodcutting near Ramoth Church.

[1291] Noah J. Fritter (c.1811-1901) lived west of the courthouse. He died at the Stafford Poor House.

[1292] John S. Graves (died 1869) died of consumption.

[1293] Thomas Gollihorn utilized his homestead exemption claiming 2 beds, 1 bureau, 1 rocking chair, 4 chairs, 1 dining table, 1 washstand, 1 clock, 1 small looking glass, 7 hogs, 1 cow, 2 calves, and 1 double plow all valued at $102.00 (Stafford County Loose Papers, Homestead Exemptions).

1843

George G. Glasscock[1294]	Charles Griffis	John Harrison
John R. Homes	Henry W. Hill[1295]	William F. Hord[1296]
Thomas Harding	Ephraim Harris	Hugh Harris[1297]
Gustavus Heflin	Marshall Heflin[1298]	William Heflin[1299]
David R. Jones	Noah Jones[1300]	William Jones
Elisha Jones	John W. Jones[1301]	Thornton Jacobs
John King	Richard King	Pearson King
Neru Kenady	James H. Lunsford[1302]	Landon Limbrick[1303]
James Limbrick[1304]	Sidney Limbrick[1305]	William Limbrick[1306]
Gustavus Limbrick	James Latham	Robert Latham
George Lightner[1307]	Joseph Lee	Jeremiah Moore[1308]
Henry C. Moore[1309]	William Morris	Edward C. Marshal
Robert S. Mills	Travis D. Moncure[1310]	George Musselman

[1294] George Garnett Glasscock (1807-1879) married Agatha Ann Moncure (1815-1859), the daughter of Edwin Conway Moncure (1787-1816) and Eleanor Edrington. George and Agatha resided at Clermont on Chappawamsic Creek.
[1295] Henry W. Hill (c.1809-after 1850). In 1850 he was living next door to Thomas Hill (c.1782-c.1870) in Hartwood.
[1296] In 1839 William F. Hord paid tax on 450 acres on Deep Run in the southern part of the county.
[1297] May be Hugh M. Harris (born c. 1822) who lived in Falmouth.
[1298] Marshall Wesley Heflin (1819-1892) was the son of Rachel Heflin and Asa Holloway and the brother of Gustavus Heflin. He lived near Rock Hill Church and Tackett's Mills.
[1299] In 1843 William Heflin paid tax on 750 acres on Aquia Run about 14 miles west of the courthouse.
[1300] Noah Jones (died after 1896) married Susan Gallahan (c.1810-1896), the daughter of John and Nellie Gallahan.
[1301] In 1850 John W. Jones (1821-1897) paid tax on 106 acres of the old Coal Trips tract on Aquia Creek about five miles east of the courthouse. During the War Between the States, he served with the 9th Virginia Cavalry. John married Susan Watson (born 1815). He was buried at Coal Trips.
[1302] James H. Lunsford (c.1810-c.1889) was the son of William Lunsford (born 1785) and Willa Lunsford (born 1795). In 1874 he made a homestead exemption that consisted of 170 acres, 1 horse, 6 cattle, 17 hogs, 1 old carriage and harness, 1 old wagon, and household and kitchen furniture all valued at $831.00 (Stafford County Loose Papers, Homestead Exemptions). His estate inventory included household and kitchen furniture, 1 side board, 1 dining table, 1 clock, 6 cane chairs, 1 looking glass, a map, 1 writing desk, 1 horse, farm implements, 1 log chain, 6 stands of bees, and 1 saddle all valued at $53.90 (Stafford Deed Book 3, p. 544).
[1303] Landon Carter Limbrick (1815-after 1880) was the son of John Limbrick (c.1780-after 1850) and Lucy Mahorney (born 1790). In 1838 he married Catherine Betts (Bettis?) in Falmouth.
[1304] James Limbrick (born 1817) was the son of John Limbrick (c.1780-after 1850) and Lucy Mahorney (born 1790) of Stafford.
[1305] Sidney Limbrick (born 1820) was the son of John Limbrick (c.1780-after 1850) and Lucy Mahorney (born 1790) of Stafford. Sidney married Celia Powell.
[1306] William Limbrick (born 1814) was the son of John Limbrick (c.1780-after 1850) and Lucy Mahorney (born 1790) of Stafford. He married Martha Cora Billingsley.
[1307] George W. Lightner (c.1805-1886), a minister, was born in Maryland. In 1860 he was granted permission to take over the mercantile license of Coons and Swetnam in Falmouth. In addition to general merchandise, he also sold "retail spirits at his said store not to be drank where sold" (Eby, Men 282). George married Mary L. Coakley (born c.1817).
[1308] Jeremiah Moore (c.1806-1879) was the son of William F. and Mary Moore of Prince William. He died in Stafford of a stroke. In 1850 Jeremiah paid tax on 31 acres of Enoch Mason's Clover Hill in what is now the Roseville area of Stafford. He never married. Jeremiah's will, recorded in Stafford, mentioned sister Angelina Moore and nephew Arthur Moore (Stafford Will Book R, p.99).
[1309] In 1850 Henry C. Moore paid tax on 190 acres on Potomac Run about nine miles west of the courthouse.

1843

Robert Musselman	Gustavus B. Newton	Abraham B. Newton[1311]
Lewis H. Perry	James Patterson	Gustavus Pates[1312]
Thomas B. Pickett	Silwelton Pearson[1313]	Martin Pearson[1314]
George Peyton	James Payne	Elijah Payne
John Pomfrey	Robert Rawlings	Benjamin Randall[1315]
Robert Randall	Richard Randall	John Randall
Thomas Rose	Selden Rains[1316]	Thomas M. Robertson[1317]
John Robertson	John Rives[1318]	Robert C. Rodgers[1319]
William Rollow	Jackson Roles	Harrison Skinner[1320]
George Stone	Sanford Stone[1321]	Thomas Stone
Charles H. Simms	Harrison G. Skidmore[1322]	Alexander Skidmore[1323]
Richard M. Scott	Strother Shackleford	Alexander Snellings
George W. Smith[1324]	Benjamin Sullivan[1325]	Thomas Sullivan
James Sullivan	John Sullivan	Daniel Sullivan
Stephen Sullivan	John F. Swift	John Shelton
Jesse Stone	James W. Stone	John H. Skinker[1326]

[1310] Travers Daniel Moncure (1811-1886) was the son of John Moncure, III (1772-1822). He was born at Clermont on Chappawamsic Creek and died at Oakwood, also in Wide Water. In 1838 he married Susan B. Carter. Travers served as a justice of the peace in Stafford. In 1870 he paid taxes on 150 acres in Wide Water.

[1311] Abraham Benjamin Newton (1809-1869) was the son of Benjamin Newton and Nancy Butler. He married Catherine "Kitty" Snellings. Abraham was the twin of Gustavus B. Newton (born 1809). While repairing his roof he fell and died a few days later.

[1312] Gustavus was the son of Chandler Pates (c.1780-after 1860) and Lucy Sullivan. He married Clementine Shelton and moved out to Pates, Spotsylvania County.

[1313] Silwellington E. Pearson (c.1821-1883) lived near Beaverdam Run of Aquia Run. He married Mary Tolson.

[1314] Martin Pearson was the son of William George Pearson (1750-c.1801), English immigrant who lived in Prince William and Fauquier.

[1315] Benjamin E. Randall (1820-1904) was the son of Abraham Randall, Sr. (1780-1855) and Sega Lygna Tarman (born 1785). Ben moved to Amissville, Rappahannock County and made saddles for a living. He was in the Confederate service for just ten days and was listed as a saddle maker (Lacy 13).

[1316] Selden B. Raines (c.1822-after 1860) is thought to be the brother of William Rowzee and John Moncure Raines. During the War Between the States, Selden served as a private in the 2nd Battalion of the Virginia Reserves.

[1317] May be the Thomas M. Robinson (born c.1802) listed in the 1850 census. He resided in White Oak.

[1318] John W. Rives (c.1812-after 1850) was a merchant.

[1319] Robert Campbell Rodgers (c.1818-1888) was born in Ireland and was postmaster at Hartwood Post Office from 1836-1841 (Eby, Men 238).

[1320] In 1870 Harrison Skinner (born c.1821) paid taxes on 33 and 24 acres in the Woodcutting near Ramoth Church.

[1321] This may be Sanford Alexander Stone (1818-1895), the son of George Stone (born 1784) of Stafford. In 1854 he married Harriet Olivia Mills (born c.1819). Sanford was a shoemaker and carpenter.

[1322] Harrison J. Skidmore (c.1816-after 1880) was the son of William Skidmore (c.1775-before 1840) and Sarah Ann Garner. By 1862 he had moved to Georgetown where he worked as a carpenter.

[1323] Alexander Skidmore (born c.1828) lived in or near Brooke. He married Mary Sullivan (c.1816-1876), the daughter of John and Susan Sullivan.

[1324] In 1849 George W. Smith paid tax on 18 acres on Long Branch of Potomac Run.

[1325] Benjamin Sullivan (died c.1848) lived in White Oak.

[1326] John Howard Skinker (1814-1867) was the son of Samuel Hampson Skinker (1785-1856) and Margaret Wilson Julian of Oakley, Stafford County. John studied law, medicine, and divinity, though he never practiced the latter two. He served as a justice in Stafford and as an editor of a newspaper in Warrenton. During the War Between the States, John was a Unionist. After the war, he practiced law in Washington and died unmarried.

1843

William Snellings	Thomas Snellings	James Snellings[1327]
Robert Smith	Benjamin Smith[1328]	John Smith
Walker Smith[1329]	Mourning Smith	Thomas Smith
Lewis Smith[1330]	Thomas W. Schooler[1331]	John Thompson
Gustavus S. Taliaferro	James M. Taliaferro	Nelson S. Timmons[1332]
John C. Tolson[1333]	James Tolson	James Tarlton
Robert Truslow	Newton Turner[1334]	Henry White
William Walker	Americus Watson[1335]	Richard Wharton
James White	George Watts	James Watson
Edward J. Whaling[1336]	William Wilson	Gustavus B. Wallace[1337]
William Young		

1844

Adjutant—John W. D. Ford
Major—James R. Benson
Captains—James Monteith
    Robert L. Waple
    James M. Taliaferro
    William Brent (Cavalry)
    John W. D. Ford (Artillery)
    George W. Conway (Artillery)—in room of J. W. D. Ford, resigned
    William S. Briggs—in room of James R. Benson, promoted
    George H. Tolson[1338]—in room of Benjamin F. Ashby, deceased

---

[1327] In 1870 James Snellings (1800-1879) paid taxes on 43 acres on Potomac Run in Hartwood District. He married Susanna Truslow (1804-1878), the daughter of Benjamin Truslow. In 1874 James claimed his homestead exemption which consisted of 2 hogs in a pen, 2 pigs, about 25 barrels of corn, and household and kitchen furniture (Stafford County Loose Papers, Homestead Exemptions).

[1328] Benjamin Smith (1804-1890) was the son of Mourning Smith, Sr. (c.1777-1853 and Sally Ann Steward (died before 1840). Benjamin worked with his father and brothers at Eagle and Smith's gold mines near Richlands Baptist Church in lower Stafford. In 1834 he married Julia Ann Marquess, the daughter of Samuel and Lydia Marquess of Stafford. Benjamin was the twin of John Smith (1804-1899).

[1329] Walker Smith (1806-1892) was the son of Mourning Smith, Sr. (c.1777-1853) of Spotsylvania and Stafford and Sally Ann Steward (died before 1840). Walker worked with his father and brothers at Eagle and Smith's gold mines in lower Stafford. Unfortunately, he bankrupted and died in the county poorhouse.

[1330] Lewis Smith (c.1812-after 1850) was a merchant in Hartwood.

[1331] In 1870 Thomas W. Schooler paid taxes on 375 acres near Hartwood.

[1332] Nelson Sedwick Timmons (c.1812-after 1850) was the son of Thomas Timmons (c.1777-1842) of Stafford. In 1843 he paid tax on 148 acres near Ramoth Church.

[1333] John C. Tolson (born c.1814) married Jane Catherine Mills. They lived many years in Prince William County.

[1334] During the War Between the States, Newton Turner (died 1863) served in Capt. Raleigh L. Cooper's Battery and died from wounds received in battle. He married Lucinda Burton (died c.1865) of Falmouth. From 1846-1850 Newton was insolvent and living in Fredericksburg.

[1335] Americus Watson (c.1815-after 1870).

[1336] Edward Jones Whaling (born c.1816) was the son of Posey Whaling (born c.1777) and Sarah Jones (born c.1780) of Charles County, Maryland and Stafford. He married Frances Ann Robey (c.1827-1882) of Stafford.

[1337] Gustavus Brown Wallace (1810-1882) was the son of John Wallace (1761-1829) of Liberty Hall and Elizabeth Hooe (c.1766-1850). He married Emily Travers Daniel (c.1806-1869), the daughter of Travers Daniel, Jr. (1763-1812) and Mildred Stone (1772-1837). Through his marriage, Gustavus became owner of Crow's Nest. Gustavus' death was brought about by an accident at home. While sleepwalking one night he stepped out of a second story window. He fell to the ground and sustained a compound fracture of one let as well as some possible internal injuries. His leg had to be amputated and he suffered greatly from the injuries, but lived for several years afterwards.

1ˢᵗ Lieutenants—William Burton
William Randall
William S. Embrey—in room of John M. Edrington, removed
Rodham P. Shelkett[1339]—(Cavalry)—in room of George W. Conway, resigned
Harrison B. Barnes
Rodney B. Bradshaw—in room of Alexander B. Jones, resigned
Jefferson W. Heflin[1340]—in room of William Ashby, removed
2ⁿᵈ Lieutenants—William B. Ball
Addison J. Sullivan[1341]
Charles T. Jones
John H. King
John F. Ficklen[1342]
Regimental Clerk—George Waller

Men fined for failure to appear at muster:

Walter Allen	John Anthony	George B. Adams
Robert Alsop	Richard B. Alexander	George A. Abbott
James T. Abbott	Francis Aufort	Richard Burton[1343]
John H. Bradshaw[1344]	Charles H. Bradshaw	William B. Ball
Elias Butchard	James W. Butcher	William Bettis
Thomas T. Brooks	John Beagle	Rawleigh Browne
Charles Browne	Thomas Browne	Thornton Browne
William Browne	Peter Bloxham	Robert Blake[1345]
Marshall Burton[1346]	Beverly Bates[1347]	Robert A. Beaty[1348]

[1338] George H. Tolson (born c.1820) was the son of George H. Tolson (c.1779-1832).
[1339] Rodham P. Shelkett (1822-1899) was the son of John Shelkett (1793-1857) and Nancy Stark (1786-1834) and lived near Stafford Store. He married Virginia Lula Daffan (1833-1875), the daughter of William Daffan (c.1777-1855) and his first wife, Nancy Davis (born c.1795). In 1870 he made his Homestead Exemption listing his farm, Locust Grove, 13 cattle, 2 horses, 16 hogs, 1 wagon, 1 cart, 1 buggy, and household and kitchen furniture (Stafford Loose Papers, Homestead Exemptions). Rodham died of cancer; his will mentioned daughters Nannie G. and Dora L. Shelkett and Lulie M. French, and sons W. H. and John R. Shelkett (Stafford Will Book R, p. 246). Rodham's estate inventory included 1 old still, a corn sheller, farm implements, 1 log chain, 34 railroad ties, 6 cattle, 3 horses, and 1 horse wagon all valued at $327.75 (Stafford Deed Book 8, p. 379).
[1340] Jefferson William Heflin (1811-1880) was the son of William and Lydia Heflin. In 1870 Jefferson paid taxes on 227 acres on Aquia Run. He was one of the original trustees of Rock Hill Baptist Church (Stafford Deed Book 26A, p. 51).
[1341] Addison J. Sullivan (died c.1870) married Elizabeth G. Roberson (1827-1889), the daughter of Thomas and Ella Roberson.
[1342] John Fielding Ficklen (c.1824-1872) was the son of James Grant Ficklen (1794-1846) and Katherine Davenport. In 1847 he married his cousin Sarah A. Slaughter (born 1824) and moved to Danville, Virginia.
[1343] Richard Burton (c.1821-1860) was a merchant in Hartwood. He died of pneumonia.
[1344] John H. Bradshaw (1814-1879) was the son of Zachariah Bradshaw of Stafford. John died in Stafford.
[1345] May be Robert Norman Blake (c.1804-1892), the son of Samuel Blake of Middlesex County. In 1861 Robert was overseer of a road in Stafford and lived at Woodend near Greenbank.
[1346] Marshall Burton (c.1808-1882) was the son of William and Susan Burton. In 1868 he bought from William and Sinah D. Irvine 24 acres of the old Lee Gold Mine tract (Stafford Deed Book 26A, p. 397). This was located to the west of Holly Corner Road (Route 655). He married Jane F. Dunnington (c.1813-1887) of Stafford. Marshall's estate included 5 chairs "very indifferent," 200 pounds of pork, 5 bushels of wheat, 1 old wagon, 13 barrels of corn, 4 hogs, 7 cattle, 4 geese, 25 hens, and an assortment of farm implements all valued at $230.90 (Stafford Deed Book 1, p. 468).

1844

Lawson Brooks	Joseph Bridwell[1349]	William M. Bridwell[1350]
Robert H. Bowling	James Bowling	Thomas Bowling
Travis Bowling[1351]	Walker L. Conyers[1352]	David Cooper
John E. Cooper[1353]	Hamilton Cooper	John E. Coakley
Harrison Coakley	John Calhoun	James M. Courtney[1354]
Thomas Colbert[1355]	Alexander Curtis	Presley J. Curtis
Fleet Cox[1356]	John Carrol	Jeremiah Carter[1357]
William Dillon	John Dillon	James Davis
John Davis	Samuel Dent[1358]	William Edwards
Francis T. Forbes[1359]	John F. Ficklen	Joseph B. Ficklen
Benjamin Franklin[1360]	Beverly Fugate	John Fugate
John R. Fitzhugh	Edward Finnel	John Furgason
William Flinch	Elijah Fines[1361]	George Fuss[1362]

[1347] Beverly Bates (c.1810-after 1850) later lived in Spotsylvania.

[1348] Robert A. Beaty (born c.1822) was the son of Robert Beaty, Sr. and his wife Charlotte (c.1782-after 1850) and resided near Tackett's Mill.

[1349] May be Joseph Jacob Bridwell (c.1824-1849), the son of Richard Bridwell (c.1785-1853) and Elizabeth Jacobs (born c.1797). Joseph married Mary Virginia Turner (died 1859) and died in Mason County, Kentucky.

[1350] William Moncure Bridwell (1825-1907) was the son of Richard Bridwell (c.1785-1853) and Elizabeth Jacobs (born c.1797). He married Mary Ann Harrison and removed to Denver, Colorado.

[1351] Travis Bowling (born c.1821).

[1352] Walker Lewis Conyers (born c.1812) was the son of John Conyers (1754-1819) and his second wife Lucy (died 1820). Walker married Alzira ___ and inherited Cedar Hedge from his father.

[1353] John E. Cooper (born c.1825).

[1354] James M. Courtney (died c.1850) lived in Hartwood. He may have been the son of Daniel Courtney (born c.1766). He had brothers Elias, Lawson, and Alexander. Around 1828 James married Elizabeth Timmons by whom he had nine children. By 1829 James was living in Fauquier and was included on that county's censuses of 1830 and 1840. He sold a tract of land in Fauquier in 1849 and returned to Stafford where he soon died.

[1355] Thomas R. Colbert (c.1818-1876) was the son of James D. and Elizabeth Colbert of Culpeper. He lived in the southwest corner of Stafford near Deep Run.

[1356] This was William Fleet Cox (1821-1905) was the son of Berryman Cox and Delila Payne. He married his cousin, Sarah Cox (c.1823-1879), the daughter of Samuel and Sarah Cox. Fleet lived across from Bethel Baptist Church on White Oak Road (Route 218). He died at his home and was buried at Bethel Church.

[1357] Jeremiah Carter (c.1810-186_) was the son of Jeremiah Carter (c.1784-after 1828) of Stafford and was a descendant of Capt. Thomas Carter (c.1630-1700) of Lancaster County. Jeremiah was a merchant and kept stores in Stafford and Fredericksburg. In 1835 he was living in his father's home near the courthouse. In the 1840s and 1850s he ran an ordinary and store at the courthouse. Jeremiah married Elizabeth Wamsley (c.1818-1886), the daughter of Benjamin Wamsley (died 1851). He suffered from serious financial problems, largely a result of national economic woes, and finally bankrupted. Late in 1850 he was charged with killing William Hewitt while trying to break up a fight in which he wasn't involved. The outcome of the case is unknown.

[1358] Samuel Dent (c.1810-before 1870) was the son of George Dent (died c.1823) who left a will in Stafford. George left property "to be equally divided between my two Sons Travis Roles [died c.1847] & Samuel Roles or Travis & Samuel Dent, whichever may be their lawful names (Stafford Deed Book GG-240). Samuel was a fisherman and married Lucy Berry.

[1359] Francis "Frank" Thornton Forbes (c.1825-1904) was the son of Murray Forbes (1782-1863) and Sally Innes Thornton (1799-1885). In 1851 he married Ann Mercer Chew, the eldest daughter of John James Chew. He served four years in the Confederate service during which time he was a captain in the commissary in Richmond. After the war, he spent four years as postmaster of Fredericksburg.

[1360] Benjamin Franklin (c.1822-after 1850) lived in Falmouth and was a miller.

1844

Alexander Graves	Robert Graves	Austin Graves[1363]
John S. Graves	James Gollihorn	Marshall Gollihorn[1364]
Leonard Garrison[1365]	Robert Guy	John D. Griffis[1366]
Hedgman Green[1367]	Harrison Groves[1368]	Duff Green, Jr.[1369]
John Garner[1370]	Samuel H. Gordon	John T. Hedgman
Henry Hill[1371]	George Hazlegrove	John R. Homes
Jackson Harding	Randall Holden[1372]	Gustavus Heflin
James Heflin	Thornton Jones[1373]	Amos Jones
Elisha Jones	David R. Jones	Fountain Jacobs[1374]
Ambrose Jackson	Stark Jett[1375]	William J. Jerrell
John S. Knox	John M. Kendall[1376]	Daniel S. Knight[1377]
Neru Kenady	James Limbrick	Robert Limbrick
Gustavus Limbrick	Thomas M. Limbrick[1378]	James H. Lunsford
Robert Latham	Philipson Latham	George Lightner
William Leitch	Joseph Lee	George Musselman
John C. Moncure[1379]	Robert S. Mills	Green Miller[1380]

[1361] May be Elijah Fines who married Lucretia Shackelford (c.1836-1888), the daughter of Dudley and Lydia Shackelford.

[1362] George Fuss (born c.1805).

[1363] Austin Graves (c.1815-1877) was a carpenter. He died unmarried in Stafford.

[1364] Marshall Gollihorn (born c.1815).

[1365] This may be William Leonard Garrison (c.1825-after 1850), the son of Yelverton Garrison (c.1799-c.1867). Leonard was a blacksmith and was buried near Reid's Road off Courthouse Road (Route 630).

[1366] John D. Griffis (born c.1820) lived in the upper part of the county near Garrisonville Road (Route 610).

[1367] Hedgman Green (born c.1795) was the son of George James Green (1754-1847) and Frances Brown (born 1776). In 1865 he married Jane Eliza Huffman (born c.1825) in Fauquier. She was the daughter of Jonas Huffman.

[1368] In 1861 Harrison Groves (1809-1893) enlisted as a private at Aquia Creek in Capt. Butcher's Battery. He was born in Stafford and died at Lee Camp Soldiers' Home in Richmond.

[1369] Duff McDuff Green (c.1832-1885) was the son of Duff Green (1792-1854), Falmouth industrialist, and Eliza Ann Payne (1806-1876). Duff, Jr. married Mary G. Howison. During the War Between the States, he served with the Fredericksburg Artillery. After the war, he moved to Brooke where he ran a store. Duff died at Brooke.

[1370] May be the John W. Garner who was the son of John Henceford Garner (c.1811-1886) and Ann Elizabeth Littrell (c.1825-1886) of Stafford.

[1371] Henry Hill (born c.1808).

[1372] Randall Holden (born c.1800) was a manufacturer in Falmouth.

[1373] Thornton Jones (c.1804-after 1880) was a cooper. He had several children by Mary Jane Bryant (c.1813-after 1880) and resided in Stafford.

[1374] Fountain L. Jacobs (c.1822-1871) was the son of William Jacobs (1760-1829) and Lavinia Colvert (1768-1830) of Culpeper. Fountain married Lucy A. Timmons (c.1828-1882). He was born in Culpeper and died in Taylor, West Virginia.

[1375] William Stark Jett (c.1814-1864) was the son of Francis Jett. He probably lived between White Oak Road and McCarty Road. Stark died unmarried in Stafford.

[1376] In 1843 John M. Kendall paid tax on 104 acres on Aquia Run about 14 miles west of the courthouse.

[1377] Daniel S. Knight may be Daniel Webster S. Knight (1824-1909) who was the son of Bailey Knight (c.1761-1839) and Elizabeth Kendall (c.1794-c.1828). In 1863 D. W. S. Knight, then of Taylor County, Virginia, signed a marriage contract with Mary M./A. Timmons (c.1831-1896) of Stafford. She was the daughter of Thomas and Lucy A. Timmons. All Mary's property was to remain under her control and not be subject to Daniel's debts (Stafford Deed Book 26A, p. 78). Mary died in Stafford.

[1378] Thomas M. Limbrick (1819-1878) was the son of John Limbrick (c.1780-after 1850) and Lucy Mahorney (born 1790) of Stafford. Thomas died in Kemper County, Mississippi.

[1379] John Conway Moncure (1827-1916) was the son of Richard Cassius Lee Moncure (1805-1882) of Glencairne and Mary Butler Washington Conway (born 1807). In 1847 John graduated valedictorian from

1844

Francis Monroe	Abraham Newton	Gustavus B. Newton
James Patterson	Horace Potts[1381]	Thomas K. Price[1382]
Charles S. Petty	James Payne	George Payne
Thomas Potts	George C. Patten	John Randall
Thomas Rose	William Rollow	Western Rodgers[1383]
William H. Robertson[1384]	John Robertson	Thomas M. Robertson
Daniel Sullivan	Robert Sullivan	Benjamin Sullivan
John F. Swift	Charles H. Simms	Thomas Snellings
John W. Smithers	Abroad Shelton[1385]	William Shelton
John Scheldtin	Walker Smith	Lewis Smith
John Smith	Mourning Smith	Robert Smith
John Shelton	James Stone	Jesse Stone
Robert Skidmore[1386]	William Skidmore[1387]	Alexander Skidmore
John Schooler[1388]	Robert B. Taylor	John Thompson
John Taliaferro, Jr.	Nelson S. Timmons	William T. Truslow
Thomas N. Towson[1389]	Robert Watson	Hamilton Watson
Benjamin Watson	Richard Wofenden	William White
James White	Henry White	Alfred Williams
Thomas Williams	William Walker	William Wilson
Americus Watson		

VMI. After graduation, he studied law with his father and was admitted to the bar in 1849. The following year he married Fannie Dulaney Tomlin and built Mont Anna on the north side of his father's Glencairne farm. He served as a trustee for the town of Falmouth from at least 1858-1859 (Town 77, 81). John served as Commonwealth's Attorney for Stafford from 1851-1860 when he removed to Shreveport, Louisiana to practice law. He was much involved with political affairs in Louisiana. John died tragically of burns from a gas stove.

[1380] This may be the Green Miller who was the son of George Miller (born c.1793) and Sidney "Sukie" Maloney (born c.1793). This family removed to Kentucky.

[1381] John Horace Potts married Susan A. Shelkett (1810-1895), the daughter of John Shelkett (1793-1857) and Nancy Stark (1786-1834). Susan and Nancy were buried at Locust Grove near Belle Plains Road (Rt. 604). In 1847 Horace attempted to kill Fredericksburg police officer Bernard Cole by stabbing him. A court found him insane and sent him to the lunatic hospital in Williamsburg (*Fredericksburg News*, Aug. 19, 1847). He remained there at least through 1880.

[1382] This may be Thomas J. Price (1805-1886), the son of Charles Price, Jr. (1783-1851) and Elizabeth Fulcher (1785-1862). Charles was listed in the militia records in 1806. Thomas married Armeady Hubbard, but little else is known of him.

[1383] Western Rogers (c.1820-after 1870) lived in or near Brooke.

[1384] May be the William H. Robinson (born c.1825) listed in the 1850 census as living in White Oak.

[1385] Abroad Shelton (c.1822-1909) was Absalom Roe Shelton. He married Martha Cox and was a long time member of the Old School Baptist Church in White Oak. He died in Stafford.

[1386] Robert Skidmore (c.1823-1898) was the son of William Skidmore (c.1775-before 1840). He died in Stafford.

[1387] This may be William H. Skidmore (c.1813-1876), the son of William and Elizabeth Skidmore of Stafford. In 1867 the younger William was overseer of the road "from Potomac Church to Crowsnest in the place of William H. Browne removed from the county" (Eby, Men 175).

[1388] John Schooler (1812-1875) was the son of Abner Schooler (1774-after 1850) and Margaret Kirk (born 1785). John married Laurinda Jones (1815-1870) and left a large family in Stafford.

[1389] Thomas Norman Towson (1822-1863) was the son of Thomas Towson (1780-1861) and Eleanor Norman (1782-1848) of Rockdale. In 1843 he married Mary Frances Smith (1824-1895) of Fauquier. Thomas N. and Mary resided at the Old Stone House on Rocky Run.

1845

Adjutant—John W. D. Ford
Colonel—William H. Stone
Major—James M. Taliaferro—in room of James R. Benson, resigned and removed from the state
Captains—William S. Briggs (Hartwood Company)
    Rodney B. Bradshaw (Infantry)—in room of James M. Taliaferro, promoted
    George W. Conway (Artillery)
    William Brent (Cavalry)
1st Lieutenants—William Villers[1390]—in room of Rodney B. Bradshaw, promoted
    James E. Waller[1391] (Artillery)—in room of James E. Towson, resigned
    Thomas N. Towson (Cavalry)—in room of Rodham Shelkett, resigned
    Humphrey Dodd[1392] (Hartwood Company)—in room of William S. Briggs, promoted
2nd Lieutenants—George W. Smith—in room off John A. Swetnam, resigned
    James W. Johnson[1393] (Artillery)—in room of Byram Harding, resigned
    Alexander B. Jones (Cavalry)—in room of Robert Jones whose place had been vacant four years

1846

Adjutant—William S. Briggs
Colonel—William H. Stone (5th Brigade, 2nd Division)
Lt. Colonels—Charles F. Suttle—in room of William H. Stone, resigned
    James M. Taliaferro
Major—William Brent (Infantry)
Captains—John M. Brooke[1394]—in room of Robert L. Waple, removed
    George W. Conway (Artillery)
    William H. Browne, Jr.[1395] (White Oak Company)—in room of James Monteith, resigned
    William Brent (Cavalry)
    Jefferson Heflin—in room of George H. Tolson, resigned
    George W. Cropp[1396]—in room of William S. Briggs, promoted
    Charles E. Gill (Artillery)—in room of George W. Conway, resigned
1st Lieutenants—Robert B. Alexander—in room of William Randall, resigned
    Patrick H. Boroughs
    William E. Moncure[1397] (Artillery)—in room of Leonard P. Alexander, resigned
    George W. Cropp—in room of Rodney B. Bradshaw, promoted
    Isaac Sullivan[1398] (White Oak Co.)—in room of Alfred Wariner, resigned
    William J. Burton[1399] (White Oak Co.)

[1390] William Villers (born c.1817) married Catherine E. Dodd (born c.1818), the daughter of Nathaniel Dodd (born c.1773) and Elizabeth Perkins (c.1774-1802). William may have been a blacksmith. In 1849 he paid tax on 106 acres on Aquia Run.

[1391] James Elias Waller (1824-1862) was the son of James Waller (1789-1824) and Ann Adie (1792-1870). He married Elizabeth Wickliffe (1834-1862) and lived at Bloomington in Wide Water.

[1392] This was William Humphrey Dodd (1815-1895) who was the son of Travis Dodd (c.1790-1859). He married Prussia Ann Maria Heflin (c.1823-1888).

[1393] James W. Johnson (1821-1856) was the son of Joseph and Sally Johnson. In 1840 he bought from John H. and Charles F. Suttle their house and lots in the town of Aquia (Stafford Deed Book MM, p. 146). James committed suicide.

[1394] John Mercer Brooke (1826-1906) was the son of Samuel Selden Brooke (1800-1861) and Angelina Edrington (c.1803-1862). He was the first postmaster of the Accokeek post office (at Brooke), filling that position from 1857-1858.

[1395] William H. Browne, Jr. (died 1852).

[1396] During the War Between the States, George Wellford Cropp (1825-1904) served with the 47th Virginia Infantry. He was the son of John Cropp (1753-1830) and his second wife Eliza Fallis (1807-c.1850). George married Caroline E. Holladay and died at Sterling, near Guinea Station, Spotsylvania County.

[1397] William Edwin Moncure (1824-1888).

[1398] Isaac Sullivan (born c.1826).

1846

2nd Lieutenants—Thomas H. Speake[1400] (Artillery)—in room of Yelverton Garrison, resigned.
    Thomas Speake was not commissioned & Charles E. Gill filled his place.
    James M. Briggs[1401]
    Harrison B. Barnes—in room of Alexander B. Jones, resigned
Lieutenants—Austin Knight
           George W. Smith
           James E. Waller

Men fined for failure to appear at muster:

John S. Arrington	James Arrington	John Atchison
Armstead A. Armstrong[1402]	Richard B. Alexander	James Atcison[1403]
Harrison B. Barnes	John Beagle	James Black[1404]
William Ball	Bernard Barber	Brockenbaugh Barnes[1405]
Robert H. Boling[1406]	James Boutyard	Henry Bowler
John Boling	James Boling	Riley Bowler[1407]
Alfred Burroughs[1408]	Charles Bruce	Daniel T. Bryant
William Bryant	William Bloxton	Rawleigh Brown
William Brown, Sr.	Thomas Brown	John A. Bramell[1409]
Joseph Bridwell	James L. Briggs	Gideon Browne
James Bullock[1410]	William Burton	William Carter
Abroad Chilton	James Chilton	Wellington Chilton[1411]

[1399] William J. Burton (c.1832-1896) was the son of William and Catherine Burton. He was a cooper and in 1867 married Drucilla Knight (born 1846), the daughter of Austin Knight (born c.1822). William lived near Lance (Mountain View) and in 1865 was granted a license to sell liquor (Eby, Men 282).

[1400] Thomas H. Speake (died 1862) died at the Seven Days Battles around Richmond. He was then serving with the 49th Virginia Infantry.

[1401] James McDonald Briggs (1822-1900) was the son of James McDonald Briggs, Sr. (1787-1845) and Charlotte Ashmore Keith (1782-1866) of the Stony Hill that was in Hartwood. In 1845 he married Louisa Ann Smith (c.1829-1888) of Fauquier and inherited and resided at Stony Hill. From 1865-1868 he served as a justice in Stafford. In 1872 he was appointed one of the commissioners of the Free Bridge between Fredericksburg and Stafford. James and Louisa were buried in Green Hill Cemetery, Berryville, Virginia.

[1402] Armistead A. Armstrong (c.1816-1885) was the son of James Armstrong (1800-1876) of Stafford.

[1403] James Atchison (died c.1841) owned 90 acres on Beaverdam Run of Aquia Run.

[1404] James Black (c.1818-1850) was the son of William Black (born c.1775). He married Delila Bussell (1819-1896) of Stafford. In 1843 James paid tax on 13 acres near Ramoth Church.

[1405] May be Harrison Brockenbrough Barnes (born c.1813) who married Lucy Peyton Conway (born 1822).

[1406] Robert H. Boling (born 1817) was the son of Frances Boling (born c.1805) and Christian Musselman (born c.1801). On Nov. 12, 1873 he submitted his Homestead Exemption which included 1 bed, 8 chairs, 2 chests, 2 tables, cooking utensils, 1 ox, 20 acres of land, 12 barrels of corn, and some fodder and shucks (Stafford Loose Papers, Homestead Exemptions).

[1407] Riley Bowler (c.1814-1891) was the son of Charles and Phoebe Bowler. He lived near Falmouth and died in Stafford.

[1408] Alfred Burroughs (1802-1867) was noted as being "overage."

[1409] In 1850 John A. Brammell (died c.1875) paid tax on 591 acres on Chappawamsic Run.

[1410] In 1850 James R. Bullock (c.1819-after 1850) paid tax on 74 ½ acres in which he held a life estate from the will of Thomas Harwood (1769-1832). James had married Thomas' daughter, Alice Harwood (1819-after 1850).

[1411] This was actually George Wellington Luke Shelton (1825-1902) who was the son of George Gustavus Shelton and lived in White Oak. He served with the 47th and 30th Virginia Infantry and was a musician. His first wife was a Sullivan. He married secondly Maria Alberta Perry. Wellington is buried under the 1950s addition on Bethel Baptist Church.

1846

William Chinn[1412]	William Clift[1413]	Albert Clift[1414]
John F. Cox[1415]	Presley J. Curtis	Lafayett Corbin[1416]
Benjamin Conyers[1417]	Enoch Cox[1418]	Hamilton Cooper
Walter M. Cox[1419]	Arthur F. Clift[1420]	William Dillon
Aldridge Dye[1421]	John Ennis	John Edwards
James Embrey	William Edwards	Patrick H. England
James Edwards	John F. Ficklen	Joseph B. Ficklen
John Finnall	John Furgerson	Edward Finnall
Edmund C. Fitzhugh[1422]	Henry Fitzhugh[1423]	William H. Fitzhugh, Jr.[1424]
Austin Graves	Hedgman Green	Samuel Gordon
John B. Gray[1425]	William Grinnan	James A. Gollyhorn[1426]

[1412] In 1843 William Chinn paid tax on 131 acres in White Oak. In October 1843 Charles Bruce of Stafford sold William 15 acres, part of the land Bruce bought from Robert E. Scott of Fauquier on Casson Ferry Road (Stafford Deed Book NN, p. 324).

[1413] This may be William A. Clift who died in 1869.

[1414] Albert Clift (c.1813-1890) was the son of Fielding Clift and Sallie Elkins. In 1850 he paid tax on 200 acres on Accokeek Run.

[1415] John Francis Cox (c.1802-after 1850) was the son of Presley Cox and Sarah Jett. From 1832-1834 he held retail and liquor licenses. John lived in White Oak near New Hope Church.

[1416] Lafayette Corbin (born 1824) was born in Culpeper County, the son of Jameson Corbin (1790-1862) and Mary Nelson Mason (born 1786). He married Catherine Ramey (born c.1824). In 1855 the Stafford court granted Lafayette a license to sell liquor in Stafford.

[1417] Benjamin Conyers was the son of John Conyers (c.1789-c.1844) and Ann Blackburn (born c.1789), widow of Christopher Blackburn of Stafford. Little is known about Benjamin.

[1418] Enoch Cox was the son of Samuel Cox (died 1844) of White Oak.

[1419] Walter M. Cox (born c.1820) was the son of Charnock Cox (born 1783) and Leah Owens (Monteith) Owens, widow of Thomas Owens. In 1854 Walter was a deputy sheriff in Stafford. During the War Between the States, Walter served in the 47th Virginia Infantry.

[1420] Arthur Fielding Clift (c.1815-1888). From around 1853 until at least 1864 he served as a justice in Stafford. From 1870-1873 he was a magistrate for the Aquia District. Arthur married Marian M. Alexander, the daughter of Fielding Alexander (died 1847) and Minnie Schooler.

[1421] Aldridge Dye (c.1827-1889) married Mary E. Cropp (Stafford Deed Book UU, p. 390). In February 1875 Aldridge made his homestead exemption which consisted of 2 horses, 2 cattle, 1 wagon, farm implements, household and kitchen furniture, "1 Lot of fodder & Straw, 5 Bbls of Corn" (Stafford County Loose Papers, Homestead Exemptions). Aldridge died of "cholera morbus."

[1422] Edmund Clare Fitzhugh (died 1883) was the son of Dr. Alexander Fitzhugh (1786-1847) and Eliza Gibbs Clare. In 1849 he moved to California, opened a law firm, and became head of the Sehome Coal Mine in Whatcom County. In the late 1850s he returned to Washington to help run John C. Breckinridge's unsuccessful presidential campaign against Abraham Lincoln. In 1862 he was appointed to the staff of Gen. George E. Pickett. After the war, Edmund returned to California where he died.

[1423] Henry Fitzhugh (1818-1883) was the son of George Fitzhugh (1784-1881) and Sarah Battaile Dade (1787-1862) of Milton, Culpeper County. He married Jane Elizabeth Downman (1817-1881), the daughter of Joseph Ball Downman (1787-c.1800) of Lancaster County. From her father Jane inherited 780 acres on what is now Route 3 east. After his marriage to Jane, Henry built a fine brick home on the tract and called it Sherwood Forest. The house survives today, but the farm has been bought by a developer who plans on building houses there. Following the War Between the States, Henry submitted a claim to the Southern Claims Commission for $65,415 worth of hogs, sheep, and other commodities taken by the Union Army. He was granted $21,810.

[1424] William Henry Fitzhugh, Jr. (1819-1882) was the son of William Henry Fitzhugh (1788-1854) and Eliza Churchill Darby (born 1795). He married first Betty Ambler Harrison, the eldest daughter of Carter H. and Janetta R. Harrison of Goochland County. He married secondly in 1859 Mary Ann Harrison (1839-1927), the youngest daughter of the same parents. The younger William bought Woodlawn on the east side of Deacon Road (Route 607) but became so indebted that his mother-in-law bought the farm and placed it in trust for Mary Ann.

1846

Robert Graves	Alexander Graves	Charles Griffis
John Guy	John W. Guy	Robert Guy
Thomas Green	William Green	Joseph W. Honey
Samuel Humphreys	Ludwell Herndon[1427]	George Herndon[1428]
Marshall Hefling	Benjamin Horton[1429]	James Homes
Thomas Harding	Strother Harding	Anderson Humphreys[1430]
Thomas H. Hewitt[1431]	Thomas B. Hay	Harris Hill
Randall Holden	Francis Jett	Thornton Jones
David R. Jones	Elisha Jones	John W. Jones
Gustavus Kearns	Daniel S. Knight	Lewis Knight[1432]
Austin Knight	Joel M. Kendall[1433]	Henry Knox
William Knox	John Knox	Benjamin Knox
Andrew B. Lunsford[1434]	Landon Limbrick	James Mills
Richard C. L. Moncure	Hugh Musselman[1435]	William F. Moore[1436]
James M. McIntire	John Murphy	Alexander Morson[1437]

[1425] John Bowie Gray (1808-1861) was the son of John Gray (1769-1848) of Gartcraig, Scotland and Lucy Robb (born 1773). The elder John resided at Traveler's Rest on the Rappahannock River. John B. Gray married Jane Moore Cave (1811-1890) and lived at Traveler's Rest.

[1426] James A. Gollyhorn (c.1822-1885) was the son of George and Elizabeth Gollyhorn. He owned land on Enon Road (Rt. 753) and died in Stafford.

[1427] Ludwell Herndon (1823-1908) was the son of John Herndon (c.1794-1882) and Lucinda "Lucy" Combs (c.1796-c.1867). He resided on the old Holloway farm, more recently owned by Milton Christy. This is located on the east side of Poplar Road (Rt. 616) near Potomac Run. Ludwell married Rosanna Rebecca Lane (c.1828-1903), the daughter of Fountain H. Lane (c.1795-1872) and Virginia "Jennie" Briggs/Bridges (died c.1853). From 1893-1903 he served as postmaster at Coakley's Post Office. Ludwell died of a stroke at the home of his son-in-law, Wallace Franklin.

[1428] George Herndon (1821-1898) was the son of John Herndon (c.1794-1882) and Lucinda Combs (c.1796-c.1862). George was born in Fauquier, died in Laurel, Maryland (and was buried in Ivy Hill Cemetery there), but spent most of his life in Stafford. In 1858 and 1859 he was one of the overseers of the road in Stafford and in 1866 was overseer "from Aquia Run to Stafford Store" (Eby, Men 173).

[1429] Benjamin Horton may be Benjamin B. Horton (c.1794-after 1870).

[1430] Anderson Humphreys (c.1822-after 1881) lived near Sanford Road (Route 670) and U. S. Route 17.

[1431] Thomas H. Hewitt (c.1819-1872) was born in Connecticut. He lived near Falmouth and was buried at Berea Baptist Church.

[1432] May be Lewis K. Knight (c.1820-1893), the possible son of William Knight. During the War Between the States, Lewis served with the 47th Virginia Infantry. In 1868 Lewis was overseer of the road for "Coal Landing road in the place of John N. Stewart" (Eby, Men 176).

[1433] Joel M. Kendall (c.1827-after 1850) was the son of Robert Kendall (c.1787-1860) and was a merchant.

[1434] Andrew B. Lunsford (born 1822) was the son of William Lunsford (born 1785) and operated a store in Hartwood. He married Mary Ann Elizabeth Smith (born 1834), the daughter of Wilford Smith (c.1797-after 1860) of Stafford. By 1870 Andrew had removed to Clay County, Missouri.

[1435] Hugh Musselman may be Hugh R. Musselman (c.1817-1862), the son of Peter Musselman (1792-1870). Around 1825 he married Mary Jane West (born c.1825), the daughter of George West of Stafford. Hugh died in Richmond.

[1436] William F. Moore (c.1812-1864). In 1846 he married Mary Frances Alsop (1823-1865), the daughter of William Alsop (c.1792-c.1860). From 1854-1856 he served as a justice of the peace in Stafford. From at least 1845-1851 William was president of the board of the overseers of the poor for Stafford. He died of consumption. His estate inventory included 10 sheep, 10 cattle, 2 mules, 1 wagon, 1 buggy, 21 barrels of corn, 30 barrels of oats, 7 hogs, 1 horse, 1 safe, 1 dining table, 1 pair sheep sheers and scales, 1 carpet and several rugs, 2 dressing tables, 1 crib and mattress, 4 beds, 1 "Teaster Bed Stead & furniture," and 1 table cloth all valued at $1,348.37 (Stafford Deed Book 26A, p. 494).

[1437] This may be Arthur Alexander Morson (1801-1864) who was the son of Alexander Morson (1759-1822) and Anne Casson Alexander (1781-1833). He married Maria Martin Scott (born 1814), the daughter of John Scott (1781-1850) and Elizabeth Pickett.

1846

Thomas Monteith[1438]	Abram B. Newton	Edward Oder[1439]
William Payne	George Payne	James Payne
Spotswood Payne[1440]	Robert Peyton	Horace Potts
Thomas Patton[1441]	John Robertson	John Randall
Gallenus Randall[1442]	Abram Randall[1443]	John Reeves
James Rolls[1444]	Isaac Reeves[1445]	George W. Smith
Richard Stark[1446]	Richard M. Shelton[1447]	Richard M. Snellings
William Snellings	James Snellings	Philip A. Snellings[1448]
Caleb Sullivan	Daniel Sullivan, Jr.	Presley Sullivan[1449]
Addison Sullivan	Thomas Sullivan	Thomas Sullivan, Jr.
Stephen Sullivan	George W. Strother[1450]	Thomas Stratton[1451]
John Scott	William Skinner	Harrison Skinner
Jackson Suddoth[1452]	Warren Slaughter[1453]	James H. Truslow[1454]

[1438] Thomas Monteith was the son of Samuel Owens Monteith (1785-1862) and Mildred Fines.

[1439] Edbert Franklin Oder (c.1823-1907) often appears in records as Edward F. Oder. He was the son of Thomas Oder (1798-after 1876) and Mary Howdershelt (c.1798-1876). Edward was a blacksmith and lived in Falmouth. His first wife was Sarah Whiting Cowne (c.1830-before 1880). He married secondly Mariah Coakley. Edbert was a Confederate veteran.

[1440] Spotswood Payne (c.1814-after 1870).

[1441] Thomas Patton (c.1822-after 1850) was a miller and lived in Hartwood.

[1442] Gallenus M. Randall (c.1792-c.1889) was a carpenter and lived near Stafford Store on Beaverdam Run in what is now the Quantico reservation (Stafford Deed Book 5, p. 49). In 1870 he paid taxes on 150 acres on Beaverdam Run in Rock Hill District. He actually moved back and forth between Stafford and Fauquier counties. His first wife was Betsy (last name unknown). Around 1787 he married secondly Harriet M. Pearson (born 1845), the daughter of Martin Pearson. Gallenus seems to have been the only one of this branch of the Randall family who could read and write.

[1443] Abram Randall (1814-1875) was the son of Abram Randall (1780-1855) and Sega Lygna Tarman (born 1785) and worked as a carpenter. He was born in Fauquier but lived on the farm his father had bought just east of Stafford Springs. By his wife, Jane, he fathered numerous children.

[1444] James Rolls/Roles (c.1810-after 1850) was the son of Rosanna Roles (c.1770-after 1850). He married Martha Ann ___ (c.1811-after 1852) and lived in the northern part of the county on what is now the Marine Corps reservation.

[1445] This may be Isaac J. Reeves who was a trustee for the town of Falmouth in 1849 and possibly other years as well (Town 67).

[1446] Richard Stark (c.1813-1877) was the son of Joseph Stark and Mary Edwards. He married Eleanor Bell, the daughter of Thomas Bell and Catherine Arrington. In 1849 Richard paid tax on 90 acres on Chappawamsic Run. His estate inventory included 1 mahogany side board, 1 cherry table, 1 mahogany bureau, 12 chairs, 2 clocks, 1 wardrobe, 1 spinning wheel, 4 bedsteads, 1 china press and contents, 2 horses, 1 ox, and household and kitchen furniture all valued at $522.25 (Stafford Deed Book UU, p. 325).

[1447] Richard Mason Shelton (c.1819-1892) was the son of Gustavus Shelton and Lucinda Pates. He ran the stable at the courthouse. He also pleaded cases in court and served as attorney for some Stafford residents who submitted claims to the Southern Claims Commission. Richard married Eliza E. Shackelford (born c.1827). In April 1878 Richard claimed his homestead exemption, which consisted of 110 acres, 1 clock, 1 cart, 4 cattle, 1 colt, 1 mule, 5 shoats, 9 sheep, 1 table, and 7 chairs all valued at $513.75 (Stafford County Loose Papers, Homestead Exemptions).

[1448] Philip A. Snellings (1827-1887) was the son of Alexander Snellings (1800:05-before 1850) and Annis Mannin(g) (1806-1853) of Stafford. Between 1850 and 1854 he married Julia A. Boutyard (born 1829), the daughter of John Boutyard and Sarah Mahorney.

[1449] Presley J. Sullivan (c.1824-1880) was killed in a fight.

[1450] George W. Strother (born c.1803) was the son of George Strother (c.1765-1811) and Sarah Kenyon (c.1770-1825) of Albion. In 1850 he paid tax on 550 acres of Albion.

[1451] Thomas Stratton married Priscilla Bradshaw, the daughter of Harberson Bradshaw (1785-1843) (Stafford Deed Book NN, p. 333).

[1452] Jackson Suddoth (born c.1825) lived in Falmouth.

John Truslow	Charles A. Tackett[1455]	Withers Waller[1456]
Thomas Williams	William White	James White
Henry White	Gustavus B. Wallace	William Young

1847

Adjutant—William S. Briggs (Cavalry)
Captains—William J. Green[1457] (Cavalry)—in room of William Brent, promoted
      Rodney B. Bradshaw
      John M. Brooke
1st Lieutenants—Fielding B. Stone[1458]—in room of William S. Embrey, resigned
      Harrison B. Barnes (Cavalry)—in room of Peter Wigginton, resigned
      Andrew B. Lunsford—in room of John H. King, resigned
2nd Lieutenant—William J. Snellings[1459]—in room of John F. Ficklen, resigned
      Thomas H. Speake—in room of Byram Harding, resigned
3rd Lieutenant—Elijah McInteer[1460]—in room of Harrison B. Barnes
Lieutenants—Isaac Sullivan
      Robert B. Alexander
      Patrick H. Burrus[1461]
      William J. Burton
      William C. Moncure[1462]
      James M. Briggs
Regimental Clerk—George Waller

[1453] May be John Warren Slaughter (1820-1866), the son of William Slaughter (born 1780) and Harriet Ficklen (1796-1881). John was born in Culpeper and married Sarah Moore Braxton (1827-1881) of Mathews County. Prior to the War Between the States, he was a partner with Walker P. Conway in the Bank of Virginia in Fredericksburg. In 1850 John paid tax on a ¼-acre island mill lot near Falmouth. By that time he was a resident of Fredericksburg.

[1454] James Henry Truslow (c.1828-c.1898) was one of ten children born to Benjamin Truslow, Jr. (c.1792-1869) and Nancy Dicken(s). In 1854 he married Mary J. Green of Stafford.

[1455] Charles Addison Tackett (1814-1896) was the son of Charles Tackett, Sr. 1780-1834) who built Tackett's Mill around 1800. C. A. Tackett served in a variety of public offices in Stafford including being clerk of the court from 1875 until around 1885.

[1456] Withers Waller (1825-1900) married Anne Eliza Stribling (1832-1903) of Fauquier and resided at Clifton on the Potomac River in Wide Water. Withers was the son of Withers Waller (1785-1827) and Catherine Barret Conway (died c.1864). For many years before and after the War Between the States, the younger Withers operated a large commercial seine fishery at Clifton. From at least 1850-1851 he was a trustee of the town of Falmouth (Town 70, 72).

[1457] William James Green (1825-1862) was the son of Duff Green (1792-1854) of Falmouth. He served as a town trustee from at least 1858 until entering Confederate service in 1861 (Town 77, 83). In 1846 he graduated from VMI and in May 1861 enlisted in the 47th Virginia Infantry. William was killed at the Battle of Gaines' Mill. He died unmarried.

[1458] Fielding Barton Stone (born c.1829) was the son of Barton Speake Stone. He married Ann M./K. Schooler (born c.1831, the daughter of Thomas E. Schooler (born c.1787) of Stafford

[1459] William J. Snellings (1821-1880) was the son of Benjamin Snellings (1780:90-before 1850). He married Elizabeth Berry (born 1820), the daughter of John Berry of Stafford.

[1460] Elijah McInteer (1828-1917) was the son of William McInteer and Ada Harding (1790-1836). He was born in Stafford and died in Hart County, Kentucky. Elijah married Sarah Wilcoxson (1831-1917).

[1461] Patrick H. Burruss (Burroughs?) (born c.1820) was a carpenter and lived in White Oak. He married Ann M. ___ (c.1819-1848) of Caroline County. She was buried in the Daffan family cemetery near Leeland Road.

[1462] William Cary Moncure (1829-1850) was the son of Henry Wood Moncure (1800-1866) and Catherine Ambler. Little is known of him and he left no children.

1847

Men fined for failure to appear at muster:

John Atchison	John S. Arrington	James Arrington
William Anderson	Joseph Armstrong	Riley Bowler
William Burton	John E. Burton	James Boutyard
Philip Bowen	John O. Banks[1463]	Charles Bridwell
Daniel T. Bryant	Robert Bowling	Travis Bowling
James Bowling	George A. Bowling[1464]	John Beagle
Joseph Bridwell	Charles G. Browne	Willis Benson[1465]
Alexander Browne[1466]	William Carter	Richard W. Carter
Benjamin Conyers	Thornton B. Cooper	David Cooper
John E. Cooper	William Cox	John E. Coakley
Walker P. Conway	John M. Conway, Jr.	Robert Chinn
George H. Deane	Alfred Dent	John S. Dent
James Davis	John Edwards	Joseph B. Ficklen
John F. Ficklen	Beverly Fugate	Edmund C. Fitzhugh
Daniel W. Ford[1467]	William H. Franklin[1468]	Henry Fitzhugh
Alexander M. Green[1469]	John W. Griffith[1470]	Samuel Gordon
William Grinnan	Alexander Graves	John B. Gray
Anderson Humphrey	Samuel Humphrey	Strother Harding, Sr.
Joseph W. Honey	George Herndon	Thomas Heflin[1471]
James T. Heflin	Walter Hore	Elias A. W. Hore[1472]
Thomas Hales[1473]	John L. Henderson[1474]	Harris Hill

[1463] John Overton Banks (1811-1886) was the son of George Banks (1779-1837) and Jemima Anne Overton (1789-1863). He married Susan Cordelia Bell (1828-1895) and died in Hines County, Mississippi.

[1464] George Allen Bowling (1817-1912). In 1865 he was overseer of the road "from Aquia road to Tackett's Mill" (Eby, Men 171). On Dec. 16, 1874 he submitted his Homestead Exemption which included 60 acres of land, household and kitchen furniture, 5 horses, 5 cattle, 7 hogs, and 1 wagon (Stafford Loose Papers, Homestead Exemptions). George married Emily Way. During the War Between the States, he served with the Stafford Light Artillery.

[1465] William Willis Lewis Benson (1815-1858) was the son of William Willis/Wilson Lewis Benson (died 1815) and Eleanor Bullard (1786-1846) of Fauquier. He married Elizabeth Sanford (c.1825-1855), the daughter of Lawrence Sanford of Stafford. William's unusual obituary read, "Sudden death by Drinking Camphor. Mr. W. W. Benson of Stafford died rather suddenly on Sunday last from the effects of drinking a glass of spirits of camphor. Mr. B. had been intemperate, and took the camphor knowingly, but not with the slightest idea it would destroy his life" (*Virginia Herald*, Oct. 27, 1858).

[1466] Alexander Browne (c.1814-1892) was the son of John and Clara Brown of Stafford. He lived somewhere in the vicinity of Greenbank in lower Stafford.

[1467] Daniel White Ford (1821-1853) was the son of Capt. William Ford (1788-1834) and his second wife, Elizabeth Allen Hore (1792-1822).

[1468] William H. Franklin (c.1834-c.1864) later served in the 9th Virginia Cavalry and died at Point Lookout.

[1469] Alexander Morson Green (c.1828-1904) was the son of Duff Green (1792-1854) of Falmouth. Alexander resided at Shepherd's Green on Potomac Creek. His father was a wealthy industrialist and businessman in Falmouth, but Alexander seems to have preferred farming to business. Although he was unmarried, he raised a large family by Nancy Ross. She may have been his slave prior to the war, but was listed as his cook thereafter.

[1470] This may be John Willoughby Griffith (c.1831-after 1903) who was a resident of Prince William County at the outbreak of the War Between the states. In his old age he resided at the Lee Soldiers' Home in Richmond.

[1471] Thomas Heflin (c.1807-1869) died in Stafford.

[1472] Elias A. W. Hore (1821-c.1891) was the son of Elias Hore (1749-1832) and Theodosia Waller (1753-1829). He was a merchant and ran a fishing business at Dipple (St. Marysville). Elias' estate included farm implements, 1 writing desk, 1 refrigerator, 1 clock, 1 old shuck mattress, 2 hogs, and 2 old muzzle-loading shot guns all valued at $36.30 (Stafford Deed Book 4, p. 559).

1847

Hugh Harris	Jackson Harding	Strother Harding, Jr.
Thomas B. Harding	Alexander Jones[1475]	Thornton Jones
David R. Jones	Joseph M. Johnson	Thomas H. Johnson[1476]
Starke Jett	Reuben Jackson[1477]	Joel M. Kendall
William A. Knox[1478]	John J. Knox	Landon Limbrick
Lewis E. Latham[1479]	Hugh Musselman	Robert Musselman
Alexander Morson	Thomas Monteith	William Monteith[1480]
William Monroe, Jr.	James Monroe, Jr.[1481]	Richard C. L. Moncure
George V. Moncure[1482]	Henry Milstead[1483]	James H. Mills[1484]
Robert S. Mills	Abraham Newton	Spotswood Payne
William Payne	George Payne	John H. Payne[1485]
Elliot Patton, Jr.[1486]	William A. Patton[1487]	John Randall
James Roles	John Roles	Noah Riley[1488]
Isaac J. Rains	Lewis Smith	Benjamin Smith

[1473] Thomas Hales (c.1805-after 1860).
[1474] John L. Henderson (c.1805-after 1850) lived in Wide Water. He married Elizabeth Milstead and was the brother-in-law of Willoughby Newton Carter (1800-1878) of Palace Green in Wide Water.
[1475] Alexander Jones (c.1804-1859) was a cooper and worked for William T. Masters. Alexander died in Stafford.
[1476] Thomas H. Johnson (c.1820-1903) lived near Falmouth. During the War Between the States, he served in the 9th Virginia Cavalry. Thomas married Enfield Honey (c.1829-1889), the daughter of George and Nancy Honey of Stafford.
[1477] Reuben Jackson (c.1804-after 1850) was a cooper.
[1478] William Alexander Knox was a merchant in Fredericksburg. He married Elizabeth J. W. Jennings of Fauquier.
[1479] Lewis Elzey Latham (1813-after 1888) was the son of Jesse Latham (born c.1785) and Betsy P. Horton of Fauquier. Lewis was a stonemason and died childless.
[1480] William Monteith was the son of Samuel O. Monteith (1785-1862).
[1481] In 1849 James Monroe, Jr. (c.1819-c.1876) was the son of James Monroe, Sr. (c.1797-1867) who was involved with the gold mines in lower Stafford. In 1849 James, Jr. paid taxes on 379 acres on the Rappahannock near Richlands Baptist Church. During the War Between the States, he served with the 47th Virginia Infantry.
[1482] George F(razier?) Vowles Moncure (1826-1901) was the son of John Moncure IV (1793-1876) of Woodbourne and his first wife, Esther J. Vowles (1795-1833). George seems to have been named for his uncle, George Frazier Vowles (1780-1825), though he didn't use the Frazier name in his signatures. The only record of his complete name is on a receipt from his father (Kendall, private collection). One of Stafford's leading citizens of the 19th century, George was born at Somerset and resided at Chelsea, both of these farms in Wide Water. In 1849 he married Mary Conway Ashby (1830-1897), the daughter of Col. Turner Ashby (1789-1834) and Dorothea F. Green (1789-1865) of Rosebank, Fauquier County. George represented Stafford in the Virginia House of Delegates, served as clerk of the court in Stafford, and was frequently asked by the courts to administer estates.
[1483] Henry Milstead (1812-1873) was from Prince William County. He married Sarah "Sally" Fendall Bell (1831-1917), the daughter of John Fendall Bell and Jane Adie of Stafford.
[1484] James H. Mills was the son of Willis Franklin Mills (c.1806-1886) and Ann D. Lewis (c.1814-after 1880) of Spotsylvania.
[1485] John H. Payne (c.1823-after 1850) was a blacksmith.
[1486] In 1870 Elliot Patton paid taxes on 283 acres on or near the Rappahannock River. He married Juliet Coppage (born c.1824), the daughter of Esom Coppage (c.1790-after 1850) and Marian Curtis (born 1808).
[1487] William Allen Patton (c.1812-1857) was the son of John Patton and Bathsheba McInteer. He married Rebecca Harriet Timmons (1821-1913), the daughter of Thomas Tarleton Timmons (1801-1853) and Hannah Elizabeth Jones (born 1804) of Stafford. William died in Stafford.
[1488] Noah Riley (1813-c.1897) was the son of James Riley. He married Cleopatra O'Byrhim (born 1839) and lived in the north end of the county in what is now part of the Marine Corps reservation. Noah also married Louisa Jane Patterson (c.1823-1858), the daughter of Perry Patterson (1776-after 1850).

1847

Thomas Smith	Robert Smith	Walker Smith
John Smith	Stephen Sullivan	Richard Starke
John W. Slaughter	Jackson Suthard	Harrison Skidmore
Samuel Skidmore	Walter Stone	Samuel Shackleford
Abroad Shelton	George W. Strother	Charles A. Tackett
William W. Turner	John Truslow	Robert Truslow
Charles Truslow	William Villers	Withers Waller
Henry White	William Young	

1848[1489]

Captain—Thaddeus J. Crismond[1490]—in room of Robert L. Waple, resigned
1st Lieutenant—Charles H. Roberson[1491] (White Oak Co.)—in room of William J. Burton, resigned

1849

Captain—Randall Holden—in room of Rodney B. Bradshaw, resigned

1850

There were "Courthouse Company," "Aquia Company," and an "Artillery Company."

Captains—John M. Homes (Artillery Co.)—in room of Charles E. Gill, resigned
Peter Wigginton (Stafford Courthouse Co.)—in room of Joseph Golatt, resigned
1st Lieutenant—Peter N. Hedgman[1492]—in room of Wofinton Kendall, resigned
2nd Lieutenant—Charles Jones—in room of Aquilla Randall, resigned

Men fined for failure to appear at muster:

James E. Anderson[1493]	John H. Armstrong	William Brown
John Brown	Richard Burton	Benjamin Barker
Thomas Berry[1494]	Lemuel Brooks[1495]	Alexander Chilton
George W. Catlett[1496]	Andrew Catlett[1497]	John F. Cox

[1489] On Apr. 17, 1848 William S. Briggs wrote that John Mercer Brooke and Robert B. Alexander never qualified to their commissions and left the county very shortly after having been elected. Patrick H. Burroughs was still in the county but refused to qualify (Box 148, Folder 58).

[1490] Thaddeus Jett Crismond (1826-1906) was the son of Charles B. Crismond (1791-1865) of King George County. For some years Thaddeus was engaged in the mercantile business in Fredericksburg and Baltimore. Later, he taught school. His first wife was Mary F. Davis of Virginia. He married secondly Sarah Louisa Embrey (born 1842) of Saline County, Missouri.

[1491] Charles H. Roberson (1823-1892). In October 1863 he enlisted in the Fredericksburg Artillery, but later transferred to the 9th Virginia Cavalry. He married Maria Turner (1820-1885), the daughter of Alexander and Elizabeth Turner. Charles and Maria are buried in White Oak near Bethel Church Road (Route 600).

[1492] Peter N. Hedgman (c.1829-1897) later served as a sergeant in the 47th Virginia Infantry and was wounded in December 1864. In 1876 he bought part of the Potomac Silk Farm near Potomac Church and Brooke Road (Route 608) (Stafford Deed Book 1, p. 343). He later lived in the Confederate veterans' home in Richmond and was buried in Hollywood Cemetery.

[1493] James E. Anderson (born c.1833) was the son of William Anderson (c.1795-after 1850) and lived in the northern end of the county.

[1494] Thomas Berry (c.1818-after 1870) married Margaret Newton, the daughter of William Newton, Sr. On Jan. 17, 1874 he submitted his Homestead Exemption which included 13 acres of land, 2 horses, 1 cow, 4 hogs, 1 cart, 3 plows, 12 barrels of corn and fodder, and household and kitchen furniture (Stafford Loose Papers, Homestead Exemptions).

[1495] Lemuel Brooks (c.1820-after 1850) was the son of Thomas R. Brooks (c.1801-after 1850) and worked in the gold mines near the Rappahannock River.

1850

George L. Cox[1498]	John B. Cox[1499]	William Cox
John E. Coakley	Alexander Curtis	Samuel Cole[1500]
Robert A. Chinn[1501]	Presley Curtis	John Chilton
James Dunnington	John Davis	James Davis
Greenhow Edwards[1502]	John Ennis	John Ellington[1503]
Walter Fugate[1504]	Albert Fugate[1505]	John Finnall
Elijah Groves[1506]	Harrison Groves	Willis Groves
George Gollahorne[1507]	John S. Graves	Edward Green
James L. Hefling[1508]	Hugh Harrison	William A. Jones
Warner Jacobs[1509]	Reuben Jackson	James Jett[1510]
Stark Jett	George Littral[1511]	Robert Latham
Lawson Lunsford	James H. Lunsford	James Latham
Philip Latham[1512]	Robert Lowry[1513]	Walker Monroe[1514]
William Monroe	Robert Mills[1515]	John S. Mills[1516]

[1496] George W. Catlett (c.1812-1871) was the son of Robert (died c.1854) and Clarissa Catlett of Bell View, just west of Belle Plains. He married Matilda Newton, the daughter of Gustavus Newton.

[1497] Andrew J. Catlett (c.1830-1883) was the son of Robert (died c.1854) and Clarissa Catlett of Bell View, Stafford. His first wife was Susan C. ___. He married secondly Sarah Ann Gains (born c.1826). Andrew served with the Fredericksburg Artillery from March to April 1862 when he deserted.

[1498] George L. Cox (born c.1832) was the son of John F. Cox (c.1802-after 1850) and lived in White Oak.

[1499] John B. Cox (1830-1914) married Ann Eliza "Nannie" Boutchard (1834-1912).

[1500] Samuel Cole (c.1810-after 1850) was a tanner and lived in the north end of the county.

[1501] Robert A. Chinn (1824-1876) was the son of James Thomas Chinn and Susan McGuire. He married Sarah Jesse Rowe (1833-1918), the daughter of Jesse Rowe and Atsey Humphries. In March 1862 William Pollock and wife Janet R. sold Robert 58 acres adjoining Ferry Farm and known as Clark's tract (Stafford Deed Book TT, p. 60).

[1502] Greenhow Edwards (born c.1832) was the son of Ann Edwards (c.1808-after 1850) and lived in or near Falmouth.

[1503] John Ellington (born c.1838) was a farm laborer.

[1504] This may actually be Walker M. Fugate (c.1817-1896) who died in Stafford.

[1505] Albert Fugate (c.1831-after 1900) moved from Stafford to Prince George's County, Maryland. He was the son of John Fugitt/Fugate.

[1506] Elijah Groves (born c.1822).

[1507] George Gollahorne (c.1818-after 1880) was the son of Solomon Gollahorn (1791-after 1870) of Stafford. In 1850 he paid tax on 80 acres on Accokeek Run about two miles south of the courthouse.

[1508] James Lee Heflin (c.1827-1862) was the son of William Strother Heflin, Sr. Around 1846 he married Elizabeth M. Bowling (born c.1825). In 1858 he was one of the overseers of the road for Stafford.

[1509] Warner Jacobs (c.1824-1872) was the son of William Jacobs (1760-1829) and Lavinia Colvert (1768-1830) of Culpeper. He married Mary Graves (c.1826-1872).

[1510] This may be James Jett who married Polly N. Cox (c.1799-1876), the daughter of Vincent and Sarah Cox of Stafford.

[1511] George Littral (born c.1828) was a miner.

[1512] Philip Latham (c.1820-after 1850) was a cooper.

[1513] May be Robert A. Lowry (1838-1907). In 1884 he was a judge of elections for Brooke Station (Eby, Men 186). He was buried in the Jones/Lowry cemetery near Brooke.

[1514] Walker Monroe (c.1830-c.1870) was the son of Anthony Monroe. Walker married Sarah Elizabeth Jones (born c.1835) and lived on part of the Richlands tract off U. S. Route 17. In 1870 Walker paid taxes on the 50-acre Philemon Leitch tract in Hartwood.

[1515] Robert Mills (c.1825-1887) married Lucy A. Lampkin (c.1829-1879) of Rockingham County.

[1516] John S. Mills (c.1806-1891) was the son of John Mills (born c.1783) and Phoebe Stevens (born c.1780). He married Elizabeth Haydon (c.1817-after 1891) and lived near Berea. In 1850 James and John S. Mills paid tax on 35 acres near Horsepen Run. John's estate inventory included 2 beds, 1 clock, 1 writing desk, 1 rocking chair, 1 cooking stove, a 2-horse wagon, 2 horses, and 3 cattle all valued at $117.25 (Stafford Deed Book 6, p. 454). John was a shoemaker.

1850

William Payne	Robert Peyton	Gustavus Pates
James Rowe	George F. Rose	George Robertson
William Robertson	John Robertson	James Sullivan
Elijah Sullivan[1517]	Wellington Shelton	Moncure Shelton[1518]
Harrison J. Skidmore	William J. Snellings	Robert Skidmore
Thomas Sullivan	John Sullivan	James Snellings
William Snellings	Abroad Shelton	Daniel Sullivan
John Sullivan, Jr.	Addison Sullivan	Isaac N. Sullivan
Caleb Sullivan	John Snellings	William Skidmore
Robert Smith	Enoch Skidmore[1519]	Thomas Smith
Walker Smith	Jesse Stone	Thomas M. D. Stephens[1520]
Thomas B. Thomkins	John F. Warters	Thomas Williams
George M. Watson	Robert Watson	Henry White

1851

Colonel Commandant—Charles F. Suttle
Adjutant—Charles E. Gill
Major—William J. Green—in room of William Brent, removed
Captains—Jefferson Heflin
    Thaddeus J. Crismond
    James Ashby[1521] (Cavalry)—in room of William J. Green, promoted
    William H. Browne, Jr. (White Oak Co.)
    George W. Cropp—Hartwood Company
1st Lieutenants—William J. H. Alexander[1522] (Stafford Store Company of Infantry)—in room of Jefferson Heflin, promoted
    John Schooler (Stafford Courthouse Co. of Infantry)—in room of Peter N. Hedgman, resigned
    William H. Franklin (Artillery Co.)—in room of James E. Waller, resigned
    Robert L. Homes[1523] (Artillery Co.)—in room of James W. Johnson, resigned
    James H. Ball[1524] (White Oak Co.)—in room of Charles H. Roberson, resigned
    John Newton, Jr.[1525] (White Oak Co.)—in room of Charles H. Roberson, resigned

---

[1517] Elijah Sullivan (c.1812-1888) was the son of Benjamin and Lucy Sullivan and died in Stafford.

[1518] Moncure D. Chilton (born c.1831) was the son of Thomas Chilton and Charlotty Limbrick, but went by Shelton. He lived in White Oak. His wife was Elizabeth Roberson who married secondly William Snellings and moved to Baltimore.

[1519] Enoch Skidmore (1832-after 1873) was the son of Alexander S. Skidmore (c.1811-before 1860) and Sarah Ann Garner. His first wife was Imsey Green. He married secondly Sarah E. Rogers. Enoch rented part of Peter D. Lowry's farm (Stafford Deed Book TT, p. 115).

[1520] Thomas M. D. Stephens (c.1824-1889) was the son of James and Susan Stephens of Stafford. In 1852 he married Harriet E. Embrey in Fauquier. Thomas was a wheelwright. During the War Between the States, he served briefly with the 30th Virginia Infantry. He died of consumption.

[1521] James Ashby (1827-1861) was the son of Col. Turner Ashby (1789-1835) and Dorothea Farrer Green (1797-1865) of Fauquier and the brother of Gen. Turner Ashby (1826-1862). James married Frances Vowles Moncure (1828-1910), the daughter of John Moncure (1793-1876) of Woodbourne. He was slated to be in command of the 9th Virginia Cavalry, but died before the unit was formed.

[1522] William J. H. Alexander is likely John William H. Alexander (born c.1827), the son of John Alexander (c.1796-after 1850). He lived near Garrisonville and later served in the 47th Virginia Infantry.

[1523] Robert Lawrence Homes (1831-1852) was the son of James Homes (1786-1843) and Mary Ratcliffe (1795-1867). Most of the Homes family lived in the Garrisonville area of Stafford.

[1524] James H. Ball (c.1831-1907) was the son of Aaron H. Ball. In 1856 James was overseer of the poor for the lower district. He later served with the 30th Virginia Infantry and then with the 9th Virginia Cavalry; during his service, he was wounded in the head and leg. After the war, James worked as a dentist in Stafford. In 1865 he used a small piece of land that straddled the Stafford/King George County line to secure a debt (Stafford Deed Book 26A, p. 18). He lived near Monteithville in lower Stafford.

2*nd Lieutenants*—Richard Ashby[1526] (Cavalry)—in room of Elijah McInteer, removed from the district
Charles W. Bridwell[1527] (Stafford Store Co. of Infantry)—in room of Frister Carter,[1528] resigned
Horace T. Roe[1529] (White Oak Co.)—in room of James Lunsford, resigned
Alexander Turner, Jr.[1530] (White Oak Co.)
John L. Lunsford[1531] (White Oak Co.)

Privates in George W. Cropp's Hartwood Company:[1532]

Harrison C. Alexander[1533]	George L. French[1534]	Robert Lunsford[1535]
John Anderson	John Garner	James H. Mills
Armstead A. Armstrong	John S. Graves	John S. Mills
James Armstrong	Willis Graves	John T. Mills[1536]
Flavius J. Ballard[1537]	John Grinnan[1538]	Robert S. Mills

[1525] John Newton, Jr. was actually John Curtis Newton (born 1829), the son of John Newton and Mildred Curtis. He married Henrietta Chinn, the daughter of James Chinn and Susan McGuire.

[1526] Richard Ashby (1831-1861) was the son of Col. Turner Ashby (1789-1835) and Dorothea Farrer Green (1797-1865) of Fauquier and the brother of Gen. Turner Ashby (1826-1862). For a few years Richard owned and resided at Mt. Experiment in northern Stafford. Prior to the War Between the States, he removed to Texas, but returned to Virginia to serve in the Confederate Army.

[1527] Charles W. Bridwell (born 1824) was born in Prince William County.

[1528] This is William Fristoe Carter (c.1818-before 1891). See his note in 1841.

[1529] Horace Thomas Rowe (born 1830) was not commissioned. He was the son of John Gasking Rowe (1788-1862) and Nancy McGuire (1800-1858).

[1530] Alexander Turner, Jr. (born c.1833) married Ellen F. Stone (born c.1827). In 1850 he paid tax on the 156-acre Hickory Hill tract on Bethel Church Road (Route 600).

[1531] John Lawson Lunsford (c.1832-1863) was the son of William and Willa Lunsford of Stafford. In 1861 he married Jennie B. Swetnam (born c.1841), the daughter of John and Sarah Swetnam. John Lunsford died at Point Lookout Prison.

[1532] From O'Grady pp. 51-53.

[1533] Harrison C. Alexander (c.1817-1903) was the last of the descendants of William Alexander of Stafford. In 1859 he was part of the old Hartwood Baptist Church congregation that met at Enon to try and re-establish that church. In 1871 he bought 182 acres of the old Randolph farm called Cedar Grove. This was located off Rt. 17 and in the southwestern part of Stafford. It doesn't appear that Harrison ever married. He died at Cedar Grove and was buried on Robert Buchan's old farm, Carmora, on Potomac Run (*Fredericksburg Daily Star*, July 3, 1903). Why he was buried at Carmora is unclear and no headstone is known to exist for him.

[1534] George Lee French (1831-1903). During the War Between the States, he served in the 9*th* Virginia Cavalry and was a scout for W. H. F. Lee. He was the son of James French (1803-1865) and Sarah Curtis (1812-1872) of Poplar Grove in Stafford. George married his cousin, Martha Margaret (Payne) McCoy (1832-1905), widow of Leonard H. F. McCoy.

[1535] Possibly Robert F. Lunsford (c.1832-c.1903) who later served with the 9*th* Virginia Cavalry. Robert's estate inventory included 2 horses, 1 mule, 2 cows, 1 spring wagon, 1 cider mill, farm implements, 1 side saddle, assorted tools, 1 washing machine, 1 range, 1 extension table, 1 cook stove, 1 desk, 1 china press, 1 sewing machine, 3 lamps, 1 organ, 5 feather beds, 5 bedsteads, and 1 double-barrel gun (Stafford Deed Book 10, p. 169).

[1536] May be John Thomas Mills (1831-1906), the son of Willis Franklin Mills (c.1806-1886) and Ann D. Lewis (c.1814-after 1880) of Spotsylvania. John was a miner and stone cutter by trade and married Mary Ann Stiars (c.1826-1899), daughter of John G. Stiars and Elizabeth Dillard of Spotsylvania. He was a Confederate veteran and was buried in the Fredericksburg City Cemetery (*Free Lance*, July 3, 1906).

[1537] Flavius Josephus Ballard (1808-1892) was the son of James Ballard (1763-1856) of Spotsylvania. His second wife was Aphia Sanford (c.1814-1846), the daughter of Lawrence Sanford (1778-1858) and Aphia Farmer (1784-1864). He held several minor positions in county government, including being

1851

William Beach	Thomas Groves[1539]	Daniel Monrow[1540]
William W. L. Benson	Jackson Harding	Francis Monrow[1541]
Thomas Bettis, Jr.[1542]	Richard Harding[1543]	James Monrow, Jr.
Thornton Bettis[1544]	Strother Harding	Strother Monrow[1545]
Zachariah Bloxton[1546]	Hugh Harris	Thomas Monrow[1547]
George A. Bowling	Absalom P. Hefling[1548]	Walker Monrow
John F. Bradshaw[1549]	James L. Hefling	William Monrow
Andrew Bridges[1550]	John Helm[1551]	William Monrow, Jr.

Commissioner of Elections for the Harwood Precinct (this was not the Hartwood Precinct) in 1870. From 1873-1875 he was supervisor of the Hartwood District.

[1538] This may be John W. Grinnan (c.1832-1907). He died at the home of his son, Charles L. Grinnan near Richlands Church (*Free Lance*, Aug. 17, 1907).

[1539] Thomas Groves (c.1828-before 1863) married Julia Ann Timmons (c.1829-after 1880), the daughter of William D. Timmons of Stafford. Julia married secondly James Barber (c.1834-after 1880) of Stafford.

[1540] This may be Daniel Monroe (born c.1829) who was the son of James S. Monroe of Stafford. He married Mary L. Sheser (born c.1833).

[1541] Francis "Frank" Monroe (c.1832-1862) was the son of James Monroe, Sr. (c.1797-1867) of Stafford. In May 1862 Frank was wounded at the Battle of Seven Pines. He died of typhoid later that year.

[1542] Thomas Bettis, Jr. (c.1832-1909) was a cooper. On Apr. 7, 1862 he enlisted in the 47th Virginia Infantry and deserted on Apr. 10 (Musselman, 47th, 104). Thomas lived near Berea. On Mar. 31, 1881 he submitted his homestead exemption which included 2 horses, 1 colt, 6 cattle, 16 hogs, farm implements, household and kitchen furniture, 20 barrels of corn, and 1 wagon and harness (Stafford Loose Papers, Homestead Exemptions).

[1543] Richard Harding (born c.1814).

[1544] Thornton Bettis (born c.1825) was a cooper. On Apr. 7, 1862 he was drafted into the 47th Virginia Infantry and deserted on Apr. 9, 1962 (Musselman, 47th, 104).

[1545] Strother D. Monroe (c.1824-before 1860).

[1546] Zachariah Bloxton (born 1815) married Arabella Oder (born 1815) in Fredericksburg in 1837.

[1547] Thomas Monroe (c.1808-1876) was the son of Benjamin and Virginia Monroe. He was born in Stafford and left a will here in which he mentioned his wife Lethe Ann Burdis (born c.1833). He also listed children Roberta Moxley, Sarah J. Hoffman, Robert W. Monroe, and grandson, Charles E. Burdis, the son of his deceased daughter, Susan Elizabeth (Monroe) Burdis (Stafford Will Book R, p. 85). Thomas died from cancer of the face.

[1548] Absalom Perry Heflin (1824-1904) was born in Fauquier and was the son of James W. Heflin (born 1786) and Nancy Anne Shelkett/Walker (1790-1831). Absalom was a carpenter and worked in a sawmill. His first wife was Mary E. Turner. He married secondly Susan E. Nash (died 1866) and thirdly Elizabeth Margaret Grimsley of Culpeper. By 1870 Absalom was a resident of Fredericksburg. He died in Jarrett, Sussex County, Virginia and was buried in the Fredericksburg City Cemetery. (*Free Lance*, May 3, 1904).

[1549] John F. Bradshaw (c.1820-c.1888) was the son of Harberson Bradshaw (1785-1843) of Stafford. He was a miller and in 1869 married Martha Burton, the daughter of James and Ann Burton. His estate was inventoried and appraised on Sept. 29, 1888 and included 3 horses, 4 cattle, 14 fowls, "1 lot cabbage," 1 saddle and bridle, 1 spring wagon, 1 new horse wagon, farm implements, 4 pictures, 1 large table, 1 clothes chest, 1 sideboard, 1 cook stove, 1 coffee mill, 1 desk, and 1 common wardrobe, all valued at $491.26 (Stafford Deed Book 4, p. 123).

[1550] Andrew Bridges' (died c.1865) name appears in the Stafford records with equal frequency as Bridges and Briggs and he seems to have been the son of the Scottish immigrant William Bridges. Andrew inherited his father's large farm, called Scotland, which straddled the intersection of Poplar Road (Route 616) and Stony Hill Road (Route 662) and included Briggs' Mill on Long Branch and now behind Long Branch subdivision on the east side of Poplar Road. In 1838 he paid taxes on 1 slave, 6 horses, and a cariole/carryall (a type of wheeled vehicle).

[1551] John G. Helm (1831-1902) was the son of Thomas Helm (1790-1848) and Joanna Hathaway (1792-1860) of Fauquier. His first wife was Paulina E. Jones of Fauquier. He married secondly Martha French (1833-1912). During the War Between the States, he served in the 9th Virginia Cavalry. John lived in Stafford for some years, moving to Fredericksburg in 1867. While there he operated a grocery store. In

1851

Franklin Brooks[1552]	Ludwell Herndon	Jesse Nash, Jr.[1553]
Lemuel Brooks	John H. Hickerson[1554]	Albert Patterson[1555]
Thomas H. Brooks[1556]	Charles Humphrey, Jr.[1557]	Eli S. Patterson[1558]
Alexander Brown	David Humphrey[1559]	John Patton, Jr.[1560]
Marshall Brown[1561]	John T. Jackson	William A. Patton
Arthur A. Burton[1562]	Reubin Jackson	John Porch
James Burton, Jr.	James Jacobs[1563]	James Powell[1564]
James A. Burton[1565]	Jefferson Jacobs[1566]	James Roberson

1871 he moved to Washington, DC where he worked for Capital Traction Company. He died in Washington, DC and was buried at Poplar Grove in Stafford (*Free Lance*, Apr. 8, 1902).

[1552] Franklin Brooks (born c.1832) was the son of Thomas R. Brooks (c.1801-after 1850). In the 1850 census Franklin was listed as a farmer, but two of his brothers were miners. This family lived at or very near the Eagle Gold Mine in the lower part of Stafford.

[1553] This may be Jesse B. Nash (1827-1908) who may have been the brother-in-law of Absalom P. Heflin. In 1850 he married Lucinda Martin (1826-1904) in Culpeper.

[1554] John Hore Hickerson (c.1818-1875) was the son of Daniel Hickerson (before 1775-1831) who lived at Green Branch near Goldvein in Fauquier. John lived near Rt. 17 just above Falmouth and was a school commissioner in Stafford in 1855. In 1860 he was listed in the Stafford census with real estate valued at $2,300 and $14,500 in personal property. John married Lucy B. Swetnam (c.1824-1878), the daughter of Levi Swetnam. John's personal estate was inventoried and appraised on Feb. 8, 1876 and included 1 wagon, farm implements, 1 saddle, 2 bridles, 5 log chains, 4 cattle, 18 sheep, 4 hogs, 1 spring wagon and harness, 55 barrels of corn, carpenter's tools and a workbench, 2 clocks, 1 desk and bookcase, 1 table, 1 gun, 2 bedsteads and bedding, 1 looking glass, and 1 dining table all valued at $410.50 (Stafford Deed Book UU, p. 203).

[1555] Albert Patterson (c.1826-1920) worked as a laborer in Stafford. During the War Between the States, he served in the 47th Virginia Infantry and was wounded at the Battle of Seven Pines. Albert deserted in March 1864 (Musselman, 47th, 146). For many years after the war he lived in Fredericksburg. He died at his daughter's home in Washington and was buried in the Fredericksburg City Cemetery (*Fredericksburg Daily Star*, Oct. 9, 1920).

[1556] Thomas H. Brooks (born c.1830) was the son of Thomas R. Brooks (c.1801-after 1850) and was a miner. He lived at or very near the Eagle Gold Mine in lower Stafford.

[1557] Charles Humphrey, Jr. (c.1828-after 1874). In 1877 he married Mary Embrey (born c.1842).

[1558] Elijah T. Patterson (1808-1870) was the son of Perry Patterson (1776-after 1850) and Winifred Shackelford (c.1782-1859) of Stafford. In 1861 he enlisted in the 47th Virginia Infantry. In May 1863 he was captured for the fourth time and was sent to Old Capitol Prison. After his parole, he rejoined his unit and served until the end of 1864. In 1858, 1860, and 1861 Elijah was granted licenses to sell liquor in Stafford (Eby 281-282).

[1559] David Humphrey/Humphries (born c.1824) lived very near the gold mines in the lower part of Stafford.

[1560] During the War Between the States, John Patton, Jr. served with the 9th Virginia Cavalry. He was captured and spent over a year as a prisoner of war at Fort Delaware.

[1561] Marshall Brown (born c.1831) was the son of William Brown (c.1798-after 1850) and lived near the gold mines in the lower part of the county.

[1562] Arthur A. Burton (c.1818-after 1897) married Mary A. Ballard (c.1806-1883). At age 66 he married Eliza V. Ballard (born c.1838).

[1563] James William Jacobs (1828-1863) was the son of William Jacobs (1760-1829) and Levinia Colvert (1768-1830). At the time of the 1850 census, James and his brother Jefferson were residing together near the gold mines. In 1856 James married Permelia Rogers.

[1564] James Powell (c.1816-after 1870) was a cooper. He was the son of Thomas Powell (born c.1794) and Elizabeth Lewis (born c.1794) of Spotsylvania. He married Mary Catherine Jacobs (c.1818-after 1870) of Stafford.

[1565] James A. Burton (died c.1896). During the War Between the States, James served with the 30th Virginia Infantry. His estate was inventoried and appraised on Nov. 24, 1896 and included 1 cook stove and fixtures, 1 sofa, 2 beds, 2 leaf tables, 1 pepper mill, 1 lantern, 1 brass skillet, 1 hand satchel, 1 shot gun, 1 eight-day clock, 1 broken clock, 40 hens and chickens, 2 hogs, 2 cows, 8 crocks, 1 wheel barrow, 1 20-

1851

Joseph S. Burton[1567]	Warner Jacobs	Robert C. Rodgers
Marshall Burton	William T. Johnson	Edmund F. Rose[1568]
Richard Burton	Charles T. Jones[1569]	Charles Schoolar[1570]
William Burton	William T. Jones[1571]	John H. Schoolar[1572]
William A. Butler	William Kelloge[1573]	Peter D. Schoolar[1574]
Walker L. Conyers	William F. Lane	John R. Smith[1575]

gallon keg, 50 gallons of vinegar, 2 whiskey barrels, farm implements, and 1 army pistol, all valued at $83.15 (Stafford Deed Book 7, p. 574).

[1566] T. Jefferson Jacobs (1824-1901) was born in Culpeper and died in "upper" Stafford (*Free Lance*, Dec. 12, 1901). He was the son of William Jacobs (1760-1829) and Levinia Colvert (1768-1830) and was a cooper by trade. Jefferson married Lucy Ann Bettis (1827-1871). Jefferson's personal estate was sold on Dec. 19, 1901 and included 3 bedsteads, 3 feather beds, 1 parlor stove, 1 dining table, 1 shot gun, 5 comforters, 2 clocks, 1 looking glass, 1 pistol, 5 rolls tar roofing, farm tools, 1 can of powder and fuses, carpenter's tools, 1 lot of honey, 1 lot of meat, 1 cow, 8 chickens, and 1 pair of medicine scales (Stafford Deed Book 9, p. 522).

[1567] Joseph S. Burton (born c.1808) lived very near the gold mines in the lower part of the county.

[1568] Edmund Fontaine Rose (1817-1893) was the son of Alexander Fontaine Rose (1780-1831) of Amherst County and Sarah Rose Fontaine (1796-1863) of Hanover County. Edmund lived at Hampstead on the west side of Poplar Road (Route 616). From 1858-1868 he served as a justice of the peace for Stafford. He was also a school commissioner for the county and in 1857 became postmaster at Spottedville (Spotted Tavern).

[1569] Charles T. Jones (born c.1838) was the son of Jerret Jones and was a carpenter.

[1570] Charles C. Schooler (c.1821-c.1904) was the son of Thomas E. Schooler (1787-1860) and Mary A. Kirk (c.1793-1857). He married Ann Payne Adams (born c.1826) and left numerous children in Stafford.

[1571] This may be William T. Jones (born c.1826) worked as a farmer and overseer in Stafford. In April 1862 he was drafted into the 47th Virginia Infantry, but was discharged the following October for chronic hepatitis (Musselman, 47th, 135). On Mar. 1, 1871 William submitted his homestead exemption. This included 313 ½ acres of land on Deep Run, household furniture, 5 horses, 9 cattle, 2 hogs, 3 sheep, 1 yoke of oxen, farm implements, and 30 bushels of oats, all valued at $1,438.00 (Stafford Loose Papers, Homestead Exemptions).

[1572] John H. Schooler (1825-1896) was the son of Thomas E. Schooler (1787-1860) and Mary A. Kirk (c.1793-1857). During the War Between the States, John served with the 30th Virginia Infantry. At the Battle of Drewry's Bluff near Richmond John was wounded in the back and neck but, after recovering, returned to service. He was accidentally killed by a streetcar in Richmond while trying to cross the Clay street line of the Richmond Railway and Electric Company. After being hit, he was pushed down the line for some distance resulting in multiple severe injuries. His obituary stated, "Mr. Schooler was a gallant soldier of Company C, 30th Virginia Regiment, of which Capt. C. Wistar Wallace was commander (*Free Lance*, July 7, 1896).

[1573] William Allison Kellogg (1827-1890) was the son of William Kellogg (1784-1848) and Mary Stadler Allison (1790-1873). He married Mary L. Kemper (1835-1883) of Fauquier. During the War Between the States, he served with the 9th Virginia Cavalry and attained the rank of sergeant.

[1574] Peter D. Schooler (1828-1894) was the son of Thomas E. Schooler (1787-1860) of Hartwood. During the War Between the States, Peter served with the 9th Virginia Cavalry. In December 1894 Peter was brutally murdered at his home. A newspaper article describing the crime noted, "Mr. Schooler was one of three brothers—all old bachelors—and all queer, but worthy men. Each of these old gentlemen lived by himself on his little place, and each had the same orderly and methodical habits…Yet one of these quiet, inoffensive, peaceful old men was singled out as the victim of the most shocking, cold-blooded murder that has ever been committed in this section." Peter's little house was "nothing but a hut—one story, two rooms. One room with a fireplace and chimney, and the other more of a shed addition. In the little room, about 8 x 10, the old man lived, surrounded by all the little odds and ends, stuck in corners and on shelves and around about, 'till you could scarcely move in the little room" (*Free Lance*, Dec. 21, 1894) William J. Hunt was charged with the crime.

1851

Broaddus Courtney[1576]	James Latham, Jr.	Lewis Smith
Carter G. Cropp[1577]	Lewis E. Latham	Robert Smith
James Cropp[1578]	Phillip Latham	Robert Smith, Jr.
James T. Cropp[1579]	Robert Latham	Thomas Smith
Lewis Cropp[1580]	Thomas Latham[1581]	Walker Smith
Alexander Curtis	Benjamin Leach[1582]	James L. Stephens, Jr.
Francis Curtis	James Leach[1583]	Thomas M. D. Stephens
George Die	James Limbrick	John A. Swetnam
Humphrey Dodd	George Litteral	Thomas L. Swetnam[1584]
Thomas L. Duerson[1585]	James Litteral[1586]	Joseph F. B. Timberlake[1587]
James Dunnington[1588]	Thomas Litteral[1589]	Lewis T. W. Timberlake[1590]

[1575] John R. Smith (c.1832-1914) was the son of Lucinda Smith (born c.1804) and was listed in the 1850 Stafford census as a miner. During the War Between the States, John served with the 30th Virginia Infantry. He was paroled at Appomattox and was buried in the family burying ground in Stafford.

[1576] May be Alexander Broaddus Courtney (c.1831-1881), the son of James Courtney (1800:10-c.1845) and Elizabeth Timmons (c.1806-after 1850) of Stafford. He married Miriam (last name unknown) and had numerous children. During the War Between the States, he served with the 30th Virginia Infantry.

[1577] Carter Grandon Cropp (1821-1902) was the son of John Cropp (1753-1830) and his second wife, Eliza Fallis (c.1798-c.1850). From his father he inherited Cropp's Tavern, which stood very near the old Spotted Tavern; Carter resided on the Cropp's Tavern tract. During the War Between the States, Carter was an avowed Unionist. He voted in favor of secession only "in view of the violence of his neighbors" and feared for his life if he didn't do so. In his Southern Claims deposition he said he was forced into Confederate service, but escaped and found employment in the Quartermaster Department at Alexandria. Although he owned slaves prior to the war, his neighbors "stigmatized him as an Abolitionist before the war. He submitted a large claim for property taken by Burnside's troops, including 5 horses, 9 cattle, 1,000 pounds of bacon, 33,400 rails, and 16 acres of timber (Southern Claims, Approved Claims, Claim #51419, p. 2). On Mar. 18, 1875 Carter submitted his homestead exemption which consisted of 195 acres of land, 2 cows, household and kitchen furniture, and 4 hogs (Stafford Loose Papers, Homestead Exemptions).

[1578] James Cropp (1822-1884) was the son of Walker Cropp. He married Mahala Humphries (died 1884).

[1579] Dr. James Thomas Cropp (1829-1865) was the son of John Cropp (1753-1830) and Rosie Thomas. He married Elizabeth J. Wharton, the daughter of John Wharton. From 1860-1862 he served as a justice of the peace in Stafford. During the War Between the States, he served as a surgeon in the 51st Virginia Infantry. James and Elizabeth were buried in the family cemetery on the former Sherman farm, now King's Grant subdivision on the western side of Stafford.

[1580] Lewis Cropp (born c.1828) was the son of Walker Cropp. In 1861 he married Elizabeth Humphries (born c.1833), the daughter of Charles and Matilda Humphries. During the War Between the States, he served in Cooper's Battery. By 1910 he was a resident of Fauquier. Lewis married Elizabeth Humphries, the daughter of Charles and Matilda Humphries.

[1581] Thomas W. Latham (born c.1834). In the 1850 census Thomas was living in the household of William Latham (c.1770-after 1850). This family lived at or very near the gold mines in the lower part of the county.

[1582] This may be Benjamin F. Leach (born c.1826) who married Amanda True in 1857.

[1583] James Leach (born c.1827). In the 1850 census, James was living in the household of Benjamin Leach (born c.1826) who may have been his brother.

[1584] Thomas Levi Swetnam (1830-1898) was the son of Levi Swetnam (1785-1838) and Frances Buckner Roane (1792-1858). Thomas moved from Stafford to Boone County, Kentucky where he ran a general merchandise store. He married Katura M. Taylor White.

[1585] Thomas L. Duerson (born c.1829). At the time of the 1850 census, Thomas was living in the household of Lawrence Sanford on the old Greenbank farm. During the War Between the States, Thomas served with the 9th Virginia Cavalry and died during the war.

[1586] May be James Wesley Litteral (died 1908). During the War Between the States, he served with the 30th Virginia Infantry.

[1587] Joseph F. B. Timberlake (c.1826-1859) was born and died in Stafford.

[1588] James Ellington (born c.1840) was a farm laborer.

1851

James Ellington	William Litteral[1591]	Roberson Timmons
John Ellington	James H. Lunsford	Stanard Timmons[1592]
John Ennis	John S. Lunsford	Thomas B. Tompkins[1593]

1852

Adjutant—Charles E. Gill—in room of Charles F. Suttle, resigned—James M. Taliaferro became acting commanding officer between Suttle's resignation and the appointment of C. E. Gill.
Captains—Rodney B. Bradshaw (Light Infantry)—in room of Randall Holden, resigned
    Charles T. Jones (Light Infantry)—in room of Thaddeus J. Crismond, resigned
1st Lieutenants—William A. Douglas[1594] (Light Infantry)—in room of Harrison J. Skidmore, resigned
    Andrew J. Catlett (White Oak Co.)—in room of Charles H. Roberson, resigned
2nd Lieutenants—Charles H. Roberson (White Oak Co.)—in room of Alfred Wariner "who left this state some six years since"
    Fleet Cox (White Oak Co.)

1853[1595]

Adjutant—Charles E. Gill
Lt. Colonel—William H. Browne—in room of James M. Taliaferro
Colonel—William J. Green—in room of Charles F. Suttle, resigned
Major—John M. Homes—in room of William J. Green, promoted
Captains—Peter Wigginton
    John W. H. Alexander (Stafford Store Co., Light Infantry)—in room of Jefferson Heflin, resigned
    William McChin (White Oak Co. Light Infantry)—in room of William H. Browne, resigned
    Robert Lunsford (Hartwood Light Infantry)—in room of George W. Cropp, resigned
    William W. Franklin[1596] (Stafford Courthouse Artillery)—in room of John M. Homes, promoted
Lieutenants—James F. Robinson[1597]—in room of Humphrey Dodd, resigned
    Alexander H. Mountjoy[1598] (Stafford Courthouse Artillery)—in room of William W. Franklin,

---

[1589] Thomas Litteral (c.1832-1888) married Lavinia E. Latham (c.1844-1886). Both are buried at Hartwood Presbyterian Church.

[1590] Lewis Thornton Woodford Timberlake was the brother of Joseph F. B. Timberlake. Before the War Between the States, he worked as a clerk in Fredericksburg. At the outset of the was he enlisted in the Fredericksburg Artillery, but was sick for much of the war. He was captured while in hospital in Richmond and paroled there on May 1, 1865. He was wounded at Reams' Station and near Fort Harrison (Krick, Fredericksburg, 110).

[1591] William Litteral (born c.1829) seems to have been the brother of the above James Litteral (born c.1832).

[1592] William Stanard Timmons (c.1833-c.1898) was the son of William D. Timmons of Stafford. In April 1862 he enlisted in the 47th Virginia Infantry, but deserted, took the oath in November 1864, and was sent to Harrisburg, Pennsylvania (Musselman, 47th, 162).

[1593] Thomas B. Tompkins (born c.1831). At the time of the 1850 census he was part of the household of William Benson (1815-1858).

[1594] William A. Douglas (born 1832) was the son of Triplett Douglas (1805-1867).

[1595] A note in this year's file read, "This company [Stafford Courthouse] of artillery has not for many years been in uniform and do not intend to uniform, therefore they wish to be commissioned as a company of malitia [sic], unless their mustering can be dispensed with, though they be commissioned as a company of volunteers" (Box 148, Folder 62).

[1596] William W. Franklin (c.1829-1890) later served with the 9th Virginia Cavalry.

[1597] James F. Robinson (born c.1833).

[1598] Alexander Hamilton Mountjoy (c.1826-c.1902) was the son of Thornton Mountjoy (1794:7-1881) and Mary Payne (1794-1856). During the War Between the States, he served in the 9th Virginia Cavalry as a private. He was wounded and discharged on July 31, 1864. Around 1850 he married Mary Frances Herndon (1826-1910). From 1879-1887 he served as a magistrate for the Aquia District. In 1865 he was overseer of the road "from Red House to H. M. Jones old shop" (Eby, Men 171).

promoted
Simeon C. Peyton[1599] (White Oak Co. Light Infantry)—in room of William McChin, promoted
1st Lieutenant—William W. Gordon[1600] (Stafford Store Light Infantry)—in room of John W. H. Alexander, resigned
1st/2nd Lieutenants—Zachariah Bridwell[1601] (Stafford Store Light Infantry)—in room of Charles W. Bridwell, removed
George R. Cooper[1602] (Stafford Store Light Infantry)
Robert Flatford (Stafford Courthouse Artillery)—in room of Robert L. Homes, deceased
Richard M. Shelton (Stafford Courthouse Artillery)
2nd Lieutenants—James E. Schooler[1603]
William B. Stewart[1604]
James Williams[1605]

1856

Colonel—William J. Green[1606]
Captains—Alexander M. Green (Potomac Church Company)
William G. Pollock[1607] (Falmouth Company)

[1599] Simeon Chancellor Peyton (1829-1905) lived in White Oak. He was the son of Thomas Peyton (1790-1864) and Sarah Maddox (1794-1877).

[1600] William Wallace Gordon (1834-1912) later served with the 9th Virginia Cavalry. After the War Between the States, he moved to Richmond where he was a physician.

[1601] Zachariah Bridwell (born 1832) was the son of Richard Bridwell (c.1785-1853) and Elizabeth Jacobs (born c.1797).

[1602] George R. Cooper (1835-1881) was the son of John C. Cooper (c.1801-1874) and Sythia Tolson (c.1815-1870). He later served with the 9th Virginia Cavalry. In February 1868 Seth B. Combs sold George a three-acre lot adjoining Stafford Store in what is now the Quantico reservation (Stafford Deed Book 26A, p. 360).

[1603] James E. Schooler (born c.1833) was the son of John Schooler (1815-1875) and Laurinda Jones (1815-1870). He married Lucy E. Hedgman (born c.1834), the daughter of John T. Hedgman. James and Lucy operated the old Garrard's Ordinary and the post office near the courthouse.

[1604] William B. Stewart (c.1830-1863) was the son of Charles Stewart (1809-before 1850). He later served in the 47th Virginia Infantry and was killed in action at Gettysburg.

[1605] James Williams (born c.1833).

[1606] On Dec. 10, 1856 William J. Green wrote, "In pursuance of an order received from the Adjutant General's office some months since, I took the necessary legal steps to have a meeting of the Companies of the 45th Regt Va Militia, for the purpose of filling vacancies in their respective companies, among the Commissioned officers. After the most strenuous efforts on the part of myself and the other field officers, the companies fail to assemble, and after such failure (after due notice), twice, it becomes my duty to recommend to your Excellency proper persons for appointments to vacancies…It shall always be my pleasure as it is my duty to lend my best endeavors to the improvement of the Materiel of our Militia Officers having been educated at that Institution which is now the pride and glory of the state. I feel and appreciate most fully the necessity for some better organisation of the defences of the State than exist at present. I look with anxious interest to events of 1860, and while I hope that nothing may occur to mar our peace and domestic quiet, yet I think it is well, 'In time of peace to prepare for war'" (Auditor. Box 148, Folder 63).

[1607] William G. Pollock (1829-1865) was born in Scotland and was the son of William Pollock (died 1885) and Janet R. Gray (1804-1878). Janet was the daughter of John and Lucy Gray. William G. Pollock died of dysentery and was buried in the Gray family cemetery at Traveler's Rest between Route 3 (east) and the Rappahannock River.

Sources:
Alexandria Gazette, Sept. 8, 1819, death of Daniel Pilcher
Auditor of Public Accounts. #477, Claims for Payments of Militia Fines Collected. Record Group 48, BC 1082233, Box 1354. Library of Virginia.
Auditor of Public Accounts. #478, Fines Collected. Records, 1797-1819. Record Group 48, BC 1082439, Box 1560. Library of Virginia.
Auditor of Public Accounts. #478, Fines Collected. Records, 1797-1819. Record Group 48, BC 1082441, Box 1561. Library of Virginia.
Auditor of Public Accounts. #247, General Militia Records, 1811-1821. Record Group 48, BC 1081523, Box 754. Library of Virginia.
Auditor of Public Accounts. Governor's Office. Militia Commissions. Record Group 3, BC 1167437, Box 148, Accession # 42222, Library of Virginia.
Boogher, William F. *Overwharton Parish Register, 1720 to 1760*. Baltimore, MD: Genealogical Publishing Co., 2000.
Bradshaw, J. Douglas. *John H. Bradshaw and Scythia Enfield Fritter of Stafford County, Virginia*. Richmond: Dietz Press, 1991.
Brent, Chester H. *The Descendants of Coll. Giles Brent, Capt. George Brent and Robert Brent, Gent*. Rutland, VT: Tuttle Publishing Co., 1946.
Coppage, A. Maxim and Tackitt, James W. *Stafford Co., Virginia 1800-1850*. Concord, CA, 1982.
Creel, Bevin. *Selected Virginia Revolutionary War Records*, vol. 1. Lulu Press, Inc., 2007.
Deyo, William L. *The Sullivan Family of Stafford County, Virginia*. Colonial Beach, VA: DeJoux Publications, 2000.
Duncan, Marion M., Miller, Adrian C., Moncure, Peyton S. *House of Moncure Genealogy*. Self-published 1967.
Eby, Jerrilynn. *Men of Mark: Officials of Stafford County, Virginia, 1664-1991*. Westminster, MD: Willow Bend Books, 2006.
_____. *They Called Stafford Home: The Development of Stafford County, Virginia, from 1600 until 1865*. Bowie, MD: Heritage Books, Inc., 1997.
_____. *Will of Travers Daniel, Sr.*, private collection.
Fancy, Steven G. *Genealogy of the Reno/Reneau Family in America, 1600-1920*. Self-published, 2001.
Ficklen, Slaughter W. *Genealogy of the Ficklin Family since 1720*. Charlottesville, VA: J. Alexander, 1870.
Fisher, Therese A. *Marriage Records of the City of Fredericksburg, and of Orange, Spotsylvania and Stafford Counties, Virginia, 1722-1850*. Bowie, MD: Heritage Books, Inc., 1990.
Fredericksburg Circuit Court Records:
    "Commonwealth vs Hore" HU-R/467-924/1842
    "Commonwealth vs Payne" HU-R/363-322/1822
    "Cox vs Wright" SC-H/59-8/1830
    "Dickinson's Admr vs Tyler's Admr" SC-H/80-3/1829
    "Dunbar vs Swan" SL-l/583-89/1820
    "Grand Jury Presentments" HU-G/356-188/1803
    "Grand Jury Presentments" HU-G/360-541/1814
    "Howe vs Buchanan" DC-L/369-152/1790?
    "Insolvent Whites" TX-TX-I/548-57/1849
    "McInteer vs McInteer" LC-H/182-28/1838
    "Morson & al vs Hewitt" SC-H/202-04/1820
    Land Causes, 1815-1815
Fredericksburg Daily Star, July 3, 1903, obituary of Harrison C. Alexander
Fredericksburg Ledger, July 24, 1867, obituary of Triplett Douglas
_____. Feb. 18, 1868, obituary of Taliaferro S. Kendall
_____. Mar. 25, 1873, obituary of James T. Abbott
Free Lance, Aug. 6, 1886, obituary of Willis Mills
_____. Mar. 10, 1893, obituary of Harrison Groves
_____. Dec. 18 and 21, 1894, obituary of Peter D. Schooler
_____. Dec. 12 and 17, 1901, obituary of Jefferson Jacobs
_____. Dec. 21, 1901, obituary of Lawrence Clift

1856

_____. Jan. 7, 1902, obituary of Noah Fritter
_____. Apr. 8, 1902, obituary of John G. Helm
_____. May 3, 1904, obituary of Absalom P. Heflin
_____. July 2, 1904, obituary of Aquilla Randall
_____. July 3, 1906, obituary of John T. Mills
_____. Feb. 7, 1907, obituary of Edward Oder
_____. Aug. 17, 1907, obituary of John W. Grinnan
_____. May 18, 1909, obituary of Thomas Bettis
_____. Apr. 18, 1911, obituary of Lafayette Franklin
_____. Oct. 12, 1920, obituary of Albert Patterson
Gov. John Floyd. Executive papers, 1830-1834. Accession #42665. Sept. 13, 1831, Box 4, Folder 7. Library of Virginia.
Hall, W. K. and Chappell, Wilma. *The Simms Family of Stafford County, Virginia.* St. Louis, MO: self published, 1969.
Hartwood Baptist Church Minutes. Virginia Baptist Historical Society. Richmond, VA: University of Richmond.
Hayden, Horace E. *Virginia Genealogies.* Baltimore, MD: Genealogical Publishing Co., 1979.
Hord, Arnold H. *The Hord Family of Virginia.* Self-published, 1915.
Kendall, Mary Cary. Private collection.
King, George H. S. *The Register of Overwharton Parish, Stafford County, Virginia, 1723-1758.* Easley, SC: Southern Historical Press, Inc., 1986.
King, Ruth C. *The Cropp Family in America.* Self-published, 1986.
Kinsey, Margaret B. *Mountjoy Omnibus.* Baltimore, MD: Gateway Press, Inc., 2001.
Krick, Robert K. *The Fredericksburg Artillery.* Lynchburg, VA: H. E. Howard, Inc., 1986.
_____. *9th Virginia Cavalry.* Lynchburg, VA: H. E. Howard, Inc., 1982.
Lacy, Ronnie L. *The Randalls of Stafford County, Virginia.* Baltimore, MD: Gateway Press, Inc., 1997.
Lee, _____ _____ Collection. Accession # _____. Richmond, VA: Virginia Historical Society.
Letter, George M. Cooke to Duff Green, Sept. 30, 1831. Private collection of Jerrilynn Eby.
Lombus, William. *Latham: a Catalog of Virginia and Ohio Families.* Self-published, 1998.
Lowe, Richard G. "Virginia's Reconstruction Convention: General Schofield Rates the Delegates." *Virginia Magazine of History and Biography*, vol. 80 (1972), pp. 341-360.
Musselman, Carl P. *Musselman-Powell & Bowling Families of Spotsylvania & Stafford Counties, Virginia.* Fredericksburg, VA: Bookcrafters, 1993.
Musselman, Homer D. *The 47th Virginia Infantry.* Lynchburg, VA: H. E. Howard, Inc., 1991.
_____. *Stafford County in the Civil War.* Lynchburg, VA: H. E. Howard, Inc., 1995.
_____. *Stafford County, Virginia Veterans and Cemeteries.* Fredericksburg, VA: Bookcrafters, 1994.
National Archives and Records Administration. Revolutionary War Pensions and Bounty Land Records. Record Group M804.
National Archives and Records Administration. Southern Claims Commission. Approved Claims. M2094. Record Group 217.
National Intelligencer, Mar. 4, 1822, Israel F. Langfit arrested
_____. Jan. 11, 1823, Temple Fouche employed by William H. Fitzhugh
O'Grady, Kelly J. "Hartwood's Venerable Ledger: Rare 1851 Militia Roll Found." *Fredericksburg History and Biography*, (2004), vol. 1, pp. 40-55.
Payne, Brooke. *The Paynes of Virginia.* Berryville, VA: Virginia Book Company, 1937.
Peyton Society of Virginia. *The Peytons of Virginia, vol. 2.* Baltimore, MD: Gateway Press, Inc., 2004.
Pippenger, Wesley E. *John Alexander, a Northern Neck Proprietor: His Family, Friends and Kin.* Baltimore: Gateway Press, Inc., 1990.
Political Arena, Jan. 1, 1836, notice regarding Fielding Hudson
_____. May 5, 1840, sale of Walker Cropp's land
Prichard, A. M. *Allied Families of Read, Corbin, Luttrell, Bywaters.* Staunton, VA: McClure Co., Inc., 1930.
Ranck, George W. *The History of Lexington, Kentucky.* Lexington, KY: R. Clarke Publishers, 1872.
Stafford County Circuit Court Records, 1850-1853. Stafford Courthouse.

Stafford County Court Minute Book 1852-1867
Stafford County Estate Accounts, 1823-1834
Stafford County Land Tax Records
Stafford County Loose Papers. Homestead Exemptions. Stafford Courthouse, Virginia.
Stafford County Personal Property Tax Records
Town of Falmouth Trustee Proceedings, 1728-1866. Accession #20588, BC 1051101. Richmond, VA: Library of Virginia.
"Virginia Executive Papers: Selected Items." *Virginia Genealogist*, vol. 17 (1973).
Virginia Herald, May 9, 1793, Fielding Fant court case
_____. Jan. 27, 1810, obituary of Henry Ward
_____. Aug. 29, 1812, obituary of Juliet Ward
_____. May 24, 1817, obituary of Thomas C. Alexander
_____. Dec. 5, 1818, William Daffin's business notice
_____. Sept. 18, 1819, obituary of Daniel Pilcher
_____. Aug. 25, 1824, advertisement of the Broadfield Races
_____. Dec. 22, 1824, obituary of Meriweather Taliaferro
_____. Jan. 14, 1829, Archibald Rollow's ferry and blacksmith advertisement
_____. Feb. 2, 1832, obituary of Thomas Pilcher
_____. Mar. 17, 1832, advertisement for James Cave's fishery
_____. Jan. 8, 1855, Harris Hill killed John Limerick
_____. Oct. 27, 1858, obituary of W. W. L. Benson
Virginia Legislative Petitions:
    "Nancy Payton" Reel 188, Box 239, Folder 67, Feb. 23, 1849. Richmond, VA: Library of Virginia.
Vogt, John and Kethley, T. William. *Stafford County, Virginia Tithables, Quit Rents, Personal Property Taxes and Related Lists & Petitions, 1723-1790*. Athens, GA: Iberian Publishing Co., 1990.
Ward, Roger G. *1815 Directory of Virginia Landowners (and Gazetteer)*, vol. 4: Northern Region. Athens, GA: Iberian Publishing Co., 1999.
Wise, Erbon W. *The Bridwell Family in America*. Sulphur, Louisiana, self-published, 1978.

Contributors:

Susan Bailey	Barbara Kirby
Gerald Carr	Robert Knight
Gene Chappell	Gene Lindsley
Albert Z. Conner	Larry Newhouse
Garry Cooper	D. P. Newton
Mary Alice Corder	Amy Patterson
Francis Courtney, II	Constance Peck
Teresa Dahlgren	Don Robey
Karen Dale	Ronald Scott
William Deyo	William Scroggins
John L. Eby, Jr.	Deborah Shelton
Betsey Ellis	Donnie Shelton
Douglas Fant	William Shelton
Ron Garrison	Jane Cloe Sthreshley
Janelle Gaughan	Danika Tolbert
Ken Gray	Lee Tyson
Linda Gunn	Aubrey R. Ward
Morgan Heflin	Ann Worthington
Mary Cary Kendall	
Scott Kendall	

INDEX

Abbot, Benjamin T. 1843
  Elijah *1803n*, 04
  Fielding *1805n*
  George A. *1843n*, 44
  James T. *1843n*, 44
  John 1826
  William *1812n*, 14, 15, 17, 19
Abel, Allen 1843
Achors, William 1802
Adam(s), Abendigo *1809n*
  George B. 1844
  James *1794n*, 04, 05
Adie, Benjamin *1786n*, 02, 03, 04
  Hugh *1813n*, 19, 26, 28, 29, 30
  Lewis *1828n*, 29
  Samuel H. *1825n*
  Walker *1822n*
  William *1797n*, 29, 30
Agin, James 1802
Alcock, Abner R. *1811n*, 14, 15, 16, 18, 19, 21, 24
Alexander, Armistead *1806n*, 08
  Harrison C. *1851n*
  James *1821n*, 22, 23, 25
  John L. *1829n*, 34, 36, 38, 41
  John W. H. 1853
  Laurence 1826, 27
  Lawrence B. *1829n*, 30
  Leonard P. *1842n*
  Lewis *1801n*, 02, 03, 04, 05, 09, 10, 11, 12, 13, 14, 15, 16
  Philip *1814n*
  Richard B. *1837n*, 40, 44, 46
  Robert B. *1843n*, 47
  Thomas 1801
  Thomas C. *1802n*, 03, 04, 05, 06, 08, 11, 12, 13, 14, 15
  Thornton *1815n*, 19, 21, 22, 23, 24, 25, 29, 33
  William *1786n*, 97, 22
  William J. H. *1851n*
Allen, James 1815
  Robert 1815, 19, 21, 23
  Walter 1843, 44
Al(l)ison, James 1817
  John 1804
  John S. *1805n*, 06, *09n*
  Thomas L. *1804n*, 05
Alsop, Benjamin 1817
  Boswell *1814n*, 15
  Walter 1844
Anderson, Albert 1826, 27
  James 1817
  James E. *1850n*
  John 1825, 26, 27, 28, 30, 51
  Luke *1826n*, 27, 43
  Richard 1797, 04
  William *1815n*, 19, 21, 26, 27, 30, 47
Anthony, John *1843n*, 44
Armstrong, Armstead A. *1846n*, 51
  Atchison H. 1819, 21
  Enoch S. *1830n*
  James *1815n*, 16, 19, 21, 26, 51
  James, Jr. 1823
  John 1798
  John H. 1850
  Joseph *1816n*, 47
  Stephen 1819, 22, 25, 26
  Stephen H. 1821, 23
Arrington, Ferdinand *1821n*, 29, 30
  James *1843n*, 46, 47
  John S. 1843, 46, 47
  John W. *1830n*
Ashby, Benjamin *1802n*, 13, 29, 30, 41
  Benjamin, Jr. 1826
  Benjamin F. *1840n*, 42, 44
  Gustavus *1822n*, 23, 24, 29, 30
  James *1851n*
  John *1801n*, 02, 03, 14, 25
  Joseph 1814
  Richard *1851n*
  Robert *1802n*, 04, 13
  William 1841
Atchison, Henry *1826n*, 28, 29, 30
  James *1814n*, *46n*
  Jeremiah *1815n*
  John *1825n*, 26, 27, 28, 46, 47
  Martin 1826, 27
  Nathan *1797n*
  Rodney *1826n*, 29, 30
  William 1828
Aufort, Francis *1843n*, 44
Backster, (*see Baxter*)
  William 1828, 29
Badger, Jesse *1797n*
Bails, Jesse *1797n*, 03
Baily, (*see also Bayly*)
  Robert 1846
  William P. *1803n*
Baker, Fielding *1817n*
Ball, Aaron H. 1814, 15, 26, 28
  Bailey F. 1814
  Benjamin 1825, 26, 27
  Edward *1797n*
  Hibbard *1811n*
  James H. *1851n*

INDEX

John	*1814n*, 15		26, 29, 30
John, Jr.	1812	Beard, Thomas D.	1821
Joseph H.	1823	Beaty, Robert	*1811n*, 14, 15, 24, 43
Reuben	1804, 05	Robert A.	*1844n*
William	*1786n*, 90, 94, 01, 23, 26, 27, 28, 29, 30, 46	Beavers, John	1826
		Samuel	*1826n*, 29, 30
William B.	*1839n*, 44	Beckwith, Jonathan	*1822n*
Ballard, Flavius J.	*1851n*	Richard	*1803n*
Banks, George	*1806n*, 21, 22, 23, 24	Richard M.	1804, 05, 14
John	1829, 30	William	1818
John O.	*1847n*	Bell, Alexander	*1803n*, 04, 06, 19, *23n*, 28
Barbee, Lameth	*1814n*		
Barber, Bernard	*1829n*, 46	Bailey	*1797n*, 03, 05
Edward	*1803n*	Charles	1801, 03, 04
Joseph	*1802n*	Daniel	*1802n*, 26, 27, 28
Nathaniel	*1825n*, 28, 29, 30	Elijah	*1825n*, *26n*
Sinclear	*1826n*	Francis	*1829n*, 30
William	*1803n*, 24, 28	George	*1797n*
Barby, Charles	*1797n*	James	1823
Elijah	*1814n*	John, Jr.	1809, 14, 17
Barker, Barney	1824	John F.	*1837n*, 39, 41
Benjamin	1850	Joseph H.	*1825n*, 25, 29, *30n*
Brooke	*1814n*	Waller S.	1805
Henry	1825	William	*1800n*, 01, 19
John	1797	Benson, James R.	*1837n*, 41, 43, 44, 45
Barn(e)s, Brockenbaugh	*1846n*	Robert	*1814n*
Harrison B.	*1843n*, 44, 46, 47	William W. L.	1851
Jesse	1797	Willis	*1806n*, 08, 09, 11, 12, 13, *47n*
Newman B.	*1794n*, 95, 96		
Williamson	1818	Benton, David	1813
Bates, Beverly	*1844n*	Bernard, James	1814
James	*1802n*, 04	Berry, James	1829, *30n*
John	1825	John	1814, 21, 23
William	1798, 19	Richard	*1819n*, 28, 29
Batley, Moses	1813	Richard, Jr.	*1826n*
Bauer, M.	1812	Thomas	*1814n*, *50n*
Baxter, (*see Backster*)		William	1797, 02
William	1826, 30	Bethel, Edward	*1797n*
Bayles, Enoch	1798	James	1805
Bayl(e)y (*see also Baily*)		Thompson	*1813n*
Josiah F.	*1837n*, 40	William	1804
William	*1822n*, 24	Bettis, Thomas, Jr.	*1851n*
William P.	*1813n*	Thornton	*1851n*
Beach, Charles	*1817n*	William	1814, 19, 21, 22, 25, 26, 27, 28, 29, 30, *43n*, 44
Daniel	1804, 05, 06		
John	1823		
Peter	*1813n*	Bettys, Thomas	1804
William	1805, 06, *43n*, 51	Billingsley, ___	1822
Beagle, James	1823, 25, 28, 29	Clement	*1814n*
John	*1797n*, 02, 03, 04, 28, 43, 44, 46, 47	George	*1810n*, 11, 14, 26, 28
		George W.	*1823n*
Joseph	*1797n*, 02, 14	James	*1797n*
Sollomon	1803	Joseph	1818, *22n*, 23
William	1804, *28n*, 29, 30, 43	William	*1814n*
Beale, James	1819	William B.	*1830n*
William C.	*1819n*, 21, 22, 23, 25,	Bisset, George	1812

INDEX 167

Black, George	*1826n*, 27, 28, 30		Reubin	*1822n*, 24, 25, 26, 27, 28
James	*1846n*		Riley	*1846n*, 47
Joseph	1802, 03		Robert	1812
William	*1802n*, 18		Thomas	*1825n*, 26, 27, 28
Blackburn, Christopher	*1805n*, 11, 14		Bowlin(g), (*see also Boling*)	
Blackston(e), Abraham	1802		Abijah	1817, 22, 23, 26, 28, 29, 30
Samuel	*1802n*			
Blake, Robert	*1844n*		Alexander	1821, 23
Bloxham, Henry	1804		Alexander W.	1822
Peter	*1843n*, 44		Charles	1814
Thompson M.	*1831n*, 34		Elijah	1802
William	*1823n*, 26, 28, 31		George	1817, 19, 22, 23, 25, 26, 27, 28
Bloxton, Abraham	*1803n*			
Abram	1798		George A.	*1847n*, 51
Henry	1803, 19, 21		James	1813, 16, 17, 18, 43, 44, 47
John	*1803n*, 05			
Samuel	*1803n*, 14		James L.	1822
Thomas	1815		James S.	1816, 17, 18, 24, 25, 26, 27
William	*1827n*, 46			
Zachariah	*1851n*		John	1814, 18, 19, 22, 25, 26, 27, 28
Boarn, Henry	1802, 03			
Boatler, Joseph	1802		Lewis	1817
Bobo, Jessey	*1804n*		Richard	*1830n*
William	1797		Robert	1847
Bohannon, John A.	1814		Robert H.	*1843n*, 44
Boling, (*see also Bowling*)			Servis	1815
Abijah	*1814n*, 21		Thomas	1822, 43, 44
Alexander	1819		Travis	*1844n*, 47
George	*1814n*, 21		William	1814
James	1814, 46		Bradley, David	1805, 06, 13
James S.	1821		Henry	*1802n*, 04, 05, 06
John	1821, 46		James	1827, *30n*
Robert H.	*1846n*		James, Jr.	1826
Booton, Henry	1815		Bradshaw, Charles H.	*1843n*, 44
Boteler, Joseph	1804		Harberson	*1802n*, 05
Botts, Charles	1806		John F.	*1851n*
James	1797		John H.	*1844n*
John	*1809n*, 11		Rodney B.	*1841n*, 43, 45, 47, 49, 52
Joseph B.	*1797n*			
Lawrence	*1806n*		Uriah	1825, 26, 27
Richard	1822		Uriah H.	*1831n*
Samuel	*1804n*, 06, 08, 09, 19		William	1829, 30
Bouchard, James	1797		Zachariah	*1802n*, 06
Boucher, John	1818		Brahan, William	1802
Bourn, Henry	1805		Bramell, John A.	*1846n*
Boutyard (*see also Butchard*)			Braniston, John	*1798n*
James	1846, 47		Branson, Isaac	*1797n*, 02, 03, 04, 05
Bowen, Burket	*1794n*, 96, 97, 03, 04		John	*1802n*, 03, 04, 05, 06
Burkett P.	*1822n*, 23, 24, 28, 31		Brawner, Alexander	*1812n*
Philip	1847		John	1814
Stephen P.	*1816n*		Brent, George	*1786n*, 94, 97, 02, 03, 04, 18, 19
Thomas	*1786n*			
Bower, Michael	*1803n*		George L.	*1816n*
Bowler, Henry	1846		Thomas L.	*1829n*
Peter	*1822n*, 23, 26, 27, 29, 30		William	*1794n*, 05, 06, 14,

INDEX

Brewin, Thomas 1797, 04
Bridges, Andrew *1851n*
  Burdit 1819, 21, 23, 25, 26, 27, 28, 30
  Charles *1806n*, 13
  John *1803n*, 04
  William *1806n*
Bridwell, Charles *1815n*, 19, 47
  Charles D. 1815, 19, 21, 22, 23, 25, 26, 27, 28, 29, 30
  Charles W. *1851n*, 53
  Isaac *1813n*
  James 1829
  John 1797, 02, 04, 14, 15
  Joseph *1844n*, 46, 47
  Lewis *1797n*, 01, 02, 03, 04
  Moses 1804
  Nelson 1818
  Peyton *1829n*
  Presly *1802n*, 04
  Richard *1814n*
  Samuel *1803n*
  Samuel, Jr. 1802
  Thomas 1798, 02, 04, 05
  Timothy *1821n*, 29, *30n*
  Westly 1821, 22, 23
  William 1806, 13, 15, 17
  William M. *1844n*
  Zachariah *1853n*
Brig(g)s, David *1805n*
  James *1815n*, 18, 19, 21, 24, 26, 27, 28, 29, 33
  James L. 1846
  James M. *1846n*, 47
  Robert *1804n*
  Thomas *1803n*, 04, 05
  William S. *1843n*, 44, 45, 46, 47
Brimer, Charles 1803, 04, 06
  John F. *1803n*, 05, 06
Brimley, William 1819
Brimmer, John F. 1803, 12
  William 1812, 13, 15, 16
Brock, Thomas *1803n*, 05
Bronaugh, Jeremiah W. *1806n*
  John, Jr. *1804n*
  John W. *1806n*
  Martin *1801n*, 02, 03
  Robert *1827n*
  William 1794, 95, 96, 97, 98, 01, 02, 03, 04, 05, 13
Brooke, John M. *1846n*, 47
  John T. *1802n*, 04, 05, 06
  Robert 1817
  Samuel S. *1818n*, 21, 22, 23, 24, *41n*, 42, 44, 45, 46, 47, 51
  Whitfield 1797, 04
  William *1851n*
Brooks, Franklin 1819, 21, 23, 25, 26, 27, 28, 30
  Jesse *1806n*, 13
  Lawson *1803n*, 04
  Lemuel *1806n*
  Richard *1815n*, 19, 47
  Thomas 1815, 19, 21, 22, 23, 25, 26, 27, 28, 29, 30
  Thomas H. *1851n*, 53
  Thomas T. *1813n*
Brown(e), Alexander 1829
  Ambrose 1797, 02, 04, 14, 15
  Bartlet *1844n*, 46, 47
  Charles *1797n*, 01, 02, 03, 04
  Charles G. 1804
  Coleman R. 1818
  Deacon *1829n*
  Dixon *1802n*, 04
  Enoch *1814n*
  Enoch J. *1803n*
  Ephraim 1802
  Fielding 1798, 02, 04, 05
  Francis *1821n*, 29, *30n*
  Gideon 1821, 22, 23
  Innis 1806, 13, 15, 17
  James *1844n*
  John *1853n*
  Marshall *1805n*
  Rawleigh *1815n*, 18, 19, 21, 24, 26, 27, 28, 29, 33

29, 30, 33
1817n, *22n*
1804n, 05, 06, *19n*, 21, 22, 23, 25, 26, 29
1851
1817, 19, 21, 22, 26
1843n, 44
1850n, 51
1802, 04
1817n, 25
1851
1843, 44
1847n, 51
1828n
1821, 22, 23, 26, 27
1844
1847
1802n, 08, 11, 12, 13, 14, 15
1826
1826n
1802
1804n
1823n
1823, 26
1803, 13
1846
1802n, 05, 13, 14
1814, 29, 30
1802n, 03, *30n*, 50
1851
1824n, 26, 28, 29, 30, 44, 46

  Raleigh T. *1797n*, 01, 02, 04
  Thaddeus 1798
  Thomas 1822, 43, 44, 46
  Thornton 1822, 23, 24, 25, 26, 27, 28, 43, 44
  Travers *1796n*
  Wallis 1813
  William 1803, 04, *06n*, 12, 13, 14, 15, 16, 17, 18, 19, 21, 22, 25, 26, 27, 28, 43, 44, 50
  William, Jr. 1798, 02, 03, 04, 05
  William, Sr. 1805, 46
  William H. 1853
  William H., Jr. *1846n*, 51
Bruce, Charles *1790n*, 94, *97n*, 01, 04
  James 1829, 30
  Robert *1790n*
Brummett, James *1813n*
Bryan, Joseph 1814
Bryant, Daniel T. *1843n*, 46, 47
  George *1826n*, 29
  Joseph *1813n*

INDEX 169

Silas	*1822n*	Butchard (*see also Bouchard*)	
William	*1814n*, 25, 26, 46	Elias	*1826n*, 27, 28, 44
Buchanan, William	*1814n*	John	1829
Buckner, Edward M.	1819	Butcher, Elias	1843
Bull, A. H.	1819	James W.	1844
Bullard, Reuben B.	1813	Butler, Augustus	*1817n*
Bullock, James	*1846n*	James	*1806n*, 14
Burges(s), Benjamin	1818	Jesse	1828, 29, 30
William	1812	John	1821
Burnham, Joseph	1814	Rolly	1819
Burr, Ezra	*1825n*	William	1797, 17, 19, 21, *22n*, 23
Burrage, Edward	*1826n*, 27, 30, 31		
Thomas	*1829n*	William A.	1851
Burroughs, Alfred	*1826n*, *46n*	William R.	1813
George	*1786n*, 14	Button, William	1815
James	1802	Byram, Baily	*1814n*, 17, 22, 23, 26
John	*1806n*	Cuthbert	*1826n*
Richard	1821	Fielding	*1813n*
Robert	*1822n*	James	1821, 22
Thomas	*1804n*, 05, 08, 10, 11	James W.	1828, 29, 30
William	*1800n*	John	1805
Burrus, Patrick H.	*1847n*	John N.	1829
Burton, Arthur A.	*1851n*	John W.	*1825n*, 26, 27, 30
Egery	1819	Mason	*1843n*
Harris	1824, 25	Nimrod	*1804n*
Harris W.	*1819n*, 22, 43	Senate	1802
Ira	1817	Bywaters, James	1797
Isaac	*1798n*, 03, 05, 14	Calender, Henry	1819
James	1829, 30	Calhoun, John	1843, 44
James, Jr.	1851	Camper, Henry	1829, 30
James A.	*1851n*	Cannady (*see also Kennedy*)	
Jesse	*1823n*, 26, 30	George	1805
John	1805, 14, 17, 19, 26, 27	Carback, Thomas	1815
		Care, Learken	1805
John E.	1847	Carney, Jessey	*1802n*, 03, 04, 05
Joseph	1826, 29	Michael	1830
Joseph S.	*1851n*	Mitchell	*1822n*
Joshua	1822	Carpenter, James	*1813n*
Marshall	*1844n*, 51	Joseph	1797, 26, 30
Nathaniel	*1802n*, 05, 06	Zachariah	*1828n*
Richard	*1844n*, 50, 51	Carrol, John	1843, 44
Strother	1819, 21, 23	Robert	1818, 19, 21
Strother M.	1826, 27	Thomas	1843
Thomas S.	1814, 24	Carter, Frister	*1851n*
William	1802, 17, 22, 44, 46, 47, 51	George	1803, *04n*
		James	1818, 26, 27
William, Jr.	*1803n*, 04, 05, 14	James P.	1814
William, Sr.	*1802n*, 03, 14	Jedediah	1797
William B.	1826, 27, 29, 30	Jeremiah	*1813n*, *44n*
William J.	*1846n*, 47, 48	John	1797, 02, 03, 04, 05, 06
Busel(l), Charles	*1813n*, 19, 21, 22, 23, 25		
		Joseph	1805
George	*1825n*	Joseph A.	1814, 15
John	1812, 15, 17	Landon N.	*1822n*
Randal	*1812n*, 14	Loyal	*1814n*, 23
William	*1829n*, 30	Richard	*1843n*

INDEX

	Richard W.	1847	Cline, Frederick	1814
	Robert W.	*1814n*	Cloe, Alexander	*1818n*, 21, 23, 24
	Sanford	*1805n*, 14	James	*1797n*, 03
	William	*1813n*, 43, 46, 47	James H.	*1843n*
	William F.	*1841n*	John	*1814n*
Cash, John		*1828n*	John H.	*1843n*
	William	1797, 06	Coakley, Daniel S.	*1843n*
Catlett, Andrew		*1850n*	George	1814, 15
	Andrew J.	1852	Harris	*1843n*
	George W.	*1850n*	Harrison	1844
Cave, James		*1826n*, 29, 30	James	*1817n*
Chadwell, Bryant		*1813n*	James M.	1830
	James	*1821n*, 26	John	1831
	Lemuel	*1827n*, 29	John E.	*1843n*, 44, 47, 50
	Taliaferro	1829, 30	Thornton	1818
	William	*1797n*, 98, 02	Coalman, John W.	*1819n*
Chadwick, William		1814	Cochran, John H.	1814
Chandler, Walter		1812	Cocks, (*see also Cox*)	
Chapman, James		1815	Charles	1798
	Philip	*1822n*	Enoch	1797
	Turner	*1822n*	Samuel	1797, 98
Charters, William		1819	Vincent, Jr.	1797
Cheshire, George		1804	Coit, David G.	1819
Childs, Robert		1814	Colbert, Thomas	*1844n*
Chilton, (*see also Shelton*)			William	1828
	Abroad	1846	Cole, Daniel	1815
	Alexander	1850	James S.	*1819n*, *22n*
	James	1846	Samuel	*1811n*, *50n*
	John	1850	Coleman (*see Coalman*)	
	Thornton	*1822n*	Collat, (*see also Golatt*)	
	Wellington	*1846n*	Joseph	*1821n*
	William	1803, 04	Collins, Sira	1806
Chinn, John		1822	Colvert, Henry	1812
	Joseph	*1798n*	Colvin, Charles	*1803n*
	Rawleigh	1821, 22	John	1813
	Robert	1847	Rawleigh	*1803n*
	Robert A.	*1850n*	Combs, Benjamin	*1818n*
	Thomas	1826	David W.	*1843n*
	William	1825, 26, 27, *46n*	Fielding	*1802n*, 03
Chis(s)om, Francis		1828, 29, 30	Harrison	*1821n*, 23
	William	1815, 17	John	1814, 15, 24, 26, 29
Christy, John		*1814n*	John H.	1804
Clanton, John P.		1817	John M.	*1830n*
Clark, Richard		1812	Seth	*1802n*, 04
Clemmons, George		1804	William	1802, 03, 43
Cleveland, William L.		1818	William R.	*1828n*, 29
Cliff, Washington		1817	Conner, James	1819, *25n*
Clift, Albert		*1846n*	John	1821
	Arthur F.	*1846n*	Conns, Joseph	1826, 27
	Chandler	1818, 19, 21, *22n*	Conway, George M	1842
	Fielding	*1804n*, 05	George W.	*1842n*, 45, 46
	Fielding L.	*1834n*, 36, 41	Henry R.	*1843n*
	Laurence	*1828n*	John M.	*1803n*, 04, 13, 33
	William	*1846n*	John M., Jr.	*1843n*, 47
Clifton, Burditt		*1811n*, 15	Thomas B.	*1803n*, 04, 07, 08, 12
	Burditt H.	1814	Walker P.	*1823n*, 24, 25, 43, 47

INDEX

Valentine Y.	*1821n*	Cowne, Austin	*1812n*	
Conyers, Benjamin	1846, 47	Thomas W.	*1821n*, *22n*	
John	1819, 21, 22, 25, 26, 26, 28, 29, 30	Cox, (*see also Cocks*)		
		Austin	*1843n*	
John, Jr.	*1813n*, 16, 17, 18	Benjamin	1804, 24	
Thomas	1815	Berryman	*1814n*, 22	
Thomas W.	*1815n*	Cary	1812, 26, 27, 28, 29, *30n*	
Walker L.	*1844n*, 51			
Cook(e), John	*1797n*, 05, 19, 21, 22, 23	Charnock	*1814n*, 19	
		Enoch	*1802n*, 03, 04, *46n*	
John, Jr.	*1805n*, 14	Fleet	*1844n*, 52	
George M.	*1812n*, 14, 15, 18, 19, 21, 29, *30n*, 31	George	1803, 04, 14, 17, 19, 21, 23, 24, 26, 27, *28n*	
Cooper, Alexander	1815	George L.	*1850n*	
Barnard	1804	John	1804, 05, 13, 19, 21, 25, 28	
Barnet	1802, 05			
David	1843, 44, 47	John B.	*1850n*	
Edward	1843	John F.	*1846n*, 50	
George R.	*1853n*	Lemuel	1813	
Hamilton	*1843n*, 44, 46	Newton	*1802n*, 03, 05, 06	
Howard	*1823n*, 29, 30	Peter	1812, 13, 18, 25, 26	
Jessey	1803	Peter P.	*1814n*, 17, 19, 22, 24	
Jessey, Jr.	1802, 04	Presley	*1798n*, 12, 13	
Jessey, Sr.	1803	Samuel	*1823n*	
John	1814, 43	Walter M.	*1846n*	
John, Sr.	1825, *26n*	William	1814, 19, 22, 23, 24, 25, 26, 27, 28, 29, 30, 47, 50	
John E.	*1844n*, 47			
Joseph	1805			
Rawleigh	*1817n*, 21	William, Jr.	1824	
Sanford	*1834n*, 41	Craig, John	1823, 26, 27, 28, 29, *30n*	
Spencer	*1802n*			
Thomas	1803, 04, 05, 06, *21n*, 22, 23, 25	Crismond, Thaddeus J.	*1848n*, 51, 52	
		Cristy, John	*1806n*	
Thornton B.	*1843n*, 47	Crop(p), Carter G.	*1851n*	
Coppage, Esom	*1825n*, 30	George W.	*1846n*, 53	
Fielding	*1798n*	James	*1851n*	
Coram, Champ	*1814n*	James, Jr.	*1804n*, 05, 06, 07	
William	*1813n*	James, Sr.	*1797n*	
Corbin, Benjamin	1826, 27, 28	James T.	*1851n*	
Benjamin S.	*1815n*, 18, 21, 22, 25, 29, 30	John	1808	
		John, Jr.	1797, 03, 05	
Harris S.	1817, 26, 27	John, Sr.	*1797n*, *51n*	
James	1821	Lewis	1802, 13, *51n*	
Jameson	*1822n*, 24, 30, 31, 32, 33	Presley	*1814n*, 22, 24, 25	
		Richard	1803, 04, 15, 18	
John M.	*1822n*	Robert	1797, 02, *26n*, 28, 29, 36, 38, 39	
Lafayette	*1846n*			
Mason	*1814n*	Silas F.	*1816n*, 18, 21, 22, 24	
Cosby, Morris	*1798n*	Thornton	1815, 18, 20, 22, 28	
Courtney, Broaddus	*1851n*	Thornton P.	1825	
Daniel	*1797n*	Thornton W.	*1815n*, 26, 27	
Elias	*1828n*	Walker	*1825n*	
James M.	*1844n*	William	*1797n*, 37	
Lewis	*1814n*, *28n*	William T.	*1829n*, 36, 41, 43	
Rawleigh	*1797n*	Croton, Charles	1804, 06	
Cowgill, George	*1804n*	Croughton, Charles	*1803n*, 05	

Robert	*1819n*, 21, 22n		Barnet	*1814n*	
Crump, Henry	1819		Barton	*1814n*, 15	
Reuben	*1803n*, 05		Henry	1824, 25, 26	
Crutcher, Robert	*1800n*, 01, 02, 03, 04, 05, 06, 07, 08, 11, 12, 14, 15		Spencer	*1797n*, 98	
			Day, Jeremiah	1802, 04, 05, 06	
Cummins, Ezekiel	1802, 03		Deakins, James	1827	
Cunninghame, Richard	1817		Deane, George H.	1843, 47	
Curkman, James	1819		Degarnet, Daniel	1804, 05	
Curry, James	1815, 16, 17, 18, 21, 22		Dekins, James	1822	
			Delany, Adonijah	*1805n*	
John	1819, 21		Dent, Alfred	*1843n*, 47	
Joseph	1813, 14, 17		John	1802, 03, 04	
Curtice, George	*1813n*		John S.	*1843n*, 47	
Richard	*1813n*		Samuel	*1844n*	
Curtis, Alexander	*1843n*, 50, 51		Scott	1828	
Fielding	*1822n*, 29, 30, 44		William	1797, 02, 04, 19, *22n*, 43	
Francis	*1828n*, 51		Dermot, John J.	*1828n*	
James	1803, 04, 12, 14, 17, 22, 23, 24, 25, 26, 30		Dickens, (*see also Dekins*)		
			Columbus	1826, 27, 29, 30	
Jessey	*1805n*, 06, 08, 11, 14		James	*1821n*, 26	
John	1822		Dickenson, Lewis	*1813n*, 17, 21	
Presley	1850		Travis	1819	
Presley J.	*1843n*, 44, 46		Dickerson, Lewis	1815	
Thomas	*1804n*, *25n*, 26, 27, 28, 29, 30		Dickinson, Edward	1830	
			John	1818	
William	1802, 14		Lewis	1824	
Dade, Alexander	1803		William	1815, 23, 24, 25, 26, 31	
Cadwallader	*1814n*				
Daffin, John	1825, 28		William, Sr.	1826	
William	*1821n*		Die (*see also Dye*)		
Dagins, John	1817		George	1851	
Daniel, John M.	*1803n*, *26n*, 28, 29, 33, 43		Dikes, (*see also Dykes*)		
			Richard	1830	
Moncure	1826, 29		Dillard, Madison	1812	
Peter V.	*1804n*, 09		Dilley, Richard	1803	
Samuel G.	*1830n*		Dillon, Benjamin	1805	
Thomas H. C.	*1831n*		Henry	1804, 05	
Travers	*1788n*		John	1826, 27, 28, 43, 44	
Walter R.	*1814n*, 15, 16, 19, 21, 24, 25, 28		William	1825, 43, 44, 46	
			Dobing, Thomas	1804	
Dasher, John	1814		Dobson, Seamor	1826	
Davis, Bailis	*1826n*, 27		Dodd, Humphrey	*1845n*, 51, 53	
Edward	1813		Travers	1821, 22	
Gervis C.	*1800n*, 01, 04, 05, 06, 08, 09		Travis	*1819n*	
			Dodson, Charles	*1802n*, 05	
George	1814		John	1802	
Hiram	1817		Seymour	1827, 28	
Hugh	1829, 30		Dogget, George	1818	
James	1828, 43, 44, 47, 50		Thomas	*1803n*, 04, 05, 15	
John	1823, 25, 28, 43, 44, 50		Wishart	*1826n*, *28n*	
			Doing, Jesse	1797	
Joseph	1803		Doniphan, Joel T.	*1822n*	
William	1797		Dorson (*see also Dawson*)		
Dawson (*see also Dorson*)			John	1806	
Bailey W.	*1815n*		Knight	1802, 03, 04	

INDEX

Lemuel	1815	John	1823, 29, 30
Douglas, Archibald	*1821n*	Joseph	1843
Mourning	*1797n*, 02	William	1825
Triplet	*1829n*	Ennever, Joseph	*1797n*, 03, 04
William A.	*1852n*	Ennis, John	1846, 50, 51
Dowdall, James	*1798n*	Ensor, Anthony	1812
Doyal(l), Dennis	*1802n*	George	*1815n*
Jesse	1797	William R.	*1815n*, 19, 23, 24, 26, 27, 30
William	1817, 19		
Dozier, John	1813	Enzor, William	1805
Duerson, Thomas L.	*1851n*	Ervin, John	*1825n*
Duffill, Edward	1797	Estredge, Meredith	*1821n*
Dunaway, Gerard	1824	Eustace, Hancock	*1788n*, 96, 97, 98, 00, 02
Joseph	1818		
Dunbar, John	*1802n*, 04	William	1824
Robert	*1804n*	Fant (*see also Faunt*)	
William	*1818n*, 22, 28	Elias	*1813n*
Dunnington, James	1850, 51	Fielding	*1801n*, 04
William P.	*1814n*	George	*1786n*, 94
Dye (*see also Die*)		George B.	*1813n*
Aldridge	*1846n*	Joel	*1813n*, 21
George	1830	John	1803, 04, 13
Dykes, (*see also Dikes*)		John P.	*1800n*, 01
Richard	*1826n*	Lovel	*1814n*, 19
Edmunson, Lewis	1805, 06, 15, 17	Richard J.	1809
Edrington, James	*1825n*, 29, 32, 33	Richard L.	*1813n*
John C.	*1801n*, 06, 08, 11, 12, 13, 14, 15, 16, *25n*, 29	Thornton	1805, 06
		William P.	1805
John M.	*1842n*, 44	Farish, George	1817
William	*1805n*, 06	Hazelwood	*1803n*
Edwards, Cylas	1814	Johns(t)on	1804, 06
Greenhow	*1850n*	Robert	1818
James	1796, 14, 46	Farnham, James	1825
John	1843, 46, 47	John	1825
Lewis	*1802n*	Faunt (*see also Fant*)	
William	*1813n*, 14, 25, 26, 28, 30, *43n*, 44, 46	George	1790
		Fennel (*see also Finnall*)	
Elkins, David	1824	John	1805
El(l)ington, James	1851	Ferguson (*see also Forgerson*)	
Jameson	*1819n*	George	1812
Joel	*1803n*, *04n*, 05, 06	George C.	1813
John	*1850n*, 51	Ficklen, Benjamin	*1794n*, 96, 97, 98, 99, 00, 01, 02, 03, 04, 06, 08, 09
Elliot, Elias	1823		
Ellis, Robert	*1805n*	John	1843
Ellison, John	*1819n*	John F.	*1844n*, 46, 47
Embrey, James	1846	Joseph B.	*1819n*, 23, 24, 33, 44, 46, 47
Joseph	1843		
William	1843	Leonard H.	*1826n*, 29, 30, 43
William S.	1842, 44, 47	Lewis	*1796n*, 97
England, Jacob	*1804n*, 05, 17	Strother	*1824n*, 25, 26, 30
John	*1813n*	William H.	*1826n*, 29, *30n*
John, Jr.	*1814n*	Filer, Samuel R.	1803, 04
John F.	1829, *30n*	Fines, Daniel	*1815n*, 17, 19, 21, 22, 26
Patrick	1828		
Patrick H.	*1826n*, 29, 30, 46	Elijah	*1824n*, 26, *44n*
English, Haden	1806		

174 INDEX

Isaac	*1825n*	John W. D.	*1841n*, 42, 44, 45
James	*1823n*, 24, 25, 26, 27, 43	William	*1813n*, 17, 19, 21, 25, 31
John	1817, 19, 21, 23, 24	Forgerson (*see also Ferguson*)	
Thomas	*1817n*, 19, 21, 23, 24, 25, 26, 27, 28, 43	George	1803
		George C.	*1804n*, 05, 06
Finks, (*see also Fixx*)		Fortune, Almond	1804
Oliver	1821	Fouche, Temple	*1825n*, 26
Finnall (*see also Fennel*)		Fouracres, James	1804, 12
Edward	1843, 44, 46	Foushee, Philip	*1822n*
James	1814, 22, 24, 25	Fox, Claiborne	*1801n*, 02, 03, 05
John	*1825n*, 27, 43, 46, 50	John	*1797n*, 98, 00, 01, 05
John, Jr.	1826	Steaphen	1804
Jonathan	1819	Thomas	1804
Robert	*1802n*, 05, 06, 14	Foxworthy, Alexander	*1817n*
Thomas	*1830n*	Philip A.	*1815n*
Walter H.	*1823n*, 24, 28	Franklin, Benjamin	*1844n*
Fishback, Martin	1812	Charles	*1826n*
Fisher, Ewel	1826, 27	George	1813, 19, 21
Robert	*1803n*, 04, 05	John	1813, 15, 24, 25, 26, 27, 29, 30
Fitzhugh, Alexander	*1813n*, 24		
Alexander H.	*1814n*, 33	Lafayette	*1843n*
Arthur	1813	Rubin	*1790n*, 94, 97, 00
Charles E. S.	*1824n*, 26, 29, 30	Thomas	*1813n*, 29
Edmund C.	*1846n*, 47	William H.	*1847n*, 51
Edwin C.	1843	William W.	*1853n*
Henry	1846, 47	Frazier, John	1829, 30
John B. S.	*1802n*, 04, 05, 06, 19, 21, 22, 23	French, George L.	*1851n*
		Samuel	1817
John R.	*1821n*, 44	Fristoe, Amos	*1813n*, 15
Thornton	*1797n*	Jessey	*1803n*, 04
William	1806	John	1830
William H.	*1812n*, 13, 14, 15, 16, 24, 25, 33	Richard	*1802n*, 04
		Thomas	*1797n*, 00, 02, 03, 04, 05, 06, 08, 09, 11, 12, *13n*, 14
William H., Jr.	*1846n*		
Fixx, (*see also Finks*)		Fritter, Arnold	*1814n*
Oliver	1819	Barnet	*1814n*, 15, 17, 23
Flatford, Robert	*1837n*, 40, 41, 42, 43, 53	Enoch	*1802n*, 19, 21
		Ephraim	*1802n*, 13, 17
Fletcher, John	1805, 12	Gustavus	*1819n*, 21
William	1802, 03, 04	John	*1814n*, 17
Flinch, William	1844	John H.	*1843n*
Fling, George	*1797n*, 98	Kenas	1819, 21
Flor(e)y, Ralph	1819, 21	Moses	*1797n*
Flurry, Edward	*1813n*	Noah	*1843n*
Fog, John, Jr.	1803, 04	Reubin	*1819n*, 21, 26
Major	1803	Travis	*1814n*, 17
Nathaniel	1803	Frost, Thomas	1803, 04, 05
Follis, Nicholas	1824	Fugate, Albert	*1850n*
Nicholas J.	*1826n*	Beverly	1844, 47
Forbes, Francis T.	*1844n*	Gerard	*1824n*
Murray	*1819n*, 21, 22, 23, 25	Jarred	1828
Ford, Daniel W.	*1847n*	John	*1819n*, 21, 22, 24, 25, 43, 44
James	*1805n*, 14, 15		
James W.	*1821n*, 22, 23, 25, 26, 29	Martin	*1821n*, 22, 24, 25, 26,

INDEX

		27, *28n*	Glasscock, Ezekiel H.	*1830n*
	Walter	*1850n*	George G.	*1843n*
	William	1803	Golatt, (*see also Collat*)	
Fuget, Martin		1823	Joseph	*1840n*, 41, 42, 50
Fulcher, George		1828	Gollahorn, Charles	1814
Furgason, (*see also Forgerson*)			George	*1821n, 50n*
	John	1843, 44, 46	James	1804, 43, 44
Fuss, George		*1844n*	James A.	*1846n*
Gaddes, Alexander		*1805n*	John	*1804n*, 13, 14, 15, 17,
Gaddis, Robert		1823		19, 21, 23, 28, 29,
Gaines, Nathaniel		*1824n*		*30n*, 43
	Richard	*1814n*, 15	Marshall	*1844n*
	Seth	*1817n*, 21, 23, 24	Robert	*1804n*, 12
	William	*1814n*	Solomon	*1818n*, 19, 22, 25, 26,
	William P.	*1817n*, 22, 24		27, 29, *30n*
Gallagher, Robert		1814	Thomas	1814, 21, 24, 26, 28,
Gardner, Jacob		1802		29, *30n, 43n*
	John	1797	William	1804, 13, 22, 23, 25,
Garner, Ezekiel		1819, 21		27
	Hansford	*1819n*, 27, 28, 29	Gordon, Alexander	*1822n*, 23
	Hensford	1830	Bazel	*1803n*, 04, 05, 06
	John	1813, 17, *44n*, 51	Jeremiah	1817
	Thomas	1814	Samuel	1825, 43, 46, 47
	William	1825, 26, 27, 29, 30	Samuel, Jr.	1803, 04, 23
Garnett, Joseph		*1806n*	Samuel, Sr.	*1803n*, 04
	Thomas	*1797n*, 03	Samuel H.	1844
	Thomas W.	*1804n*	William	1812, 14
Garrard, James		*1781n*	William K.	*1819n*, 22, 25
	William	*1786n*	William W.	*1853n*
Garrison, Aaron		*1805n*	Gough, James	1803
	Alexander	1814	John	1802
	Amos	1814	William	1821
	George	1814	Gravatt, Ellis	*1814n*
	James	*1813n*, 14, 26	Graves, Alexander	1844, 46, 47
	James H.	*1834n*	Austin	*1844n*, 46
	John	1803	Edmund	1804, 05, 06
	L___	1814	Henry	1803, 05
	Leonard	*1844n*	James	*1817n*, 18, 19, 24, 26,
	Moses	*1813n*		27, 28, 29, 30
	Richard	1843	John	*1803n*, 04, 05, 26, 27
	Robert	*1804n*, 05	John S.	*1843n*, 44, 50, 51
	Yelverton	*1813n*, 30, 37, 42	Joseph	1797, 02, 03, 04, 05,
George, Fielding		1815		14, 28
Geter, Samuel		1813	Robert	1844, 46
Gibs, John		1806	Rodham	*1814n*
Gilbert, Benjamin		1812, 14	Sidney	1825
Gill, Charles E.		*1842n*, 43, 50, 51, 52,	Thomas	1813
		53	Townsend	1825, 26, 27, 28, 29,
	Philip E.	*1825n*		30
	Presly	*1802n*	Townson	1819, 21
	Thomas	1815, 19, 21, 24, 25,	William	1818, 19, 21, 23, 25,
		26, 27, 28		43
	Thomas, Jr.	1822, 23	Willis	*1828n, 30n*, 51
	Thomas, Sr.	1822, 23	Gray, Atchison	*1819n*
	Washington	1812	Jesse	*1815n*
	William	1822, 24, 28, *30n*, 43	Joel	1813, 14, 19, 21

INDEX

John B.	*1846n*, 47		Charles	*1802n*, 04, 05
William	1819		James	1802
Grayson, Robert O.	*1825n*, 26, 27, 28, 30		John	1846
Green, Alexander M.	*1847n*, 56		John W.	1846
Duff	*1819n*, 22, 24, 26, 30		Joseph	*1797n*, 02, 03
Duff, Jr.	*1844n*		Luke	1822
Edward	1850		Mason	1822
Elisha	1828		Moses	*1819n*, 21, 22, 25
George	*1804n*, 13, 19, 21, 28, 43		Robert	*1821n*, 22, 25, 26, 44, 46
Hedgman	*1844n*, 46		Walter	*1797n*
James	1813, 21, 22, 23, 25, 26, 27, 28		William	*1814n*, 15
			Haborn, Robert	1823
Jesse	*1797n*		Hale, Corbin	1824
John	1843		Daniel	1814
Jones	*1818n*		Warner	1829
Robert	1825, 26, 27, 43		Hales, Thomas	*1847n*
Sydney	1830		Warner	*1830n*
Thomas	1816, 46		Hall, Benjamin H.	*1813n*, 14
William	1817, 27, 29, 46		Daniel	*1814n*
William J.	*1847n*, 51, 53, *56n*		John	1804
Gregg, John	*1781n*		Joseph	*1825n*
Gregory, John	1813		Haner, William	*1786n*
William	1814		Han(e)y, James	1818, 19
Griffin, John	1813		Jessey	1805, 06
Martin	1797		Hansborough, George	*1802n*, 03, 04
Griffis, Charles	1843, 46		Peter	*1791n*
John D.	*1844n*		Harding, Alfred	1830
Perry	1817		Bennet	1804
Ralph	1826, 27, 28, 29, *30n*		Boswell	*1825n*
Richard, Jr.	1828		Byram	*1842n*, 45, 47
Robert	*1828n*, *30n*		Elijah	*1801n*, 02, 04, 05, 06, 08, 11, 12, 13, 14, 15, 16
Thomas	*1837n*, 42			
Griffith, John W.	*1847n*		Enoch	*1796n*, 01, 04, 05, 06, 07, 08, 09, 10, 11
Ralph	1813			
Grigsby, Daniel	1797, 04		Harrison	*1814n*, 19
Moses	*1797n*		Jackson	1844, 47, 51
Peter	1814		Joel	*1803n*
Weeden	1819		John	*1796n*, 00, 02, 04, 15
William	1821		Mark	*1816n*, 18, 21, 26
Grinnan, Daniel	*1814n*		Mason	*1802n*
John	1851		Philip	*1813n*, 19, 21
William	1843, 46, 47		Richard	*1851n*
Groves, Alfred	1843		Rosall	1827, 28
Benjamin	1815, 19, 21, 22, 23, 24, 25		Strother	*1827n*, 29, 30, 46, 51
Elijah	*1850n*		Strother, Jr.	1847
Harrison	*1844n*, 50		Strother, Sr.	1847
Thomas	*1817n*, *51n*		Thomas	*1798n*, 05, 25, 43, 46
William	1819, 21		Thomas B.	1847
Willis	1850		William	*1814n*, 24, 25
Gun(n), Jacob	*1802n*, 03, 04		William, Jr.	1825, 26, 27
James	*1814n*		Harmage, Philip	1815
Guy(e), Benjamin	*1797n*, *14n*, 22, 25		Harreld, Samueld	1805
Benjamin, Jr.	1830		Willis	1813
Branson	*1825n*		Harris, Ephraim	1843

INDEX

Hugh	*1843n*, 47, 51		John L.	*1847n*
John W.	*1815n*		Hening, Robert	*1794n*, 95, 98, 00
Harrison, Daniel P.	*1815n*		Hensey, Thomas	1814
Hugh	1850		Hepborn, Robert	1821, 22
John	1843		Herndon, George	*1846n*, 47
Robert	1798		John	*1815n*
Thomas P.	*1813n*, 15, 16, 18, 19, 21		Ludwell	*1846n*, 51
			Hewe, James	1802
Harry, John	1813		Hewitt, James	*1815n*, 19
Hartly, George	1802		James E.	1814
Harwood, James H.	1823		James R.	*1821n*, 22
Thomas	*1803n*, 04, 05, 06		Jesse	1818
Haslip, Charles	1815		John E.	*1814n*, 24, 26, 28, 29
Hawkins, James	*1814n*		Joseph	1819, 23, 25, 26, 27, 28
James, Jr.	1817			
Hay, Alexander	*1796n*, 02, 04		Thomas H.	*1846n*
Charles T.	*1822n*, 24		William	*1786n*, 94, 96, 14, 15, 17, 18, 19, 21, 22, 23, 24, 25, 26
Thomas B.	*1819n*, 46			
William	*1794n*, 96, 97, 02, 04			
Hayden Ambrose	*1827n*		Hickerson, John H.	*1851n*
Jarvis	1826		Ransom M.	*1825n*
Hayes, Alfred C.	*1819n*, 23, 24, 25, 26, 30		Hiks, William	1819
			Hill, Brooke	1812
William H.	1829		Charles	1807
Hazlegrove, George	1844		Francis	1825, 29
Heb(b)ron, Robert	1822, 24, 26, 27		Frank	*1805n*
Hedgman, George	1803		George	1827
George F. G.	*1826n*, 28, 30, 34		Harris	*1830n*, 46, 47
George G.	*1807n*, 08, 09, 14		Henry	*1844n*
John	1797, 01, 24		Henry W.	*1843n*
John G.	*1800n*, 04, 06, 09, 22, 24, 25		Pitman	*1802n*
			Richard	*1821n*, 22, 26, 27
John T.	*1825n*, 28, 44		Thomas	*1808n*, 11, 12, 13, 14, 15, 16, 18, 19, 21, 28
Peter D. G.	*1824n*, 26, 28, 29, 30			
Peter N.	*1850n*, 51		William	1800, 01, 03, 06
Heffernon, Martin	1797		Hines, Charles B.	1817
Heflin(g), Absalom P.	*1851n*		Hite, William	1821
Gustavus	*1826n*, 29, 30, 43, 44		Hobs, James	1806
James	1814, 17, 19, 44		Hockman, James	1821
James L.	*1850n*, 51		Hogans, Edmund	1819
James T.	1847		Holden, Randall	*1844n*, 46, 49, 52
Jefferson	1846, 51, 53		Holloday, Bazil	1827
Jefferson W.	*1844n*		John	1797, 12, 13
John	1812		Robert	*1802n*, 04, 13
Marshall	*1843n*, 46		Samuel	1797
Robert	1837		William	1802, 14, 15
Strother	*1819n*, 21, 23		Zacheus	1819
Thomas	*1847n*		Holloway, Aaron	*1802n*, 03, 04, 05, 06
William	1814, 22, *43n*		Abel	*1798n*
Heifornon, James	1802		Daniel	*1804n*
James, Jr.	1804		George	*1804n*, 05, 06
John	1802		Jessey	*1805n*, 06
William	1802		John	*1802n*, 26, 27, 28, 29, *30n*
Helm, John	*1851n*			
Henderson, George	1821		Nathan	*1802n*, 03, 04
John	1826		Samuel	1813

INDEX

Thomas	*1802n*, 03		Joshua	*1826n*
Holly, Charles	1821		Huffman, Daniel R.	1825
Ho(l)mes, Edmund	*1814n*		Humphrey(s), Anderson	*1846n*, 47
Edward	*1813n*		Charles	*1802n*, 03, 04
George	1813, 19, 21		Charles, Jr.	*1851n*
James	1815, 16, 46		Daniel	*1803n*
James S.	*1814n*, 21, 22		David	1851
Jeremiah	*1814n*		John	1825
John M.	*1843n*, 50, 53		Samuel	*1841n*, 46, 47
John R.	1843, 44		Humphries, Rawley	*1827n*
Joseph	1814, 28		Samuel	*1837n*
Robert L.	*1851n*, 53		Hunt, William	1823, 24, 25, 27
William	1805		Hunter, William	1797
Honey, Joseph W.	*1830n*, 46, 47		Hutchison, John	1798
Hooe, Edwin C.	*1825n*		Ingalls, Lemuel	1817
Fantlyroy	1816		Jackson, Ambrose	*1827n*, 44
Francis	1804		Francis	*1814n*, 15
Francis H.	*1812n*, 15, 22, 26, 28		George	1797
Moore F.	*1813n*, 18, 19		James	1814, 29
Robert H.	*1794n*, 96, 04, 05, 06, 26		John	1816, 21
			John, Jr.	1814, 15
Robert S.	1819, 25, 27, *28n*		John T.	1851
Hooms, William	1803, 04		Reuben	*1847n*, 50, 51
Hord, Alexander	*1805n*, 06		Richard	1829, 30
Daniel	*1794n*, 97		Robert	1819, 21
James M.	1824, 25, 27, 28		Samuel	1812
James N.	1823		Thomas	1802, *25n*
John	1810		William	*1814n*, 18, 19, 21, 26, 27, 28
Lewis	*1800n*, 01, 02			
Reuben	*1798n*		Jacobs, Fountain	*1844n*
Rhoadham	*1803n*, 08		James	*1851n*
William F.	*1843n*		Jefferson	*1851n*
Hore, Elias	*1813n*		Robert	1805
Elias A. W.	*1847n*		Thornton	1843
James	*1786n*, 94, 97, 00		Warner	*1850n*, 51
John	*1794n*, 01, 02, 03, 04, *30n*		James, Benjamin	*1799n*, 02, 04, 05
			George	*1797n*
Walter	*1819n*, 21, 25, 47		Isaac	1797
William	*1822n*, 25		John	*1800n*, 01
Horton, Benjamin	*1846n*		Thomas	1815*n*, 19, 21, 29
Cossom	*1821n*		Jameson, Joel J.	*1828n*, 31, 33, 34, 37, 38
George	1798			
Hezron	1802, 03		Janens, Reuben	1806
James, Jr.	1803		Jenkins, George	1814
John	1814		Leroy	1823
Joseph	1803		Lewis	1819
Leonard	1816		Thomas	*1817n*
Marshall W.	1827		Jeredine, ___	1797
Peter	1802, 03, 04, 05		Jerrell, William J.	1844
Roy W.	*1825n*		Jett, Archibald	*1805n*, 06
Thomas	1819, 21		Benjamin	1806
William	*1797n*, 00, 01, 02, 03, 05, 06, 14, 21, 28		Berryman	*1804n*, 05
			Francis	1803, 04, 05, 19, 28, 29, 46
Howerson, John	1829			
Howison, John	1830		George	1819, 21, *22n*, 24, 27, 28, 29, *30n*
Hudson, Fielding	*1814n*, 19, 28			

INDEX

James	*1797n*, 04, 05, *50n*	
Jessey	*1797n*	
Peter	*1803n*, 04, 05, 06, 13, 14, 15, 16, 21, 29	
Peter, Jr.	1814, 19, 21, 26	
Peter J.	1822	
Stark	*1844n*, 47, 50	
William	*1813n*, 19, 21, 22	
Jewel, Bartimus	1805	
Cornelius	*1818n*	
Elijah	1821	
Peter	1805	
Johns(t)on, Barton	1814	
Burkit	*1830n*	
George	*1822n*	
Jacob	1817	
James	1829, *30n*	
James W.	*1845n*, 51	
Joseph	1818	
Joseph M.	*1819n*, 22, 26, 27, 29, 30, 47	
Littleton	1826	
Samuel	*1797n*, 03, 04	
Thomas	1815	
Thomas H.	*1847n*	
Walker	1803	
William T.	1851	
Jones, Alexander	*1847n*	
Alexander B.	*1841n*, 45	
Allen	*1805n*, 14	
Amos	*1836n*, 37, 41, 44	
Azariah	*1823n*, 26, 27, 29, 30	
Charles	1823, 24, 26, 29, 50	
Charles F.	*1838n*	
Charles T.	*1851n*, 52	
Charles W.	*1841n*	
Daniel	1818	
David R.	1843, 44, 46, 47	
Edward	1823, 26, 27, 28	
Elias	1829	
Elijah	1821	
Elisha	*1823n*, 25, 27, 28, 29, 30, *43n*, 44, 46	
Elisia	1822	
Esra	1824	
Ezra	1828	
Ezekiel	1825	
George	1797, 98, 04, 15, 21, 22, 23, 25, 28	
Gerrard	1821	
Henry	*1802n*, 03, 04, 05, 14, 19	
Isaac	1802, 03, 04	
James	1802, 24, 29, 37, 41	
John W.	*1843n*, 46	
Lewis	*1804n*	

Meriwether	1829, 30	
Noah	*1814n*, 22, 26, 27, 28, 29, *43n*	
Robert	1845	
Roy	*1829n*	
Samuel	1802	
Stanfield	*1797n*, 00	
Thomas	1802, 03, 11, 14, 21, 22, 23	
Thomas, Jr.	1824, 25, 26	
Thornton	*1844n*, 46, 47	
Travers	*1798n*	
William	1802, 03, 04, 15, 18, 19, 21, 23, 24, 27, 29, 43	
William A.	1850	
William T.	1816, *51n*	
Zachariah	*1804n*, 06, 14	
Jordan, Isham	1815, 17, 18, 19, 21, 22, 23, 24, 27, 28, 29, 30	
Jeremiah	*1815n*, 17	
Jesse	1812	
Jordin, Baily	*1802n*, 03, 04, 05	
John Scot	1802, 04	
Kearns, Gustavus	1846	
Kellogg, William	*1819n*, *51n*	
Kelly, Alexander	1825	
Alexander D.	*1826n*	
Kemper, John F.	*1815n*, 17	
Samuel	1813	
Kendall, Alexander	*1817n*	
B. B.	*1812n*	
Barnet	*1814n*	
Charles	*1794n*, 96, 97	
Joel M.	*1846n*, 47	
John	1813, 14	
John M.	*1844n*	
Joshua	*1814n*, 21, 25	
Moses	*1802n*	
Robert	*1828n*	
Toliver S.	*1825n*, 26	
Travis	*1814n*	
William	*1815n*, 28	
Wofinton	*1843n*, 50	
Kenady, Neru	1843, 44	
Kennedy (*see also* Cannady)		
Benjamin	*1802n*, 03	
George	1802, 04	
Kenney, John	1806	
Ker, Enoch	1818	
William	1803	
Kerns, Thomas	1825	
Keshaw, William	1797	
Keys, Amos	1817	
King, Absalom	*1819n*, 23, 25, 26, 29,	

John	30	Israel F.	1823, 25
	1814, 18, 19, 21, 29, 30, 43	William	*1811n*, 12
		Langford, William	1815
John H.	1847	Lanz, Alexander	1823
Pearson	*1805n*, 43	Latham, Anthony	*1805n*, 29, 30
Richard	1843	Daniel	1818, 19, 21, 22
Kinner (*see also* Skinner)		Edward	*1836n*
Abel E.	1819	Edward W.	*1837n*
Kirk, Jeremiah	*1786n*, 94	George	*1830n*
John	1823	James	1805, 24, 43, 50
William	1824	James, Jr.	1851
Kisshuck, George	1798	John, Jr.	1797, 04
Knight, Austin	*1843n*, 46	Lewis E.	*1847n*, 51
Baily	*1802n*, 03, 04, 13, 15	Philip	*1850n*, 51
Benjamin	*1802n*, 03, 06	Philipson	1844
Branson	1822, 28	Rawleigh	*1814n*, 19, 21, 22, 23, 25, 26, 29, 30
Christopher	*1802n*		
Daniel S.	*1844n*, 46	Robert	1843, 44, 50, 51
Elijah	*1806n*, 13, 15, 17, 18, 19, 21	Rowsy	*1819n*
		Thomas	*1851n*
Fielding	1802, 03	Thornton	1814, 16, 17, 23, 25, 26, 28, 29, 30
Gustavus	*1805n*		
James	1803, 14	Weadon	1805
John	1802, 03, 13, 19, 23, 26, 27, *28n*	William	1805, 15, 26
		Lavender, James	*1797n*, 98
Lewis	*1846n*	Lawless, Lewis	*1814n*
Peter	*1797n*, 02, 03, 04	Leac(t)h, Benjamin	*1797n, 51n*
Thomas	*1798n*, 03, 04	Elijah	1821
Uriah	1813	George	*1802n*, 19, 21, *22n*
Valentine	*1802n*	George H.	*1840n*
Wesley	1829, 30	James	*1790n*, 94, 15, *51n*
Westly	1827, 28	John	1797, 02, 14, 19, 21
Knox, Benjamin	1846	Philemon M.	*1822n*
Henry	1846	William	1813, 21
John	1846	Lee, Joseph	1843, 44
John J.	1847	Syrus	1817
John S.	*1813n*, 14, 15, 44	Thomas Ludwell	*1786n*
Thomas F.	*1814n*	Lei(t)ch, Abner	*1814n*
William	1846	Elijah	*1822n*
William A.	*1847n*	George	1823, 41
Knoxville, James	1829, 30	James	*1805n*
John	*1828n*	John	*1819n*, 22
Lakenan, Allen	1814, 17	Philip	1815
John	1802	William	1816, 44
Joseph	*1822n*	Lewis, Charles	1805
William	1802, 03	George	*1814n*, 16, 17, 22, 23, *25n*, 28, 29, 30
Lance, James	1805		
Lane, Alexander	1821, 25	John	1806, 10, 12, 14, 15, 17, 22, 23, *25n*, 28
George	*1802n*, 04		
John	1825, 29	Robert	*1804n*, 05, 06
William F.	1851	Thomas	1813
Lang, Alexander	1824, 26, 28	Lightner, George	*1843n*, 44
John	1819, 21, 23, 27, 28, 30	Limbrick, Daniel	1826, 27
		George	1804, 21, 22, 23, 24, 25, 26, 28
Robert	*1814n*		
Langfit, Fulsom	*1815n*	Gustavus	*1828n*, 43, 44

James	*1814n*, 21, *22n*, 23, 24, 25, 26, *43n*, 44, 51	Lyon, James	*1786n*
		Maccaboy, Robert	*1814n*
James, Jr.	1815	Mannen, Cornelius	*1823n*, 30
John	1814, 15, 17, 18, 22, 24, 25, 26, 28	Philip	1802, 03
		Manning, Cornelius	1828
John, Jr.	1826	Markham, Allen W.	*1810n*, 14, 15, 16
Landon	*1843n*, 46, 47	John	*1813n*
Po(a)rch	*1797n*, 98, 03, 04, 05, 06, 12, 13	Marmaduke, John	1829
		Marquess, Elijah	*1802n*
Robert	1844	John	*1816n*, 19, *21n*, 22, 23, 24, 25, 26, 27
Sidney	*1843n*		
Thomas	1804, 05, 06, 25, 26, 27, 28	Joseph	1802, 28, 28, 29, *30n*
		Samuel	*1802n*, 04
Thomas, Jr.	1827, 28	Thomas	1828
Thomas M.	*1844n*	William	*1811n*, 16, 19, 21
Vintson	*1804n*, 05, 12, 15, 26, 29	Marshal, Edward C.	1843
		Marston, Joshua	1797
William	1797, 02, 03, 14, 16, 19, 22, 23, 24, 25, 27, 28, 29, 30, *43n*	Martain, John	1798
		Martin, Francis	*1804n*, 05, 06, 18, 19
		George	1806, 13
William, Jr.	1822, 23, 24	John	1802, 12, 13
William, Sr.	1823	Joseph	1805
Linch, John	1819	Lewis	1805
Litteral, George	1851	Lewis G.	*1814n*
James	*1851n*	Robert	1805, 06
Thomas	*1851n*	Thornton	1813, 15, 16, 17, 18, 19, 21, 22
William	*1851n*		
Littleton, Sollomon	1802, 03, 04	Travis	1821
Littral, George	*1850n*	William	*1819n*
Loga, John	1819, 21	Mason, Alexander H.	*1833n*
Lomax, Gerard	*1813n*	Bartlet	*1803n*
Richard	1814	Daniel	*1800n*, 03, 04, 05, 06, 08, 10, 12, 13, 14, 16
Loury, (*see also Lowry*)			
James	1805	Daniel, Jr.	1802
Lo(w)e, Benjamin	1812	Enoch	*1786n*, 94, 96, 98, 99, 00, 01, 03, 04, 06, 07, 31, 33, 37
Edward	*1804n*, 05		
Lowry, (*see also Loury*)			
Moses	*1798n*	Enoch, Jr.	*1822n*
Peter D.	*1842n*	Henry	*1786n*, 94, 96, 97, 98, 00, 01, 02
Robert	*1806n, 50n*		
Thomas	*1797n*	Joel	*1794n*, 96, 00, 02, 08
William	1814	John	1814
Lunsford, Andrew B.	*1846n*, 47	Lewis	*1786n*, 91, 94, 96, 97, 98, 00, 01
George	1824, 27, 28, 29, 30		
James	1806, 30, 51	Nelson	*1806n*, 14, 21
James H.	*1843n*, 44, 50, 51	Wiley R.	*1827n*
John	1802, 03, 04	William	1797, 04, 05
John L.	*1851n*	Yelverton	*1805n*
John S.	1851	Massey, Alexander W.	*1822n*, 25, 26, 28, 29
Lawson	1850	Edmund	*1829n*
Lewis	*1830n*	Robert W.	1812
Moses	*1803n*	Masters, John	1825, 26
Robert	*1851n*, 53	John G.	1827
William	*1802n*, 04, 05	Thomas	*1814n, 37n*, 41
Lyle, Robert	*1802n*, 04	Mattocks, Henly	1798
Lynn, Joseph R.	*1814n*	Mattox, Henry	1797

INDEX

Maury, James	1821		Burwell	1823
James F.	*1812n*, 22		Mills, Gustavus	*1829n*, 30
McCarney, Michael	1826		Henry	1819, *22n*, 23, 24, 25
McCart(e)y, Daniel	1802, 03, 04		James	1814, 25, 27, 46
James	1802, 03		James H.	1847, 51
John	1803, 14		John	1805, 26, 29, 30
Nathaniel	1823		John S.	*1850n*
McCaulay, John	1804		John T.	*1851n*
McChinn, William	1853		Robert	*1850n*
McCoy, Benjamin	1814		Robert S.	*1837n*, 41, 43, 44, 47, 51
Daniel	*1812n*		William	1803, 05
Eliot	1802		Willis	*1821n*, 22, 27
Mason G.	*1815n*, 21		Milstead, Henry	*1847n*
William	1804, 13		Mintern, Henry S.	1836
McDaniel, George	1802		Mitchel(l), Horace	*1813n*, 17
John	1824		James	*1802n*, 04, 05, 06
Ozborn	1802, 03		John	1802
William	1806, 19, 21, 23, 25, 26		Samuel	1813
William, Jr.	1821, 22		Moncure, Edwin C.	*1804n*, 05, 13, 15
William, Sr.	1822		George V.	*1847n*
McDermott, Shadrick	1803, 04, 05		Henry	*1830n*
McFee, John	*1813n*, 17, 25, 27		John	*1796n*, 28, 29, *30n*
McGee, Alexander	1804, 05		John, Jr.	*1813n*, 14, 15, 17, 19, 22
McGuire, John	1804		John C.	*1844n*
McInteer, Elijah	*1847n*, 51		Richard C. L.	*1828n*, 29, 30, 46, 47
Henry S.	*1840n*		Thomas G.	*1823n*, 24, 26, 28, 29, 30
Henry W.	*1836n*		Travis D.	*1843n*
William	*1806n*, 08, 12, 14, 15		William A.	*1829n*
McIntere, John	*1814n*		William C.	*1847n*
McIntire, Elijah	1813		William E.	*1846n*
James M.	1846		Monett, James	1827
McIntosh, Francis	1797		Monroe (*see also Munroe and Monrow*)	
McKenny, Michael	1825		Alexander	*1821n*, 47
McNeil, William W.	*1815n*		Daniel	*1814n*
Mcoboy, Robert	1815		Daniel, Jr.	1816
McPherson, Alexander	*1830n*		Fielding	1825, 28, 29, 30
McRobertson, James	*1797n*, 00, 03, 04, 05, 06		Francis	1844
Meizings, John	1825		James	1826
Melion (*see also Million*)			James, Jr.	*1847n*
William	*1802n*, 04, 05		Walker	*1850n*
Mentharpe, Jacob	1786		William	1850
Mercer, John F.	*1786n*		William Jr.	1847
Mickie, John	1828		Monrow (*see also Monroe and Munroe*)	
Mif(f)lin, Charles	*1813n*		Daniel	*1851n*
George S.	*1821n*		Francis	*1851n*
James	1813		James, Jr.	1851
John	1813		Strother	*1851n*
Sanford	1813, 28		Thomas	*1851n*
Miller, Green	*1844n*		Walker	1851
John	1821		William	1851
John D.	1819		William, Jr.	1851
Joshua	1812		Monteith, Enos	*1798n*, 03, 04, 05, 17, 18
Million (*see also Melion*)				
Burrel	1824, 25			

INDEX

James	*1826n*, 27, 39, 41, 42, 44, 46		Jesse	*1814n*, 15, 25, 28, 29, 30
Samuel	*1819n*, 21, 22, 24		John G.	1814
Thomas	*1846n*, 47		John J.	*1813n*
William	*1847n*		Peter	*1828n*, 29, 30
Moody, Stephen	1818		Robert	1843, 47
Moore, Henry C.	*1843n*		Myers, Rhodam	1812, 14
Jeremiah	*1843n*		Napier, William P.	*1827n*
William F.	*1846n*		Nash, James	1824
More, Edward, Jr.	*1805n*		Jesse, Jr.	1851
John	1814		Nelson, James	1804
Morris, William	1843		John	*1805n*
Morson, Alexander	*1803n*, 23, 25, 26, 28, 46n		Newton, Abraham	1844, 47
			Abraham B.	*1843n*, 46
William	*1828n*		Benjamin	*1802n*, 03, 04
Morton, James	*1816n*, 17, 21		Gerrard	1821, 22
Joshua	1798		Gustavus	*1826n*
Richard	*1786n*, 94, 96, 99, 04		Gustavus B.	*1833n*, 43, 44
Robert B.	*1786n*		Gustavus V.	*1841n*
Thomas M.	*1813n*, 15		Isaac	*1794n*, 95, 96, 97, 02, 03, 04, 06
Moss, James	*1803n*, 04, 05, 07			
John	1803, 04, 05		James	1815, 23, 24, 25, 26, 27, 28, 29, 30
Mountjoy, Alexander H.	*1853n*			
Arrington	*1829n*, 30		Jarred	1828, 29, 30
Branson	1825		Jerrard	1823, 26
Edward	1802, 04		John	1821, 22, 24
James	*1811n*, 14, 19, 21, 22, 23, 24, 26, 28, 29		John, Jr.	*1851n*
			Marsena	*1818n*, 21, *22n*
Lemuel	*1828n*		Thomas	*1796n*, 99, 00, 03, 04, 17, 18
Lemuel S.	1826			
Ransom	1826, 28		Thomas K.	*1819n*, 33, 41
Thomas	*1804n*, 05, 06, 07, 08, 09, 11, 12, 13, 26, 28, 29, 30		Thomas T.	1821
			Nichols, Thomas	1803
			William	1827
William	*1798n*, 99, 00, 01, 02, 03, 04, 05, 13		Nicholson, George	1805
			William	1825
William B.	1813		Norman, Allen W.	*1815n*, 16, 17
Moxley, James	1826, *27n*		Edward	*1794n*, 00
Mozingo, John	*1817n*, *26n*		James S.	*1814n*
Thomas	*1812n*		Matthew	*1802n*, 03, 05, 06, 11
Mullin, Edward	*1798n*		Thomas	*1814n*, 15, 16, 24
Munns, James	1798		William	*1797n*
Munroe, Alexander	1819		Obyrhim, Alexander	*1814n*, 15, 17, 21, 22, 23, 25, 27, 28, 29, 30
Murphy, Amos	1828, 29, 30			
Benjamin	1821		Oder, Edward	*1846n*
John	1846		Ogden, Manuel	1828
Thomas	*1819n*, 21		Oglevy, James	1802
William	*1813n*, 17, 19, 21, 24		John	1816
Murray, Ebanezer	1814		Oliver, John	1813
James	1805		John, Jr.	*1824n*
James F.	1816, 19, 21, 25, *28n*		Owens, James	*1798n*
William	1814		Thomas	*1803n*, 04
Musselman, Christopher	*1819n*, 30		Pain(e), (*see also Payne*)	
George	1843, 44		John	1814
Henry	*1797n*		Lewis	1814
Hugh	*1846n*, 47		Rubin	1814

INDEX

William	1814	John W.	*1797n*, 04
Parker, Amos A.	1816	Led G.	*1815n*
Amos H.	1817	Led W.	1806
Parsons, George M.	*1814n*	Merryman	1803, 04
Pates, Aaron	1814	Perry	1805
Chandler	*1802n*, 04	Reuben	*1813n*, 23, 26
Gustavus	*1843n*, 50	Robert	1827, 29, *30n*
John	1812, 17, 19, 21, 22, 23, 24, 26, 27, 28	San(d)ford	*1825n*, 26, 27, 29, *30n*
		Spotswood	*1846n*, 47
John S.	1821	Theodocius	*1804n*, 05, 06
Reuben	1802	Thomas	1817, 21, 22, 25, 26, 27, 28, 29, 30
Patten (*see also Patton*)			
George C.	1844	Thomas J.	*1822n*, 26, 30
Patterson, Albert	*1851n*	William	1802, 03, 04, 06, 12, 19, 22, 23, 26, 27, 28, 29, 30, 46, 47, 50
Eli	*1814n*, 17		
Eli S.	*1851n*		
Fielding	1819	William S.	1816, 17, 18
James	1843, 44	Payton, (*see also Peyton*)	
Jesse	*1826n*, 28	Daniel	1796
John	1802	John	1812
Perry	*1805n*, 17	William W.	1821
Perry, Jr.	1823	Pearson, Asa	*1819n*, 21
Richard	1827	Martin	*1843n*
Thomas	*1813n*	Silwelton	*1843n*
William	1817	Watson	*1813n*
Patton (*see also Patten*)		Pemberton, W.	1814
Alexander	*1826n*, 27, 28	Perks, Coleman	1817, 18
Elliott	*1813n*	Perry, Eli P.	*1821n*, 22, 25, 26, 27
Elliot, Jr.	*1847n*	Frederick	1822
James	1813, 29	Lewis H.	1843
John	1829	William	1821
John, Jr.	*1851n*	Pettit(t), Benjamin	*1801n*
Richard	*1812n*, 28	Benjamin D.	*1803n*, 08, 09, 10
Robert M.	*1827n*	Hezekiah	1828
Thomas	*1846n*	Jacob	1798
William A.	*1847n*, 51	Jessey	*1803n*, 04, 05
Paulding, George	1813	Petty, Charles S.	*1840n*, 41, 42, 44
Payne, (*see also Paine*)		Peyton, (*see also Payton*)	
Daniel F.	*1818n*	Absalom	1828
Edmund R.	1823	Alexander	1821, 22, 23, 24, *25n*
Elijah	1802, 04, 05, 43	Bernard	*1811n*, 12
Francis	*1797n*	Daniel	1822
George	1805, 06, 13, 16, 18, 19, 21, 23, 24, 26, 27, 44, 46, 47	Garnett	*1797n*, 98, 99, 00, *02n*, 03, 04
		George	1843
George S. M.	*1840n*, 42	Henry	1795, 96
Harris	1827, 28	James	1803, 05
James	1798, 43, 44, 46	John H.	*1802n*, 03, 04, 05, 22
James L.	1826, 27, 28, 29, *30n*	John N.	1825
Jesse	*1826n*	Robert	1846, 50
Jessey, Jr.	1806	Rowzee	*1814n*, 15, 22, 23, 26, 27, 29, 30
John	1798, 06, 14, 23, 28, 29		
		Samuel H.	*1786n*, 94, 96, 97, 98, 99, 00, 01, 03, 06, 07, 08, 12, 14, 15, 16, 17, 18, 19
John A.	1821, *22n*		
John H.	*1847n*		
John N.	1822		

INDEX   185

Simeon C.	*1853n*	Thomas	*1805n*
Thomas	*1786n*, 94, 95, 19, 21, 23, 25, 26, 28, 29, 30	Primm, James	*1786n*, 94, 97, 98, 99, 01
Valentine	*1786n*, *22n*, 24, 25, 27, 28, 29, 30	William	*1802n*, 04, 05, 06, 08, 12
William	1814, 19, 23, 24, 28, 29	Proctor, Thomas	1805
		William	1805
William W.	*1818n*, 19, 23, 24, 25, 28, 29, 30	Puller, James	1816
Phillips, John	1802	Pumfrey (*see also* Pomfrey)	
John S.	*1814n*	John	*1824n*, 25, 26, 27
Silem G. F.	*1814n*	Purley, Frederick	*1819n*
William	*1786n*, 19, 21	Purnell, William	1816
Pickett, Thomas B.	*1840n*, 41, 42, 43	Pursley, James	1805, 06
Pierce, Isaac	1804	Purvis, George	*1824n*, 25, 28
Pilcher, Daniel	*1804n*	Strother	*1818n*, 19
Frederick	*1805n*	Travis	1821
Mason	*1781n*, 86, 89	Puzey, Aldom	*1797n*
Moses	*1804n*, 05	Gerard	*1803n*
Richard	*1804n*	Richard	1827
Sidney	*1817n*	Queen, Henry W.	*1831n*, 34, 36
Thomas	*1802n*, 05, 08, 11	John	1828
Pollard, Thomas	1826, 27	John R.	*1834n*
Pollock, William G.	*1856n*	John W.	1833
Pomfrey, (*see also* Pumfrey)		Washington	1828
John	1843	Rains, Isaac J.	1847
Pope, Humphrey	1813	Selden	*1843n*
Por(t)ch, Ezelburton D.	1819	Ralls, (*see also Rauls*)	
John	1851	Charles	*1786n*, 94, 97
Thomas	*1804n*	Daniel	*1813n*
Yearly	1797	Henry	*1790n*
Yelverton	*1812n*, 15	Kenaz	*1790n*, 91, 94, 96
Yelverton B.	1815, 16, 17, 18, 19, 21, 22	Randall, (*see also Randoll*)	
		Abram	*1846n*
Porter, Samuel	1812	Aquilla	*1841n*, 43, 50
Thomas	*1794n*	Benjamin	*1843n*
Potes, Henley	*1819n*	Charles	1824, 28, 29, 30
John	1819, 21	Gallenus	*1846n*
John H. S.	1819, 21, 23	John	*1829n*, 30, 43, 44, 46, 47
Lemuel	*1815n*		
Lewis	1819, 21	Richard	*1797n*, 14, 43
Valentine	*1814n*	Robert	1843
William C.	*1815n*, 17	Thompson	1824
Potts, Horace	*1844n*, 46	William	1804, *25n*, 28, 29, 30, 41, 42, 44
John H. S.	*1816n*, 26		
Richard	*1822n*	Randolph, Charles C.	*1824n*, 25
Thomas	1844	John	1828
Powel, Elishea	1806	Rankins, George	1817
James	1817, *51n*	Peter	1813
John	1812	Randol(l), John	1805
Pratt, Burkett	*1817n*	Richard	1806
Stephen	*1814n*	William	1822
Presley, James	1813	Rat(c)liff, Alexander G.	*1813n*
Price, Charles	*1806n*	John A.	*1804n*, 06, 08, 11
Thomas K.	*1844n*	Richard	*1805n*
Prichard, Ishmael	*1819n*, 23, 24, 25	Thomas H.	1819, 21
		Rauls, (*see also Ralls*)	

Moses	*1806n*	Robison, George	1805
Rawlings, Robert	1843	James	1805, 24
Read, Gustavus	*1819n*	Thomas M.	1824
Lewis	1802	Ro(d)gers, Aaron	1797
Reamy, John	1806	Caleb	1803
Reaves, Hiram	1821	Christopher	1797, 02
Red, William	1812	Henry L.	*1823n*, 30
Redder, John	1812	James	1797
Reder, Hezekiah	1821	John	1805, 12, 15, 23, 25, 28
Reddish, Fielding	1797, 02, 03, 04, 06		
Joseph	*1808n*, 09, 11, 12, 13, 14, 15, 16	Lyburn	1830
		Robert C.	*1843n*, 51
Ransom	*1801n*, 02	Western	*1844n*
Reed, Gustavus	1826, 28	Roles, (*see also Rolls*)	
Noah	1813	Jackson	1843
Reeves, George	1815	James	1847
Isaac	*1846n*	John	1813, 19, 47
John	1846	Valentine	*1814n*
Reid, Gustavus	1823	Rollow, Archibald	*1809n*, 11, 14, 15
Reiley, Hugh	1805	Archibald, Jr.	*1813n*
Renno(e), Scarlet	*1819n*, 21	Francis	*1813n*, 28, 29, *30n*
Zele/Zelia	1823, 24, 28, 29, 30	Peter J.	*1819n*
Richards, Franklin	*1830n*	Rossall	*1813n*, 29, 34, 36
William	1803, 04, 05, 29, 30	William	1843, 44
Richar(d)son, Henry W.	1817	Rolls, (*see also Roles*)	
James	1815, 18	Daniel	1821, 23, 25, 28
John	1814	Jackson	*1828n*, 30
Riley, Henry	1806	James	*1846n*
Hugh	1803, 04	John	1813, 21, 23, 24, 25
Noah	*1847n*	William	*1822n*, 23, 25
Rives, John	*1843n*	Rolly, Peter	1819
Roach, Jesse	1812	Rose, Alexander	1804
Roberson, Barcelius	*1828n*	Alexander F.	*1819n*, 21
Charles H.	*1848n*, 51, 52	Benjamin	1826
George	1813	Edmund F.	*1851n*
James	1822, 51	George F.	1850
John	1825, 26	Henry	1814, 17
Philip	1829, *30n*	Jessey	*1804n*, 06
Thomas	1816, 28, 29, *30n*	Robert	1797, 02, 03
Thomas N.	1825	Thomas	1843, 44
William	1827, 29, 30	William	1805, 15
Roberts, William	1804	William, Jr.	1818
Robertson, George	1797, 02, 03, 04, 50	Ross, Andrew	*1805n*, 14, 15
James	1803	John	*1811n*, 14, 15
James M.	1801, 02, 03, 08, 11	William	1786, 94, 03
John	1843, 44, 46, 50	Ro(w)e, Horace T.	*1851n*
Lawson	*1794n*, 97, 01, 02, 03, 04	James	1805, 50
		James P.	*1814n*, 22, 24, 26
Orasid	1797	Jesse	*1814n*, 25, 28
Thomas M.	*1843n*, 44	John	1822
William	1798, 50	John G.	*1814n*
William H.	*1844n*	Keilding	*1815n*
Robeson, George	1806	Perry	1825
Robinson, James	1819, 21, 23	Rowley, Archibald	1800, 01
James F.	*1853n*	Richard	1804
Thomas M.	1823	Theophilus	1797

INDEX

Rucker, George A.	1817		William	*1803n*, 04, 05, 23, 27, 29, 30
Ruder, Hezekiah	*1822n*			
Rye, Alfred	1825, 26, 27		Sharp, Arthur	1813
Archibald	*1814n*, 15, 17, 21, 22, 23, 25, 27, 28		Benjamin	1804
			John	1803, 05
Gustavus	1813, *28n*		Richard	1812, 14
James	1822, 23, 25, 28		Thomas	*1812n*
James A.	1827		William	*1804n*, 05
Sam, Alfred S.	1817		Shelkett, George	1811, 14
Sanders, Robert	1822		George G.	1815
William	1797		George T.	*1815n*, 17
San(t)ford, Joseph	*1823n*, 24		James	*1819n*, 21, *22n*
Lawrence	*1813n*		John	*1797n*, *29n*
Saunders, Robert	*1822n*		Rodham	1845
Scheldtin (*see also* Shelton)			Rodham P.	*1844n*
John	1844		Shelton, (*see also* Scheldtin *and* Chilton)	
Schoolar, Charles	*1851n*		Abroad	*1844n*, 47, 50
John H.	*1851n*		Augustin	1821, *24n*, 25
Peter D.	*1851n*		Edward	*1797n*
Schooler, Abner	*1805n*, 14		George G.	*1813n*, 19, 22, 30
James E.	*1853n*		Gustavus	*1816n*, 17, 18, 26
John	*1844n*, 51		John	1805, 24, 28, 29, *30n*, 43, 44
Thomas W.	*1843n*			
Thornley	1798, 02		John C.	*1822n*, 23, 25
Thornley E.	*1826n*		Moncure	*1850n*
Scott, Gustavus	*1796n*, 97		Richard M.	*1846n*, 53
George	1821		Thomas	*1804n*, 05
John	1827, 28, 29, 30, 46		Thornton	*1824n*, 25, 28
Richard M.	*1828n*, 29, 30, 43		Wellington	1850
Thomas C.	*1817n*		William	1797, 05, 08, 12, 13, 15, 44
Scrivner, John	1827			
Seddon, George	*1819n*, 21		Yelverton	*1826n*
John	*1804n*, 06, 08, 09		Shoemate, Daniel	*1803n*
Thomas	*1803n*		Shumate, Triplett	*1816n*
Thomas, Jr.	1804, 05, 06		Shurlock, George	1798
William	*1803n*, 04, 13, 14		Sidebottom, William	*1814n*, 28, 29, 30
Servis, George	1815		Silmon, Joseph	1815
Settle (*see also* Suttle)			Simmons, William D.	1815
John	1805		Sim(m)s, Benjamin	*1814n*
Shackelford, Benjamin H.	*1821n*, 22		Charles H.	1843, 44
Coleman	*1829n*, 30		Claibourn	1828
Dudley	*1836n*, 40		Daniel	*1803n*
James	*1832n*		Hanson	1825, 26, 27, 29, 30
James H.	*1836n*, 42		John D.	*1819n*, 21, 22, 23, 24, 25, 26
John	1819, *22n*			
Samuel	1847		John H.	1813
Solomon	*1813n*, 21		Presly	*1814n*
Strother	*1828n*, 30, 43		Rodham	*1802n*
Thomas	*1827n*, *30n*		William	1821
Thornton	*1819n*, 28		Simpson, Jesse	1798
Toliver	1825		Sinclare, James	1802, 03, 04
Uriah	*1828n*, 29		John	1804, 05, 06
Vincent	1814		Thomson	1814
Shacklet(t), Benjamin	*1797n*, 03, 04		Skidmore, Alexander	*1843n*, 44
Benjamin H.	*1822n*, 23		Alexander W.	1834, 41
Edward	*1805n*		Enoch	*1850n*

Harrison	1847		Thomas	1825, 28, 29, 30, 43, 44
Harrison G.	*1843n*			
Harrison J.	1850, 52		William	*1821n*, 22, 23, 24, 25, 26, 27, 28, 29, 30, 43, 46, 50
John	1819			
Joshua	1822, 24			
Robert	1827, *44n*, 50		William J.	*1847n*, 50
Samuel	1847		Snipe, Nathaniel	*1824n*
Thornton	1814		Snoxall, Sarsfield	*1802n*, 06, 12
William	1812, *44n*, 50		Sorrel, Alexander	*1805n*
Skinker, John H.	*1843n*		James	*1822n*
Samuel	1804, 05		John	1815
Samuel H.	*1814n*, 16, 24		Speake, Thomas H.	*1846n*, 47
Skinner, (*see also Kinner*)			Spencer, John	1805
Abel	1823, 24		Spilman, James	*1803n*, 04, 05, 06
Abel E.	*1825n*		Stadler, William	1814
Ezekiel	*1819n*, 21		Stadlow, William	1805
Harrison	*1843n*, 46		Stanly, Thomas	*1822n*
William	1846		Stark(e), James	*1802n*
Slade, William	1804		James B.	*1814n*
Slaughter, David	1821		Jeremiah	*1797n*, 02
David C.	*1823n*, 24, 25		John	1813, 18
John F.	*1805n*		John A.	*1818n*, 21, 28
John W.	1847		Newman B.	*1819n*, 21
Warren	*1846n*		Richard	*1846n*, 47
Smith, Absalom	*1828n*, 29, *30n*		Robert	1804
Benjamin	*1843n*, 47		Thomas	*1800n*, 01
Elias	1813		William	*1794n*, 01, 02, 03, 04
George W.	*1843n*, 45, 46		Ste(a)phens, Allen	1802
Harris	1814, 29, 30		James L., Jr.	1851
James	1804, 25		John	1819, 21
John	1794, 14, 17, 43, 44, 47		John M.	1822
			Robert	1804
John R.	*1851n*		Thomas M. D.	*1850n*, 51
Jonas	1803, 04, 05		Stern(e), Francis	*1809n*, 19
Joseph	1786, 17		John	*1794n*, 96, 01, 02, 03, 05
Lewis	*1843n*, 44, 47, 51			
Mourning	*1797n*, 04, 43, 44		Stevens, James	1823
Robert	1843, 44, 47, 50, 51		John	1818
Robert, Jr.	1851		John M.	*1822n*
Thomas	1818, 22, 23, 25, 29, 30, 43, 47, 50		William S.	1813
			Stewart, Barnett	*1823n*, 24, 25, 27
Thomas A.	*1819n*, 23, 25, 28		Charles	1813, 22, 23
Walker	*1843n*, 44, 47, 50, 51		Charles B.	*1825n*
William	1797, 04, 18, 19, 21, 22, 23, 29, *30n*		James	1797, 01, 03
			James N.	*1801n*, 02
Smithers, John W.	1844		Joseph	1804
Worthington G.	1828		Robert	*1828n*, 29, 30
Smithson, Shelah	1805		Stephen	1813
Smoote, John H.	*1825n*		Thomas	*1814n*, 22, 23, 24, 25, 26, 27, 30
Snelling(s), Alexander	*1818n*, 28, 29, 43			
Benjamin	*1804n*, 13, 14, 21, 22		William	1804, 06, 07, 22, 23, 29, 30
James	*1843n*, 46, 50			
Jesse	1825, 27, 28, 29		William B.	*1853n*
John	*1825n*, 50		Stilman, Joseph	1816
Philip A.	*1846n*		Stone, Alexander S. H.	*1811n*, 14, 15
Richard M.	1846		Barton S.	*1808n*, 09, 10, 11, 12,

INDEX

Charles W.	13, 14, 15, 16
	1836n
Elias	*1817n*, 18, 23, 24, 25, *26n*, 28
Fielding B.	*1847n*
George	*1823n*, 26, 30, 43
James	1828, 30, 44
James W.	*1821n*, 24, 27, 29, 32, 33, 36, 37, 41, 43
Jesse	*1797n*, 02, 43, 44, 50
Joseph	1826, 28
Richard	*1830n*
Sanford	*1843n*
Thomas	1843
Walter	1847
William	*1802n*, 19, 27, 28, 29
William B.	*1819n*, 21, 24
William H.	*1830n*, 33, 37, 38, 40, 41, 45, 46
Stork(e), Bailey W.	*1814n*, 15
John A.	1817
Thomas	*1814n*, 15
Stratton, Thomas	*1846n*
Stribling, George	1812
Stringfellow, William	*1812n*, 22
Strother, Anthony	*1794n*
George	1825
George W.	*1846n*, 47
John F.	*1828n*
Strullow, William	1813
Stuart, William	1821
Styers, Robert	1826
Sudduth, (*see also Suthard*)	
Allen	1804, 05
Francis	1802
Jackson	*1846n*
John	*1806n*, 19, 26
Suell, Josias	1823
Sullivan(t), Addison	1846, 50
Addison J.	*1844n*
Augustin	1815
Benjamin	*1843n*, 44
Caleb	*1839n*, 41, 42, 46, 50
Carson	*1815n*
Daniel	*1822n*, 26, 43, 44, 50
Daniel, Jr.	1846
Dawson	*1819n*, 21, 22, 23
Derby	*1803n*
Elijah	*1850n*
Gabriel	*1797n*, 98, 06
George	1802
Gustavus	*1814n*, 16, 17, 18, 19, 21, 22, 23, 24, 27, 28
Isaac	*1846n*, 47
Isaac N.	1850
James	1804, 14, 17, 18, 19, 21, 43, 50
John	1797, 04, 05, 06, 43, 50
John, Jr.	1850
Lewis	1812
Marmion	*1805n*, 14, 15, 21, 22
Martin	*1806n*, 18, 19, 21, 22, 24, 25, 26
Martin, Sr.	1823
Presley	*1846n*
Robert	1844
Rodney	1813
Stephen	*1829n*, 30, 37, 41, 43, 46, 47
Thomas	1797, 03, 04, 05, 21, 24, 25, 43, 46, 50
Thomas, Jr.	1846
William	1804, 13, 15, 19, 21, 23, 24, 25, 26
Suthard, (*see also Suddoth*)	
Jackson	1847
John	1822
Suttle (*see also Settle*)	
Charles F.	*1836n*, 37, 41, 43, 46, 51, 52, 53
Ellis	1821
John	*1802n*, 03, 29
John H.	*1830n*
Sweatman, Neri	*1805n*
Swetnam, John A.	*1843n*, 45, 51
Levi	*1811n*, 12, 13, 14, 16, 27, 29
Thomas L.	*1851n*
Swift, John F.	1843, 44
Swillavant, Jonas	*1814n*
Swope, George	1798
Tackett, Charles A.	*1846n*, 47
John	*1815n*, 17
Sennet	*1819n*, 21
Taliaferro, Gustavus S.	*1841n*, 43
James M.	*1842n*, 43, 44, 45, 46, 52, 53
John, Jr.	1844
Meriweather	*1802n*, 03, 04
Tal(l)marsh, Mark	1821, 22
William	1819, 21, 22, 23, 24, 25, 26, 27, 28, 29, 30
Tarlton, James	1843
Tarrier, Benjamin	1804
Taulmarsh, William	*1806n*
Taylor, Ezekiel	*1823n*
George	1797
Henry	1797
James	1814
John	1816
John B.	*1815n*

Robert	1837, 41			02, 03, 04, 05, 06, 07, 08, 12, 13, 14, 15, 21
Robert B.	*1841n*, 44		Benjamin, Jr.	1818, 25, 27
Sidney H.	*1826n*		Benjamin P.	*1834n*
Thornton	*1814n*, 26		George, Jr.	1819, 21
Vintson	1802, 03, 04		George H.	*1802n*, 06, *44n*, 46
William	1786		James	1843
Templeman, Edward	*1812n*, 14, 19		James N.	1830
Ephraim	*1817n*		John C.	*1843n*
Henry N.	1824		John L./D.	1815
James	1803, 04, 06, *19n*, 21, 22, 25, 26, 28, 29, 30		John N.	*1816n*, 19, 21, 27
Jeremiah	1822		To(o)mbs, Robert	*1803n*, 05, 15, 16
Jeremiah B.	*1809n*, 10, 13, 14, 15, 24, 26, 28, 29		Tompkins, Thomas B.	1851
			Towson, James E.	*1828n*, 30, 36, 45
John	1797		Thomas N.	*1844n*, 45
Lewis	1803, 04		True, Crede	*1814n*
Moses	*1825n*		Dolphin	*1822n*, 23, 24, 25, 27
William	1797, 02		William	1798
Tharp, James	*1814n*, 15, 19		Truslow, Benjamin	*1818n*, 21, 22, 27, 28, 29, 30
John	*1813n*			
Richard	1815, 17		Charles	1847
Thomas	*1805n*		James H.	*1846n*
William	1815, 18		John	*1814n*, 28, 46, 47
Thomas, Benjamin	*1803n*, 04, 05, 06, 10, 11, 14		Robert	*1839n*, 43, 47
			William	1818, 24, 30
William	*1826n*		William T.	1844
Thomkins, Thomas B.	*1850n*		Z.	1812
Thompson, James	1814, 15, 21, 28, 29, 30		Trussel, John	1812
			Thomas	1812, 24
James M.	1829, 30		William	1814, 25, 26, 29
John	1805, 24, 43, 44		Trussle, Thomas	1823
Rodney	1815		William	1828
William	*1812n*, 14		Turner, Alexander	1822, 23, 28
Thornton, Charles	1804, 13		Alexander, Jr.	*1851n*
George	*1802n*, 03, 04, 05		Henry	1806, 12
George W.	*1806n*		Jessey	*1805n*, 06
Henry R.	*1825n*		Joseph	1802
John	1804		Newton	*1843n*
Threlkeld, Elijah	*1786n*		Rowland T.	*1803n*
Jesse	*1802n*		Thomas	1803, 04, 05, 21
Tiltcomb, Lewis	1812		William	1802, 14
Timberlake, Joseph F. B.	*1851n*		William W.	1847
Lewis T. W.	*1851n*		Tut(t), John	1812
William	*1812n*, 21		Richard J.	*1802n*, 03, 04, 08, 09
Timmons, Lewis	*1825n*, 26, 27, 29, 30		Thomas	*1815n*
Nelson S.	*1843n*, 44		Tyler, John C.	*1813n*
Roberson	1851		Sepleman	1812
Stanard	*1851n*		Thomas G. S.	*1781n*, 86, 94, *96n*, 97
William D.	*1824n*, 25, 26, 30		William H.	*1821n*
Tippett, Thomas	1797		Tyson, (*see also* Tison)	
Tison, Edward	*1804n*		James	1813, 19, 21, 24, 29, 30
James	1814, 16			
John	*1814n*		Joseph	1805, 12, 15, 18, 19
Joseph	*1804n*, 16, 17		Robert	*1830n*
Joseph, Jr.	*1806n*		William	1821, 22, 28, 30
Tolson, Benjamin	*1790n*, 94, 97, 98, 99,		Vant, (*see also* Fant)	

INDEX

Joel	1819	Ward, Henry	*1781n*
Lovel	1821	Wardell, Patrick G.	1813
Vass, Edwin B.	*1824n, 26n*	Ware, Robert	1806
James	*1803n*, 04, 05, 06	Thomas	1805
James C.	*1824n*, 26	William	1796, 01
Penrose	*1826n*	Wariner, Alfred	1842, 52
Villers (*see also Willers*)		Warren, Charles	*1823n*, 28, 29, 30
William	*1845n*, 47	Robert	1823
Vinyard, Samuel	1806	Washington, Bailey, Jr.	*1797n*, 06
Voss, Robert	*1822n*	Henry	*1815n*
Vowles, Charles	*1788n*	Warters, John F.	1850
George	*1803n*, 04, 05	Wat(t)ers (*see also Walters*)	
George F.	1806	James	*1786n*
Thomas	*1805n*, 08, 09	Sandy	*1830n*
Zachariah	*1803n*, 04, 05, 06	Thomas	*1814n*
Walker, Alexander	*1794n*, 96	Wat(t)s, Anthony	1824, 25
James	1797	George	1843
John	1822, 25, 26	William	1803, 04, 28, 29, 30
Thomas	1814	Watson, Americus	*1843n*, 44
Landon	1814	Archibald	*1802n*
William	1814, 43, 44	Baily	1814, 17, 21
Wallace, Gustavus B.	*1843n*, 46	Benjamin	*1819n*, 44
John	*1794n*, 95, 03, 04, 05	George M.	1850
John H.	*1810n*	Hamilton	1844
Michael	*1823n*, 28, 29	James	1814, 43
Stewart	*1798n*	John	1804, 13
Thomas	*1815n*, 28, 29, 30	Robert	1844, 50
William B.	*1802n*	William	1802, *26n*
Waller, Edward	*1787n*, 94, 96, 97, *25n*, 28, 31	Waugh, David	1797
		George L.	*1790n*
George	*1807n*, 08, 11, 13, 15, 16, 18, 19, 21, 22, 24, 25, 26, 28, 29, 43, 44	James	1803, 04
		Way, Allen	1815
		John	1814
James	*1811n*, 12, 14, 15, 19	Weaks, Benjamin	*1803n*, 04
James E.	*1845n*, 51	John	1803, 04, 05
William	*1797n*, 01, 02, 04, 16	John H.	1822
Withers	*1825n*, 26, *46n*, 47	Wealch, Joseph	1812, 13
Walters (*see also Waters*)		Weeks, John	1816
Bladen	1803	John H.	*1819n*, 21, 23
Juniper	*1826n*	Weir, Robert	1805
Landon	*1814n*, 15, 19, 24, 25, 26, 27	Welch, Joseph	1814, 17
		Wells, Benjamin	*1802n*, 04
Mark	*1797n*	Went, William	1825, 28
Mason	1815	West, Charles	1797, 98, 02, 03, 04
Sandy	1828	Edward	*1786n*
Sanford	1813	George	1804, 23
Seamor	*1826n*	James	1830
Silas	*1803n*, 04, 05, 06, 13	John	1790, 94, 02, 03, 04, *05n*, 06
William	*1827n*, 28	Joseph	1812
Wamsley, (*see also Wormsley*)		Oliver	1823, 26, 27
Benjamin	*1840n*	Walter	1827, 30
Joseph	*1815n*, 21	William	1801, 04, 25
Waple, Hezekiah	1813, 17, 19, 21	Whaling, Edward J.	*1843n*
Robert	1833	Pozey	*1803n*, 19
Robert L.	*1832n*, 37, 40, 41, 42, 43, 44, 46, 48	William J.	1824

Wharton, Joseph	*1806n*	Wishart, Sidney	*1797n*
Richard	1843	Withers, Allen	*1797n*, 00, 01
Samuel	1814	Allen W.	1808
Wheatly, Lawson	*1813n*, 16, 19	Benjamin	*1786n*, 94, 96, 04, *06n*
White, George	1814	Daniel F.	*1826n*
Henry	*1824n*, 25, 26, 27, 28, 43, 44, 46, 47, 50	Edward	*1797n*, 00
		Jenings	*1813n*
James	*1813n*, 27, 28, 43, 44, 46	Joseph D.	*1828n*, 29
		Samuel	1817
Thomas	1805, 06	Thomas A.	*1837n*, 41
William	1822, 23, 24, 25, 26, 28, 44, 46	William A.	1802, 03, 04, 05, 06, 09, 11
Whitecotton, Harris	*1796n*	Wofenden, Richard	1844
Whorton, William	1819	Wolfe, William	1824
Wiat, John	1806	Wood, Rhoadham	1803
Wiggenton, Peter	*1841n*, 47, 50, 53	Wood(w)ard, James	1802
William	1805	John	1797
Wilder, Horace	1825, 26	William	1823
Wilhite, Martin	*1816n*	Woodroe, Henry	*1802n*, 03, 04
Willcocks, Samuel	*1812n*, 14	Woodyard, James	1806
Williams, Alexander P.	*1830n*	Wormsley, (*see also Wamsley*)	
Alfred	1844	Joseph	1802, 03, 12, 19, 22, 23
Benjamin	*1805n*, 15		
Benjamin, Jr.	*1830n*	Wort, John	*1803n*
Benjamin, Sr.	1815	Wray, Allen	1814
Charles	*1819n*, 21, 24, 27, 28	Wright, John	*1804n*, 05
George	*1786n*, 02, 10	Joseph	*1802n*, 03, 04, 05
George, Jr.	1807, 08	Yarby, Thomas	1814
Henry	*1800n*, 02, 04, 07, 08, 10, 11, 12, 13, 14, 15, 16	Yeastis, Woodford	1805
		Yost, John	1797
James	1814, 24, *53n*	Young, George	1823
Jessee	1814, 17	Linsfield	*1814n*, 15
John	1798, 13, 17	Rhoadham	1804, 05, 06
John P.	*1815n*, 19, 21, 30	Richard	1812
Nathaniel	1828	William	1802, 12, 19, 21, 22, 43, 46, 47
Nathaniel P.	*1794n*, 97, 01, 11, 19, 24, 25, 26, 27	Zatum, Robert	1821
Nathaniel P., Jr.	1821, 22, 23, 30		
Thomas	1821, 44, 46, 50		
Walter	*1813n*		
William	1790, 94, *97n*, 98, 01, 02, 03		
Willers (*see also Villers*)			
Richard	1817		
Willis, William	1805		
Wilson, George	1818, 27		
James	1804, 05, *30n*		
Moses	*1821n*		
Thomas	1815, 16, 21		
Wesley	1813		
William	*1828n*, 30, 43, 44		
Wine, Abner	1819		
Hosea	1802		
William	1804, 05		
Winlock, Joseph	1813		

www.ingramcontent.com/pod-product-compliance
Lightning Source LLC
Chambersburg PA
CBHW051927160426
43198CB00012B/2065